UNHAPPY INDIA

AMS PRESS
NEW YORK

Unhappy India

by

LAJPAT RAI

Second Edition
(*Revised & Enlarged*)

BANNA PUBLISHING CO.
CALCUTTA
1928

Library of Congress Cataloging in Publication Data

Lajpat Rai, Lala, 1865-1928.
  Unhappy India.

  A reply to K. Mayo's Mother India.
  1. India--Social conditions. 2. India--Economic
conditions--1918-1947. 3. Women in India.
4. Mayo, Katherine, 1868?-1940. Mother India.
I. Title.
DS421.M42   1972   915.4'03'35   72-171642
ISBN 0-404-03803-4

Reprinted from the edition of 1928, Calcutta
First AMS edition published in 1972
Manufactured in the United States of America

International Standard Book Number: 0-404-03803-4

AMS PRESS INC.
NEW YORK, N.Y. 10003

CONTENTS

CHAPTER		PAGE
	PREFACE	ix
	INTRODUCTION	xiii
I	THE ARGUMENT	1
II	THE LIGHT THROUGH THE AGES	15
III	THE LIGHT THAT FAILED	42
IV	LEARNING AND EARNING—AND HARD-HEADED AMERICANS	49
V	A COUNSEL OF PERFECTION	57
VI	HISTORY OF COMPULSORY PRIMARY EDUCATION	69
VII	'WHY IS LIGHT DENIED?'	74
VIII	THE HINDU CASTE SYSTEM	81
IX	THE UNTOUCHABLES—HIS FRIENDS AND HIS EXPLOITERS	93
X	LESS THAN THE PARIAH	104
XI	LESS THAN THE PARIAH (*concluded*)	132
XII	WOMAN IN INDIA—A RETROSPECT	151
XIII	WOMAN AND THE NEW AGE	175
XIV	EARLY TO MARRY AND EARLY TO DIE	186
XV	THE HINDU WIDOW	192
XVI	THE DEVADASI	199
XVII	'SCHOOLING, FREE OF CHARGE'	206
XVIII	THE SEX URGE IN THE WEST	210
XIX	A PRESENT TO MR. WINSTON CHURCHILL	254

CONTENTS

CHAPTER		PAGE
XX	MUCK-RAKERS WHOM WE KNOW	269
XXI	THE HYGIENE OF THE HINDUS	278
XXII	WHY THE COW STARVES	290
XXIII	INDIA—HOME OF PLENTY	301
XXIV	INDIA—'HOME OF STARK WANT'	319
XXV	POVERTY—THE ROCK BOTTOM PHYSICAL BASE OF INDIA'S ILLS	350
XXVI	SOME ASPECTS OF THE DRAIN TO-DAY	373
XXVII	SOME ASPECTS OF THE DRAIN TO-DAY (*concluded*)	382
XXVIII	'DIVIDE ET IMPERA'	399
XXIX	'THE SONS OF THE PROPHET'	411
XXX	BRITISHERS ON BRITISH RULE	426
XXXI	THE STORY OF THE REFORMS	440
XXXII	'CUMBROUS, COMPLEX, CONFUSED SYSTEM'	465
XXXIII	INDIA—A WORLD-MENACE	470

APPENDICES

I	SOME OPINIONS ABOUT 'MOTHER INDIA'	487
II	DEPRESSED CLASSES	518
III	THE GOVERNMENT OF INDIA AND CASTE	537
IV	MASS EDUCATION IN INDIA	543
	INDEX	545

DEDICATED

With love and gratitude to those numberless American men and women who stand for the freedom of the world; who know no distinctions of colour, race or creed; and who profess a religion of love, humanity and justice. To them the oppressed people of the earth look for sympathy in their struggle for emancipation, and in them is centred the hope of world-peace.

LAJPAT RAI.

PREFACE

Not many words are needed to send out this book into the world. I claim neither originality nor literary merit for it. In my judgment it is easier to write an original thesis than to hunt up authorities, verify and quote them. But being the member of a subject race, writing a book in defence of my motherland, in refutation of the calumnies invented and circulated throughout the world from base motives, I could not but refer to, and quote from authorities. There are not many statements in this book (in fact I doubt if there are any) in support of which reputed and reliable authority has not been quoted. It is easy to speak ill of the under-dog. It is difficult to defend him. The very fact that he is an under-dog goes against him. Nothing is more humiliating than the necessity of quoting the testimony of foreigners in defence. The process in itself involves an admission of inferiority. But there is no use hiding the fact that the white peoples of the West are not prepared to accept and believe any testimony but that of persons of their own race and colour. The book has been written mainly for them, and so it has been necessary to keep their needs in view. The foreign editions are to be larger in size and to contain extra matter that, for various reasons, could not be embodied in this edition.

Efforts are also being made to collect illustrations for the foreign edition. My best thanks are due to my fellow-worker and friend, Lala Feroz Chand, Editor of *The People*, but for whose collaboration the book might not have been prepared, printed and published so soon.

One word more and I have done. It is with extreme reluctance, amounting to pain, that I have referred to certain phases of American life. There is another side of American life—beautiful, noble, humane, full of the milk of human kindness for all races, all colours and all peoples of the world, of which I had personal experience during my five years' residence in that country. In order to expiate the sin of noting down some of the dark spots of American life in this book I may have to write another book depicting the bright traits of American character in the shape of personal narrative and character sketches. In this book these would be out of place. They would not fit in with my argument. I hope my American friends will pardon me for giving only one side of American life. America was not the theme of this book. I have spoken of certain phases of American life only by way of comparison.

The book has been prepared, printed and published in great hurry. No one is more conscious of its defects than my humble self, but there is one satisfaction that nothing is stated herein which I do not believe to be true.

In referring to *Mother India* I have used the English edition.

New Delhi:
January, 1928. LAJPAT RAI.

INTRODUCTION

I.

Subjection to foreign yoke is one of the most potent causes of the decay of nations.—Prof. E. A. Ross.

Speaking from a national point of view, no curse is greater than that of political subjection to another people. The marching hordes of a monarch are nothing in their ruinous effects on the country they overrun as compared with the gradual loss of a country's freedom by the complete subjugation of its people by a foreign army and its governance through the fear of bayonets. The invader comes, plundering, devastating, uprooting and sweeping everything before it like a hurricane. But he either goes away with his plunder or settles down in the country and identifies himself with the people. To the first type belonged invaders like Alexander, Mahmud of Ghazni, Timur, Chengiz Khan, Nadir Shah and Ahmad Shah Abdali; to the second belonged men who led the Scythians and the Huns into India and settled down here and became a part and parcel of the Indian nation, or like Mahmud of Ghor and Babar laid the foundations of dynasties deep on the soil of India.

It is true that in either case a great deal of humiliation, degradation and economic loss is suffered by the people of the country, but eventually the people and the invader become one. They mingle their blood one with the other, they exchange their cultures and ways of life, and strive for the evolution of a new culture and a new people with the strong points of both. In either case the curse of foreign rule is neither so keen and poignant, nor so devastating and humiliating as it is when a nation imposes its rule over another and maintains it by all her political, economic and military resources. An appeal to the generosity, magnanimity and sense of justice in an individual sovereign or ruler may for once meet with success, but that to a nation or a democracy never can. No rule over a foreign people is so exacting and so merciless in its operations as that of a democracy. A democratic form of government may be good for domestic purposes, but the domination of a democracy over other peoples is disastrous in its effects, and is fraught with possibilities of infinite mischief.

Political subjection is the punishment of social evils and national crimes, but once imposed, it adds to their volume and intensity. It effectively checks any rejuvenation or reconstruction. It accentuates social evils and weaknesses. It leads to poverty in all its hideous forms, mental, moral and physical. If ever an awakening comes, it is delayed, or checked and crushed by all the forces of law and diplomacy, and of cunning and fraud. It is a part of the imperial game to paint the subject people in the blackest colours, and to slander and libel them most shamelessly. The object is to produce and perpetuate the slave mentality of the subject people, and to obtain the moral sanction of the rest of the world for usurping the rights, properties and liberties of other peoples. This is the genesis of the cult of the white man's burden. This is the mentality which stimulates the Empire-builder. This is the material with which the ' steel frames' are forged to keep the subject peoples in bondage and to prevent them ' from doing harm to themselves ' by aspiring to, and working for their freedom. That is how Britain made her Empire in India; that is how the U. S. A. took possession of the Philippine Isles and now refuses to vacate them.

It is true that sometimes empire-making begins in a fit of self-forgetfulness, for temporary purposes of safety or trade, but soon, very soon, it becomes wilful and unscrupulous empire-building. Empires built and made have to be maintained and managed and fresh territories added to it. Sometimes, however, empires based on fraud and maintained by force, have the knack of awakening the political consciousness of the subject peoples. Political domination leads to economic exploitation. Economic exploitation leads to dirt, disease and distress, until they drive even the meekest people on earth to rebellion, passive or active, and create the desire for freedom. The rulers resent this. At first they try to crush this spirit for emancipation out of existence by ridicule and contempt, or by ignoring it altogether. Then comes the stage of control, which is followed by a policy of repression *cum* conciliation leading to cunning and fraud, chicanery and charlatanism. The struggle goes on. The Imperialists divide themselves into two parties: (*a*) The advocates of pure force and no nonsense; (*b*) The liberals who trot out the plea of trusteeship by convincing the 'wards' inside, and the world outside, that the people are unfit to rule themselves, and that the best interests of the ruled themselves demand a never-ending continuance of the trusteeship. Certain theoretical conditions are laid down, the fulfilment of which might lead to the ending of the period of trusteeship, but the actual policy is directed to check and prevent the fulfilment of these conditions, and thus a vicious circle is created by which both the people affected and the world at large are deceived. Want of literacy, lack of social purity and social solidarity, the existence of depressed and suppressed classes, the low nature of private and public morality, and incapacity to build arms, to lead armies and to organise scientific defence, all these are trumped up as justifying a denial of freedom; every effort is at the same time made to perpetuate these disqualifications. The subject people are declared deficient in character, which alone is said to enable people to rule themselves, or to deal fairly as between one class and another. The lesson of their own domestic history or that of other peoples is clean forgotten by the ruling race, and great point is made of the so-called backward condition of the aspiring nation. It is declared from housetops that these people have got into the slough of slave-mentality: they hug their chains; they love their ignorance; they adore their poverty; they are devoted to dirt, disease and distress; they are afraid of freedom, and they hate the classes which cry for liberty and raise the standard of revolt against established absolutism, entrenched foreign autocracy, and personified exploitation. Such is the curse of political subjection and economic bondage that the slaves themselves fail to recognize that the only way to develop a character for self-government and a free life is to break their chains and throw off the yoke. Such is the process of imperial hypnotism and of sophisticated, well-organised and well-planned propaganda that the subjects themselves, while disgusted with their chained life, are yet afraid of freedom. Thus things keep moving in a vicious circle until Nemesis overtakes all and starts a fresh chapter in history.

Every schoolboy knows that for ages Europe was plunged in barbarity, ignorance and bondage. When we say Europe, we mean the white races of the world—Europe and America, for America is only a child of Europe. The white races got their religion from Asia; arts and industries they copied from Egypt; moral standards they borrowed from India and Palestine. Whatever is really good and moral among the modern nations of the world is largely a gift of the East. According to some, even their blood is Asiatic in origin. Even casual students of history know that only three centuries back Asia ruled and dominated at least half of modern Europe. Alexander's were the only armies that ever met with victory in pre-Christian

Asia. They affected but a small part of Asia, and that also only for a short period of a few years. Alexander's raid was well recompensed by the raids and victories of the Huns, of Chengiz Khan and Timur, and then of the Moors and Turks. For centuries Russia, Turkey, Sicily, Spain and the Balkans were ruled and dominated by the Asiatics. Europe's dominance over Asia is not more than two centuries old. It virtually began with the conquest of India, and, God willing, will end with her emancipation. It is this fear which is the motive behind an unholy combination of all the white peoples of the earth against India's aspirations to political freedom. India is the crux of the problem of the clash of colour. India's freedom means the freedom of the whole coloured world. This explains the great popularity and success which Miss Katherine Mayo's book, *Mother India*, has gained throughout the West.

Miss Mayo's mentality is the mentality of the white races as a whole against the black or brown or yellow peoples of Asia. She is only the mouthpiece of the oppressors of the East. The awakening of the East has frightened both Europe and America. Hence this hysterical exhibition of temper, and this studied, deliberate, infamous propaganda against a race so ancient and so cultured.

II.

Miss Katherine Mayo is by her antecedents a tool of the Jingoes of America. She is a journalist whose only claim to authorship is a facile pen, a

familiarity with sensational catch-words and a
habit of telling doubtful stories in a crackling
style. Even a superficial reader can point out her
ignorance of history, psychology and politics. Yet
she is an able writer of sorts. Her first debut into
the realm of authorship was made by the publication of a volume of her ' researches ' into the
condition of the Filipinos who have been knocking at the door of America for their promised
freedom. The book was named *The Isles of Fear*.
Mr. S. K. Ratcliffe, sometime Editor of the Calcutta *Statesman*, and a famous English journalist,
now popular in the U. S. A., by his lectures and
contributions to the American Press, tells us in the
course of his review of *Mother India* (published in
the New York, *New Republic*) :

" Two years ago, when I read Katherine
Mayo's propagandist volume on the Philippines,
it seemed to me certain that she would go next to
India and produce a book enforcing a conclusion
precisely similar to the one reiterated in *The Isles
of Fear*. The thesis of that vigorous manifesto, it
will be remembered, is that the United States
must keep its governing hand upon the archi-
pelago, for, if it did not, the Filipinos would be
skinned alive by their own landlords, lawyers,
usurpers."

We have reason to believe that Miss Mayo's
visit to India was not a spontaneous one, and that
she was urged to come to India by those Britishers
with vested interests, who think that the development of self-government in India is a menace to

them and their pockets. Obviously we can have
no direct evidence in support of this allegation.
But of strong circumstantial evidence there is no
dearth. Mr. Lionel Curtis is one of those
' progressive ' gentlemen who are interested in the
integrity and prosperity of the British Empire. He
is a member of the Round Table Group in Great
Britain. This Group is vitally interested in the
problems of the Empire, and its members devote
their time and energy to bringing the different
parts of the Empire together and to making them
understand each other better. The Empire, however, for which they stand is a ' Commonwealth of
Nations ' in which the white, British as well as
Colonial, shall rule and exploit the ' natives.'
Mr. Curtis visited India in 1916-17—about the time
of the famous pronouncement of Mr. Montague in
August 1917, in the House of Commons, pledging
the word of Great Britain to grant self-government
to India in progressive stages. Mr. Montague came
to India to study the situation and to report to
Parliament how best to give effect to that pledge.
Mr. Lionel Curtis also made somewhat similar
professions. While the Secretary of State tried to
give something, it was the Round Table knight's
concern to see that little was given, and even that
little rendered ineffective. He entered into a
conspiracy with two eminent Britishers of the
Indian Civil Service, members of the Round Table
Group, both in charge of high offices in one of the
provinces of India. The object of this conspiracy
was to give a voice and share to the white
Dominions of Great Britain in determining the

future of India and to strengthen the chains with which she was bound down for the glorification of the Empire. One of the documents which contained the infamous story of this conspiracy fell by chance into the hands of Mr. Gandhi, and he made it public. Mr. Curtis was caught red-handed, and had to explain away the Round Table circular as a private letter to 'intimate friends.' By repute he and his fellow-conspirators of the Indian Civil Service were the authors of dyarchy and such other features of the Montague-Chelmsford Report as have been the bane of the Reforms Act of 1919.

In August 1925 Mr. Curtis happened to be in Massachusetts, U. S. A. He met Miss Katherine Mayo, and was at once so much enamoured of her production, *The Isles of Fear*, that he wrote a foreword for the English edition of that book. The language of the foreword makes it highly probable that Mr. Curtis—even if he did not find the money for Miss Mayo's expensive voyage to India—had something to do with the idea that Miss Mayo's Philippine work be followed by a visit to India with similar motives and aims. Said Mr. Curtis in the foreword :*

" The British Government is responsible for more dependencies than all the other nations put together. Our experience is centuries old. [May we ask how many centuries old, as the beginning of the British Empire in Asia is not even full two centuries old?] we can hardly afford to ignore

The Isles of Fear, (London : Faber and Gwyer) pp. ix—xii.

the experience of others, especially that of the young light-hearted masters of the West... In discussing the Indian or Colonial estimates a Minister might well be expected to show Parliament that he knew how American or Dutch administrators were handling analogous problems in the Philippines or Java. In 1917 the policy pursued by America in the Philippines was a commonplace of nationalist propaganda in India. In the following year when retiring from the Indian Government, Sir W. Meyer visited the Philippines, but if he reported on American methods the fact has never been disclosed by the India Office."

In the following paragraph Mr. Curtis makes it clear how valuable Miss Mayo's book on the Philippine Islands could be to the English administrators of India:

"The Jones Law passed by the American Congress in 1916 transferred the control of legislation and supply to a legislature answerable to a Philippine electorate, while leaving the executive power to a governor responsible to the President of the U. S. A. A system, the close equivalent of the Jones Law was the only alternative to that embodied in the constitution which was given to India in 1920. For this reason alone the operation of the Jones Law in the Philippines deserves to be studied by observers who bring to their task an adequate knowledge of Indian conditions. I commend this book to English readers in the hope of provoking such enquiries."

Mr. Curtis is conscious that ' Miss Mayo's account of the results which have followed the American attempt to "hasten" self-government in the Philippines will probably be used to discredit the policy applied to India in the pronouncement of 1917.'

Miss Mayo protests that she has written the book only for the use of her own people, but she has not yet told us of what use a wholesale denunciation of the Indian people could be to the people of the United States, unless it was the same kind of use for which Mr. Curtis recommended *The Isles of Fear* to the British-Indian administrators.

Anyhow we are justified in concluding that in August 1925 there was some kind of mutual discussion and understanding between Mr. L. Curtis, the champion of British imperialism, and Miss Mayo, the author of *The Isles of Fear*, which led to Miss Mayo's visit to the India Office, *en route* to India ' early in October 1925.' Who introduced her to the authorities of the India Office? Who persuaded the latter to give her introductions to her for use in India? These are questions that Mr. Curtis may answer for the benefit of the curious if he chooses. Be that as it may, Miss Mayo ' called at the India Office ' ' early in October 1925.' The good people of the India Office asked her, " What would you like us to do for you?" She answered:

" Nothing, except to believe what I say. A foreign stranger prying about India, not studying ancient architecture, not seeking philosophers or poets, not even hunting big game, and commissioned by no one, anywhere, may seem a queer figure. Especially if that stranger develops an acute tendency to ask questions. I should like to be accepted that I am neither an idle busybody nor a political agent, but merely an ordinary American citizen seeking test facts to lay before my own people."

On her own admission the India Office were not slow to give introductions.

This sounds suspicious enough. But here are a few further facts that I found out on enquiry. Miss Mayo was the guest of a member of the Government of India and his wife during her stay at Delhi in the winter of 1926. She was a guest at least at one Government House in India. The Home Member of the Government of India has admitted in the Legislative Assembly that the government officials in India did give her help and showed her courtesies,—though he contends these were not different from those that are given or shown to other publicists or visitors. This statement cannot be accepted at its face value when we find Miss Mayo admitting that sometimes she accompanied ' a District Commissioner on his tours of chequered duty,' sometimes she ' sat in ' ' at village councils of peasants, or at an Indian Municipal Board meeting.' How could an American woman, an utter stranger to the country, absolutely ignorant of its many vernaculars, ' sit in ' at the village councils of peasants, unless she was taken to these (probably prearranged) councils by English-speaking Indian officials deputed by higher officers?

Miss Mayo was at the India Office in London in October 1925. In her foreword she gives no date or year to show when she completed her manuscripts. Inside the title sheet of the American edition ' May 1927 ' is given as the month when it was first printed. From October 1925 to May 1927, exclusive of both months, the total period which Miss Mayo spent on this book (from the date of her starting for India to the date of the first publication of her book) seems not to have exceeded 18 months. And during this period we must understand she toured in India from the North-Western Frontier Province to Madras, visited many towns and villages, studied the history of the various communities and their social, industrial and political life. She visited homes and hospitals and discussed metaphysics and philosophic outlooks on life. She managed to include in this stupendous task printed debates of the nine provincial councils, the two chambers of the Indian legislature, the blue books and reports of the numerous government departments of all the provinces quite extending over a period of two decades. This period of 18 months includes the voyage back to America and the writing and printing of the book. Has any writer ever performed such a feat in such a short time single-handed?

To some these facts would be a conclusive proof of Miss Mayo's coming to India through some agency of Anglo-Indians, official and non-official, who wanted her to write a book of the kind she had written about the Philippines in 1924. For our more sceptical readers we shall add—

1. That her book was first boomed in the British Isles by the leading Tory organs which had been agitating against the advanced Indian political parties and their claims for Swaraj.

2. That the chief of these Tory papers, The London *Times*, refused to give publicity to an important letter* of protest, signed by almost all the influential Indians, officials and non-officials, then present in London. The letter ran—

" Our attention has been drawn to the recent publication, entitled *Mother India*, by an American tourist, Miss Kaherine Mayo, who paid a visit to India during the cold weather of 1925-26. It has never been our lot to read a book which indulges in such a wholesale, indiscriminate vilification of Indian civilization and Indian character.

---

*The letter was signed by Sir A. C. Chatterjee, High Commissioner for India; Sir Tej Bahadur Sapru, ex-Member of the Viceroy's Executive Council; Sir Chimanlal Setalvad, ex-Member of the Executive Council of the Governor of Bombay; Mr. Sachchidananda Sinha, ex-Member of the Executive Council of the Governor of Bihar and Orissa; Sir M. M. Bhowanagree; Mr. Dube, Barrister-at-Law, practising before His Majesty's Privy Council; Mr. Kamat, Member of the Royal Commission for Agriculture; and all the Indian Members of the Council of the Secretary of State for India, namely, Sir Mahomed Rafique, Mr. S. N. Mullick and Dr. Pranjpaye. The *Times* refused to publish this letter although it was an important statement by prominent people. Reuter's propagandist news service gave it absolutely no publicity.

INTRODUCTION   xxvii

"We concede that like other cold weather tourists, Miss Mayo was entitled to form and express her own opinions. But when a foreigner, who spends not more than a few months in our country, uses the material gleaned from hospital cases, culled from criminal trial reports and deduced from her own observation of isolated happenings, and seeks to fortify herself with quotations divorced from context, and then proceeds on such slender basis to formulate a general indictment against the character and culture of a great country like India, possessed of an ancient civilization, it is time that we protested.

'She depicts the entire nation of 320 million people as physical degenerates, moral perverts and unabashed liars. If an Indian could have the temerity to pass a similar judgment on any nation of the West, after but a few months' residence in any country in Europe or America, and to indict the Western people, their civilization and character on the strength of the reports of sensational cases and crimes, moral perversions and physical degeneracy as evidenced by the proceedings of the courts, hospital and personal experiences, official reports, newspaper paragraphs and other special instances he would be rightly condemned as unworthy of serious attention...

'We should not have felt called upon to take any public notice of a book of this character, but when we find that the publication is receiving serious attention of the British Press to the obvious detriment of India, at this juncture, we think it our duty to warn the British public against what strikes us as being a singularly mischievous book."

3. That the book has been distributed free both in Great Britain and America. The Rt. Hon. Col. Wedgwood, M.P., received three copies—all free. It is only propaganda books that are supplied gratis so generously.

II.

In the last section I quoted a letter which a number of responsible Indians sent to The London *Times* in August 1927 when Miss Mayo's book was being boomed by the benevolent British Press. Three of the signatories were members of the India Council at Whitehall (two Hindus and one Mussalman). They had, before their appointment to their present offices, held high offices in India. One had been the Judge of a High Court established by Royal Charter; another a Minister of Education to the Government of Bombay. Two of the other Indians had been Executive Councillors of the Government of India and one of the Government of Bombay. One of them is at present holding the exalted office of the High Commissioner of India in London; and so on. Their opinion on *Mother India* is weighty. They cannot be brushed aside as mere agitators or men of no position. It would not be a compliment to the Government of India to say that the opinion of these eminent gentlemen who had held such high offices under the Government, is false or untrustworthy.

INTRODUCTION   xxix

Now I propose to refer to the opinion of one whom a great American Christian leader has compared with Christ, and whom several Westerners have characterized as the greatest man of the age. I mean Mahatma Gandhi. In the course of a signed article in his own weekly, *Young India*, under the caption 'Drain Inspector's Report,' Mahatma Gandhi made the following remarks about this book:

" The book is cleverly and powerfully written. The carefully chosen quotations give it the appearance of a truthful book, but the impression it leaves on my mind is that it is the report of a drain inspector sent out with the one purpose of opening and examining the drains of the country to be reported upon or to give a graphic description of the stench exuded by the open drains. If Miss Mayo had confessed that she had gone to India merely to open out and examine the drains of India, there would perhaps be little to complain about her compilation...

' I feel that no one who has any knowledge of India can possibly accept her terrible accusations against the thought and the life of the people of this unhappy country. *The book is without doubt untruthful, be the facts stated ever so truthful.* If I open out and describe with punctilious care all the stench exuded from the drains of London and say, ' Behold London,' my facts will be incapable of challenge, but my judgment will be rightly condemned as a travesty of truth. Miss Mayo's book is nothing better, nothing else. The authoress says she was dissatisfied with the literature she read about India and so she came to India ' to see what a volunteer unsubsidized, uncommitted and unattached could observe of common things in daily human life.'

' After having read the book with great attention, I regret to say that I find it difficult to accept this claim. Unsubsidized she may be. Uncommitted and unattached she certainly fails to show herself in any page. We in India are accustomed to interested publications patronized —' patronized ' is accepted as an elegant synonym for ' subsidized '—by the Government. We have become used to understanding from pre-British days, that the art (perfected by the British) of government includes the harnessing of the secret services of men learned, and reported to be honest and honourable for shadowing suspects and for writing up the virtues of the Government of the day as if the certificate had come from disinterested quarters. I hope that Miss Mayo will not take offence if she comes under the shadow of such suspicion...

' [*Mother India*] is doubly untruthful. It is untruthful in that she condemns a whole nation, or in her words ' the peoples of India ' (she will not have us as one nation), practically without any reservation, as to their sanitation, morals, religion, etc. It is also untruthful because she claims for the British Government merits which cannot be sustained and which many an honest British officer would blush to see the Government credited *with*...

INTRODUCTION xxxi

'Miss Mayo is an avowed Indophobe and Anglophil, refusing to see anything good about Indians and anything bad about the British and their rule...

'Nor are all the authoress's quotations or isolated facts truthfully stated. I propose to pick up those I have personal knowledge of. The book bristles with quotations torn from their context and with extracts which have been authoritatively challenged.

'The authoress has violated all sense of propriety by associating the Poet Rabindra Nath Tagore's name with child-marriage. The Poet has indeed referred to early marriage as not an undesirable institution. But there is a world of difference between child-marriage and early marriage. If she had taken the trouble of making the acquaintance of the free and freedom-loving girls and women of Shantiniketan she would have known the Poet's meaning of early marriage.

'She has done me the honour of quoting me frequently in support of her argument. Any person who collects extracts from a reformer's diary, tears them from their context, and proceeds to condemn, on the strength of these, the people in whose midst the reformer has worked, would get no hearing from sane and unbiased readers or hearers.

'But in her hurry to see everything Indian in a bad light she has not only taken liberty with my writings but she has not thought it necessary even to verify through me certain things ascribed by her or others to me...

'The nineteenth chapter is a collection of authorities in praise of the achievements of the British Government, almost every one of which has been repeatedly challenged both by English and Indian writers of unimpeachable integrity. The seventeenth chapter is written to show that we are a 'world menace.' If as a result of Miss Mayo's effort the League of Nations is moved to declare India a segregated country unfit for exploitation, I have no doubt both the West and the East would be the gainers. We may then have our internecine wars. Hindus may be eaten up, as she threatens, by the hordes from the North-West and Central Asia—that were a position infinitely superior to one of evergrowing emasculation. Even as electrocution is a humaner method of killing than the horrid method of roasting alive, so would a sudden overwhelming swoop from Central Asia upon the unresisting, insanitary, superstitious, and sexuality-ridden Hindus, as Miss Mayo describes us to be, be a humane deliverance from the living and ignominious death which we are going through at the present moment. Unfortunately, however, such is not Miss Mayo's goal. Her case is to perpetuate white domination in India on the plea of India's unfitness to rule herself...

'The picturesque statements that this clever authoress puts into the mouths of the various characters read like so many pages from a sensational novel in which no regard has to be paid to truth. Many of her statements seem to me to be utterly unworthy of belief and do not put the men and women to whom they are ascribed in a favourable light. Take for instance this statement put into the mouth of a prince :

' " Our treaties are with the Crown of England," one of them said to me, with incisive calm. " The princes of India made no treaty with a Government that included Bengali *babus*. We shall never deal with this new lot of Jacks-in-office. While Britain stays, Britain will send us English gentlemen to speak for the King-Emperor, and all will be as it should be between friends. If Britain leaves, we, the princes, will know how to straighten out India, even as princes should." '*

' However fallen Indian princes may be, I should want unimpeachable evidence before I could believe that there can be in India a prince so degraded as to make such a statement. Needless to say, the authoress does not give the name of the prince.

' A still more scandalous statement occurs on page 314 and reads as follows :

' " His Highness does not believe," said the Dewan, " that Britain is going to leave India. But still, under this new regime in England, they may be so ill-advised. So His Highness is getting his troops in shape, accumulating munitions and coining silver. And if the English do go, three

* *Mother India*, p. 316 (Amer. Edition).

months afterward, not a rupee or a virgin will be left in all Bengal."

'The reader is kept in darkness as to the name of His Highness or of the enlightened Dewan.

'I should be sorry indeed to think that there are many Englishmen and Englishwomen who say one thing to their Indian friends and another to their Western confidants. Those Englishmen and Englishwomen who may chance to read the sweepings gathered together by Miss Mayo with her muck-rake will recognize the statements I have in mind. In seeking to see an India degraded Miss Mayo has unconsciously degraded the characters whom she has used as her instruments for proving her facts, which she boasts cannot be 'disproved or shaken.' I hope I have given sufficient *prima facie* proof in this article to show that many of her facts stand disproved even in isolation. Put together they give a wholly false picture...

'I do not remember having given the message Miss Mayo imputes to me. The only one present who took any notes at all has no recollection of the message imputed to me. But I do know what message I give every American who comes to see me: "Do not believe newspapers and the catchy literature you get in America. But if you want to know anything about India go to India as students, study India for yourself. If you cannot go, make a study of all that is written about India, for her and against her, and then form your own conclusions. The ordinary literature you get is either exaggerated vilification of India or exaggerated praise." I warn Americans and Englishmen against copying Miss Mayo. She came not with an open mind as she claims, but with her preconceived notions and prejudices, which she betrays on every page, not excluding even the introductory chapter in which she recites the claim."

I have given these copious extracts from Mahatma Gandhi as by common consent he is accepted to be the greatest, the most saintly and the most truthful of all the living Indians. Miss Mayo may not consider him saintly enough to compete with the Indian Civil Servants or the Christian missionaries working in India, as she insinuates in one of the interviews she gave to a Press reporter. But her estimate of Gandhi is in line with the relative estimates of Indians and Westerners made in her book. Next to Mahatma Gandhi the two other Indians who enjoy such international fame as is unique for the sons of an Asiatic and subjugated country are the poet, Rabindranath Tagore (knighted by the British Government and doctored by its universities), a winner of the Nobel Prize, and Dr. Sir J. C. Bose, F.R.S., the great scientist.

Tagore has expressed his opinion of the book on two occasions—(a) in a letter to the *Manchester Guardian*, (b) in a letter to *The Nation*, New York. Elsewhere we give extracts from both.

Dr. Bose calls it a filthy book not worthy of attention.

In the Appendix to this book we are putting together the opinions some prominent people, who know India much better than Miss Mayo, have expressed about *Mother India.* Rabindranath Tagore accuses her of 'deliberately untruthful irresponsibility' in handling his writings. The late Lord Sinha, the only Indian ever appointed as Governor of a province, entirely agrees with Mr. Gandhi that 'Miss Mayo has had a good sniff at all the filthy drains of India.' He calls her book 'a lie, and a false picture.' The Executive Committee of the National Christian Council of India, which is presided over by the Lord Bishop of Calcutta and Metropolitan of India, asserts that 'the picture of India which emerges from Miss Mayo's book is untrue to the facts and unjust to the people of India.' Eminent foreigners who know India intimately have condemned the book in strong terms. Mr. Edward Thompson, novelist and playwright, author of *An Indian Day*, calls *Mother India* 'one long nagging,' and expresses the opinion that Miss Mayo lost her case 'when she wove into it a bitter conviction that the white man's rule is so overwhelmingly good for inferior breeds that it is only wickedness that makes them dissatisfied.' Sir John Maynard, retired Executive Councillor, finds it hard to write with restraint about Miss Mayo's book. Col. Wedgwood, M.P., writing (in the *Hindu Annual*, 1927) of Miss Mayo's generalizations about sex life in India says:

"It has always been the habit of civilized peoples to attribute to neighbours whom they feared and hated just those vices which were unpopular. In that way contempt could take the place of fear. The Germans said of the French that they were exhausted by sexual excesses,—only they put it more shortly. In the time of the Crusades all followers of the ' false Mahound ' were addicted to unnatural vice; so were the Bulgarians or the Albigenses, when Christianity had to be worked up against them. French medieval dislike of the raiding English led them to speak of us as ' tailed monkeys,' though that particular form of sexual perversion is one from which we are exceptionally free."

The reader will find the opinions of several other people about *Mother India* in the Appendix.

III.

While dealing with Hindu life, customs and manners, Hindu religion and Hindu philosophy, Miss Mayo has chiefly relied on the authority of the Abbé Dubois and has quoted from his book on these subjects profusely. It seems proper, therefore, to deal with the authority of the Abbé once for all in this place and to point out what value can be attached to his opinions and comments.

Dubois was a Jesuit missionary. A refugee from the French Revolution, he came and settled down in India. There is reason to believe that all the time he lived among the Hindus he posed as a Brahman. There is also reason to believe that he was ' a Tamil, far more than a Sanskrit, scholar,'*—which is a polite way of saying that he was not much of a Sanskrit scholar. His opinions about Hindu religion and Hindu learning are not of much value. European knowledge of Hindu literature and religion in Dubois's days was extremely limited. Since then much that is of great scientific value has been discovered and made known, and Western scholars have written a great deal about Hindu religion, Hindu philosophy and Hindu law. The investigations of Western scholars are now being supplemented by Indian savants. Max Müller, Deussen, Welkins, Rapson, Colebrook, Sir William Jones, Lanman, Macdonnel, Keith, Foucher, Sylvian Levi and a host of others among the Europeans; Jayaswal, B. N. Seal, R. G. Bhandarkar, Sarkar, R. L. Mitter, and a host of others among the Indians, are far better authorities on these subjects than the Abbé Dubois. Miss Mayo does not know any one of them. She does not refer to their writings and opinions. She relies almost exclusively on M. Dubois, whose knowledge was gleaned mostly from what translations of Sanskrit works into European languages existed then. About his personal observations also it should not be forgotten that he lived the whole of the time he spent in India in that part of the Deccan which is situated south of the Kistna. The editor of the Oxford edition of his work remarks :*

" At the same time he [Dubois] disclaims for his work any general applicability to the whole of

*Page iv of the *Introduction* to the **Oxford** edition of Dubois's book.
Ibid., p. xiii.

India. His observations extend, broadly speaking, to the India that lies south of the Vindhyan range; and even within those limits he is careful to remark that local differences are so many and so marked that there is no class or sect or community of Hindus that has not, in addition to the general rules of Hindu society, some domestic usages peculiar to itself. So that, as he says, it is impossible to generalize with complete accuracy on any subject connected with them."

Mr. K. Nataranjan, Editor of *The Indian Social Reformer*, who is himself an advanced social reformer, remarks in the course of a series of articles on Miss Mayo's book published in his weekly :*

" [The Abbé] was an impostor from first to last.... ' I had no sooner arrived among the natives of India,' he writes, ' than I recognised the absolute necessity of gaining their confidence. Accordingly I made it my constant rule to live as they did. I adopted their style of clothing, and I studied their customs and methods of life in order to be exactly like them. I even went so far as to avoid any display of repugnance to the majority of their peculiar prejudices. By such circumspect conduct I was able to ensure a free and hearty welcome from people of all castes and conditions, and was often favoured of their own accord with the most curious and interesting particulars about themselves.'†
Notwithstanding all this camouflage, the Abbé's

* Mr. Nataranjan's articles have been published as a book by Messrs. Natesan & Co., Madras.
†Dubois, *op. cit.*, p. 8.

work as a Christian missionary was, on his own
admission, a humiliating failure. ' The restraints
and privations under which I have lived,' he wrote,
' by conforming myself to the usages of the country; embracing, in many respects, the prejudices
of the natives; living like them, and becoming all
but a Hindu myself; in short by being *made all
things to all men that I might by all means save
some*—all these have proved of no avail to me to
make proselytes. During the long period I have
lived in India, in the capacity of a missionary, I
have made, with the assistance of a native
missionary, in all between two and three hundred
converts of both sexes. Of this number two-thirds were pariahs or beggars; and the rest were
composed of Sudras, vagrants, outcastes of several
tribes, who being without resource turned
Christian in order to form connections, chiefly for
the purpose of marriage, or with some other
interested views.'* The Abbé, foiled in his missionary work, thought of serving Christianity in
another way. He writes : †

 "There is one motive which above all others
has influenced my determination [to write the
book]. It struck me that a faithful picture of the
wickedness and incongruities of polytheism and
idolatry would by its very ugliness help greatly to
set off the beauties and perfections of Christianity.
It was thus that the Lacedæmonians placed
drunken slaves in the sight of their children in

* Editor's Introduction to 3rd (Oxford) edition of Dubois's
book, pp. xxvi, xxvii.
† *Ibid.*, Author's Preface, p. 9.

INTRODUCTION xli

order to inspire the latter with a horror of intemperance.' "

No reader of Miss Mayo's book can afford to forget these admissions which altogether vitiate the conclusions in Dubois's book as well as that of its new version called *Mother India*.

The code by which the Jesuit missionaries in India went may be judged from the fact that one of Dubois's predecessors, the great missionary, Robert de Nobili (seventeenth century), who also, like Dubois, worked in the southern presidency, and anticipated his methods by simulating the Brahman mode of life, and even wearing the sacred thread, ' went so far as to forge a fifth Veda in Sanskrit and to insert into it Christian truths.'*

Mr. Nataranjan draws attention to a few more facts about the Abbé:

"The period during which the Abbé lived in India was also the period of greatest rivalry between the British and the French. The fact that the Abbé retired with a pension from the British East India Company ' in recognition of many services he had rendered to India' may be regarded either as a testimony to the disinterested generosity of the East India Company, or to the judicious patriotism of the Abbé himself."

The Abbé stands convicted out of his own mouth. Mr. Nataranjan pertinently asks:

" Suppose a Hindu were to spend some years in the United States with a like motive to produce

---

* *Indian Problems*, Bishop Whitehead: (Constable), p. 172.

3

a faithful picture of the wickedness and incongruities of Mammon-worship so that by its very ugliness it may help greatly to set off the beauties and perfections of the Vedanta, no serious student of American culture and civilization would think of relying on him as an authority on the subject. The Abbé's book is the last source to which any foreigner, after reading this candid avowal, should look for a true and faithful account of Hindu manners and customs."

It is not only the personal history of the Abbé, but also that of his book that is relevant here. I shall let the reader have it in Mr. Nataranjan's language:

" Even such a hostile witness as the Abbé Dubois is obliged to admit that Hindu women were treated with the greatest consideration, at least in public. In the first translation of his work published in 1817 by the East India Company occurred the following passage:

' But, degraded as the Hindu women are in private life, it must be admitted that they receive the highest respect in public. They certainly do not pay them those flat and frivolous compliments which are used amongst us, and which are the disgrace of both sexes; but, on the other hand, they have no insults to dread. A woman may go wheresoever she pleases; she may walk in the most public places (must I except those where the Europeans abound?) and have nothing to fear from libertines numerous as they are in the country. A man who should stop to gaze on a woman in the street, or elsewhere, would be universally hooted as an insolent and a most low-bred fellow.*

'*In the revised version from which the late Mr. Beauchamp made the present translation in 1897, and from the third edition of which Miss Mayo makes her citations, the uncomplimentary reflections on contemporary European manners are carefully omitted.* The passage is recast as under :

" But if women enjoy very little consideration in private life, they are in some degree compensated by the respect which is paid to them in public. They do not, it is true, receive those insipid compliments which we have agreed to consider polite; but then, on the other hand, they are safe from the risk of insult. A Hindu woman can go anywhere alone, even in the most crowded places, and she need never fear the impertinent looks and jokes of idle loungers. This appears to me to be really remarkable in a country where the moral depravity of inhabitants is carried to such lengths. A house inhabited solely by women is a sanctuary which the most shameless libertine would not dream of violating."*

Miss Mayo, while busy muck-raking from Dubois's book, carefully omitted to note his opinion when she made the assertion that no Hindu woman of child-bearing age could venture

* Abbe Dubois's book, 1817 edition, p. 220.
† 3rd Oxford edition, pp. 339-340.

within reach of Indian men. Here she forgot to consult her Dubois.

To Dubois's propagandist unscrupulousness Miss Mayo adds cleverness in handling quotations. Referring to the way she cites Dubois's authority in season and out of season, Mr. Nataranjan very rightly remarks :

"The deliberate disingenuousness of Miss Katherine Mayo is clear from the fact that in all her several references to the Abbé Dubois's book, she not once tells the reader that *the manuscript of the book was submitted to the East India Company in 1807*, and that the account in it relates to a period separated from our time by a century and a quarter. In one place at least she implies that the account relates to a period not very remote from ours. We refer to her statement that the Abbé found ' this ancient law [relating to the behaviour of a wife towards her husband] *still the code of nineteenth century Hinduism*,'* while the greater part of the Abbé's Indian career belongs to the eighteenth century. It may be nothing to Miss Katherine Mayo to skip over a century in order to achieve her purpose of blackening the Hindus in the eyes of the world, but one might ask what the position of women and social condition were generally in Europe, or even in Miss Mayo's own country, a hundred years ago. But comparisons are odious." [Italics are ours.]

For another instance of Miss Mayo's 'caution' in handling even her fellow Hindu-phobe, Dubois,

* *Mother India*, p. 74.

the reader may compare her quotation from the Abbé's book regarding learning among the Hindus. Thus she quotes:

"'[The Brahmans] saw well enough,' says Dubois, 'what a moral ascendency knowledge would give them over the other castes, and they therefore made a mystery of it by taking all possible precautions to prevent other classes from obtaining access to it.'"

The first two sentences of the paragraph from which this quotation is taken have been omitted as they credit the Hindus with having cultivated learning from the earliest time and the Brahmans with having 'always been as it were its depositories.'†

Miss Mayo evidently did not want to let this kind of 'damaging' statement to go in her book. The excerpt reproduced above is followed by another quotation from Dubois, which in Miss Mayo's book reads thus:

"'I do not believe that Brahmans of modern times are, in any degree, more learned than their ancestors of the time of Lycurgus and Pythagoras. During this long space of time, many barbarous races have emerged from the darkness of ignorance, have attained the summit of civilization, and have extended their intellectual researches...yet all this time the Hindus have been perfectly stationary. We do not find amongst them any trace of mental or moral improvement,

† Oxford edition, p. 376.

any sign of advance in the arts and sciences. Every impartial observer must, indeed, admit that they are now very far behind the peoples who inscribed their names long after them on the roll of civilized nations.' "

The words omitted, marked by dots, have perhaps been deleted because they would have shown that Dubois was very much lacking in the habit of exactitude. In the original the sentence reads, ' have extended their intellectual researches almost to *the utmost limits of human intelligence.*'

While on this subject I would like to give some more instances of Miss Mayo's dishonest use of quotation marks, and her lack of scruples in ascribing statements to people she met in India. Her usual method is to omit names—' one whose veracity cannot be questioned,' 'a Mussalman landlord,' ' a lawyer,' ' a prince ' come in as anonymous witnesses. But the few cases in which she does mention names are quite enough to let us judge her general standard of honesty and veracity.

I have taken some pains to investigate as to how she has reported or quoted other people, and my investigation has lent strong support to the charges I have made against Miss Mayo in the above paragraph.

The Rajah of Panagal happens to be among those quoted in *Mother India* by name.* Here is what he tells me about the statements ascribed to him by Miss Mayo:

---

* Page 165.

"Your letter of the 13th instant to hand. Miss Mayo is not accurate in reproducing my replies. The language used in the dialogue is, I think, her own. I wrote to you in my last letter what, to the best of my recollection, I told her."

The 'last letter' referred to reads:

"When Miss Mayo was at the Government House in Madras I had an occasion to meet her. On that occasion I remember having stated in reply to her questions that the present deplorable state of illiteracy in this Province is in some measure due to the superstitious ideas prevailing among the masses, and that according to Varnashrama Dharma the lower classes, who form the bulk of the population, could not take to literary pursuits. I told her too that even to this day sections of people are precluded from being admitted to Hindu schools, particularly to schools where Sanskrit and Shastras are taught; that non-Brahmans are enjoined by Smritis to avoid even listening to the recitation of Vedas, the punishment for disobedience to the injunction being to have the ears of the listeners filled with molten lead; and that after the British association with the administration and the broadcasting of higher education in the country the superstitions regarding Varnashrama Dharma are gradually losing ground, with the result that the non-Brahman classes do not now hesitate to take advantage of the existence of the various schools and colleges."

Another story about which I made some investigation is that found on page 319 of *Mother India*. Says Miss Mayo:

"Then I recall a little party given in Delhi by an Indian friend in order that I might privately hear the opinions of certain Home Rule politicians. Most of the guests were, like my host, Bengali Hindus belonging to the Western educated professional class. They had spoken at length on the coming expulsion of Britain from India and on the future in which they themselves would rule the land. 'And what,' I asked, 'is your plan for the princes?' 'We shall wipe them out!' exclaimed one with conviction, and all the rest nodded assent."

In the absence of any names it was not easy to get a clue for verification. But from enquiries from all the possible people who could have arranged such a party or who could have attended it, I learn that Mr. K. C. Roy of the Associated Press arranged a lunch to which a number of Indian gentlemen were invited. The only other *Bengali* present was Mr. Sen, Mr. K. C. Roy's assistant. Mr. K. C. Roy has assured me that Miss Mayo's story of what transpired at the meeting (if she really refers to that party) is absolutely untrue. Mrs. K. C. Roy in a letter to me writes:

"We gave a luncheon party to Miss Mayo at Maiden's Hotel, Delhi, during her short stay in the Capital. She came to us with excellent introductions. At the lunch there were only two Bengalis, namely, my husband and Mr. Sen. All the others were non-Bengalis. Prominent among our guests were Mr. M. A. Jinnah, leader of the Independent Party and Mr. S. Chetty. As I can recollect, the discussion ran on Indian constitutional development, her defence, communal harmony, child-welfare, and art and culture in Delhi. I do not recollect whether the position of the Indian princes was discussed. At any rate, I know that there was no discussion as to their being ' wiped out.' "

To both Gandhi and Tagore Miss Mayo has ascribed opinions regarding physicians and surgeons that they protest are not theirs. No wonder Gandhi should be impelled to say in his comment on her method:

"But in her hurry to see everything Indian in a bad light, she has not only taken liberty with my writings, but she has not thought it necessary even to verify through me certain things ascribed by her or others to me. In fact she has combined in her own person, what we understand in India, the judical and the executive officer. She is both the prosecutor and the judge."

Take the following statement made by Miss Mayo about the operation on M. Gandhi while he was in prison. Mark the inverted commas:

" As he happened to be in the prison at the time, a British surgeon of the Indian Medical Service came straightaway to see him. ' Mr. Gandhi,' said the surgeon, as the incident was then reported, ' I am sorry to tell you that you have appendicitis. If you were my patient, I should operate at once. But you will probably prefer to call in your Ayurvedic physician.' "

" Mr. Gandhi proved otherwise minded.

"' I should prefer not to operate,' pursued the surgeon, because in case the outcome should be unfortunate, all your friends will lay it as a charge of malicious intent against us, whose duty is to care for you.'

"' If you will only consent to operate,' pleaded Mr. Gandhi, ' I will call in my friends now, and explain to them that you do so at my request.'

"So Mr. Gandhi wilfully went to an ' institution for propagating sin,' was operated upon by one of the ' worst of all,' an officer of the Indian Medical Service, and was attentively nursed through convalescence by an English sister whom he is understood to have thought after all rather a ' useful sort of person.'"

Gandhiji comments on this:

"This is a travesty of truth. I shall confine myself to correcting only what is libellous and not the other inaccuracies. There was no question here of calling in any Ayurvedic physician. Col. Maddock, who performed the operation, had the right, if he had so chosen, to perform the operation without a reference to me, and even in spite of me. But he and Surgeon-General Hooten showed a delicate consideration to me and asked me whether I would wait for my own doctors, who were known to them and who were also trained in the Western medicine and surgical science. I would not be behind-hand in returning their courtesy and consideration, and I immediately told them that they could perform the operation without waiting for my doctors whom they had telegraphed, and that

I would gladly give them a note for their protection in the event of the operation miscarrying. I endeavoured to show that I had no distrust either in their ability or their good faith. It was to me a happy opportunity of demonstrating my personal goodwill."

Miss Bose, Principal of the Lahore Victoria School, has likewise protested against the distorted version in *Mother India* of the talk Miss Mayo had with her. Miss Bose was interviewed by the Rev. H. A. Popley about the statements ascribed to her by Miss Mayo. Here is what the Rev. Popley writes in the *Indian Witness*, a Methodist weekly published at Lucknow:

" On pages 132 and 133 she gives an account of the Victoria School, Lahore, and quotes, in inverted commas, statements of the Principal, Miss Bose. I have consulted this lady and find that a great many of the things printed in inverted commas were never spoken. Further, Miss Bose is not of the third generation of an Indian Christian family. The statement, in para third of that page (132), in regard to lower caste children is not accurate and was never made. On the top of page 134 she says that male pandits have to teach behind a curtain. Miss Bose informs me that ' Hindu girls are always taught Sanskrit by male pandits without purdah, and that the statement in regard to the pandit of tottering age, *that used to be the case 40 years ago.* The third para on page 133 dealing with the aim of the school is quite inaccurate, says Miss Bose; and she adds ' sewing has been an art among Indian women for ages', in reference to Miss Mayo's remark that 'sewing is almost unknown to most of the women of India.' The quotation in inverted commas, on the top of page 134, that ' their cooking in later life, they would never by nature do with their own hands, but would leave it entirely to filthy servants, whence come much sickness and death,' is entirely imaginary. Miss Bose says in reply to it, ' Cooking is done by ladies of every class, even when they have servants. Servants are not filthy in any good house, and certainly not in Hindu houses.'

"I have felt it necessary to deal with this rather extensively because it is a case which I have been able to investigate, and here we find an entire lack of appreciation for strict accuracy. It is most likely that in the innumerable quotations given without names the same inaccuracy would be found."

Miss Mayo makes some statements about the finances of the Victoria School to show that educated Indians are not prepared to spend anything on the education of their girls. The facts cited here by Miss Mayo have been challenged by Dewan Bahadur Kunj Behari Thapar, O.B.E., who is connected with the management of the Victoria School. I have reproduced Mr. Thapar's letter on page 209.

In a previous section we have quoted what Gandhi and Tagore have written about *Mother India*. Both of them have accused Miss Mayo of misquotation. Tagore, in any case, has been quoted by her in a thoroughly dishonest way, and made to represent opinions he has never held. Here are some excerpts from Tagore's letter which appeared in the New York *Nation* of January 4, 1928 :

" I happen to be one of those whom the writer has specially honoured with her attention, and selected as a target for her midnight raid. Difficult though it is for me completely to defend myself from such a widespread range of mischief, I must try through your organ to reach the ears of at least some of my friends, who are on the other side of the Atlantic, and have, I hope, the chivalry to suspend their judgment about the veracity of these shocking statements made by a casual tourist against a whole people, before lightly believing them to be honourable.

' For my own defence, I shall use the following extract from a paper written by Mr. Natarajan, one of the most fearless critics of our social evils. He has incidentally dealt with the incriminating allegation against me, deliberately concocted by Miss Mayo out of a few sentences from my contribution to Keyserling's *Book of Marriage*—cleverly burgling away their true meaning and shaping them into an utterly false testimony for her own nefarious purpose. Mr. Natarajan writes as follows :

" 'Tagore sets forth his own ideal of marriage in five long pages at the end of his paper (Keyserling, pages 117 *et seq.*) 'Let me,' he says, 'as an individual Indian, offer in conclusion my own personal contribution to the discussion of the marriage question generally.' He holds that the marriage system all over the world—and not only in India—from the earliest ages till now, is a barrier in the way of the true union of man and woman, which is possible only when ' society shall be able to offer a large field for the creative work of women's special faculty, without detracting from the creative work in the home.'

' If Miss Katherine Mayo was not a purblind propagandist but an honest enquirer, and if she had not the patience to read Tagore's essay, she might have asked any one in Calcutta what the age of marriage of girls is in Tagore's own family. That she was determined to discredit the poet is evident."

' Let me ask some of your readers to read my paper on Hindu marriage in Keyserling's book and challenge, in fairness to me, Miss Mayo to prove that it was my own opinion, as she asserts, that child-marriage is " a flower of the sublimated spirit, a conquest over sexuality and materialism won by exalted intellect for the eugenic uplift of the race," implying " the conviction, simply, that Indian women must be securely bound and delivered before their womanhood is upon them, if they are to be kept in hand."

' Let me in conclusion draw the attention of your readers to another amazing piece of false statement in which she introduces me, with a sneer, as a defender of the " Ayurvedic " system of medicine against Western medical science. Let her prove this libel if she can.

'There are other numerous witnesses who, like myself, if they find their access to the Western readers, will be able to place their complaints before them, informing them how their views have been misinterpreted, their words mutilated, and facts tortured into a deformity which is worse than untruth.

SANTINIKETAN,
9 November, 1927.

RABINDRANATH TAGORE.

The Englishman, a Calcutta Anglo-Indian daily, publishes, in its issue of March 7, an appreciation of the late Lord Sinha written by Mr. N. N. Sircar, 'one of the leaders of the High Court Bar in Calcutta.' Mr. Sircar, we are told, ' was closely associated with Lord Sinha, and had an intimate knowledge of his activities and views.' Mr. Sircar's appreciation exposes yet another of Miss Mayo's lies; we are reproducing below the part relevant here:

"I refer to his [Sinha's] abhorrence of being in the limelight, and a deep-rooted objection to publicity of any matter in which he was concerned. In Miss Mayo's *Mother India*,...there is a chapter headed ' A Counsel of Perfection ' (Ch. XVI. In this chapter Miss Mayo narrates a conversation with a ' Hindu nobleman who is an eminent lawyer,' and whose name Miss Mayo has not dis-

closed as ' it would be a graceless requital of
courtesy to name the gentleman just quoted.'

" This Hindu lawyer is no other than Lord
Sinha—a fact confirmed by him. It is known to
some of his friends that the interview took place
at 17, Elysium Row, Lord Sinha's residence.

' At this interview Lord Sinha is reported to
have complained about the condition of villages in
Bengal—and the inadequate attention paid to
them by the Government. Lord Sinha, it is stated,
said : ' But surely, they could have done more and
faster. And they let my people starve.' Miss
Mayo then proceeds to cover Lord Sinha with
ridicule and sarcasm by stating that this wealthy
man, ' with the income of an eminent lawyer of
New York,' has done nothing for his village
[Raipur] though it is ' but a comfortable after-
noon's ride away from his home.'

' As Lord Sinha never cared to advertise
himself, he did not care to inform Miss Mayo that
the facts are that the pucca school building at
Raipur has been constructed at Lord Sinha's
expense, that both the village school and the
village dispensary have always been maintained
by him, and permanent provision has been made
for them, that he paid Rs. 10,000 to the Agricultural Institute of his district, and that his acts of
help and charity to his village and villagers have
been too many to be mentioned.

' When Miss Mayo's book was published in
London I happened to be there. Lord Sinha's

INTRODUCTION lvii

attention was drawn to the gross injustice done to him by Miss Mayo: in fact a contradiction for publication in the press had been drafted for him, but Lord Sinha refused permission for its issue."

This nails another lie to the counter.

IV.

The question of discussing European sex morality in this book has cost me many anxious nights. I have far greater respect for Miss Mayo's sex than she seems to have, irrespective of race, colour or caste. I believe that there is nothing so beautiful and so sacred as woman. Motherhood places her above everything else in this world and that is why motherhood is held in such high esteem in India. Ancient Hindus worshipped woman in different forms. Shakti (energy), Saraswati (learning), Lakshmi (wealth), Durga (motherhood), are all female deities. The mother, the wife, the sister, the daughter, each has a separate festival dedicated to her. I have no hesitation in admitting that Hindu society has fallen from its social ideals. In my judgment this is primarily a reflection of political bondage, and it is not easy to effect a radical change for the better unless a: d until India is politically free.

We have been actively engaged in reconstructing Hindu society socially, at least since the foundation of the Brahmo Samaj in 1830. The Arya Samaj has been very active in this respect since 1877. Other agencies for social reform too have been quite active in this matter. We have denounced early marriage from thousands of platforms, and even though we got practically no help from the legislature, we have made substantial progress in raising the marriageable age of boys and girls. Marriage at the age of 12 is common now only among certain communities and castes. Personally I consider it a social crime to marry a girl under the age of 16, even though Indian girls reach puberty at about the age of 12. We have carried on an incessant war against the restrictions imposed upon the remarriage of widows, and surely some improvement is visible, though there is still a lot to do. The restrictions on widow remarriage are to be found in a few castes and communities, not in all. All the same, thousands of widow remarriages are reported every year among all classes and castes and sections of the people. There are castes among Moslems and Christians too. Some of them do not allow their widows to remarry. But there is progress all round. There is not one orthodox caste or community in which widow remarriages have not taken place. During the last decade the struggle between the orthodox Hindus and the reformers has been very keen, and the former have considerably lost ground.

The age of consent in India is 13, as fixed by statute. There is a bill before the Central Legislature to raise it to 14. It is being opposed by the Government. There is another bill to fix the marriageable age of girls at 12. Both are private bills introduced by Hindu members of the Legislative Assembly.

INTRODUCTION lix

Similarly, the movement to remove untouchability is very widespread and influential. Large sums of money have been spent by private Hindu agencies to remove untouchability and provide general and special educational facilities for the depressed classes, and otherwise to uplift them socially and economically. The statement that the movement is opposed by a ' myriad ' tongues is a wicked lie because even the most orthodox are now anxious to do justice to the depressed classes. Personally I do not believe in caste. I am in favour of its complete abolition. Nor do I believe in any distinction between the rights of men and women as regards marriage.

All these matters have been discussed in detail in the body of the book, and Miss Mayo's statements challenged and refuted. If Miss Mayo had confined herself to a *bona fide* criticism of Hindu social life the Indian social reformer would have stood by her and taken advantage of her criticisms without ever thinking of exposing the social vices of the West in retaliation. It is no business of ours to throw mud at other nations. There are evils in every society. Rightly or wrongly, we Indians believe that, even with some objectionable customs, sex life in India is much purer, much healthier and much more moral than it is in the West. We honestly believe that the ' sex stimulus ' in India is not so morbidly strong as it is in the West. As for venereal diseases we believe there is no comparison between the East and the West. The disparity is simply huge, and our medical men think that except among some hill tribes the diseases were pactically unknown in Indian life before the advent of the British. Syphilis is called ' Bad-i-Farang,' being a disease of Farangis (Europeans).

If, however, Miss Mayo had said that our social life was rotten and needed reform and reconstruction, we would not have felt so much annoyed as we do now at the base use she has made of her imperfect knowledge and at her wicked generalizations for political and racial propaganda. Even the India Office in London had warned her against such generalizations but she did not heed that and has run down a whole nation of 315 millions of human beings. She has invented false charges against us to show that we are unfit for political freedom, and that the British Government is the very best thing for us. During my recent visits to Europe in 1924, 1926, and 1927, I have observed that a wide-spread, well-organized, well-financed and influentially backed propaganda is being carried on, not only in Great Britain, but also in other countries of the West, especially in the United States of America, against India's right and claim to self-government. All kinds of agencies are at work in this campaign of vilification. Anglo-Indians retired from service or still in service, missionaries and commercial magnates, all have joined hands. The methods employed are very subtle and insidious. Political and economic troubles are kept in the background and social evils are brought out in the limelight. As usual, exaggerated and false pictures are put on the screen, which create a feeling of loathing and disgust against the Indian people. Press, platform, pulpit, the stage and cinema are all being used against us. There is no doubt that Miss Mayo's *Mother India* is a part of that propaganda. It seems that her mission in life is to oppose and bring into ridicule and contempt all the Asiatic movements for freedom from the Anglo-Saxon yoke.

As I have already said, Miss Mayo came in contact with Mr. Lionel Curtis in August 1925. In his foreword to the English edition of the *Isles of Fear* Mr. Curtis remarked as follows :*

" Here [in Williams Town] and elsewhere in the United States I have met such friends who can speak with official and first-hand knowledge of the events and conditions described in the book. In two opinions they all agree. Miss Mayo, they tell me, has written nothing which in their opinion is not the truth... They add, however, that there are other facts of the situation which Miss Mayo could scarcely be expected to observe unless she had visited the Islands in previous years... All of my informants had been in India and had met several of the Nationalist leaders. To my question, how they compared with the Philippine leaders, they, each, replied (on separate occasions) that the Indian leaders stood on a different and altogether higher plane."

Mr. Curtis knew, and Miss Mayo must have known that a revision of the Reforms was due and

---

* Curtis *op. cit.*

that the Statutory inquiry into the working of the
reforms was about to be undertaken. The London
Times and other Tory papers had been agitating
for some time past over the constitution of this
commission. They wanted no Indians on it.
They had been prejudicing the British public
against India by their attacks on the Hindu social
system and by laying special emphasis on the disabilities of the untouchables. *The Times* had been
devoting column after column to the exposure of
these so-called evils. It seems probable that the
British Tory Press knew that a book of the kind
was in preparation. So when the book came out
they began to boom it as the work of a ' disinterested ' foreigner. It was the most valuable
support to their cause. Such was their anxiety to
shut out any criticism of the book from its readers
that they threw all journalistic ethics to the winds
and refused to publish the criticisms of *Mother
India* though signed by the most influential and
reliable Indians, official and non-official, then
present in London. The book has been distributed
free by the thousand. All these facts leave no
doubt in the mind of an Indian that the real
motive behind the book is political and racial.

In these circumstances should we not hit back
by stating what is perfectly true—that the vices
attributed to us by Miss Mayo are to be found,
some of them even more widely and intensely,
also in European society and that they are not
considered to be a bar to national and political
freedom? As I have said, the question has cost
me many sleepless nights, but I have finally come

to the conclusion that my duty to my country and to truth requires that I should not leave my rejoinder incomplete, and that even though the task be not congenial to my nature, I must do it.

When I returned from America in 1920 I was repeatedly asked to write my impressions of Western life, but I declined to do so as such action might involve me in the unpleasant task of discussing the dark side of sex morality in the West. I believe in seeing the best in every nation. That is how we can improve international relations and advance the cause of international peace. If I am, therefore, for the first time in my life, going to depart from that rule, the responsibility is entirely Miss Mayo's or that of her Anglo-Indian supporters.

V.

Not only in the use, rather more aptly in the abuse, of her authorities, but also in her own writing Miss Mayo's one endeavour is to draw a dark and dreary picture of our life. Her sweeping generalizations are often without a shred of truth in them. Her mind is obscured by our excessive sensuality, and on the Freudian hypothesis her frequent references to this topic, in season and out of season, suggest morbidity of an uncommon order. For our readers we reproduce below a few typical statements:

Page 25.—If you do employ them [women teachers for primary education] you invite the ruin of each woman that you so expose.

Page 30.—The infant that survives the birth strain......[is] often venereally poisoned.

Page 30.—The child growing up in the home learns, from earliest grasp of word and act, to dwell upon sex relations.

Pages 32-33.—In many parts of the country, north and south, the little boy, his mind so prepared, is likely, if physically attractive, to be drafted for the satisfaction of grown men, or to be regularly attached to a temple, in the capacity of prostitute. Neither parent as a rule sees any harm in this, but is, rather, flattered that the son has been found pleasing.

This, also, is a matter neither of rank nor of special ignorance. In fact, so far are they from seeing good and evil as we see good and evil, that the mother, high caste or low caste, will practise upon children—the girl ' to make her sleep well,' the boy ' to make him manly,' an abuse which the boy, at least, is apt to continue daily for the rest of his life.

This last point should be noticed. Highest medical authorities in widely scattered sections attest that practically every child brought under observation, for whatever reason, bears on its body the signs of this habit.

Page 34.—Little in the popular Hindu code suggests self-restraint in any direction, least of all in sex relations.

Page 34.—After the rough outline just given, small surprise will meet the statement that from one end of the land to the other the average male Hindu of thirty years, provided he has means to command his pleasure, is an old man; and that from seven to eight, out of every ten such males between the ages of twenty-five and thitry, are impotent. These figures are not random, and are affected by little save the proviso above given.*

Page 61.—[Indian women] commonly experience marital use two and three times a day.

Page 67.—Until the Pax Britannica reached so far [the Khyber Pass], few Hindus came through alive, unless mounted and clad as women.

Page 84.—An inmate of her husband's home at the time of his death, the widow, although she has no legal claim for protection, may be retained there on the terms above described, or she may be turned adrift. Then she must live by charity— or by prostitution, into which she not seldom falls. And her dingy, ragged figure, her bristly, shaven head, even though its stubble be white over the haggard face of unhappy age, is often to be seen in temple crowds or in the streets of pilgrimage cities, where sometimes niggard piety doles her a handful of rice.

Page 86.—The remarriage of a Hindu widowed wife is still held to be inconceivable.

Page 91.—Therefore, in total, you have the half-blind, the aged, the crippled, the palsied and

---

*Even a sympathetic British reviewer of Miss Mayo's book, Mr. Rushbrook Williams, formerly Publicity Agent of the Indian Government, is forced to point out the evident absurdity of such a staement. See his review in the *Asiatic Review*, London.

the diseased, drawn from the dirtiest poor, as sole ministrants to the women of India in the most delicate, the most dangerous and the most important hour of their existence. [This is about midwives.]

Page 154.—To-day the defenders of untouchability are myriad, and, though Mr. Gandhi lives his faith, but few of his supporters have at any time cared to follow him so far.

Page 308.—" Without the British no Hindus will remain in India except such as we [Pathans] keep for slaves."

Page 325.—"If we protect our babies the gods will be jealous and bring us all bad luck"!!! [These words are put into the mouth of a Bengali mother.]

Page 332.—No orthodox Hindu, and certainly no woman, will consent to wear shoes.

We have given only a few samples. These and many more of such statements we shall notice in the body of our book. But can a writer, who indulges in such wild generalizations on such a lavish scale, be taken seriously by serious people?

A POSTSCRIPT.

In *Liberty*, a weekly magazine owned by the *Chicago Tribune*, in its issue of the 14th January, 1928, Miss Mayo has an article that attempts to meet some of the criticisms on *Mother India*.

She refers in particular to Mahatma Gandhi's review of her book from which we have already quoted at length. Being clever at quibbling she tries to hoodwink the public by throwing the real issues involved in the background when protesting that she had not said that the Mahatma always had two secretaries about him to take down all that he said, a fact which is a mere side issue. 'If Mr. Gandhi were to look on page 222 [page 202, English edition] he would discover that he has inserted the word "always" into my text.' Nothing of the kind. Mr. Gandhi has inserted nothing into her text; he merely says that without using the word 'always' Miss Mayo conveys the impression that she is not merely describing the occasion of her visit to his 'Ashram.'

But that, however, is a trivial thing. Much more important is the message incident. And in this Miss Mayo certainly does not come out with credit to herself. Says she:

"......I duly received back the corrected and expanded report of the interview, over Mr. Gandhi's own signature.

'The first sentence of this document of several typed pages, now before me, is his reply to my opening question: 'Have you any message for America?' It reads as it was spoken, and as I have printed it: 'My message to America is the hum of this spinning-wheel.'

'Mr. Gandhi now seeks to disavow the 'message' as the invention of an enemy. 'I do not remember having given the message......The only one present who took any notes at all has no recollection of the message imputed to me,' he says."

But what are the facts about this message? At the time of writing his review on *Mother India*, Mahatma Gandhi—being on tour—had not the notes of the interview with him. But in his recent article in *Young India* (February 2, 1928) written in reply to Miss Mayo's article in the *Liberty* he has given the facts thus:

" Her adherence to the statement that I did give her the message she ascribes to me proves her to be guilty of gross suppression of truth. She seems to have thought that I would not have a copy of the corrected interview between her and me. Unfortunately for her I happen to possess a copy of her notes. Here is the full quotation referring to the hum of the wheel :

" ' My message to America is simply the hum of this wheel. Letters and newspaper cuttings I get from America show that one set of people overrates the results of Non-violent Non-co-operation and the other not only underrates it, but imputes all kinds of motives to those who are concerned with the movement. Don't exaggerate one way or the other. If, therefore, some earnest Americans will study the movement impartially and patiently, then it is likely that the United States may know something of the movement which I do consider to be unique, although I am the author of it. What I mean is that our movement is summed up in the spinning-wheel with all its implications. It is to me a substitute for gunpowder—for it brings the message of self-reliance and hope to the millions of India. And when they are really awakened they would not need to lift their little finger in order to regain their freedom. The message of the spinning-wheel is, really, to replace the spirit of exploitation by the spirit of service. The dominant note in the West is the note of exploitation. I have no desire that my country should copy that spirit or that note.'

'The first sentence only of the foregoing extract, which Miss Mayo quotes without the most important commentary on it, is intended to ridicule me. But the whole paragraph, I hope, makes my meaning and message clear and intelligible... I claim, however, that the message, as it appears in the full paragraph quoted, is not different from what I have stated in the article Miss Mayo attempts to shake."

The message, as is now plain, was not 'invented' by Miss Mayo; but her offence remains as grave as it was—for her dishonest parody of the message is in no way more honourable than an outright invention. Having no defence to offer she has only quibbled again. And yet this 'trivial quibble,' as she calls this episode, releases her 'from the necessity of further considering Mr. Gandhi's criticism at this writing.'

Mahatma Gandhi's protest that the *Mother India* 'story' of the Sassoon Hospital operation on him was grossly misleading has not been noticed by her, she having released herself from the further necessity of considering Gandhi!

And, again, what about her taking liberty with Tagore's paper in Keyserling's book? If Miss Mayo's article in any way seeks to make amends for the grave wrong she did Tagore, or even if she has some quibble in defence of her indefensible mishandling, we do not find it in the excerpts from her article that we have seen.

CHAPTER I

THE ARGUMENT

The first two parts of Miss Mayo's work (chapters I—X) deal with the social life—that is to say the social evils—of the Hindus. Most of the evils dealt with by her, so far as they exist, are really common to all classes of Indians, but she generally singles out the Hindus for her malicious attacks. These chapters are full of rash and vile generalizations against the manhood and womanhood of India. Sometimes these charges contain just that dash of truth which makes a statement more dangerous than an utter falsehood. No Indian, however keenly conscious he may be of the evils of the existing social order, and however great may be his ardour for radical reform, can, in any case, accept the picture drawn by Miss Mayo as anything but grossly exaggerated and untrue.

The fact is that Miss Mayo began with entirely wrong premises and presumptions. We have seen in the *Introduction* that there is good reason to suppose that this 'unsubsidized, uncommitted, and unattached' woman journalist from America came on a mission of political propaganda. Her object was to whitewash British imperialism, and in the fulfilment of that mission she has ignored all the decencies of a writer's art. For illiteracy, misery and disease in India she assigns no responsibility to the State. To her all that there is in India is wrong, and is so because the Hindu is either a savage sensual beast, or a pervert, or both.

The details of her picture of Indian social life form the subject of discussion in the chapters that follow. But Miss Mayo's logic, according to which the Indian Government is absolved from all responsibility in the matter, must be examined at the very outset, for it is fundamental to her argument.

On page 23 of *Mother India* we find Sir Chimanlal Setalvad and Mahatma Gandhi quoted. The ultra-moderate politician, Sir Chimanlal, is reported to have stated: "What this country suffers from is want of initiative, want of enterprise, and want of hard, sustained work."

This is put in juxtaposition with a sentence taken from Mahatma Gandhi's weekly, *Young India*. "We rightly charge the English rulers for our helplessness and lack of initiative and originality."

Then follows another statement attributed to 'other public men of India,' who demand:

" ' Why are our enthusiasms so sterile? Why are our mutual pledges, our self-dedications to brotherhood and the cause of liberty so soon spent and forgotten? Why is our manhood itself so brief? Why do we tire so soon and die so young?' Only to answer themselves with the cry: 'Our spiritual part is wounded and bleeding. Our very souls are poisoned by the shadow of the arrogant stranger, blotting out our sun. Nothing can be done—nothing, anywhere, but to mount the political platform and faithfully denounce our tyrant until he takes his flight. When Britain has abdicated and gone, then, and not till then, free men breathing free air, may we turn our minds to the lesser needs of our dear Mother India.'"

To all this Miss Mayo's glib reply is:

"The British administration of India, be it good, bad, or indifferent, has nothing whatever to do with the conditions above indicated. Inertia, helplessness, lack of initiative and originality, lack of staying power and of sustained loyalties, sterility of enthusiasm, weakness of life-vigour itself—all are traits that truly characterize the Indian not only of to-day, but of long-past history. All, furthermore, will continue to characterize him, in increasing degree, until he admits their causes and with his own two hands uproots them. His soul and body are indeed chained in slavery. But he himself wields and hugs his chains and with violence defends them. No agency but a new spirit within his own breast can set him free. And his arraignments of outside elements, past, present or to come, serve only to deceive his own mind and to put off the day of his deliverance.

'Take a girl-child twelve years old, a pitiful physical specimen in bone and blood, illiterate, ignorant, without any sort of training in habits of health. Force motherhood upon her at the earliest possible moment. Rear her weakling son in intensive vicious practices that drain his small vitality day by day. Give him no outlet in sports. Give him habits that make him, by the time he is thirty years of age, a decrepit and querulous old wreck—and will you ask what has sapped the energy of his manhood?

' Take a huge population, mainly rural, illiterate and loving its illiteracy. Try to give it primary education without employing any of its women as teachers—because if you do employ them you invite the ruin of each woman that you so expose. Will you ask why that people's education proceeds slowly?

' Take bodies and minds bred and built on the lines thus indicated. Will you ask why the death-rate is high and the people poor?

' Whether British or Russian or Japanese sit in the seat of the highest; whether the native princes divide the land, reviving old days of princely dominance; or whether some autonomy more complete than that now existing be set up, the only power that can hasten the pace of Indian development toward freedom, beyond the pace it is travelling to-day, is the power of the men of India, wasting no more time in talk, recriminations, and shiftings of blame, but facing and attacking, with the best resolution they can muster, the task that awaits them in their own bodies and souls.''

To avoid doing her any injustice we have quoted Miss Mayo at length.

Now it is quite plausible to argue that we Indians have by our disunion and foolishness invited foreign rule, and must blame ourselves if that rule has dwarfed our stature, emasculated our bodies, made us incapable of initiative, blocked our way to progress and national efficiency. If such were Miss Mayo's argument, we would admit its force. In fact, it is because this argument is so strong that we want to throw off the foreign yoke and be free to develop to our full stature as a nation.

But Miss Mayo seems to argue in quite a different way. To her, political environment has nothing to do with national inefficiency and helplessness. Are initiative and enterprise in a nation wholly independent of its political environment? Are literacy, health, national efficiency in no way influenced by those who run the legislative and administrative machinery? Are these things dependent wholly on social custom, as Miss Mayo would have us believe? Are not, on the other hand, even social customs largely determined by the political conditions prevailing in a country and the literacy of her people?

These questions go to the very root of the matter. For, to us, it seems that the Indian problem is primarily a politico-economic one, and one of social customs is only secondary.

To suit her purpose Miss Mayo assumes the existence of certain facts which do not exist at all. Secondly, she fancifully traces them to ' long-past history '—of which she is utterly ignorant. Thirdly, she entirely ignores the effects of economic and political bondage on the *whole* life of a people, including even the social and spiritual.

Miss Mayo argues in a most superficial way when she thus lightly dismisses the political factor. It must have been women like Miss Mayo that elicited this unenviable tribute from a very distinguished psychologist, Professor Münsterberg, in his sympathetic but frank study of America:* "The American woman who has scarcely a shred of education, looks in vain for any subject on which she has not firm convictions already at hand... The arrogance of this feminine lack of knowledge is the symptom of a profound trait in the feminine soul, and points to dangers springing from the domination of women in the intellectual life..."

Why is a girl-child of 12 years 'a pitiful physical specimen in bone and blood?' asks Miss Mayo. The causes may be: (*a*) heredity, (*b*) insufficient food, (*c*) unhygienic conditions of life, (*d*) illiteracy and ignorance. Leaving (*a*) alone can anyone say, that (*b*), (*c*) and (*d*) are not affected by political conditions? It is an admitted fact that children born of weak parents can to a great extent make up for inherited weakness if they are well looked after afterwards. But if to hereditary weakness are added the disabilities which result from political bondage and economic

The Americans, p. 587.

penury then God help such children. It is the duty of a national government to see that every child that is born is well looked after, and, if the parents are too poor to bring it up in a healthy atmosphere and to fit it for the duties of citizenship, the responsibility is the State's. It is the recognition of this principle that has led in modern times to the establishment of 'national nurseries' for the benefit of deficiently born children, and of national public schools for the free and compulsory education of all children, irrespective and regardless of their parents. The prohibition of child labour, the compulsory physical education of all the citizens, the State or municipal feeding of the insufficiently fed children, the compulsory and periodical medical examination, and, last but not least, a provision by the State for unemployment, are everyday facts in free and progressive lands. Why are the States taking so much trouble to root out drunkenness, to remedy and cure venereal disease, to regulate marriage and to prevent overcrowding? Why have the different governments in the world established Ministries of Health? Why has the government in Britain taken up the problems of milk supply and the provision of good sanitary houses for all and sundry? Why has all this been done if Miss Mayo's premises are correct?

If the national governments of the world were justified in undertaking these responsibilities, why has the Government of India shirked them? The explanation is obvious. The Government of India is a foreign government whose chief business in India is to get the most out of her and to exploit her for the benefit of the Empire. When Sir Austen Chamberlain (an ex-Secretary of State for India) speaking at the Savoy Hotel on March 29, 1917, said that India would not and ought not to remain content to be a hewer of wood and drawer of water for the rest of the Empire, the implication was clear that so far India had been no better than a hewer of wood and drawer of water for the Empire. In that position she continues to be to this day. The whole economic history of British rule in India is evidence of that.*

Given the fact that for the last 200 years India has been exploited by the British for the benefit of their Empire, her social degradation, the physical degeneration of her sons and daughters and the lack of initiative and spirit in them can be easily explained. Everyone knows, perhaps Miss Mayo not excepted, what social legislation in Great Britain, Germany, France, the United States, and Japan has done within the last 75 years. There is no sphere of child or adult life, the ' sanctity ' of which has not been invaded by law and administrative orders. It is only a national State that identifies itself with the nation. The interests of the two are so inter-dependent as to make them wholly identified with each other. Even in

---

* In subsequent chapters I shall have occasion to refer to this. But for fuller particulars I must refer the reader to documents quoted from, and referred to by me in my book *England's Debt to India*, published by B. W. Huebsch, New York, 1917.

ancient India the State had a great deal to do with social life and public health. Hindu law-givers and commentators devoted volumes to public education in all its branches, student life, public and personal hygiene, marriage, etc.

To-day every political thinker and every statesman recognizes the responsibility of the State in equipping the citizen properly for the race of life. The thing is so obvious to-day that it may seem superfluous to labour the point and cite authorities. However, in view of the fact that the question is vital to Miss Mayo's argument it may be worth while to have the opinion of some recent writers.

The American sociologist, Professor Scott Nearing, remarks in one of his best books, *Social Adjustment:**

" In a large community, maladjustment [i.e., social maladjustment] can be removed *only* by concentrating public opinion *in the form of legislation.* Among large groups public opinion may relieve maladjustment temporarily but *permanent reform can be effected only through legislative expression.*" [Italics are ours.]

Discussing modern social philosophy, Mr. L. T. Hobhouse, the great Liberal thinker of England, has often pointed out how the present ideas of the responsibility of the State in social matters have developed. In one of his books† he

* Macmillan, 1911, p. 323.
† *Social Evolution and Political Theory,* Columbia University Press, 1911, pp. 178 *et. seq.*

speaks of the extension of the sphere of common responsibility in the remarkable growth of State control, and discusses the principles on which the responsibility of the State for employment is based leading to a State provision for old age pensions, etc. He refers to the report of the minority on the Poor Law Commission which recommended that ' the labour exchanges, themselves constituting a new State agency for the provision of employment, should be constituted the centre of a machine by which no adult, healthy working man or woman would be left without means of support in periods of industrial crises. Speaking of the duties of a modern State, Professor Hobhouse remarks :

"The determined idler must not be allowed to prey upon society, he must not go cadging about for odds and ends of useless jobs or for bits of charity; he must not be allowed to keep his wife and children in rags, ill-housed and underfed. The children must be cared for; the mother, if she is doing her duty by them, is doing one woman's work and may fairly claim public maintenance with no possible question of a return. As to the man, he is a fit subject for discipline and restraint. For him a labour colony must be provided, where he must learn to work and gain his discharge as soon as he can prove himself efficient enough in mind and body to stand the stress of industrial competition."

In that strain he goes on to define the duty of the State towards people of different types and

different ages. The gist of his survey is that
recent years have witnessed a ' remarkable extension of the functions of the State as the organizer
of certain great departments of life.' Foremost
amongst these is public education. ' Within the
lifetime of men who still survive the function of
the State in education was conceived as being
adequately discharged by the grant of a few
thousands a year in support of the poor. Within
my lifetime the State has made itself responsible
for the elementary education of three-fourths of the
community, and from elementary education it has
advanced to secondary education, and at least to
an active interest in and a modest financial
support of education of a university type.'
As Professor Hobhouse points out, a good deal
of the burden on the State to-day would have
been regarded by earlier thinkers as ' a necessary
incident of parental responsibility.' To-day ' the
older liberty of the family is impaired by the
principle of compulsion.' ' No more striking
illustration of the extension of State functions
could be given than a comparison of the budget of
an Education Minister of the present day with
that of 1850 or 1860.'

The testimony of history is clear. If one
studies the condition of England, religious, social,
hygienic, intellectual and industrial, before 1870—
or still earlier, before the Reform laws of 1830—one
would find that the condition of the masses was
worse in most respects than that of the people of
India to-day. Illiteracy was rampant, disease and
destitution were wide-spread, the condition of

women and children in the factories was indescribable, and morality of any kind seemed almost non-existent. Down to 1870 education of the people was in a sad state. In speaking of the achievements of England in the nineteenth century, Mr. G. M. Trevelyan, the historian, says :*

"A characteristic of the new national machinery, fully apparent towards the end of Queen Victoria's reign, was the close inter-relation that had grown up on the one hand between private philanthropic effort and State control, and on the other between local and central governments. As Parliament and local government began to respond to the needs of the community as a whole, and as the State became more and more intelligently interested in the work of private effort in education, medicine, sanitation and a hundred other sides of life,—an elaborate system of State aid, enforcement and control came into being, through Treasury grants-in-aid to local bodies, State inspection of conditions of labour and of life, industrial insurance and the modern educational system."

Again :

"The advance in humanity, democracy and education, and the changes in industrial method, bringing large crowds of wage-earners of both sexes together in offices and factories, led to a new conception of the place of woman in society. The education of women, from being *almost totally*

* *History of England*, G. M. Trevelyan, Longmans, 1926, p. 617.

neglected, became in a couple of generations comparable to that of men. The position of women in the family was altered in law, and was yet more altered in practice and opinion."*
[Italics are ours.]

Some of the Continental countries started work on these lines earlier than Great Britain. Germany passed a law for the compulsory education of her children in 1717. Discussing the tendencies of the British dominions to entrust the State more and more with social duties, Charles Pearson in his book on *National Life and Character* says : †

" Let it be remembered, however, that every Continental State—even those of Germanic origin—has worked for centuries upon these lines, and that in England itself the first entrenchments of the *laissez faire* system have been forced."

These principles are recognized to-day by every State and every statesman. Individualist and Socialist, Fascist and Bolshevik countries alike recognize that it is the duty of the State to see that its people are not illiterate. This principle finds acceptance in the over-prosperous United States of America as much as in its indigent neighbour, Mexico, and as much in the Far Eastern Japan as in the Western lands. A politically free India, would, no doubt, be no exception to it. Indians no more love illiteracy

* *Ibid.*, p. 618.
† Macmillan, 1913, p. 19.

and ignorance than do the masses in the Western countries. But it must be recognized that progress in literacy in India, as in the West, cannot be altogether without compulsion.

CHAPTER II

THE LIGHT THROUGH THE AGES

Chapters XIII to XVI of Miss Mayo's book deal with education in India. The first of these is headed, ' Give Me Office or Give Me Death.' Miss Mayo betrays a lack of humour, when she unwittingly chooses a heading which in itself is the strongest condemnation of the educational policy of the British Government in India. But she does not seem to recognize that the Government in India owes a duty to the people in matters educational. Her sole concern is to find fault with the Hindus and throw the whole blame for the inadequacy of education and of the defects of the British Indian educational system on their broad shoulders. Chapter XIII of *Mother India* opens thus:

" Education, some Indian politicians affirm, should be driven into the Indian masses by compulsory measures. 'England,' they say, ' introduced compulsory education at home long ago. Why does she not do so here? Because, clearly it suits her purpose to leave the people ignorant.' "

A ' hot reply ' to this, Miss Mayo tells us, was given her by the Raja of Panagal, the ' then anti-Brahman leader of Madras Presidency':

" ' Rubbish!' he exclaimed. ' What did the Brahmans do for our education in the 5,000 years before Britain came? I remind you: *They asserted their right to pour hot lead into the ears of the low caste man who should dare to study books.* All learning belonged to them, they said. When the Muhammadans swarmed in and took us, even that was an improvement on the old Hindu regime. But only in Britain's day did education become the right of all, with State schools, colleges, and universities accessible to all castes, communities, and peoples.' " [Italics are ours.]

This is supported by two quotations from the book of the Abbé Dubois. The first quotation, torn, as is not unusual with our authoress, from the context, runs thus :

" '[The Brahmans] saw well enough,' says Dubois, 'what a moral ascendancy knowledge would give them over the other castes, and they therefore made a mystery of it by taking all possible precautions to prevent other classes from obtaining access to it.' "

Miss Mayo omits the first two sentences of the paragraph from which this quotation is taken, for they credit the Hindus with having cultivated learning from the earliest times, and the Brahmans with having been always as ' it were its depositories.'* Miss Mayo evidently did not want to let this kind of ' damaging ' statement go into her book.

We have already discussed the credentials of the Abbé in the *Introduction*, and it is unnecessary

* *Hindu Manners*, etc., 3rd edition, Oxford University Press, p. 376.

to emphasize again that no unprejudiced enquirer can afford to rely on that tainted source. The Raja of Panagal, Miss Mayo's other authority, has, as will be seen from his letter reproduced in the *Introduction*, made it clear that Miss Mayo, as seems her wont, has in this case too been guilty of a dishonest use of the inverted commas. The language put within the commas is not that of the Raja to whom it is ascribed, but of the American journalist herself. The Raja had referred only to the ban against the study of the Vedas by the Shudras, but Miss Mayo, by resorting to tricks of the trade so familiar to her, makes the statement far more sweeping. Surely reciting the Vedas is not equivalent to ' all learning,' and 'study of books.' Besides, what has the present day illiteracy to do with what the Brahmans did or did not do ages ago? But Miss Mayo was anxious to supply a background for her subsequent conclusions in which she eulogizes the Government of India's work in the matter of education in India and throws the whole blame of the educational backwardness of the Hindus on themselves.

Panagal's statement is at best that of a partisan, and Dubois's remarks are irrelevant. Assuming that the Brahmans were so wicked as to shut the doors of knowledge upon all non-Brahmans—which is a lie in itself—can that justify the behaviour in this century, of a Western government that poses to be civilized and up to date, and is no mild critic of the Brahmans? Are we to conclude that the modern white Brahmans have taken the place of the yellow and black

Brahmans of old India and are treading in their footsteps in keeping the people of non-European origin in ignorance and bondage?

But the charge against the Hindu Brahmans has no leg to stand upon, and we have excellent authority for proving its baselessness. I have before me a small book* written by a Christian missionary, Rev. F. E. Keay, on this subject. Rev. Keay is no apologist for the Brahmans. I shall base the account that follows on his book.

Rev. Keay traces the Brahmanic system of education to the very remotest past. By the time the 'various portions of the Veda had been completed, Brahmanic education was not only of long standing but was highly organized.'†

It is unnecessary to go into details here regarding the curricula at the Brahmanic seats of learning. As a rule the young Brahmans specialized in the Vedic and the philosophical studies. For the Kshatriyas and Vaishyas 'it is probable that...the study of the Veda was something far less serious than [it was] for the young Brahmans, and the duties which the former had to perform in life must have necessitated their receiving the education suitable for their special callings before they became adults. Probably they tended less and less to attend the Brahmanic schools, and vocational schools, or at least domestic training,

---

Ancient Indian Education, Oxford University Press, 1918.
† *Op. cit.*, p. 27.

for their future duties in life were developed.'*
'By the time that the earliest *Dharmasutras* which are extant were composed (*circa* 500 B.C.) the system was in full working order, and it had become customary for Kshatriyas and Vaishyas, as well as for Brahmans to be initiated with the sacred thread as a preliminary to entering upon the period of life under Brahman teachers, which was to occupy at least twelve years.'†

Later on (between the sixth and fourth centuries before Christ), Kshatriya education came to attract special attention. The science of politics had grown up. 'The education of the young Indian nobles was not inferior to that of the European knights in the times of chivalry... The idea that the king and the nobles had a duty to perform to society in the protection of the weak, and that their position was not one so much of glory and of ease as of service to others, is very prominent.'‡

"A Vaishya," says Rev. Keay on the authority of Manu, "must know the respective value of gems, of pearls, of corals, of metals, of cloth made of thread, of perfumes, and of condiments. He must be acquainted with the manner of sowing seeds, and of the good and bad qualities of fields, and he must perfectly know all measures and weights. Moreover, the excellence and defects of commodities, the advantages and disadvantages of different countries, the probable profit and loss on merchan-

* *Op. cit.*, p. 57.
† *Op. cit.*, p. 59.
‡ *Op. cit.*, pp. 71-72.

dise, and the means of properly rearing cattle. He must be acquainted with the proper wages of servants, with the various languages..."*

Brahman schools of learning known as *tols* were 'indeed scattered all over the land in numerous towns and villages.'† Sometimes in a town of special sanctity, or even of political importance, *tols* were established side by side and constituted a kind of university. Benares and Nadia furnish examples.

Rev. Keay sees in the educational system of ancient India ' an interesting and pleasing picture of the life of pupil and teacher...dating back to many centuries before Christ.'‡ The teacher had no mercenary motive to impel him to teach, but was to perform his office solely as a duty. He was forbidden to accept a fee. The pupil, on the completion of his course, would offer a present to his preceptor. But ' except possibly in the case of rich pupils it could never have been in any sense an adequate remuneration.'§ The pupil was trained to a simple life, whether he was rich or poor, and habits of discipline, reverence and self-respect were inculcated. The discipline was somewhat rigorous, but had nothing harsh or brutal about it. In the matter of the punishment of the pupil the Hindus were far more humane than Britons of the time of Dickens. Keay quotes

* *Op. cit.*, pp. 72-73.
† *Op. cit.*, p. 51.
‡ *Op. cit.*, p. 36.
§ *Op. cit.*, p. 35.

Gautama as laying down that, ' as a rule, the pupil shall not be punished corporally. If no other course is possible he may be corrected with a thin rope or cane. If the teacher strikes him with any other instrument he shall be punished by the king.' Manu agrees with this in substance and forbids beating on a ' noble part ' of the body. Apastamba, however, allows as punishments 'frightening, fasting, bathing in cold water, and banishment from the teacher's presence.'*

What of the Shudras, the impatient reader will ask? Replies Rev. Keay: " The Shudras were always shut out from Brahmanic education, and they also developed their own system of training for the young craftsman. The popular system of education, which will be noticed in a later chapter, also grew up to meet a need for which the Brahmanic schools made no provision."† The caste system, its disadvantages notwithstanding, helped in keeping up high standards in craftsmanship which even the Abbé Dubois praised. " The spirit of fine art and of craftsmanship has existed in India for long centuries, and has still a future before it," says Keay. The system of education for the lads of each trade was a domestic one. Generally they were 'brought up to the same trade as their fathers.' 'The boy was taught by observing and handling real things,' and the training was free from the artificiality of the school-room.' The

* *Op. cit.*, p. 35.
† *Op. cit.*, p. 57. The quotations that follow about the craftsman's education are from Keay's book, pp. 78-80.

father would take a great delight in passing on to his son his own skill. ' In the collection of jade at the Indian Museum there is a large engraved bowl on which a family in the employ of the Emperors of Delhi was engaged for 3 generations.' In several crafts there was a systematic course in drawing for the lads. ' The education of the young craftsman in India was entirely vocational, and even narrowly so.' In many occupations ' a knowledge of reading and writing would not be required for the direct purposes of the craft, and would not be learnt. But certain Sanskrit works would, in some occupations, be learnt by heart.'

Rev. Keay sums up his survey of the Brahmanic system:*

" Like the Muhammadan education with which it has many points of similarity, it [the Brahmanic education] was at least not inferior to the education of Europe, before the Revival of Learning. Not only did the Brahman educators develop a system of education which survived the crumbling of empires and the changes of society, but they also, through all these thousands of years, kept aglow the torch of higher learning, and numbered amongst them many great thinkers *who have left their mark not only upon the learning of India, but upon the intellectual life of the world.*" [Italics are ours.]

When Buddhism came, it had also to organize and develop a system of education. The Buddhist

---
* *Op. cit.*, p. 57.

system was very much like the Brahmanical system from which it borrowed largely. Some of the Buddhist universities were of enormous size. Their high standards of learning attracted many scholars from China, some of whom have recorded descriptions of these seats of learning. Buddhist education was by no means merely theological education. The study of medicine received special attention at the Buddhist universities. The Buddhist seats of learning did not shut their doors upon any caste or creed. The high caste, the low caste, the Buddhist, the would-be Buddhist, the non-Buddhist, all were welcome. The contribution of Buddhist monks to elementary mass education was also considerable. Because of its Buddhist monasteries practically every male adult in Burma was literate when the British set foot there. "In Burma," says Rev. Keay, "before the country came under British control, almost the whole male population passed through the monasteries, and were taught by the monks."* Under British rule of course that universal literacy has not survived.

These systems continued tenaciously even when political power passed on to the Muslims. Says Rev. Keay:†

"Some of the more ruthless, or more orthodox, of Muhammadan sovereigns destroyed Brahman places of learning, and scattered their students, but in spite of this interruption, Brahman

* *Op. cit.*, pp. 50-51.

† The quotations (from Keay) about elementary education are from chapter V of the work referred to.

learning continued." The Buddhist institutions 'gradually decayed and disappeared, a process which was helped by the assimilation of Buddhism in India with Hinduism. But the Brahman education continued in spite of difficulties, and, as the Buddhist centres of learning decayed, those of the Brahmans became more prominent.'

*

A reference has already been made to the system of *popular* elementary education, which flourished side by side with that of higher Sanskrit learning. We must now go into it more fully to see whether mass literacy was such an unknown thing in India as writers like Miss Katherine Mayo would have us believe.

Says Rev. Keay:*

" Side by side, however, with these [the Brahmanic, Buddhistic and Muslim systems] there grew up at some time and in most parts of India, a popular system of elementary education *which was open generally to all comers.* It must have arisen to supply a popular demand for instruction in reading, writing and arithmetic, and was made use of chiefly by the trading and agricultural classes."

The italics are ours, and are intended to make it clear that the contention that it is the caste system and the Brahmans that are responsible, wholly or largely, for the present day illiteracy in India, is nothing short of a gratuitous lie. As

* *Ibid.*, p. 107.

THE LIGHT THROUGH THE AGES

Rev. Keay points out, this indigenous system of mass elementary education was independent of the Sanskrit school. ' There was no mutual dependence or connection between them.' The elementary school catered to the trading and artisan classes, the Sanskrit school to the religious and the learned.

It is difficult to trace when this system of national literacy originated, but there can be no doubt that it continued in full vigour all through the Muslim period and had not died out when the British came into power. Official records, incomplete as their account of the disappearing system is, leave no room for doubt about its having been wide-spread Rev. Keay refers briefly to the evidence furnished by British-Indian records and British officials:

" There was then, before the British Government took over control of education in India, a wide-spread, popular, indigenous system. It was not confined to one or two provinces, but was found in various parts of India, though some districts were more advanced than others. In the inquiry made for the Madras Presidency in 1822-26, it was calculated that rather less than one-sixth of the boys of school-going age received education of some sort. In the similar enquiry made for the Bombay Presidency (1823-28) the number of boys under instruction was put down as about one in eight. In one of the districts in Bengal, where Adam carried out his inquiry, he found 13.2 per cent. of the whole male population receiving instruction. In another district he found 9 per cent. of all children of school-going age under instruction. William Ward says that it was supposed that about one-fifth of the male population of Bengal could read. In some parts of India the number under instruction would probably be less than that in the three provinces mentioned. Wide-spread, therefore, as elementary education was, it did not include a very large proportion even of the male population, and amongst females of course it hardly existed at all."*

The conclusion in the last sentence is based on the evidence available at the time when the indigenous system was on the decline; even then, as we shall presently see from official evidence, at least in the case of the Punjab, the reference to literacy amongst women as almost non-existent is not warranted by facts. However, the following quotation from Rev. Keay's closing chapter is interesting : †

*There is reason to believe that in these surveys the number of indigenous schools and of scholars receiving education therein was under-estimated. Even where the survey was directed by a sympathetic official at the top, the subordinates collecting data did not evince the needed sympathy for the indigenous system; besides, the agency engaged in such surveys was often looked at askance by the people themselves. Dr. Lietner, speaking of these difficulties, refers to the returns of Rawalpindi district in the Punjab : " Of this district the public returns gave 171 schools with 3,700 pupils; the first returns of the district officers for 1878-9 gave 302 schools with 5,454 pupils, but when Mr. Miller took the matter in hand, the existence of 681 schools with 7,145 pupils was ascertained." Leitner's *History of Indigenous Education in the Punjab*, p. 14.

† *Ibid.*, p. 169.

"*Few countries, and certainly no Western ones, have had systems of education which have had such a long and continuous history with so few modifications as some of the educational systems of India.* The long centuries through which they have held sway show that they must have possessed elements which were of value, and that they were not unsuited to the needs of those who developed and adopted them. They produced many great men and earnest seekers after truth, and their output on the intellectual side is by no means inconsiderable. They developed many noble educational ideals, which are a valuable contribution to educational thought and practice." [Italics are ours.]

These quotations from an authority who could not even remotely be accused of a pro-Hindu or pro-Indian bias, ought to be sufficient to convince any seeker after truth of the absurdity of Miss Mayo's position and of the utter unreliability of the foundations on which she has built.

Fortunately we have some official documents also that show how fairly wide-spread education in India was, and how well the indigenous system fulfilled our needs, till the British took charge of this country and made a clean sweep of the indigenous structure without substituting for it anything that could be called satisfactory or adequate. A remarkable publication amongst these is Dr. Leitner's *History of Indigenous Education in the Punjab*. Dr. Leitner was an eminent educationist in the Punjab, who served as the first

Principal of the Lahore Government College, and later as the Director of Public Instruction in the province. The very thorough and painstaking investigations made by him about the indigenous system in the Punjab surviving to his day,—the eighties—were issued as a blue-book by the Government in 1882. Incidentally Dr. Leitner also put together the observations of several earlier administrators and writers that were relevant to his subject. We need offer no apologies for drawing largely upon Dr. Leitner's valuable document to give the reader an idea of the educational position at the time the British came into political power in India; for to arrive at truth one has to turn to facts revealed by firsthand investigation, and not to the propagandist clap-trap that Miss Mayo has treated us to.

The indigenous system of elementary education was so much bound up with the Indian village system* that a paragraph about the latter will not be irrelevant.†

"One of the great characteristics of Hinduism, according to Mr. Ludlow, "is its municipal institutions, as embodied in the village system...which deals with the soil in an essentially personal way... The occupants of a given space of land are no mere aggregation of human units, but an organised body, to which certain func-

---

*"Where the village system has been swept away by us, as in Bengal, there the village school has equally disappeared." (Ludlow in *British India*, quoted by Leitner, p. 18).

† *Ibid.*. p. 18.

tionaries are necessary, which enjoys, as a body, certain rights over the soil...even though within that community (certain persons) should be entitled to rights of what we should call absolute ownership. Everywhere the community has certain officers representing all those functions which appear to be most essential to village life. First is the headman, representing the whole community as towards the government; next is the accountant keeping a description of all the village lands, with the names of holders and terms of holding, and the accounts of individuals and of the village, drawing up deeds, writing letters. Then the police officer, not a mere paid watchman, but a member of the village, hereditary, as I have said, in his functions, enjoying as the price of them a certain definite amount of land. The priest, often a Brahman, is another of these officers, hereditary in like manner; in like manner holding the priest's land. The *schoolmaster*, often also the astrologer (though in other cases they are distinct functionaries), *is another*. And do not suppose that this is an office which has fallen into desuetude... *In every Hindu village which has retained anything of its form...the rudiments of knowledge are sought to be imparted;* there is not a child, except those of the outcastes (who form no part of the community), who is not able to read, to write, to cipher; in the last branch of learning they are confessedly most proficient..."
[Italics ars ours.]

The Directors of the Company Bahadur were certainly no pro-Indian propagandists, and yet

Mr. A. P. Howell,* writing in his book entitled *Education in British India prior to 1854, and in 1870-71*, quotes passages from the First Education Despatch of the Court of Directors of the Company (June 1814), which bear glowing testimony to the efficiency of the indigenous system, and incidentally explain how it was financed. The reader will find that they form a refreshing contrast to the ignorant glib talk of Miss Mayo:

"We refer with particular satisfaction upon this occasion to that distinguished feature of internal polity which prevails in some parts of India, and by which the instruction of the people is provided for by a certain charge upon the produce of the soil, and by other endowments in favour of the village teachers, who are thereby rendered public servants of the community.

'The mode of instruction that from time immemorial has been practised under these masters has received the highest tribute of praise by its adoption in this country, under the direction of the Reverend Dr. Bell, formerly Chaplain at Madras; and *it is now become the mode by which education is conducted in our* [English] *national establishments*, from a conviction of the facility it affords in the acquisition of language by simplifying the process of instruction.

'This venerable and benevolent institution of the Hindus is represented to have withstood the shock of revolutions, and to its operation is as-

---
*Quoted by Dr. Leitner, *op. cit.* pp. 21-22.

cribed the general intelligence of the natives as scribes and accountants. We are so strongly persuaded of its great utility, that we are desirous you should take early measures to inform yourselves of its present state, and that you will report to us the result of your inquiries, affording in the meantime the protection of government to the village teachers in all their just rights and immunities, and marking, by some favourable distinction, any individual amongst them who may be recommended by superior merit or acquirements; for, humble as their situation may appear, if judged by a comparison with any corresponding character in this country, we understand those village teachers are held in great veneration throughout India." [Italics are ours.]

Mr. Howell comments on this as follows:

" There is no doubt that from *time immemorial* indigenous schools have existed, as here alleged. In Bengal alone, in 1835, Mr. Adam estimated their number to be 100,000; in Madras, upon an enquiry instituted by Sir Thomas Munro in 1822, the number of schools was reported to be 12,498, containing 188,650 scholars; and in Bombay Presidency, about the same period, schools of a similar order were found to be scattered all over it. It is much to be regretted that, as each province fell under our rule, the Government did not take advantage of the time when the prestige of conquest or gratitude for delivery from war and oppression were strong in the popular mind, to make the village school an important feature in the *village system that was almost everywhere transmitted to us.*" [Italics are ours.]

The second paragraph in the excerpt from the Education Despatch deserves special attention Says Dr. Leitner: "Just as the introduction of specimens of the art-industry of India has tended largely to develop the present artistic taste among English workmen, so did the *methods of instruction pursued in indigenous schools influence the schools in England.*"*

A Bengal Inspector of Schools, deputed to visit the schools of the Punjab in 1868, remarked in the course of his report:

" The indigenous education of India was founded on the sanction of the Shastras, which elevated it into religious duties and conferred dignity on the commonest transactions of everyday life. The existence of village communities which left not only their municipal, but also in part their revenue and judicial administrations, in the hands of the people themselves, greatly helped to spread education among all the different members of the community. He will see the fruits of the indigenous system in the numberless *pathshalas, chatsals* and *tols* which still overspread the country, and which, however wretched their present condition, prove by their continued existence, in spite of neglect, contempt, and other adverse circumstances of a thousand years, the strong stamina they acquired at their birth. At

---

* *Op. cit.*, p. 20.

the present day, the religious sanction is growing weak, the village communities are nearly gone, manufacturing industry has come to the verge of ruin, the heaviest incidence of taxation is falling upon land, and a foreign language has become the language of court and commerce. The natural incentives to popular education being thus weak, its progress will depend on the efforts of an enlightened Government inclined to compensate to the people for their losses under foreign rule. Until a healthy political, economical and social condition has been regained under the security of British administration, artificial stimulants must supply its place as well as they are able."*

Miss Mayo's malicious libel that Indians love ignorance and illiteracy is a lie which has no leg to stand upon. We read in Dr. Leitner's report :†

" I cannot forbear from bearing any testimony to the great desire and appreciation of education among all classes of the Hindu, Muhammadan and Sikh communities, as also to the great talents which this ' land of the sun ' has so prodigally bestowed among its children.... Now, as 3,000 years ago, the East is the home of mental discipline, culture and repose, where genius is as universal as it is ignored, in consequence chiefly of the want of publicity and of easy communication. Without these advantages we should now be behind the Orientals, whom we despise. The one intelligent European among a thousand of his dull

* *Ibid.*, p. 42.
† *Ibid.*, p. 85.

brethern is able to pass off his views and inventions as the embodiment of the civilization of his continent. When the whole East will have its cheap Press and railways—provided always that it does not seek to slavishly imitate the West in its reforms—it must resume the position it once held, owing to the native genius of its peoples."

One could cite more testimonies like that. But those given above will suffice; Miss Mayo must be more royalist than the King, if she thinks these British writers and administrators and the Directors of John Company were all pro-Hindu. However, to give the reader a more concrete and detailed idea we shall copy here Dr. Leitner's calculation regarding literacy in the Punjab in the days immediately preceding annexation by the British. Dr. Leitner in his day found a sad contrast with the wide-spread literacy of the pre-annexation days. On page 3 of his report we read :

" In backward districts, like that of Hushiarpur, the Settlement Report of 1852 shows a school to every 19.65 male inhabitants (adults and non-adults), which may be contrasted with the present proportion of one Government or Aided school to every 2,818.7 inhabitants."

Speaking of the entire province Leitner says :*

" Including the since-incorporated Delhi and Hissar Divisions, which now contain 4,476 towns and villages, there were, in 1854 (when an incom-

Ibid., p. 145.

plete census was taken), 33,355 towns and villages, and presumably the same number in 1849. Assuming, at least, the existence of 33,355 mosques, temples, *dharmsalas* and other sacred edifices in which some teaching was carried on (not to count the 3,372 indigenous secular schools which were ascertained to exist in 1854 or to speak of the large number of schools held in the houses of teachers), and giving each ' Collegium ' of pupils an average attendance of 10, we shall get, at least, 333,550 persons under instruction in a province in which we have now about 113,000 assumed to attend Government and Aided schools, and a much smaller number in indigenous schools (according to the last census the total number ' under instruction ' of every kind would only be 157,623). What the state of education was in the time of Ranjit Singh may be inferred from the enumeration of Sikh authors in a previous chapter. The list of men distinguished for learning in other denominations is even more lengthy; whilst the evidence of our own Administration and Settlement Reports (so far as I have been allowed to see them) is conclusive *as to the general spread* of the elements of education in the province."

The British rulers did India a grave wrong when they rooted out the useful old system, and did not even care to replace it by a new one. Dr. Leitner discusses the passing away of the old system in the Punjab, and concludes among other things*—

* *Ibid.*, p. 148.

(1) That elementary, and sometimes high, Oriental, classical and vernacular education was more widely spread in the Punjab before annexation than it was in his day.

(2) That the Board of Administration in the Punjab was ordered to resume rent-free tenures of land, even in the case of schools and religious edifices when their endowments were large, thus following the example of the land resumption in Bengal.

(3) That in consequence most of the endowments of indigenous schools were gradually destroyed.

(4) That the action of the *Educational Department of the Punjab, in spite of constant reminders, tended to destroy the indigenous schools whilst neglecting its own primary schools.*

This in the years of grace *circa* 1880.

Miss Mayo seems to imply that the chapter on the education of Hindu women must be something like the proverbial blank chapter on ' Snakes in Iceland.' Says she, ' The people of India, as has been shown '—presumably by the remarks of the discredited Abbé Dubois—' have steadfastly opposed the education of women.' This is lie No. 1 (in chapter XV). She adopts a characteristically wicked method of accounting for India's illiteracy. Of the 247,000,000 people in British India, 50 per cent. are women; so she excludes 123,000,000 from those who can be made literate.

Next she proceeds to exclude the '60 million untouchables.' This is lie No. 2.

We are just now concerned only with lie No. 1. We shall later on give the Hindu idea of the position of women. Here we are concerned only with the present-day problem of women's literacy.

Dr. Leitner, from whose valuable report we have already quoted so much, has some very illuminating observations to make on the education of women in the Punjab, during the period just preceding annexation by the British :*

" The Panjabi woman has, however, not only been always more or less educated herself, but she has also been an educator of others. In Delhi, for instance, we find that, before the annexation of the Punjab, six public schools for girls were kept by Panjabi women, who had emigrated to the South for this purpose."

" In other places, similarly, Panjabi women were to be found as teachers, just as the *Guru* or the *Padha* spread his instruction beyond the precincts of a province where he was becoming a drug in the market. Among Muhammadans, very many widows considered it a sacred duty to teach girls to read the Koran, and though Delhi, like the rest of the North-Western Provinces, was far behind the Punjab in female education, we find that it had in 1845 numerous schools for girls, kept in private houses."

* *Ibid.*, pp. 97-8.

The following from Dr. Leitner's evidence before the Education Commission of 1882 will give interesting details of the indigenous system for girls :*

"*Q*. 41. Is there indigenous instruction for girls in the province with which you are acquainted; and, if so, what is its character?

"*A*. 41. Yes; the wives of Maulvis and Bhais, for instance, are generally taught by their husbands and instruct their children up to a certain age in reading and religious duties. The wives of the respectable Muhammadans generally can also read and write (though the latter attainment is not so much encouraged as the former for reasons into which it is not necessary to enter). Some of the ladies are good Persian scholars, and in a distinguished Muhammadan family that I know, I have been given to understand that several of the ladies are excellent poets. The position of women is far higher among Muhammadans and Sikhs than is supposed, and there is no prejudice against their being educated, provided this can be done without interfering with the privacy of their domestic life. There are in proportion as many women that can read in Native States, where there has been no fuss made about female education, as there are in British territory, whilst in the latter also I have no doubt that many respectable women can read and write... There have always been indigenous schools for Sikh females in the districts between the Chenab and the Attock. That the

* *Ibid*., pp. 103-4.

wives of priests should visit females of their community and teach them, is right and proper, but that girls, especially of a marriageable age, should cross bazaars in order to assemble in a school, is, I think, objectionable. Much reading of elementary religious books, sewing, embroidery, cooking with extreme care for the household, great neatness, tenderness in trouble, and gentle mediation in family disputes, constitute the chief features of female home rule and education in the better classes, who regard their female relatives with a respect and a religious affection of which we have not even the outward profession in Europe."

The British occupation was actually followed by a decline in women's education. That was the conclusion forced upon Dr. Leitner by facts brought out during his investigation. The causes of this decline, as they appeared to Dr. Leitner, are thus summarized in his blue-book :*

" There has been a decline in female teaching since annexation, for the following reasons :

(*a*) Formerly the mother could teach the child Panjabi. Now, wherever the child learns Urdu, the teaching power of the mother is lost.

(*b*) The weakening of the religious feeling has caused the decrease of all indigenous schools, including those conducted by women.

(*c*) Formerly a woman guilty of misconduct was criminally punished, so that the safeguards

* *Ibid.*, pp. 108-9.

against it were strong, and there could be less objection to granting women more education and greater freedom. Since the introduction of our law, adultery, for instance, can, comparatively speaking, be committed with impunity, and the necessary consequence is that the male population watches with greater jealousy any attempt towards emancipating the female sex.

(*d*) The female education given by us was avoided by the more respectable, because it too closely resembled that enjoyed by a class, which, if not criminal, to which our system is now reducing it, was not reputable...

(*e*) By keeping the female schools in public places, and by always attempting in spite of any pledges that may have been given at the commencement of the ' female education movement ' to inspect them, thus preventing the very patrons of the schools from sending their own daughters to them.

Female education has, therefore, been brought into discredit with the respectable classes by official interference, which has already done so much mischief in the Punjab in various other respects, and which the boon of self-government given at the eleventh hour can alone remedy, provided all officials combine in a measure of temporary self-effacement for the sake of the common good."

These extensive quotations have been occasioned by extreme caution on our part. We did not wish to give the impression that we were improvising facts to prove our thesis or to give the lie direct to Miss Mayo's ignorant but mischievous generalization. The least attention to the study of the subject forces one to the following conclusions :

(*i*) That from the earliest times there was a well-organized and wide-spread system of education throughout India.

(*ii*) That this system was a two-fold system—one for the aristocratic, cultured and priestly classes aiming at religious learning and culture, the other for the trading and working classes aiming at economic efficiency and dexterity in the use of tools—something akin to the system of apprenticeship in Tudor England.

(*iii*) That this system, as a part of our village system, had lasted as a living organization till the British occupancy of this country.

(*iv*) That this system was easily mistaken as a part of the body politic and uprooted by the British administrator, particularly anxious since the days of Lord Macaulay to create a class of subordinate officials and hirelings.

CHAPTER III

THE LIGHT THAT FAILED

We suppose the quotations we have given from British official publications and British writers make it abundantly clear that Miss Mayo's insinuations that before the advent of the British the Hindus had no system of education and that even now they are resisting all attempts to spread education and literacy are entirely misleading. In several provinces literacy was more widespread at the time the British took possession of them than it is to-day after 175 years of British rule. The old Indian system was admirably adapted to the genius and the needs of the people. The British of course did not destroy the old system without any aim in view. Their vandalism was for the greater part deliberate. To find out the motives underlying the educational policy we have to turn to its authors, the British administrators of the last century, and of the last years of the eighteenth century.

Charles Grant in his book on the education of the Indian people, published towards the end of the eighteenth century, remarked: " In the success [of the new educational policy] would lie our safety, not our danger." " We shall take the most rational means to remove inherent great disorders, *to attach the Hindu people to ourselves, to ensure the safety of our possessions,** to enhance continually their value to us."

Some forty years later, Sir Charles Trevelyan, a relative of Lord Macaulay, who served John Company in various capacities and rose to be the Governor of Madras, and a member of the Supreme Council in India, discussed this question in his book, *On the Education of the People of India*, and came to the conclusion that a million sterling annually expended on the education of Indians would 'render them at once amenable to our rule and worthy of our alliance.' Very shrewdly he remarks :

" In following this course we should be trying no new experiment. The Romans at once civilized the nations of Europe and attached them to their rule by Romanizing them, or, in other words, by educating them in the Roman literature and arts and teaching them to emulate their conquerors instead of opposing them. Acquisitions made by superiority in war were consolidated by superiority in the arts of peace, and the remembrance of the original violence was lost in that of the benefits which resulted from it. The provincials of Italy, Spain, Africa and Gaul, having no ambition except to imitate the Romans, and share their privileges with them, remained to the last faithful subjects of the Empire, and the union was at last dissolved, not by internal revolt, but by the shock of external violence, which involved conquerors and conquered in one

*Chapter IV. Italics in these quotations are throughout ours.

common overthrow. *The Indians will, I hope, soon stand in the same position towards us in which we once stood towards the Romans.* Tacitus informs us that it was the policy of Julius Agricola to instruct the sons of leading men among the Britons in the literature and science of Rome and to give them a taste for the refinements of Roman civilization. We all know how well this plan answered. From being obstinate enemies, the Britons soon became attached and confiding friends; and they made more strenuous effort to retain the Romans than their ancestors had done to resist their invasion."

The Roman parallel was recalled also by Rev. Alexander Duff—the pioneer of English education in Bengal. In his paper, *An Exposition of the late Governor-General of India's Last Act*, published at about the same time as Trevelyan's book, he observed :

" When the Romans conquered a province, they forthwith set themselves to the task of Romanizing it; that is, they strove to create a taste for their own more refined language and literature, and thereby aimed at turning the song and the romance and the history, the thought and the feeling and the fancy, of the subjugated people into Roman channels which fed and augmented Roman interests. And has Rome not succeeded?"

Trevelyan thought the indigenous education would not make for the safety of the British Raj. He therefore wanted Indian youth to be nurtured on English education :

"*The spirit of English literature...cannot but be favourable to the English connection.* Familiarly acquainted with us by means of our literature, the Indian youth almost ceases to regard us as foreigners... From violent opponents...they are converted into zealous and intelligent co-operators with us.*"

The political motive in this policy could not be more clearly emphasized.

And we have the more graphic and more quotable words of Trevelyan's more illustrious relation, Lord Macaulay :†

"We must at present do our best to form *a class who may be interpreters between us and the millions we govern; a class of persons Indian in blood and colour but English in taste, in opinions, in morals and in intellect.*"

The Rt. Hon. Charles Grant, whom we have already quoted, wanted to '*attach* our subjects by affection, by *interest*, by winning them to our religion, and our sentiments.' That, in his opinion, 'would have the effect of *rendering our authority permanent and secure.*'

With these political motives underlying the educational policy, it was in vain that H. H. Wilson, the great Sanskritist, protested :

" I have noticed for some time past repeated effusions in the Calcutta newspapers, advocating a departure from principles hitherto considered

---

*Minutes of 1835.   †Evidence before Parl. Com., 1853.

sound and just, and recommending the exclusive encouragement of English as the first stage of a very feasible project for the annihilation of all the languages of India, vernacular or classical, and the universal use of our native tongue throughout the East. As long as the reveries were confined to the columns of a newspaper they were inoffensive or even amusing; they assumed more importance when, in order to prepare for the extermination of the languages, the suppression of the alphabets was seriously undertaken and Oriental works were printed in characters which the natives could not read."

These quotations leave no doubt as to what motives inspired the founders of the British-Indian educational policy. Their hostility to the prevailing systems of education sprang from political motives. The new system that they devised for India was intended not to help cultural or material progress of the Indian people, but merely to make the work of administration easy. Sir John Malcolm, Governor of Bombay, in a Minute he wrote in 1828, recorded:

" One of the chief objects...of diffusing education among the natives of India, is our increased power of associating them in every part of our administration. This I deem essential on grounds of economy, of improvement, and of security.

"I cannot look for reduction of expenses in the different branches of our Government from any diminution of the salaries now enjoyed by

European public servants, but I look to it from many of the duties they now have to perform being executed by natives on diminished salaries."

'Natives on diminished salaries' was the goal the educational system had in view! The authors of the Despatch of 1854 were driving at the same thing when they wrote :

" We have always been of opinion that the spread of education in India will produce a greater efficiency in all branches of administration by enabling you to obtain the services of intelligent and trustworthy persons in every department of Government, and, on the other hand, we believe that the numerous vacancies of different kinds which have constantly to be filled up may afford a great stimulus to education."

Sir John Malcolm in the course of the Minute from which we have already quoted said :

" From English schools being established at no place but Bombay the pay of writers and accountants is immoderately high, and when these move from the Presidency they require still higher wages; and when well qualified they can from their limited numbers, command almost any pay they demand. This introduces a tone of extravagance of demand from this class of persons in all our departments. Of some remedies of this evil I shall speak hereafter, but *the real mode to decrease price is to multiply the article.* English schools should be established or encouraged at Surat and Poona."

The British administrators aimed at producing the Give-Me-Office-or-Give-Me-Death type! The educational machine constructed by them was admirably suited to this end.

Add to this the fact that the British Government in India pursued a deliberate policy of destroying Indian industry. Lancashire arose on the ashes of the Indian cotton industry. In the name of 'Free Trade' they refused to afford protection to the infant industries, and prevented their development. The banking policy, the currency manipulation, have meant no small handicap to the Indian manufacturer. Recent advances in science that have revolutionized agriculture elsewhere have not benefited Indian agriculture to any appreciable extent. The Indian Government seems to be beginning to take some interest in practical scientific agriculture, but hitherto the few agricultural institutes that we have, produced graduates more proficient in theory than in practical knowledge. I believe it was the late Sir Ganga Ram—' that fine old Punjabi,' as Miss Mayo calls him—who, while speaking at the Agricultural College, Lyallpur, a few years ago, narrated the painful fact that graduates in agriculture of that institution sometimes approached him to get chits for jobs in the police department Such being the condition of agriculture and industries, is it any wonder that young educated Indians depend so much on clerical jobs under the bureaucracy?

CHAPTER IV

LEARNING AND EARNING—AND HARD HEADED AMERICANS

It is always easy to talk of education for education's sake, but surely it does not lie in the mouth of an American to indulge in that cant. The ancient Hindu ideal in this respect was much higher and nobler than the present European or American ideal. In the West the chief values are money values—in the United States of Miss Mayo they may be said to be almost the sole values. Even universities are judged by the amount of money spent on, and provided for them. The typical American is a creature of money, judging everything by its money value. The cost of production, whether of a book, a picture, a film, or a play or even a university, is the real and the only understandable test of its value. Electric signs in Broadway, New York, in Chicago, in Philadelphia, in San Francisco and every other big town abound with announcements of a million dollar productions. A certain multi-millionaire couple took it into their heads to perpetuate the memory of their deceased son by establishing a university and naming it after him. They undertook a tour of the United States to inspect its various centres of university activities and to select a model for the proposed memorial. Everywhere they made it a point to enquire about the total cost of the university,—permanent and recurring. At the entrance of a famous university library in Massachusetts they put the same question to the gentleman who was showing them the different departments of the institution, and the husband was overheard saying to his wife, 'Dear, we can do this,' i.e., build a university involving the cost of the one they were inspecting! The university established by them is a well-known educational institution in the West but its chief claim to the gratitude of humanity is its money cost. The average American is only interested in making money or in spending it when made.

The sermon of education for education's sake is so often preached to us by men in high position who ought to know better that it will not be out of place to discuss it at some length, though I am afraid I cannot burden this book with too many quotations on this subject. I will ask the reader's indulgence for a quotation from my own book, *The Problem of National Education in India*, so frequently quoted by Miss Mayo herself.* In chapter XII of that book I discussed the 'Money Value of Education,' quoting largely from the United States Bureau of Education Bulletin No. 22 of 1927 (called 'Money Value of Education'). Introducing the excerpts from that Bulletin I said in my book:

" The first requisite of an efficient system of national education is that it enables every citizen

---

**The Problem of National Education in India*, George Allen and Unwin, London, 1920.

to live better, and to help others in living better. To live well, one requires a certain minimum of food, clothing, shelter, leisure, recreation, and means for the satisfaction of higher tastes and higher cravings. A nation which does not secure enough to enable every one of its members to live well, is a drag on the rest of the world. But when a nation of 315 millions of human beings, as well developed as the Indians, in possession of a country so rich in soil as that of India, with abundant natural resources of all kinds, cannot produce sufficient to satisfy even the minimum demands of half of its population, it is a sight for the gods to weep at. India's phenomenal proverty is one of the tragic facts of its life; and it is mainly due to the lack of means of education.

" Under the circumstances, the first aim of all publicly imparted education in India should be to increase the productive capacity of its citizens. Education is the first necessity of such a nation, and it should be the first charge on all national revenues. The nation should strive every nerve to go without all *luxuries*, nay, even without secondary necessities, in order to place this first necessity of national life within the reach of every boy and girl, and of every adult capable of learning. This is only possible by a general widespread system of vocational education, and by a general dissemination of practical, scientific knowledge applicable to the ordinary needs of life and vocational efficiency.

" Such a wide-spread system of education requires huge funds. These funds are to be furnished (*a*) from existing revenues, (*b*) from new taxes, (*c*) by practising economy in other departments of public administration, (*d*) and from national or provincial loans. In order to prepare the public mind to meet the demands for funds for education, it is necessary to bring home to the people 'the material and measurable rewards of education.'"

The last words, within quotation marks, are the words of the American Bulletin. Then follow the results of the world-wide investigation on the subject made by Dr. A. Caswell Ellis, Professor of Philosophy of Education in the University of Texas, with reference to Germany, Japan and Russia, the United States and other countries. Speaking of Germany he says :

" The concrete evidence of the effect of education in increasing industrial efficiency is overwhelming, whether considered from the national standpoint or from that of the individual citizen. For example, how else to account for the fact that a nation like Germany, with limited natural resources, but with excellent public schools, has grown in wealth and power so much more rapidly than her neighbour, Russia, which has a vigorous and talented national stock and vastly better resources but poor educational facilities? That the phenomenal success of Germany is the direct result of her thorough educational system is generally admitted."

About the United States he tells us :

"The relation of productive power to education is shown by the enormously increased rate of production that has come about everywhere since education became more generally diffused. The total wealth accumulated in America from 1492 to 1860, a period of 368 years, was $514 per capita. From then till 1904, a period of only 44 years, this increased to $1,318 per capita, or an addition in 44 years of $804...

'Since that time the increase has been even more striking. This increase is partly due to increased valuations or the smaller purchasing power of the dollar; to the use of accumulated capital, and to many other things; but after due allowance is made for all these the conclusion is inevitable that the education of the nation is largely responsible for vastly increasing the productive power of its citizens. The productive power of illiterate countries is not increasing at such rates."

Dr. Caswell Ellis rightly holds that natural resources are worthless without education. The Indian Government alone refuses to recognize that the grinding poverty of the people of India is mostly due to their ignorance and illiteracy, and that for this appalling ignorance and illiteracy the British Government of India is *wholly* responsible. The Government of India has never seen that—

"the efficiency of an illiterate people in competition with an educated nation is as the crooked stick against the sulky plough; the sickle against the reaper; the bullock cart against the express train, the ocean greyhound, and the aeroplane; the pony messenger against the telegraph, telephone, and wireless; the individual harangue against the printing press, the newspaper, the library; the spinning-wheel against the factory; the pine faggot against the electric light; the peddling of skins and herbs from the ox-cart against the bank, the cheque book, the railroad, the department store; the log hut against the steel skyscraper; the unaided eye against the microscope and telescope; incantations and magic against the chemist, the hospital, the modern physician and surgeon. Take away from one entire generation all education, and society must revert to the stick plough, the ox-cart, and such primitive means, because steel implements, locomotives, steamships, electricity, telephones, telegraph, waterworks, steel buildings, mining and chemical industries, factories, modern sanitation, hygiene and medicine, books, newspapers, courts of justice, and laws that protect property and defend the rights of the weak are all impossible without education, and are efficient only in proportion as educated intelligence is applied to them."*

 Instead of carrying on a propaganda showing the money value of education, like the one carried on by the United States Government, the high officials of the Government of India are constantly bemoaning the tendency of the people of India to judge the value of education by its material returns. What a difference there is between a

*Dr. A. Caswell Ellis, *op. cit.*

national government and a foreign government of exploiters imposed from without!

On page 184 Miss Mayo, commenting on a quotation from my book, *The Problem of National Education*, writes:

" In 1923-24, India's total expenditure of public funds on education, including municipal, local, Provincial and Central Government contributions, reached 19.9 crores of rupees, or £13,820,000. This sum is much too small for the work to be done. Nevertheless, when taken in relation to the total revenue of British India, it compares not unfavourably with the educational allotments of other countries."

This is Miss Mayo's characteristic way of dealing with figures. She not only includes municipal and local contributions *but also the income from tuition fees and private endowments.* The total contribution of the government from Central and Provincial funds in 1923-24 was only Rs. 9,74,76,000, i.e., less than one half of the total amount.

In 1924-25—later figures are not yet available —it was Rs. 9,98,02,000 out of a total from all sources of Rs. 20,87,48,000. In the official report for 1924-25 it is observed (page 4): " The total expenditure by Government on education in India is Rs. 9,98,01,594, a sum which represents only four annas per head [about 4d. in British currency and about 8 cents in American currency]...Meanwhile the percentage of the total expenditure on education borne by Government has declined from 48.9 to 47.9, while the contribution from fees has risen from 21.8 to 22.4." For less than 50,000 European pupils in all stages of instruction in India nearly Rs. 50 lakhs are spent annually *from the government funds alone.* This gives an annual sum of about Rs. 100 per pupil. Distributed over the entire European population in India—less than 2 lakhs of souls—it gives you more than Rs. 25 per head per year. Compare it with the beggarly four annas per head spent on the education of the Indian population! It is unthinkable that any national government could ever treat education so shabbily as the present government in India is doing. Leave aside the rich and resourceful governments of America, Britain and France. Even then you know what the enlightened Calles government is doing in a poor country like Mexico. Can the Indian government's effort compare even with that of the Mexican government?*

*Mr. J. W. Brown in his recent book on *Modern Mexico* (Labour Publishing Co., 1927) says that the '28 Mexican States are now spending 40 per cent. of their budgets on education, in addition to what the Federal Government does.'

CHAPTER V

A COUNSEL OF PERFECTION

Private agency in India has done, and is doing a good deal for the spread of literacy as also for higher and technical education. The late Mr. J. N. Tata spent a good part of his fortune in making provision for higher scientific education. The Bangalore Science Institute owes its existence to him. The Bose Institute, the Calcutta Technological Institute (with which the well-known Chemist, Dr. P. C. Ray is connected), the National Medical College, all owe their existence solely or mainly to private effort. Even official universities owe a good deal to the munificence of people like Sir Gooroodas Banerjee. The Hindu University of Benares not only has arrangements for high class literary education but also runs an Engineering college. But Miss Mayo gives you the impression that Indians themselves are doing nothing for the spread of education, and blames the Indian Nationalists for unfairly criticising the British administration for a supposed neglect of duty. Her charge against educated Indians, as usual, rests on a talk, she says, she had with a Bengali lawyer of unknown identity, who made good money at the Bar but gave no attention to the education or sanitation of his village.

In the introductory chapter of my book, *The Problem of National Education in India*, I gave a resume of what had till then (1918) been attempted by private enterprise in the matter. But when all is said, it is no use denying that education is mainly the business of the State of the first and foremost importance. Private effort, however earnest, is utterly helpless to meet the educational requirements of a modern nation. In chapter V of my book on education I gave copious extracts from the then recent speeches of the Rt. Hon. H. A. L. Fisher, at that time President of the British Board of Education, to emphasize how in all the civilized countries education in all its branches is regarded to-day as the business of the State. It is the right as well as the duty of the State to see that the citizens do not grow up illiterate and uneducated. In one of his speeches Mr. Fisher, Britain's leading authority on educational problem, said :*

" But though the State cannot forbid wage-earning among young people [why?] it should and must assign a value to learning as well as to earning. *It has a right and a duty to affirm that it believes in education for the masses*, and that by education it means not a sham and make-believe, but something substantial, something which will leave a durable mark on mind and character, and that the claim of this education on the child is paramount... The State should not allow itself to be diverted from its great object of diffusing knowledge and intelligence among the people by the fear of being involved in some expenditure based on personal circumstances. It should first

---

* In quoting from Fisher's speeches I am using the material in chapter V of my *Problem of National Education in India*.

devise a course of education, as thorough and effective as the object demands and the available means of instruction furnish, and then, having settled on a plan likely to give to each of its citizens the fullest chance for self-development. it should be prepared to give adequate assistance in special cases." [Italics are ours.]

Adequate education for the masses is a *right* as well as a *duty* of the State. So it is not the Indian politicians only who demand that education ' should be driven into the...masses by compulsory measures.' British statesmen also affirm the same thing about their own country.

We get a glimpse of the educational ideals that the modern statesman has before him in the further excerpts from Mr. Fisher's speeches, which I made originally for my book on education:

" The province of popular education is to equip the men and women of this country for the tasks of citizenship. All are called upon to live, many are called upon to die, for the community of which they form a part. That they should be rescued from the dumb helplessness of ignorance is, if not a precept of the eternal conscience, at least an elementary part of political prudence, to which the prospective enfranchisement of several million new voters...adds a singular emphasis. But the argument does not rest upon grounds of political prudence alone, but upon the right of human beings to be considered as ends in themselves and to be entitled, so far as our imperfect social arrangements may permit, to know and enjoy all the best that life can offer in the sphere of knowledge, emotion and hope."

Speaking at Bradford Mr. Fisher said :

" When I began my survey of national education I was struck—as I suppose everybody is struck —by the fact that there are millions and millions of men and women in this country [Great Britain] —who are not getting as much out of life as life can afford to give them. There are millions of men and women who derive no profit from books, no pleasure from music or pictures, very little cultivated joy from the ordinary beauties of nature. They pass their life bound down to dull mechanical toil, harnessed to iron and steel, without a gleam of poetry, without a touch of imagination, without the faintest sense of the glories and splendours of the world in which we live, unable to attach to their ordinary dull task the interest which belongs to a scientific appreciation of the principles upon which that task is founded, unable equally to turn their leisure to any rational or cultivated account, and I ask myself this : Ought we to be content with a state of civilization in which these things are possible, and should it not be part of our duty so to provide for posterity that they may have within their reach a happier, more cultivated, and wider life?"

Again he expressed the same ambition when he said in the House of Commons :

" What is it that we desire, in a broad way, for our people? That they should be good citizens, reverent and dutiful, sound in mind and body, skilled in the practice of their several avocations, and capable of turning their leisure to a rational use."

In making a plea for an additional grant for education (1917), after citing the figures relating to the expenditure on education in England—some £16,000,000 paid out of the taxes, another £17,000,000 out of the rates and perhaps £7,000,000 out of fees, voluntary contributions and endowments, making a total of £40,000,000, or 60 crores of rupees in Indian coin, the Rt. Hon. Mr. Fisher rightly pointed out: " But when we are considering a form of productive expenditure which is *not only an investment but an insurance*, that question cannot stand alone. We must ask a supplementary question. We must ask not only whether we can afford to spend the money." And he called the ' supplementary ' question the ' more important and more searching.' In spite of the universal cry 'for ' economy ' Mr. Fisher maintained that ' we should economize in the " human capital " of the country, our most precious possession, which we have too long suffered to run to waste.'

Some of the passages in Mr. Fisher's speeches are very relevant to those trying to find out how far national efficiency to-day depends on adequate mass education. While introducing a new Education Bill on August 10, 1917, when England was in the midst of the titanic struggle of the World War, Mr. Fisher discussed some aspects of this question :

"Attention has been increasingly directed to the close connection between educational and physical efficiency. One of the great dates in our social history is the establishment of the school medical service in 1907. We now know what we should not otherwise have known, how greatly the value of our educational system is impaired by the low physical condition of a vast number of the children, and how imperative is the necessity of raising the general standard of physical health among the children of the poor, if the great part of the money spent on our educational system is not to be wasted."

To Mr. Fisher one of the lessons of the War was the clear indication of how education improves national efficiency. Speaking at Bradford he said :

"Have you ever reflected, ladies and gentlemen, upon the astonishing influence which education has exercised over the course of this titanic conflict? how those countries have best succeeded who have equipped themselves with a modern provision of education, and how those countries have succeeded least who have been most backward in their provision of popular education? I suppose there has never been a war in which the contending armies have been so well educated, or in which the contending armies have owed so much to science and education. And whether you talk to the officers at the front—who will all speak to you of the value which they attach to a well-educated non-commissioned officer or private—or whether you go to the headquarters staff, or whether you go to the great munition factories and sources of military supply, you always have the same answer to the same question. Always you will be told that *education is the keynote of efficiency.*" [Italics are ours.]

Miss Mayo has ventured to offer some remarks on learning and earning. She tries to concentrate her scorn for Indians in her chapter head, ' Give Me Office or Give Me Death.' Infinitely nobler is the following from Mr. Fisher's Manchester speech :

" I venture to plead for a state of society in which learning comes first and earning comes second among the obligations of youth, not for one class only but for all young people. At present the rich learn and the poor earn.

"Education is the eternal debt which maturity owes to youth. Now I do not care whether youth be poor or rich, we owe it education—all the education which it can afford to receive and all the education which we can afford to give."

It is no use expecting youth to put learning before earning where the eternal debt of education is so inadequately discharged as in India under British administration.

One would have thought that coming from America Miss Mayo would bring to bear on the problem of education in India a broad and en-

lightened outlook. But her sole object was to
whitewash British rule and to denounce Indians.
She makes much of the fact that by the Reforms of
1919 education is a Transferred subject in charge
of Indian Ministers and that now the responsibility of neglecting it lies on their shoulders. Here
again she has shown an utter lack of understanding
of the real problem. She has failed to see that the
Indian Ministers are not quite free agents in the
matter. Nationalist India has been crying itself
hoarse over the unjust distribution of revenues
between the Reserved and the Transferred subjects. The latter have no chance of being rapidly
improved, because the distribution of revenues
rests neither with the representatives of the people
nor with the Ministers, but with the autocratic
executive. The top-heavy administration which
readily sanctions an addition of over a crore
of rupees to the already exorbitant emoluments
of the Imperial services and which has been
spending about eighty crores per year on the military has never allowed sufficient money to the
nation-building departments made over to the
Ministers. Says Mr. Richey, the Education Commissioner to the Government of India :*

"The straitened finances of the central and
local governments of India at the present time
preclude any hope of striking educational developments in the immediate future. The new provincial ministries of education, after successfully
combating the attack on their schools, are now

---

* Para. 39 of the Eighth Quinquennial Review of the Progress
of Education in India, volume I.

taking stock of their educational position with a view to systematic advance when the necessary funds are forthcoming. In such an advance, it is evident from the keen interest shown by the new Councils, they will have the support of public opinion..."

In England a Fisher might tell his people that education is an investment even in the time of the Great War. The universal cry of economy would not deter him from planning out new and big programmes of mass education. If he were an Indian Minister he would be told by Mr. Richey, ' There is no short cut to educational reform.'

That the Ministers' chief difficulty is that of finding finances is again made clear by Mr. Richey when he says :*

" The financial inequalities of the provinces cannot but profoundly affect their educational policies. While Bombay with its large and growing revenues can contemplate the early and general introduction of compulsory primary education, it is out of the question for Bengal with its restricted and inelastic resources to consider any such project. Since a well-organized system of education is one of the most potent factors in economic, social and political development the ultimate effect of such provincial divergencies can hardly be over-estimated."

* Para. 20 of the Eighth Quinquennial Review of the Progress of Education in India, volume I.

Commenting on the excerpts from Mr. Fisher's speeches I wrote in my book :*

"To us in India Mr. Fisher's words are of greater significance than those of educators, equally well placed, of other countries, because of our political connection with England. Here is the chief educational authority of the Empire laying down certain principles and expounding truths which are, according to him of general application in all self-respecting, progressively-minded communities. We, the Indians in India, are not yet free to determine our educational policy. Even with the promise of educational autonomy to the provinces, the last word will practically remain with the Imperial Government. The progress of popular education in India must, for a long time, depend on the goodwill of the British officials in charge of policies and vested with powers over revenues and funds."

The words are as true to-day as they were in 1918. Having studied the educational policies of the various civilized nations of the world I stated in my book on Indian education certain general principles which I may here summarize :

1. National education, being the surest and the most profitable national investment, is as necessary for national safety as the military provision for physical defence. Universal popular education must be provided for by the State, and should be the first charge on State revenues. Any attempt to provide for nation-wide education by

National Education in India, pp. 104 et seq.

private agencies and private funds is futile, and to attempt it is to attempt the impossible. Moreover it diverts public attention from the duty of the State. A national system of education must be provided for, enforced, financed and controlled by the nation, and in performing that function the nation must be represented by the State.

2. The old idea that the State was concerned with making provision for elementary education alone is also gone. All over the world it is recognized that the duty of the State does not end with elementary education. The economic and industrial efficiency of the nation depends upon technical and industrial education, and that also must be provided for by the State. Nor can the State ignore the necessity of higher education, for intelligent and efficient leadership depends on that.*

3. Education does not consist in imparting a certain amount of book knowledge and teaching the three R's. It includes provision for the physical development of the young. It embraces a provision for the general health of the child, including feeding, if necessary, to such an extent as to ensure the fullest benefit to the child from the provision for his education made by the State.

* The United States Federal Government in 1923-24 spent $1,808,321,420 on academic education alone as compared with $555,077,146 spent in 1913, and from 1918 to 1926 the Federal Government alone spent about 38 million dollars on vocational education and now spends over 7 million dollars every year. See *American Year Book*, pp. 1072 and 1110.

4. In short, the duty of bringing up and educating the child with a view to helping him to become an efficient, intelligent and prudent citizen rests with the State and the State must be made to fulfil it. It no longer depends on the capacity or willingness of the parents.

CHAPTER VI

HISTORY OF COMPULSORY PRIMARY EDUCATION

The history of compulsory primary education in India is sufficiently illustrative of the stepmotherly intentions of the British Indian Government. The first Bill for this reform was introduced by the late Mr. Gokhale in the old Imperial Legislative Council in 1911. It was opposed by the Government on the usual specious grounds : 'time is not yet for such a measure,' 'funds are not available to meet the necessary expenses,' 'the masses are opposed to compulsion on religious grounds,' etc.

The second attempt was made in 1916 by the Hon'ble Mr. V. J. Patel, whose Bill sought permission for certain advanced portions of the Presidency of Bombay to introduce legislation through municipalities for making primary education free and compulsory if the local authorities so desired and if they were willing to abide by certain conditions laid down by the Government. The Bill was thrown out by the official majority in the Bombay Provincial Council on the pretext that the passage of such a Bill would be a violation of the educational policy of the Imperial Government, which had declared in 1913 ' that time for such compulsory legislation in primary education has not yet arrived.'

The subsequent history is given in paras. 190 and 191 of the Education Report for 1917-1922, which shows that in most cases the initiative in pressing these measures was taken by a Hindu member. The working of the compulsory primary education measure has been left to the discretion of local bodies. In speaking of the working of this measure Miss Mayo quotes one paragraph from Mr. Richey's report relating to the Punjab. She very wisely omits to mention the progress made in other provinces and also of the reasons why progress has not been more rapid. For example, in para. 195 Mr. Richey observes :

"Compulsion has been introduced under the Act of 1920 in a number of wards in the city of Bombay. There has been a fifty per cent. increase in the number of schools and school-children, and in the number of trained teachers and a proportional increase in the general and medical inspectorate; a novel feature has been the appointment of lady superintendents. The total expenditure on education in the municipality has increased 350 per cent."

The statement made by Miss Mayo on page 176 about 'the Hindu element in the Punjab Legislative Council' having attempted to exempt from school attendance all ' untouchables ' otherwise known as 'depressed classes' is a lie, pure and simple. On the other hand, the following questions and answers taken from the proceedings of the Punjab Legislative Council for 1922-23 will show how keenly the Hindu members have interested themselves in the cause of the depressed classes:

Q. 2211. *Lala Atma Ram:*

(*a*) Will Government be pleased to enquire as to what is being done by other provincial governments to ameliorate the educational condition of the depressed classes?

(*b*) Will Government be pleased to consider the advisability of ameliorating their educational condition by means of special scholarships and stipends in the Primary and Secondary Schools of the Punjab?

The Honourable Khan Bahadur Mian Fazl-i-Hussain, the Government Minister for Education:

(*a*) Enquiry has been made from other provincial governments whose replies are awaited.

(*b*) The education of the depressed classes is already engaging the attention of the Government which has taken two steps in the direction of encouragement. Aid and recognition have been given to the training classes for the depressed classes at Moga, and under the new grant-in-aid rules increased financial assistance may be given to private schools which entertain trained teachers. Government has also laid down the principle that its grants for the introduction of compulsory education are meant for the benefit of all classes of the community without any exception, but it is for the local bodies concerned to decide how the education of the depressed classes should be provided for, whether in separate schools or in the ordinary schools. Government does not desire to lay down any rigid rules.

As early as January 1922 (the Reformed Councils began to operate only from 1921) Mr. K. L. Rallia Ram moved a resolution asking the Government to set apart a sum of 10 lakhs for the benefit of the depressed classes. An amendment was proposed to reduce the sum to 3 lakhs. Rao Bahadur Lt. Balbir Singh and Mr. Motilal Kaistha, Hindu members of the Council, opposed the amendment and supported the original resolution. This resolution was opposed on behalf of the Government, but, the latter giving an assurance of sympathetic consideration, was withdrawn. In 1923 again a Hindu member asked the following question :

" Q. 2721. *Rai Sahib Lala Thakur Das*:

Will Government be pleased to state :

"(a) what has been done since 1st January, 1921 for the education of the depressed classes;

"(b) how much money has been spent in this behalf since January 1st, 1921, up till now, and also how much it is proposed to be spent during the remainder of the current financial year;

"(c) what results have been achieved so far?

" *The Honourable Khan Bahadur Sir Fazl-i-Hussain:*

It is hoped that the information required by the honourable member will be found in a circular letter, a copy of which is laid on the table."

The last paragraph of the circular letter referred to in the above answer is worth quoting :

" The Minister desires to take this opportunity of expressing his appreciation of the efforts made by local bodies and philanthropic societies on behalf of depressed classes and communities; and he is anxious, even in this time of acute financial stringency, to afford them all the encouragement and assistance at his command. In this noble work, he relies much on the co-operation of private effort; and much also on the desire of the community to help itself, a desire which has already expressed itself in some parts of the province. He trusts, therefore, that the satisfactory results of the last few years are merely a prelude to a far greater improvement in the near future, and that the Punjab will rise to its opportunities and will, as a whole, take a lead in the removal of illiteracy and ignorance from its midst, and in the breaking down of the barriers between the depressed classes and those more fortunately circumstanced in life."

This is only with regard to one province. Similar efforts have been made in other provinces by Hindus of light and leading to uplift and educate the depressed classes. Yet Miss Mayo deliberately tries to give an impression that the Hindus are opposed to this. As one engaged in this work I can say that lakhs of rupees have been spent by me and my co-workers on this work ever since I returned from America in 1920. I started on this work as early as 1910 with large donations from my own purse.

CHAPTER VII

' WHY IS LIGHT DENIED?'

Miss Mayo ignores all these facts recorded in the Indian Government's own official documents. Sober truth does not produce shilling shockers. For these the *Mother India* method of putting down everything to the exaggerated sexuality of Indians comes so handy. In her chapter, ' Why is Light Denied?' Miss Mayo tries to account for the wide-spread illiteracy in India. Village education cannot be undertaken without women teachers, she tells us. And women teachers would not go out to villages, for ' Indian women of child-bearing age cannot safely venture without special protection, within reach of Indian men.'* This wicked libel on the Indian nation is totally unwarranted. In sex morality the average Indian villager is infinitely firmer, stronger and nobler than men in Europe and America. I say this after experience of nearly half the inhabited world. Miss Mayo quotes in her support a sentence from the *Calcutta University Commission Report*, which in her context passes for the opinion of the Commission

---

*Mother India, p. 186.

themselves,* whilst the fact is that Miss Mayo's excerpt is part of a paragraph *quoted* by the Commission. Their own remarks are confined to saying that 'the lot of the women teacher is made extraordinarily hard *by the prejudices which environ her.*' The words italicised by us are something substantially different from the contention Miss Mayo seeks to support. They also give the real meaning of the passage from the witness's evidence—which Miss Mayo has cited as the Commission's opinion—deploring the lack of a sense of ' chivalry and respect ' for a woman who does not live in the zenana. Rightly or wrongly zenana-life is the test of respectability in rural Bengal.† Does this statement, made with reference to Bengal only, justify the sweeping accusation that Miss Mayo makes against all Indians?

Equally wicked and malicious is the statement ascribed to the head of an American Mission College in Northern India. There is no means of verifying its authenticity.

On page 191 Miss Mayo quotes from *The Education of India*, by Mr. Arthur Mayhew, late Director of Public Instruction in the Central

---

* " The Calcutta University Commission...expressed the point as follows : ' The fact has to be faced that until Bengali men generally learn the rudiments of respect and chivalry toward women who are not living in zenanas, anything like a service of women teachers will be impossible.' " (*Mother India*, p. 188).

† Though not very much in the towns, nor in Madras and several other provinces, as admitted by Miss Mayo herself.

Provinces. In quoting Mr. Mayhew she omits just a few words to convey a wrong impression. Let the pillory of parallel columns expose her trick :

"A far more serious objection is the difficulty...to safeguard these ladies who take up work outside the family circle. Their employment without offence or lapse seems possible only in mission settlements and schools under close supervision. In a general campaign they [widows] can play only an insignificant part." [As found in *Mother India*.]	"A far more serious objection is the difficulty *of providing suitable residence and companions, in order* to safeguard these ladies who take up work outside the family circle. Their employment without offence or lapse seems possible only in mission settlements and schools under close supervision. In a general campaign they [widows] can play only an insignificant part." [As in the original.]

Dishonest dots! How by keeping out just four words they give quite a different meaning to the passage! But it is a trick of the trade Miss Mayo specialises in. That an Indian widow going out to an out of the way village cannot live without suitable residence and wihout companions certainly does not mean that being of ' child-bearing age ' she ' cannot safely venture within reach of Indian men.'

The nature of the prejudice against women teachers is described thus in the Census Report for the U. P. in a passage cited by Miss Mayo :*

" It is said that there is a feeling that the calling cannot be pursued by modest women. *Prima facie*, it is difficult to see how such a feeling could arise, but the Indian argument to support it would take, probably, some such form as this : ' The life's object of woman is marriage; if she is

* *Census of India*, 1911, vol. XV, p. 229.

married her household duties prevent her teaching.
If she teaches, she can have no household duties
or else she neglects them. If she has no household duties she must be unmarried, and the only
unmarried women are no better than they should
be. If she neglects her household duties, she is,
though in a different way, no better than she
should be!"

Perhaps the real strong reason for the paucity
of women teachers is that there are no spinsters in
India.*

The sex ratio in Great Britain and other
European countries gives rise to certain complications, no doubt. But it also provides a contingent of women teachers who do useful work. In
India the sex ratio leaves no army of spinster
teachers. The *married* woman teacher is not so
common in several European countries. We
understand in the post-War years educational
authorities in the United Kingdom have been
imposing restrictions afresh to discourage the
married woman teacher.

It is notoriously difficult, says Miss Mayo,
quoting the authority of the *Qinquennial Review
of Education in Eastern Assam and Bengal*, ' to

---

* " It is safe to say that after the age of seventeen or eighteen
no females are unmarried who are not prostitutes or persons
suffering from some bodily affliction such as leprosy or blindness;
the number of genuine spinsters over twenty is exceedingly
small. and an old maid is the rarest of phenomena!" (*Census
of India, 1911*, vol. XV, *re* the United Provinces, p. 229.)

induce women of good position, other than Christians and Brahmos, to undergo training for the teaching profession; and even of those who are trained...the majority refuse to go to places where they are wanted.'

Yes. But how could 'women of good position' be induced to go to distant villages when the scale of pay for the village primary schools is so low? Says Mr. Richey,* in the *Eighth Quinquennial Review on Education* (covering the years 1917-22) : ' The rise in cost does undoubtedly represent in most provinces a real improvement in the conditions of the teaching profession...According to the latest scales introduced in April 1921 [in the U. P.] untrained assistants receive as a minimum Rs. 12 [$5.00] *per mensem*, trained assistants Rs. 15 to Rs. 20 [$5.00 to $6.50] and headmasters Rs. 20 rising to Rs. 30.' In Madras, it is stated, the pay has been raised to Rs. 10 (about $3.00) a month for untrained teachers and Rs. 12 a month for trained ones. In Bengal the estimated pay is Rs. 8 to Rs. 16 per mensem. In Assam, for trained teachers the minimum monthly pay has been raised from Rs. 8 to Rs. 12. So on for other provinces. We know as a fact, before this 'real improvement' was effected, primary school teachers used to be paid Rs. 6 to Rs. 8—a scale of wages lower than that of coolies! While a man might have managed to eke out this miserable scale of income by other work, a woman may not. So Rs. 6 to Rs. 12 a month determines the

---

* Paras. 202 *et. seq.*

ability and the skill in the teaching staff insisted upon by Mr. Paul.*

When Miss Mayo speaks of the Indian village school teacher as a ' dreary incompetent,' and as a ' heavy blanket slopped down ' upon a helpless mass of weaklings she has to keep in mind that one month's wage of the village teacher is in general not enough to buy a copy *Mother India.* You cannot get 20 dollars worth of competence if you pay only 2 dollars a month.†

There is a moral to Miss Mayo's story of Indian education, which is sought to be brought home to the reader by two contrasted pen-pictures In the first of these, with which the chapter, " A Counsel of Perfection," opens, we are shown a " respected Hindu nobleman," of unknown identity whom she charges with having neglected his village home with its ' disease, dirt and ignorance,' in spite of his prosperity in the legal profession. In contrast we are shown a ' Mussalman land-owner ' in the Punjab who is alleged to have done so much for his tenants in his village. But unmistakably the land-owner's chief qualification to earn Miss Mayo's approval is that he ' strongly objects to Government's new policy of rapid [!] Indianization of the public services,' and ' takes no interest in Swaraj politics.' The whole object

* Quoted by Miss Mayo on p. 4.

† In Great Britain the minimum salary of certificated teachers is £250 per annum and that of uncertificated ones £145 (*Labour Year Book for 1926*, p. 273). In America, the average salary of teachers exceeds $1,243 a year. (*American Year Book for 1925*, **p. 1092**).

of Miss Mayo's visit to India and of writing her book is once again emphasized when we find this study in contrasts is followed by the following chit to the British Deputy Commissioner:

" But it is only to the Briton that the Indian villager of to-day can look for steady, sympathetic and practical interest and steady reliable help in his multitudinous necessities. It is the British Deputy District Commissioner, none other, who is 'his father and his mother' and upon the mind of that Deputy District Commissioner the villagers' troubles and the villagers' interests sit day and night."

CHAPTER VIII

THE HINDU CASTE SYSTEM

Considered historically, the present caste system is a remnant of medieval times. In ancient India caste was by no means so rigid or exclusive. In Buddhistic and post-Buddhistic periods the castes and sub-castes multiplied and gradually became more rigid. Originally there were only four castes. Then developed a large number of occupational castes corresponding to the medieval trade guilds—institutions which have given the central idea for the school of modern thinkers known as Guild Socialists, whose leaders, like Mr. Penty, want to bring back the social organization of the ' merrie England ' days and call it ' post-industrialism.'

Scholars differ as to what exact part each of the various factors—race, occupation, etc.— played in the evolution of Indian castes. Sir Denzil Ibbetson, Census Commissioner, and later Lieutenant-Governor of the Punjab, discussed the question at length in his Census Report.* According to him the various factors were tribal divisions common to all primitive societies; the guilds based upon hereditary occupation ' common to the middle life of all communities;' the exaltation of the priestly office and of the Levitical blood, and

---

* *Punjab Castes* (reprinted from Ibbetson's Report), Government Press, Lahore, 1916, pp. 9 *et. seq.*

the ' preservation and support of this principle by the elaboration from the theories of the Hindu creed or cosmogony of a purely artificial set of rules regulating marriage and intermarriage, declaring certain occupations and foods to be impure and polluting, and prescribing the conditions and degree of social intercourse permitted between the several castes.' " Add to these," says Ibbetson, " the pride of social rank and the pride of blood which are natural to man, and which alone could reconcile a nation to restrictions at once irksome from a domestic, and burdensome from a material point of view; and it is hardly to be wondered at that caste should have assumed the rigidity which distinguishes it in India."

Mr. Nesfield, however, who studied the question as Census Commissioner for Agra and Oudh. considers that the classification into castes is based solely on occupation. " Function and function only," says he, " was the foundation upon which the whole caste system of India was built up."* To him ' each caste or group of castes represents one or other of those progressive stages of culture which have marked the industrial development of mankind not only in India, but in every other country in the world wherein some advance has been made from primeval savagery to the arts and industries of civilized life. The rank of any caste as high or low depends upon whether the industry

---

*Nesfield, *A Brief View of the Caste System in North-Western Province and Oudh.* (Quoted in *The People of India* by Sir Herbert Risley, 2nd edition, Calcutta, 1915, pp. 265 *et. seq.*)

represented by the caste belongs to an advanced or backward stage of culture.'

From Census officials we turn to historians. M. Senart,* the French Indologist, sees in Hindu caste only a parallel of the Roman and Greek systems. Risley represents M. Senart as maintaining that caste is the ' normal development of ancient Aryan institutions, which assumed this form in the struggle to adapt themselves to the conditions with which they came into contact in India.' M. Senart relies greatly upon the general parallelism that may be traced between the social organization of the Hindus and that of the earlier Greeks and Romans. He points out a close correspondence ' between the three series of groups, *gens, curia,* tribe at Rome; family, *phratria, phuli* in Greece: and family, *gotra,* caste in India.' He seeks to show ' from the records of classical antiquity that the leading principles which underlie the caste system form part of a stock of usage and tradition common to all branches of the Aryan people.' Regulation of marriage by caste was by no means peculiar to India, for, as M. Senart points out, the Athenian *genos* and the Roman *gens* present striking resemblances to the Indian *gotra.* ' We learn from Plutarch that the Romans never married a woman of their own kin, and among the matrons who figure in classical literature none bears the same gentile name as her husband. Nor was endogamy unknown. In Athens in the time of

* *Les Castes d'ans l'Inde.* (Quoted by Risley, *op. cit.*, pp. 267 *et. seq.*)

Demosthenes membership of a *phratria* was confined to the offspring of the families belonging to the group. In Rome, the long struggle of the plebeians to obtain the *jus connubii* with patrician women belongs to the same class of facts; and the patricians, according to M. Senart, were guarding the endogamous rights of their order—or should we not rather say the *hypergamous* rights?—for in Rome, as in Athens, the primary duty of marrying a woman of equal rank did not exclude the possibility of union with women of humbler origin, foreigners or liberated slaves. Their children, like those of a Shudra in the Indian system, were condemned to a lower status by reason of the gulf of religion that separated their parents. We read in Manu how the gods disdain the oblations offered by a Shudra: in Rome they were equally offended by the presence of a stranger at the sacrifice of the *gens*.' 'The Roman *confarreatio* has its parallel in the *got kanala* or "tribal trencher" of the Punjab, the connubial meal, by partaking of which the wife is transferred from her own exogamous group to that of her husband.'

M. Senart traces the parallel in notions about food also. ' In Rome as in India, daily libations were offered to ancestors, and the funeral feasts of the Greeks and Romans...correspond to the *Shraddha* of Hindu usage, which...is an ideal prolongation of the family meal.' M. Senart seems even to find in the communal meals of the Persians and in the Roman *charistia*, from which were excluded not only strangers but any members of the family whose conduct had been unworthy, the analogue of the communal feast at which a social offender in India is received back to caste.' Regarding outcasting and the powers of the caste *panchayat* M. Senart points out: " The exclusion from religious and social intercourse symbolized by the Roman interdict *aqua et igni* corresponds to the ancient Indian ritual for expulsion from caste, where a slave fills the offender's vessel with water and solemnly pours it out on the ground, and to the familiar formula *hukka pani band karna*, in which the modern luxury of tobacco takes the place of the sacred fire of the Roman excommunication. Even the caste *panchayat* that wields these formidable sanctions has its parallel in the family councils which in Greece, Rome and ancient Germany assisted at the exercise of the *patria potestas* and in the chief of the *gens*, who, like the *matabar* of a caste, decided disputes between its members and gave decisions which were recognized by the State."

Risley quotes Sir S. Dill* as pointing out 'how an almost Oriental system of caste' had made all public functions in Rome hereditary, 'from the senator to the waterman on the Tiber or the sentinel at a frontier post.' 'The Navicularii who maintained vessels for transport by sea, the Pistores who provided bread for the people of Italy, the Pecuarii and Suarii who kept up the supply of butcher's meat were all organized on a system as rigid and tyrannical as that which

* *Roman Society in the Last Century of the Western Empire*, 1899. See Risley, *op. cit.*, pp. 271 *et. seq.*

prevails in India.... Each caste was bound down to its characteristic occupation, and its matrimonial arrangements were governed by the curious rule that a man must marry within the caste, while if a woman married outside of it, her husband thereby acquired her status and had to take on the public duties that went with it.' The rigidity of caste in Rome can be imagined from the account that follows : †

" The man who brought the grain of Africa to the public stores at Ostia, the baker who made it into loaves for distribution, the butchers who brought pig from Samnium, Lucania or Bruttium, the purveyors of wine and oil, the men who fed the furnaces of the public baths, were bound to their callings from one generation to another. It was the principle of rural serfdom applied to social functions. Every avenue of escape was closed. A man was bound to his calling not only by his father's but by his mother's condition. Men were not permitted to marry out of their guild. If the daughter of one of the baker caste married a man not belonging to it, her husband was bound to her father's calling. Not even a dispensation obtained by some means from the imperial chancery, not even the power of the Church, could avail to break the chain of servitude."

Even to-day where is the country in which caste does not play a prominent part? The European critics forget the beam in their own eye

† Sir S. Dill, quoted by Risley.

when they chide us for the mote in ours. In another chapter we shall say something about the attitude of the white people towards the coloured races and of the treatment the Negro ' citizens ' of the United States get from their white 'Brahmans.' But even if one excludes coloured people—there is no justification for such exclusion—do not wealth and birth very largely regulate classes in European society? They call them ' classes " instead of castes. but spades would be spades, call them by whatever name you please.

Caste in India was a form of social and industrial organization just like 'class' in modern industrial society. The forms differ because the conditions of production have changed. Neither the primitive tribal order nor the feudalism of the middle ages would suit the new economic conditions. Caste in India perfected the artistic sense in the craftsman, such as was not found on such an extensive scale elsewhere. Its principal evil was that it stereotyped society. The present system of classes is by no means a perfect system and one of the great problems of the modern thinker is to find out how to save civilization from being wrecked by class antagonism.

To-day the Indian caste system is beyond doubt an anachronism. The debris of the ages cannot be mopped away in a day, because India is not free to put her house in order. The caste system has varied through the ages with the changing conditions, and there is no reason why it should not once again be made to yield place to a new order for the new conditions. If a Vedic Indian happened to visit India any day in the post-Buddhistic period he would feel bewildered at the new and complicated system of caste prevailing in society. And there can be no doubt that a politically free India will lose no time in effecting fresh adjustments. As it is, caste has ceased to do us any good at all, and its evils have in certain respects become accentuated.

It is said the Hindus are caste-ridden, and therefore unfit for democracy. It is forgotten that the Hindus in the past had at least as much of democracy as the Romans and the Athenians. The West used to talk like that also of Japan. Not very long ago, that gifted writer, Lafcadio Hearn wrote :*

"There was a division also into castes— *Kabane* or *Sei.* (I use the term 'castes,' following Dr. Florenz, a leading authority on ancient Japanese civilization, who gives the meaning of *Sei* as equivalent to that of the Sanskrit *varna*, signifying 'caste' or 'colour.') Every family in the three great divisions of Japanese society belonged to some caste; and each caste represented at first some occupation or calling."

Large classes of persons existed in Japan, who were literally known as 'less than men.' Says Mr. Hearn :

"Outside of the three classes of commoners, and hopelessly below the lowest of them, large

**Japan: An Interpretation* (Macmillan), p. 260.

classes of persons existed who were not reckoned as Japanese, and scarcely accounted human beings. Officially they were mentioned generically as *chori*, and were counted with the peculiar numerals used in counting animals: *ippiki*, *nihiki*, *sambiki*, etc. Even to-day they are commonly referred to not as persons (*hito*) but as 'things' (*mono*)... To English readers (chiefly through Mr. Mitford's yet unrivalled *Tales of Old Japan*) they are known as *Eta*; but their appellations varied according to their callings. They were pariah people." The *Eta*, we are told, "lived always in the suburbs or immediate neighbourhood of towns, but only in separate settlements of their own. They could enter the town to sell their wares or to make purchases; but they could not enter any shop, except the shop of a dealer in footgear. As professional singers they were tolerated; but they were forbidden to enter any house—so they could perform their music or sing their songs only in the street or in a garden. Any occupation other than their hereditary callings was strictly forbidden to them. Between the lowest of the commercial classes and the *Eta*, the barrier was impassable as any created by caste tradition in India; and never was *ghetto* more separated from the rest of a European city by walls and gates, than an *Eta* settlement from the rest of a Japanese town by social prejudice. No Japanese would dream of entering an *Eta* settlement unless obliged to do so in some official capacity."

The *Eta*, and then the 'pariahs,' called

Hinin—a name signifying ' not-human-beings.' ' Under this appellation were included professional mendicants, wandering minstrels, actors, certain classes of prostitutes and persons outlawed by society. The *Hinin* had their own chiefs and their own laws. Any person expelled from a Japanese community might join the *Hinin;* but that signified good-bye to the rest of humanity.'

Were the caste-ridden Japanese fit for 'progress' and democracy? Says Hearn:

" Those who write to-day about the extraordinary capacity of the Japanese for organization and about the 'democratic spirit' of the people as natural proof of their fitness for representative government in the Western sense mistake appearances for realities. The truth is that the extraordinary capacity of the Japanese for communal organization is the strongest possible evidence of their unfitness for any modern democratic form of government. Superficially the difference between Japanese social organization and local self-government in the modern American or the English colonial meaning of the terms appears slight; and we may justly admire the perfect self-discipline of a Japanese community. But the real difference between the two is fundamental, prodigious, measurable only by thousands of years."

Hearn's gloomy prophecies notwithstanding, all these caste and class distinctions have now practically disappeared in Japan because the

Government co-operated with the people in the matter and used all its influence towards the abolition of the distinctions and divisions. Japan has been able to overthrow this system because of her political and economic independence. If India had been free she would have done the same.

In India the reformers are working against heavy odds, for they have to contend against prejudice and ignorance without absolutely any help from the State. In fact, the alien bureaucracy have devised new methods of perpetuating the old system and making it subserve their own ends. Recruitment for the army is confined to castes called the 'military castes.' It is not every man who can pass the fitness tests that will be accepted by the recruiting officer. He must come from one of the 'military castes,' who are expected to be more ignorant and 'loyal' than the other castes. Then the right to buy land is also regulated by caste. In the Punjab they have a list of castes for the Land Alienation Act, which are supposed to be 'agricultural castes.' People who have not been actual cultivators for several generations, whose chief vocation now is commerce or industry or state service are privileged under this Act because of their caste label. Such absurdities derive their sanction not from the Indian caste system but from the imperialist policy of playing off 'military and agricultural' against 'non-military and non-agricultural castes' and of trying to create a caste of 'loyalists.'

Those who think that the British Government and the Christian missionary will rid India of the evils of caste, build castles in the air. The bureaucracy only want to give caste a new orientation to make it subserve their ends. And it is only the superficial observer who thinks that 'Christianity' has 'emancipated' the lower caste people, whereas Christianity in India is even more superficial than these observers. The foreign missionary, who depends on patronage from his own country, is anxious to show results in figures, and solid qualitative work is neglected.

Caste in India is by no means confined to the Hindu. So far as the industrial order of hereditary vocational guilds is concerned Islam did not affect it much. Caste plays an important part even in the life of the Mussalman though he has avoided its grossest forms like untouchability. Christianity has done not even that much. As we shall see in the next chapter, caste and untouchability have been affected but little among the converts.

Hope lies only in a politically free India in which the progressive elements will be as free to effect new adjustments as they were and are in Japan. Till that day comes we have to continue doing our best to overcome the impediments, but we know all the time that the results cannot be proportionate to our efforts.

CHAPTER IX

THE UNTOUCHABLE—HIS FRIENDS AND HIS EXPLOITERS

Miss Mayo has devoted some chapters to an account of untouchability in India. The main thesis of the chapters, namely, that untouchability exists in India, is true. But Miss Mayo would not be her own good self if she stuck to truth alone. Her training as a yellow journalist and her love of revelling in imaginary melodramatic scenes has led her into wild exaggerations and fantastic inventions. In her picture the shades are deepend much beyond what is warranted by reality. The brighter side—the rapidly increasing sympathy for reform movements and uplift work—seems to be entirely non-existent. She is most reluctant to give due credit to Indian reformers. She naively thinks Christianity has always meant the complete emancipation for the low caste and the untouchable. She gives you the impression that the British administrator is the truest friend of the untouchable whom he is ever trying to rescue from the tyranny of the high caste people. Her account, here as elsewhere, consists of truths. untruths and the most dangerous class of untruths which are called half-truths.

Take, for instance, her statement on page 152 of her book. She would have us believe that the untouchable converts to Christianity are ' all set free from caste bondage.' Alas, they are not.

The following observations of Mr. V. N. Narasim Iyengar in the *Mysore Census Report** are as true of the Madras Presidency as of Mysore. They are more or less applicable to the whole of India. Says Mr. Iyengar:

" Roman Catholicism is able to prevail among the Hindus more rapidly and easily by reason of its policy of tolerating among its converts the customs of caste and social observances, which constitute so material a part of the Indian social fabric. In the course of the investigations engendered by the census several Roman Christian communities have been met with, which continue undisturbed in the rites and usages which had guided them in their pre-conversion existence. They still pay worship to the *Kalasam* at marriages and festivals, call in the Brahman astrologer and *Purohits*, use the Hindu religious marks, and conform to various other amenities, which have the advantage of minimizing friction in their daily intercourse with their Hindu fellow-caste brethren."

In the *Census Report of India* (*1911*) we read : " Broadly speaking, it may be said that the Catholic Church tolerates, and Protestant Church condemns the idea of caste."† In the same report a Roman Catholic Bishop is quoted as having said that ' the congregations of Southern India have been founded on the principle that to be

* *Mysore Census Report, 1891* (quoted in the Oxford edition of Dubois's *Hindu Manners*, etc.), p. xxvii.
† *Ibid.*, p. 60.

baptized a man need not renounce his own caste and nationality. They, i.e., the Christian converts, have always been so (i.e., Hindus in its natural and geographical sense) and are accepted to be so with the ranks and rights of their respective castes. In 1921 the total number of all classes of Christians, Europeans, Anglo-Indians and Indians in British India was 4,754,064 of whom nearly 30 lakhs were in the Madras Presidency (and Southern States) alone. The Roman Catholics in the whole of India numbered 1,823,079. Besides these there is a large number of Syrian Christian and other sects which are under the influence of caste. In many of the Roman Catholic churches in Southern India special seats are set apart for the different castes of Christians.

The encomiums that Miss Mayo has lavishly showered on the British Administration for sympathetic zeal for the depressed classes are still more unwarranted by facts. Miss Mayo insinuates that the concern now being shown by the Hindus of upper castes for their low-caste brethren is due not so much to humanitarian feelings as to the consciousness that in neglecting the untouchables lies a political danger to their community. But if political motives influence a certain section of the Hindus, they govern entirely the love and hate and all the predilections of the bureaucracy. The untouchable is a very recent discovery to the bureaucratic sympathies. The bureaucracy have now realised the great value of the untouchables as a weapon against the Indian aspirations for Swaraj. Their existence comes handy as an argument against nationalist claims for democratic government in India. In their name they can reserve some seats for their own nominees in the legislatures. To enfranchise the untouchables might be dangerous for the government, but the paternal pose is good enough when it can give it more nominated allies by its side in the legislatures.

One form which the bureaucratic sympathy for the depressed classes has taken is to increase the numbers of people belonging to these classes, arbitrarily. We know the story of the Census Commissioner, who, at his sweet will by one stroke of pen transferred thousands of people belonging to certain tribes returned as Hindus to the category of 'animists.' Quite as whimsical seems to be the attitude adopted in giving the numbers of untouchables. Perhaps there is method and political motive in this whimsicality. In 1917, perhaps for the first time, the Government of India made an attempt to give their numbers in their *Quinquennial Report on Education*. The total population classed according to the list in the *Quinquennial Education Report* as depressed amounted to 31 million persons or '19 per cent. of the Hindu and tribal population of British India.'*

Since then the number has swollen, and in the report of 1921 itself the total figures mount up to nearly 52.7 millions. This figure possibly includes many classes that are really not untouchables at

* *Census of India, 1921*, vol. I, p. 225.

all. The fact is that 'a caste reckoned as untouchable or depressed in one locality is not necessarily so in another.' But the Census Commissioner *guesses* that the number may be between 55 and 60 millions. We may also hazard a guess here. Sir Henry Sharp's education report put the total of depressed classes for British India at 31.5 millions. The table giving this figure put the aboriginal population at nearly 10 millions, and the criminal tribes at nearly half a million. All three categories were for good reason kept separate. But if you wanted one big figure for the untouchables what could be easier than to add up these three totals? This simple process would give you about 42 millions for British India—which means about 52 millions for the whole of India. Was it by this simple process that the Census Commissioner of 1921 got his 'conservative' estimate for the untouchables?†

Mr. Coatman, who edits the Government of India's official year-book, has simplified the situation by accepting the higher figure. He throughout refers to the 60 million untouchables. Miss Mayo goes further and throughout refers to the 60 million untouchables of *British* India. The official figures, 53 to 60 millions, are for the whole of India including the States. Miss Mayo cleverly manipulates figures to warrant more sweeping generalizations.

In 1917, i.e., just before the Reforms were inaugurated, the State had not yet fully realized

† See the Appendix on this subject.

the political value of the untouchable, and so was wasting no patronage on him.

In the United Provinces, out of an alleged total number of 8,374,542 belonging to the depressed classes, the total number of persons at school was only 10,924, i.e., about 1 in 800. In the Punjab out of a total population of over 2 millions (2,107,593) there were only 3,453 at school. In the Central Provinces out of a total population of over 3 millions there were only 26,668 at school. In Madras alone out of a total population of 5,686,342 about one-fifth were at school. These figures probably include also Christian converts. In Bengal out of a total population of 6,742,913 about 81,000 were at school. In Bombay out of a total of 1,635,896 some 30,568 were at school; in Bihar and Orissa out of a total of 1,236,300 persons 19,841 were at school. It will be interesting to read the whole paragraph in which the measures adopted to promote education among these classes were enumerated in 1917.

The one thing to be noted is that while Miss Mayo speaks of the efforts of Christian missionaries in this field, amongst Hindu agencies, she mentions only the Servants of India Society and omits all mention even of the Arya Samaj work.

The *Quinquennial Report** thus briefly describes the educational work among untouchables organised by different agencies:

* For 1912-17.

" The problem is of special importance in Madras, where the Paryars, Pallas, Malas, Madigas, Holayas and others form the great class known as Panchamas. Missionaries, both Roman Catholic and Protestant, have been very active among this class and have gained many converts. The number of departmental schools has increased and the Hindu community, as represented in the depressed classes mission, is evincing greater interest in these classes. The number of Panchama children at school has risen from 72,190 to 120,607. The total expenditure on special schools has risen from Rs. 6.08 lakhs to Rs. 8.74 lakhs, to which Government contributes Rs. 4.8 lakhs. In Bombay there are 576 special schools and classes, of which 211 are maintained by local boards, 85 by municipalities and 280 by private agencies. These last though conducted mainly by Christian Missions, are also run by the Depressed Classes Mission Society of Poona and Bombay, aided by State grants. The number of pupils has risen from 26,204 to 30,568. It is reported that there is no great difficulty about the admission of the lowest castes to primary schools in Bengal. Nevertheless, where these are settled in large numbers, Government opens special schools for them. Among Indian societies the Bengal Social Service League and the Society for the Improvement of the Backward Classes, Bengal and Assam, have opened 19 and 62 schools, respectively. In the United Provinces Boards have recently been required to open special schools without fees for backward or depressed classes when there is a demand. The report enumerates the efforts made in this direction, but admits that the results are as yet deplorably small. The Punjab report mentions 44 special schools with 1,022 pupils, and the table shows 3,491 pupils under instruction in all kinds of schools. The movement for the education of low-caste children is gaining strength, chiefly through the exertions of Christian Missions and the Arya Samaj. In Bihar and Orissa there are 41 special schools, and Rs. 7,590 was spent on these and other special measures. There are 42 special schools in the Central Provinces, of which more than half are maintained by missionaries. But this policy has received little encouragement, as the administration consistently maintains the principle that boys cannot be excluded from the common schools on grounds of caste prejudice— a principle which the institution of special schools would seem to weaken. The effects of such prejudice are gradually disappearing, and low-caste boys are less often than previously deterred from joining schools for fear of degrading treatment. In Delhi there are 16 mission schools and one municipal school."

Since 1917 when the British Government made the famous declaration about the political goal of British policy in India, great political capital has been made out of the depressed classes. They are a ready weapon in the hands of the reactionary Britons against the Home Rule movement. Not only the officials in India but the British papers like the London *Times* also frequently use the backwardness of these classes and their ' loyalty parades ' as arguments against the Indian Nationalists. Special demonstrations are got up on special occasions, the expenditure being defrayed from secret service and publicity funds at the disposal of the Imperial and Provincial governments. One of these got up demonstrations provides Miss Mayo with one of the captions for her chapters, ' Behold, a Light,' and fills some half a dozen pages in her book. The Prince of Wales is the light whom the untouchables behold with surprise and grow ecstatic. Miss Mayo waxes eloquent, she transforms their surprise into delight, delight into ecstasy and ecstasy into frenzy.

When the Prince paid India a visit in 1921, the Indian Nationalists declared a boycott of all functions and receptions arranged in his honour. The officials had, therefore, to fall back upon questionable methods, and at several places they imported ignorant people from villages, providing free transport for them, and where necessary free refreshments, and even new liveries. The people came for the sake of the *tamasha* (i.e., show). The loyalty parade described by Miss Mayo possibly did take place. But the minute descriptions in detail, of the Prince's smile and all that, must have been provided by her own imagination, and were probably intended only to create the impression on the reader that it was perhaps an eyewitness that was writing the description. Anyway her account of the *feelings* of the untouchables on seeing the Prince and their ecstatic dances appears to people in India to be a mere figment of her imagination.

Nobody but a political propagandist—and Miss Mayo undeniably is one—would attach much value to such manufactured demonstrations. But Miss Mayo in describing the work of the Britisher for the untouchable, devotes most of her space to such parades and addresses. The whole tenor of the chapter betrays the political motive behind her venture.

Yet it cannot be denied that the problem of untouchability is a real, live problem which the Hindus are grappling with, with all the seriousness that it deserves. Thousands, literally thousands, of Hindus are engaged in carrying on active propaganda against it and in organizing educational and economic facilities for the untouchables on which private citizens spend hundreds of thousands of rupees every year. Miss Mayo's statement that ' to-day the defenders of untouchability are myriad ' is a miserable lie as also the assertion that ' few of his [Gandhi's] supporters have at any time cared to follow him so far.' What happened at the annual Hindu Convention of 1926 has also been described by her very inaccurately. The ' squabble ' over the resolution relating to the untouchables was certainly not ' directed against those who would relax the pains of the untouchables.' The dispute was over one part and only one part of the resolution—the part relating to the right of the ' untouchable ' to enter the Hindu temples.

All educated Hindus recognize that untouchability is a blot on the fair name of Hinduism which must go. Mahatma Gandhi was perfectly right when he told Miss Mayo that 'in spite of opposition untouchability is going, and going fast.' The opposition is becoming weaker and weaker, and the movement for the removal of untouchability is rapidly coming to fruition.

CHAPTER X

LESS THAN THE PARIAH

One would have thought that the Americans would be the last people to declare Hindus to be unfit for *Swaraj* and democracy because of the existence of a class of untouchables among them. Americans never abdicated their right of self-government or allowed other people to question it, in spite of the existence among them of a larger proportion of ' untouchables ' and a severer form of untouchability than that in India. When they issued their famous Declaration of Independence slavery was an established institution in their country. It is less than seventy years ago that the American Civil War, costing hundreds and thousands of lives and millions of dollars, was fought because of this institution. Even to-day the untouchables in India are neither lynched nor treated so brutally as the Negroes in the United States are.

I have visited the United States twice. During my second visit I lived there for about five years, with an interval of six months spent in Japan. I went touring all over the country and made a special study of the Negro problem. In a book I finished in March 1916 I said :* " One of the things that prompted me to pay a second visit to the United States of America was my desire to study the Negro problem on the spot and to acquaint myself with the methods that are being adopted for the education and uplift of the Negro population of these States." My keen interest was due to the fact that—

" The Negro is the pariah of America. There is some analogy between the Negro problem in the United States of America and the problem of the depressed classes in India. The two cases are not on all fours with each other, but there is a great deal common to both. The social problem in the United States is, in some of its phases, very similar to the social problem in India. Hence my desire to study it in all its bearings on the spot and to come in contact with the Negro leaders in these States, so as to know their point of view from first-hand knowledge."

In my book I devoted a special chapter to ' The Negro in American Politics.' The account that follows is largely drawn from that chapter.

Very stringent laws were made to keep the Negro down, to prevent his escape, to secure his recapture after escape, to assure the master a complete dominion over him. In 1829 when a master was indicted for beating a slave, the

*The United States of America: A Hindu's Impressions and a Study (2nd edition, Calcutta, 1919), p. 88.

Supreme Court of North Carolina acquitted the former and ' affirmed the master's right to inflict any kind of punishment upon his slave short of death.' It was not right to suppose, the Court went on to say, that the relations of master and slave were like those of parent and child. The object of the parent in training his son was to render him fit to live the life of a free man, and, as a means to that end, he gave him moral and intellectual instruction. With a slave it was different. Chief Justice Ruffin summed up his opinion upon this point in these words :

" The end is the profit of the master, his security and the public safety; the subject one doomed in his own person and his posterity to live without knowledge and without capacity to make anything his own and to toil that another may reap the fruits... Such service can only be expected from one who has no will of his own, who surrenders his will in implicit obedience to that of another. Such obedience is the consequence only of uncontrolled authority over the body... The power of the master must be absolute to render the submission of the slave perfect."

The treatment which the Negro received at the hands of his master under these conditions of law may better be imagined than described.

The cruelties that were inflicted during all this period of slavery from 1619 to 1865 on the Negroes beggar description. There is nothing parallel to that in the history of India, or for the matter of that in the whole history of Asia. When in 1865 the Northern States of the United States were engaged in a civil war with the Southern States on the ostensible ground of Negro emancipation, liberty-loving Great Britain sided with the South—the same Great Britain whom Miss Mayo extols to the seventh heaven for philanthropic and humane work in India. Humane indeed!

Between 1792 and 1834 the four bordering States, Delaware, Maryland, Virginia and Kentucky denied suffrage to the Negro. In 1835, North Carolina excluded him from the suffrage. New Jersey took away the suffrage of the Negro in 1807, Connecticut in 1814 and Pennsylvania in 1838. "These changes," says Booker T. Washington, "were all evidences of the steady growth in the United States, both North and South, of a caste system which excluded the Negro from the ordinary privileges of citizenship exclusively upon the ground of his colour. In 1802 Ohio demanded a bond of 500 for Negroes who came into the state. A Negro, even though a free man could not at that time testify in a case in which a white man was a party, and Negroes were not admitted to the public schools." Similar provisions were made in other States. In 1833 it was judicially decided that a free Negro was a 'person' and not a 'citizen.'

" In some States [the Negroes] were forbidden to sell drugs, in others they might not sell wheat and tobacco, and in still others, to peddle market produce or own a boat was against the law. In several States it was against the law for a free Negro to cross the State line; in others a slave who was emancipated was compelled to immediately leave the State."

Slavery was abolished in theory only. For there started a campaign of depriving the Negro of what he had acquired in theory, bit by bit, showing, in the words of Miss Mayo, 'that there are more ways than one to keep the under-dog in his kennel.'

" The resentment and reaction of the South," says Mr. Usher,* " caused the insertion of clauses in the New Constitution denying with vehemence the equality of the white and the black races and affirming that Negroes could not be citizens of the United States. To coerce the Negroes into working ' Vagrancy ' Acts were passed in several States in the fall of 1865 which declared it an offence for Negroes over 18 years old to be without ' lawful employment or business ' or to be found ' unlawfully assembling themselves together—either in the day or night time.' Negroes under 18 years of age, ' orphans or the children of parents who could not or would not support them ' were to be apprenticed until 21 years old by the clerk of the Probate Court at his discretion, preferably to the former owners. Mississippi made a similar provision for the Negroes who did not pay their taxes, and then

*The Rise of the American People.

levied a poll-tax of one dollar a head on all Negroes
'for the support of the poor.' The criminal
statutes provided fines and compulsory work to be
done by the criminal, for the man who would pay
in return for the shortest period of service, in such
elastic offences as ' malicious mischief,' ' insulting
gestures,' ' seditious speeches,' ' or any other
misdemeanour.' "

Under the guise of apprenticeship or as a
punishment for debt or crime, they put Acts on the
statute book defining poverty and crime in broad
and comprehensive terms which *ipso facto* made
every Negro guilty. They provided compulsory
work for Negroes in debt and then had laws passed
which instantly put every Negro in debt. The
South, besides, very naturally proceeded to elect
those very men as senators and representatives to
the United States Congress who had been prominent in the administrative and military service of
the Confederacy, and organized a State militia, in
whose ranks were naturally to be found a large proportion of confederate veterans who had fought in
the war on their side. All this raised the suspicion of the North. They thought that everything
gained by the war was likely to be lost if they were
not vigilant: the South was still in rebellion and
would do everything possible to reduce the Negro
to the old conditions that obtained before the abolition. Hence the tug-of-war between the Republican Congress and the South.

The methods resorted to for reducing the
Negro majorities have been persistently followed

to practically disfranchise the Negro population altogether. *To-day the Negro is politically as much a zero in the South as he was before the emancipation.* The present political position of the Negro in the United States may be stated in the words of another American writer, Mr. Paul Leland Haworth :

" The provisions of the fifteenth amendment prohibiting the denial to citizens of the right to vote ' on account of race, colour, or previous condition of servitude ' would seemingly stand in the way of any legal discrimination against the Negro's political rights; but, as everybody knows, ways have been found for evading the constitutional prohibition. Following the downfall of the Reconstruction Governments the Negroes in the Southern States were virtually disfranchised by force or fraud, but in 1890 Mississippi evolved a plan whereby the end sought could be attained in a quasi-legal manner. To-day every one of the former Confederate States, except Florida, Arkansas, Tennessee and Texas have suffrage requirements which practically eliminate the Negro from politics, while even in the four States named as exceptions he is not much of a factor. By educational or property tests the mass of ignorant and poor Negro voters are excluded, while loopholes are provided for ignorant and poor whites in the shape of ' Grandfather clauses,' or ' Understanding clauses,' which last, white registration officers can apply rigidly to Negroes and leniently to whites. The avowed purposes of these ' suffrage amendments' was to eliminate the Negro from politics and, in spirit, they certainly violate the fifteenth amendment, and also lay the States which have adopted them liable to that section of the fourteenth amendment which provides for a reduction in representation in proportion to the number of citizens excluded from the suffrage; but the Supreme Court has always carefully evaded the constitutional issue, while Congress has not seen fit to reduce the representation of any State. In view of the existing political situation it is improbable that anything will be done to nullify the suffrage requirements."

But that is not all. In addition to disfranchising the Negro and eliminating him from politics 'by force or fraud' the Southern legislatures have passed numerous discriminating laws against him. In 1910, 26 States (out of 52) either by statute or provision in the constitution forbade the intermarriage of the Negroes with whites. Such mixed alliances are declared void, while the contracting parties are held guilty of a 'misdemeanour' in some States, of 'felony' in others, and of 'infamous crime' in yet others. The punishment varies from imprisonment for ten years at one extreme in certain Southern States to a minimum fine of $50 in one, and to no penalty on the Negro participant in another. Regarding inter-mingling of the races, M. Siegfried remarks that 'the woman may be successfully defended, but the case of the negress is very different.' To get corroboration 'we have only to compare the colour of the primitive Africans with that of the civilized Negroes of America.'*

Besides these, 'Jim Crow Laws' are in force in all the former Slave States providing for separate accommodation for the two races on railway carriages and (in some States) on steamboats and street-cars. Separate waiting-rooms and railroad dining-rooms are also the general rule. Separate cars are usually provided and on streetcars white passengers are usually given front seats and coloured passengers the rear seats. It is usually impossible for a Negro passenger, however rich, to obtain a sleeping berth in railway carriages, and in case such a passenger in Illinois railway, for example, crosses the Ohio river into Kentucky, he must give up his berth and retire to the coloured coach. Very often also, the railway companies provide better accommodation for white passengers than for coloured ones even though they both pay the same fare.

No Southern State permits coloured and white children to attend the same public schools and some States extend the provision to private schools also. One State only recently enacted a law forbidding white persons to teach in coloured schools and *vice versa*.

Legal distinctions and discriminations are mostly confined to the South, but race prejudice

---

* *America Comes of Age*, A. Siegfried (Jonathan Cape, 1927), p. 99.

is to be found practically throughout the United States. Negroes are excluded from hotels, from Y. M. C. A.'s and Y. W. C. A.'s, from theatres and saloons, and are even refused interment in cemeteries for the white, in some cases in direct violation of local laws! Because of public sentiment Negroes attend separate churches and put up at separate hotels and get special seats in the theatres. They are segregated in cities and even in country places and kept apart from white people in all relations of life. The Negro in the United States is worse than a pariah.

The worst form taken by this race prejudice is the 'lynching' of Negroes accused or suspected of crimes against white people, before they have been tried and adjudged guilty by any court of justice. The 'Ku Klux Klan' with its wide organization shows American efficiency in this job. They have the methods of a secret revolutionary society, only they know they can defy 'law and order' with much greater impunity. Speaking of this mob violence against the Negro, the author of *America Comes of Age* assures us that ' the best elements of the community often take part—society people, high officials, and even judges... they have told me this themselves... The cordial, polished gentleman with whom you are talking is possibly a murderer who has gone into the wood at night to kill a man outnumbered a hundred to one; and thousands of others, your friends among them may have been his accomplices.'*

* pp. 98-99.

The table appended below and the accounts following it will give the reader an idea of the extent to which 'lynch law' obtains and of the flimsy pretexts on which lynching is indulged in.

Coloured men lynched without trial.

Year.	No. of lynchings.	Year.	No. of lynchings.
1885	78	1902	86
1886	71	1903	86
1887	80	1904	83
1888	95	1905	61
1889	95	1906	64
1890	90	1907	60
1891	121	1908	93
1892	155	1909	73
1893	154	1910	65
1894	134	1911	63
1895	112	1912	63
1896	80	1913	79
1897	122	1914	69
1898	102	1915	80
1899	84	1916	55
1900	107	1917	44
1901	107	1918	64
		Total	... 2,975

The alleged causes for 1914 were:

	No.	Percentage in total.
Murder	30	43½
By rioters and night raiders	13	19
Personal assaults	10	14½
Rape, attempts at rape, and presence in women's rooms	8	}
Robbery and theft	5	} 23
Arson	2	}
Resistance to search	1	}

ILLUSTRATIVE MATTER, 1911

The Crime of being a Negro.

October 20, Manchester, Ga.—Because he was accused of knocking down a white man last night, Jerry Lovelace, a Negro, was taken from jail at 2 o'clock this morning and lynched. There were about thirty men in the mob.

Woman and Child Hanged.

May 26, Okeman, Oklahama.—A coloured woman accused of having shot a sheriff was taken by a mob and, together with her fourteen year-old son, was hanged from a bridge. The woman was raped before she was hanged.

Five Innocent Men Lynched.

May 20, Lake City, Fla.—Six men were taken from jail and lynched ' for complicity in the

---

* These figures are taken from the Chicago *Tribune.* The *Crisis* (the organ of the National Association for the Advancement of Coloured People) believes that the numbers given by the *Tribune* are estimated too low.

murder of a prominent citizen.' The lynchers came in automobiles and showed the sheriff's young son, who had been left in charge of the jail, a forged telegram purporting to come from the governor and ordering that the prisoners be given up. On investigation it was found that only one of the six men murdered was even accused of a crime. A quarrel between a white man and a coloured man had been brought up before a local court and the coloured man had been exonerated. Immediately afterwards the white man went into the coloured man's yard with a gun. Shots were exchanged and the white man was killed. The coloured man gave himself up at once and the five men with him were being held merely as witnesses.

Wounded Negro Burned to Death.

August 13, Coatesville, Pa.—There is no need to repeat the story of the Coatesville horror. You all remember the man who was taken from a bed in the hospital and burned alive for having shot a watchman when drunk. His writhing body was poked back into the flames as he tried to drag himself away. His teeth and charred bones were kept for souvenirs. All arrested for this frolic have been *acquitted.*

What a Judge Said.

July, Lawrenceville, Ga.—Judge, Charles H. Brand of Lawrenceville Ga., refused to call for troops to protect two Negroes who came before him for trial, one on a charge of an alleged attack on a white woman; the other for ' loitering in a suspicious manner.'

They were lynched; one was taken from a train where he was in charge of two officers (the train stopping while the passengers saw the lynching): the other was dragged out of jail by a mob several hundred strong.

Judge Brand defended his failure to secure a safeguard for the prisoners, saying:

" I don't propose to be the engine of sacrificing any white man's life for all such Negro criminals in the country... I am in perfect accord with my conscience and my God. I would not imperil the life of one white man to save the lives of a hundred such Negroes."

What Governor Blease Says.

November 11, Honeapath, S. C.—Governor Blease of South Carolina says, in regard to a recent lynching in his State, that rather than use the power of his office in deterring white men from ' punishing that Nigger brute,' he ' would have resigned his office and come to Honeapath and led the mob.'

These barbarities continue to-day as they were at the time I wrote my book from which I have extracted the illustrative matter given above. The following accounts taken from some issues of

The Crisis for 1927 will leave no room for doubt in the matter.

We read in the August issue of that magazine:

Lynchings.

" The recent horrible lynchings in the United States, even the almost incredible burning of human beings alive, have raised not a ripple of interest, not a single protest from the United States Government, scarcely a word from the pulpit and not a syllable of horror or suggestion from the Defenders of the Republic, the 100 per cent. Americans, or the propagandists of the army and navy. And this in spite of the fact that the cause of the Louisville, Mississippi, bestiality was, according to the Memphis *Commercial-Appeal*, ' wide-spread indignation at the refusal of the Negroes travelling in slow, second-handed Fords to give road to faster cars.' And yet hiding and concealing this barbarism by every resource of American silence, we are sitting in council at Geneva and Peking and trying to make the world believe that we are a civilized nation."

Here is another paragraph from the same issue:

Mob Tactics.

"There has been developed in the United States a regular technique in matters of mob violence. Matters move somewhat as follows:

' A crime is committed. The police hasten to accuse a Negro. This, of course, is popular because the white public readily believes in Negro crime. A Negro is arrested. If he is promptly lynched the police are vindicated and the guilty white persons saved from fear of detection. If lynching is delayed but threatened, a mob usually attacks the Negro district. This gives a chance for looting and stealing. If any Negroes defend themselves, immediately the police, often assisted by the militia, promptly disarm all Negroes and charge a number with rioting. If any white people are arrested for rioting nearly all of them are discharged; but the Negroes are held and prosecuted. This serves to intimidate the Negro population and keeps it from attempting any self-defence, however innocent the defenders may be, and in no matter how grave danger to life, limb and property."

The following is from the September issue of *The Crisis:*

The Aiken Lynching.

"The latest effective piece of agitation which we have been able to launch was against lynching. We have been fighting lynching for a generation but we still have to fight it, and we agitated against the Lowman lynching at Aiken, South Carolina. South Carolina, known as one of the proud States of the South, the home of Southern aristocracy, Aiken the winter resort of Northern aristocracy. Yet it was in this old State and in this select community in this State that within these recent months occurred an incident which should cause every American to hang his head in shame. Three humble Negroes were accused of a crime, accused of murder, hastily tried, farcically tried, convicted and condemned; a few days still awaiting them when their cases were taken up by a coloured lawyer of South Carolina, Mr. N. J. Frederick. Mr. Frederick appealed these cases to the Supreme Court of South Carolina and to the credit of that court and to the State, the cases were remanded to the Circuit Court for trial. And so, in the re-trial Mr. Frederick, assisted by a Southern white lawyer, Mr. L. G. Southard, represented the Lowmans. These three Negroes, two of them men and one a woman, were being re-tried in the courts of South Carolina and in the course of the trial, upon motion of Mr. Frederick, the Judge directed a verdict of not guilty for one of the defendants, and it is most probable that the other two would have been acquitted. But what happened? On that night a mob gathered and entered the jail through the connivance of the officers of the law and those two men and that woman were taken out and shot to death."

This is what we read about what happened in ' dark and benighted Mississippi ' in the September issue of *The Crisis.*

" Take the case of lynching a few days ago in dark and benighted Mississippi. While in New York City millions of people were acclaiming Lindbergh who had made an achievement which added to the glory of America, to its name throughout the whole world, and which added to scientific effort and achievement, at that very hour when millions of Americans, not only white but black, in the City of New York were acclaiming Lindbergh, a mob of a thousand or more barbarians in Mississippi had taken charge of two Negroes, brothers, accused of killing a slave-driving overseer in a sawmill. They took them from the hands of the constituted authorities, and what did they do with them? They chained them to a telegraph pole, baptized them in gasoline and set them afire."

The following account will be found in Dr. Du Bois's editorial ' postscript ' in *The Crisis* for July 1927 :

Coffeeville, Kansas.

" Two white high school girls in a Kansas city of 20,000 inhabitants claim to have been raped by Negroes on March 17. Bloodhounds are brought. They lead to the Negro quarter and three Negroes are arrested. Two of them are discharged but the other is held. On March 18 a mob of 2,000 attack the City Hall in order to lynch this black man. The mob damages the City Hall, loots stores and chases Negroes. Twenty or more Negroes arm themselves and gather in a pool room. Two of their leaders, Anderson and Ford, shoot into the mob and check it, although themselves desperately wounded. They are now under arrest and on trial for 'inciting to riot.'...

"Then the truth begins to leak out. The white people try to hush the matter up but the Negroes petition for a Grand Jury. The Coffeeville *Daily Journal* acknowledges, May 30, that white men and not Negroes were the bedfellows of the two girls and one white man is to-day in jail charged with rape while one of the girls is also in jail as accessory. What comment is adequate?"

A brief account of the Massacre of East St. Louis in 1917 will serve to disillusion those who believe in the moral superiority of the white man. In this account mark the part played by white women and children :

Massacre of East St. Louis.

"The happenings in East St. Louis, Illinois, in July 1917, were lynch-law on a wholesale scale. The trouble arose because the employers in East St. Louis had imported from the South large numbers of Negro workers to replace the white strikers. The white workers took the law into their own hands, and started Negro hunting. Women, children, the aged, none were spared. Negroes' houses were set fire to—in many cases the inmates could not escape. The white police, it was admitted even by white journals, for the most part, merely stood by or perhaps even helped the white rioters. The following account appearing in *St. Louis Star* throws light on the attitude of the police and militia :

' Some of the militia were active in the fray. Miss Gruening tells of the two soldiers, members of Troop L, from Loney. She passed them a few days after the riot near Cabokia Creek and entered into conversation with them. They boasted that here 7 ' niggers ' were thrown into the creek and every time the niggers came up people rocked them till they were all drowned.... ' And how many niggers did you, boys, kill? ' she asked. They were modestly uncertain—they were not quite sure how many, but they had certainly shot to kill. That had been their orders. ' What,' asked Miss Gruening, ' to shoot to kill niggers?' They grinned cheerfully. ' Oh, no. Only to kill all we saw starting fires.' ' And did you see any starting fires?' ' No, all we saw was niggers flying.' "

Miss Gruening reported to the Military Board of Enquiry, and offered to identify the boys. The Board put her off with evasive replies.

The National Association for the Advancement of Coloured People deputed Miss Gruening and Dr. W. E. B. Du Bois, the gifted Negro writer, to investigate into the outrages. The facts and pictures collected by these two were published in Dr. Du Bois's magazine, *The Crisis*, for September, 1917, and make most gruesome reading. The accounts here given are summarized from an article in *The Crisis*.

The Crisis compares the East St. Louis outrages with the so-called German atrocities, and says : " Germany has nothing on East St. Louis when it comes to 'frightfulness'... In all the accounts given of German atrocities, no one, we believe has accused the Germans of taking pleasure in the sufferings of their victims. But these rioters combined business and pleasure." This is supported by Carlos F. Hurd, staff reporter of the *St. Louis Post-Despatch*, who, writing in his paper as an eye-witness, says :

" The East St. Louis affair, as I saw it, was a man hunt, conducted on a sporting basis, though with anything but the fair play which is the principle of sport... There was a horrible, cool deliberateness and a spirit of fun about it... ' Get a nigger,' was the slogan and it was varied by the recurrent cry, ' Get another.' It was like nothing so much as the holiday crowd, with thumbs turned down, in the Roman Colosseum except that the shouters were their own gladiators and their own wild beasts."

There you have the American love of slogans and lust for excitement. The jaded senses of the American rioters were athirst for something striking. They wanted to revel in their grim sport. The extreme mechanization of life in America creates an abnormal craving for crazes, stunts, sensation-mongering, and produces yellow journals, and shilling-shockers like *Mother India*. Such orgies have always a peculiar fascination for American crowds. But for utter joy let it be white *versus* black.

The *St. Louis Post-Despatch* writer, continuing the grim tale of what he himself saw, graphically gives the following gruesome account :

"A Negro, his head laid open by a great stonecut, had been dragged to the mouth of an alley on Fourth Street and a small rope was being put about his neck. There was joking comment on the weakness of the rope and everyone was prepared for what happened when it was pulled over a projecting cable box, a short distance up the pole. It broke, letting the Negro tumble back to his knees and causing one of the men who was pulling on it to sprawl on the pavement.

"An old man, with a cap, like those worn by street-car conductors but showing no badge of car service, came out of his house to protest. 'Don't you hang that man on this street.' He shouted. ' How dare you to?' He was pushed angrily away, and a rope, obviously strong enough for its purpose, was brought.

"Right here I saw the most sickening incident of the evening. To put the rope around the Negro's neck one of the lynchers stuck his fingers inside the gaping scalp and lifted the Negro's head by it, literally bathing his hand in the man's blood.

"'Get hold, all pull for East St. Louis,' called a man with a black coat and a new straw hat, as he seized the other end of the rope. The rope was long, but not too long for the number of hands that grasped it, and this time the Negro was lifted to a height of about seven feet from the ground. The body was left hanging there."

There are numerous accounts as gruesome as this quoted in the article in *The Crisis*.

Even women were not behindhand in this savage saturnalia. Writes Mr. Hurd:

" I saw Negro women, begging for mercy and pleading that they had harmed no one, set upon by white women of the baser sort, who laughed and answered the coarse sallies of men as they beat the Negresses' faces and breasts with fists, stones and sticks. I saw one of these furies fling herself at a militia man who was trying to protect a Negress and wrestle with him for his bayoneted gun, while the other women attacked the refugee.

" ' Let the girls have her,' was the shout as the women attacked one young Negress. The victim's cry, 'Please, please, I ain't done nothing,' was stopped by a blow in the mouth with a broomstick, which one of the women swung like a baseball bat. Another woman seized the Negress's hands, and the blow was repeated as she struggled helplessly. Finger nails clawed her hair and the sleeves were torn from her waist, when some of the men called, ' Now let us see how fast she can run.' The women did not readily leave off beating her, but they stopped short of murder, and the crying, hysterical girl ran down the street.

" An old Negress, a few moments later, came along with two or three militiamen, and the same women made for her. When one of the soldiers held his gun as a barrier, the woman with the broomstick seized it with both hands, and struggled to wrest it from him, while the other, striking at the Negress, in spite of the other militiamen, frightened her thorougly and hurt her somewhat."

One wanted to ' cut the heart out ' of a Negro lying paralyzed from a bullet wound!

When the mob were tired of mere Negro-beating, they added to it the excitement of incendiarism. It was good fun seeing ' Negroes ' being burnt in their houses, or trying to escape from the flames only to fall victims to the fury of the mob. Even here women took a hand. ' They pursued the women who were driven out of the burning houses with the idea not of extinguishing their burning clothing, but of inflicting added pain, if possible. They stood around in groups, laughing and jeering, while they witnessed the final writhings of the terror and pain-wracked wretches who crawled to the streets to die after their flesh had been cooked in their own houses.'

Dr. Du Bois and Miss Gruening collected testimonies of many people in the hospital. The victims examined by them included a large number of women. One of them, Narcis Gurley, in her seventy-first year, thirty years a roomkeeper and laundress in East St. Louis, related that she did not stir out of her house—being afraid—till the blazing walls fell in. She got her arms burnt.

Edward Spencer, a Negro worker, five years a resident of East St. Louis, had taken his family, seven children and his wife, to friends out from East St. Louis, and walked down the street with a white man whom he thought to be a friend. When he passed this man's gate, he was shot by this same man in both arms and back.

We have not space to reproduce or summarize more statements and accounts of fancy cruelties at East St. Louis. The recital of facts in *The Crisis* is followed by this terse comment, to aid the imagination of the reader in forming a vivid idea of what happened:

"First the mob, always a frightful thing, lowering in dense cowardly ranks through the streets. Then the fleeing Negroes, hunted, despairing. A hoarse sullen cry, ' Get the Nigger!' A shower of bullets, of bricks and stones. The flash of meat-cleavers and pickaxes. The merciless flames. And everywhere bodies, blood, hate and terrible levity.

"All our hunting-songs and descriptions deal with the glory of the chase as seen and felt by the hunters. No one has visualized the psychology of the quarry, the driven, hunted things. The Negroes of East St. Louis have in their statements supplied the world with that lack."

And yet it must not be concluded that East St. Louis was the worst thing for these distressed folk. A worker in a tobacco factory whom the rioters hit with clubs and bricks and stamped upon the head, and who had his arm broken, stated:

"I shall never return to the South, whatever may happen to me here, for in the South it is always killing and burning some of our people. I shall stay in St. Louis."

That was the resolve of many other victims also. Asked a woman aged sixty-five, whom Miss Gruening saw poking almost in the desolate ruins of what had once been her home, she replied, " What are we to do? We can't live South and they don't want us North. What are we to do?"

The above facts have, we presume, given the reader some idea of the magnitude of the problem of the Negro in the United States. Both the parties to the question, the whites and the blacks, are conscious of the gravity of the situation. The whites themselves are divided into three classes : first those who have nothing but condemnation for the prejudice against the Negro; second, those who condemn the prejudice and yet condone it—in its milder forms—on the ground that there is such a difference between the white man and the Negro that it is impossible for the former to treat the latter as an equal. These people would discriminate in favour of the better class of Negroes, the educated and the cultured among them. Last, but not least, is the class which condemns the Negroes on racial grounds and would in no circumstances have any sort of social relations with them. This class believes that 'no amount of education of any kind, industrial, classical, or religious, can make out of a Negro a white man or bridge the chasm which separates him from the white man in the evolution of human history.'

The Negroes were brought to America as dejected and expatriated individuals. The imported slaves represented the conquered and subdued, the despised and outcast of their own country and race. In America, during the period of slavery, they were denied freedom of education, freedom of motion, means of inter-communication and the privilege of unrestrained assemblage. Generally speaking, everything which tends to civilize a man was denied to the Negro. The master was bound by no law or ethics in his treatment of the slave, man or woman, and to-day a large number of coloured men in America are the standing proof of the immoral lawlessness of their former white masters. Under the institution of slavery the Negro was suppressed below the level of self-respect. The black woman often felt a superior importance in becoming the mother of a tawny child. The white master or overseer felt no legal, social, or conscientious constraint in victimizing the female chattel. " The Negro in this country," says Dean Miller, " is the sacrificial race. He is the burden bearer of the white race. He constitutes the meek sill of society and suffers the ills of that lowly place. He performs the rough work of society. He suffers the affliction and even commits the crimes which always fall to the lot of his status!"

In another place the same writer says :

" The Negro woman has been made to bear the brunt of the evil passions of all the races of men living or sojourning in this country. Within the veins of the so-called Negro race there course traces of the blood of every known variety or sub-variety of the human family. Not only within the limits of the race itself, but even within the veins of the same individuals, the strains of blood are mingled and blended in inextricable confusion."

CHAPTER XI

LESS THAN THE PARIAH—*concluded*.

The Ku Klux Klan which bursts into front-page headlines several times in a year in every country, is a typically American product—not of the America that produced Whitman and Emerson, but of the America that has produced other types, Babbitt, and W. R. Hearst and Katherine Mayo.

The most important and sensational news that filter to all the countries about the Klan relate to Negro lynching. But in reality the Klan is not merely a lynching secret society—it is the embodiment of the exclusive spirit in America. It is America's Protestant Nationalism of a very aggressive type. It aims at showing the alien, the Catholic, the Jew and the Negro his place. Perhaps some readers will not readily understand the inclusion of Catholics in this list of undesirables. It must, however, be remembered that the feeling against Catholics is not yet past history in America. In spite of their considerable numbers*

---

* "According to the *Year Book of Churches*, 1924-25, there were, in the year 1923, 18,261,000 Catholic Communicants and 28,366,000 Protestants, though the latter figure would be increased to almost 80,000,000 if we took account of the innumerable adherents who are in sympathy with Protestant ideals, though not officially registered as Communicants." A. Siegfried in *America Comes of Age* (Jonathan Cape, 1927), p. 38.

the Catholics have not so far been permitted to provide even one President in American history. Al Smith, the Catholic candidate finds it hard to overcome these prejudices in spite of his protestations that he is a good Catholic as well as a good American.

The Klan, in its present phase, was organized in 1915. But it is a direct lineal successor of the nineteenth century Secret Society of Know Nothings. The original aim of maintaining the 'supremacy of the white race in the old slave States,' the original ideals, the original methods, the original vocabulary have all survived to this day. So William Joseph Simmons—called 'Colonel' Simmons because he had been a volunteer in the Spanish-American War—the Protestant lay preacher who reorganized the Klan in 1915, was trying no new experiment.

The Klan is a secret society with a mysterious, grandiloquent, solemn, though ridiculous, ritual evolved with a view to filling the ignorant Negro with awe. The mysterious letters of warning and anonymous threats, the white cowls, the silent and solemn torch-light processions, the skeleton hands which clutch at the Negroes, the lynchings and horse-whippings and executions, the defiance of all law and order—have lent the Klan uncanny powers. This secret society has office-bearers with gradiloquent titles. On top, the Grand Sorcerer commanding the Invisible Empire. Then a Grand Dragon for each Kingdom, a Grand Titan for each Dominion, a Grand Cyclop for each Cave.

Also the Grand Monk, the Grand Turk, the Grand Sentinel...

The ritual of this queer but barbarous freemasonry is contained in the *Kloran*, re-written by Colonel Simmons ' to contain all the requisites of an anti-Catholic and anti-Jewish movement.' The anti-Negro part of course needed no addition, being already sufficiently strong.

The Klan is ' consecrated as Protestant to the teaching of the Christian religion, and pledged as white men to the eternal maintenance of white supremacy.' Its numbers* are constantly increasing or decreasing, but it is by all account an organization with considerable influence on politics. Politicians ' are careful to watch their step where the Klan is concerned.'†

The attitude of the Klan towards the Catholics is revealed by the following choice pearls culled by M. Siegfried from *The American Standard*, the fortnightly organ of the Klan.‡ The first is taken from its issue of August, 1925 :

---

* " In 1921 the New York *World* estimated its membership at half a million; in 1922 a Congressional Committee of inquiry could not find more than 100,000; in 1923 *The World's Work*, suggested the figure of 2,500,000; in 1924 Mecklin, in his excellent book on the Klan, speaks of 'millions.' Decadence had however set in, first in the South and then in the Southwest. In September, the Klan was still able to fill the streets of Washington with an immense procession, but in February 1926, an inquiry made by the New York *Times* reveals an absolute rout." *America Comes of Age.*

† *Ibid.*, p. 135.

‡ Siegfried, *op. cit.*, p. 138.

"Do you know that Rome looks upon Washington as the future centre of her power and is filling our government departments with Papists, that the hierarchy for many years has been buying strategic sites in our capital, that in our Department of State at Washington, 61 per cent. of the employees are Roman Catholics, that in our Treasury Department, in which the duty of enforcing prohibition is vested, 70 per cent. of the employees are Roman Catholics?"

The next one is from its issue of October 1, 1925:

"We again take the occasion to attack the sinister purposes and persistent efforts of the Roman Catholic hierarchy, to foist upon us the belief that Christopher Columbus was the discoverer of America, and through this fraudulent representation to lay claim to inherent rights which solely belong to Nordic Christian peoples, through the discovery of this continent by Leif Eriscon in the year 1000."

M. Siegfried humorously suggests that there were no Protestants in the year 1000, and therefore Leif Eriscon must have been a Catholic! The reader will appreciate this reference to the Papal claims more readily when he is told that a false encyclical was once produced (towards the end of the last century) in which the Pope was made to claim the entire American continent on the ground that Columbus was a Catholic.

This controversy evokes much lively interest. One may try to imagine whether if an alien third party, like the British in India, were in power at Washington for a couple of decades, the Catholics and Klansmen of America would not be flying at each other's throats even more furiously than the Hindus and Muslims of India?

That is rather a digression. What however is very relevant to ask here is, ' Is the unjustifiable and cruel attitude of the Brahman towards the pariah more unjustifiable and more cruel than that of the Klansmen of America towards the Negroes?'

*

Yet another class of America's mercilessly persecuted untouchables is that of the Red Indians. Ever since the discovery of America by Europeans they have been exterminated as ruthlessly as the bison and other wild animals of the land. The record of the government and of the citizen is equally black.

Now they are not chased and hounded like wild animals. They have come up to the level of the African natives. Just as for the Masai in East Africa, special land reserves are set aside on which these people are herded. As in East Africa the richest lands are under the white men, so the Red Indian gets the ' worst lands in which life could be sustained at all.' (Though, much to the discomfiture of the whites, some of this bad land had concealed within its bosom rich deposits of mineral oil, and they have added largely to the Red Indian wealth.)

The Red Indians are made to live in insanitary surroundings. Their death-rate is much higher than the white death-rate. Tuberculosis and trachoma are said to be specially prevalent among them.

The United States Government is spending money on the education of the Red Indians. But the expenditure is made through unsympathetic agency and does not produce adequate results. The New York correspondent of the *Manchester Guardian* recently quoted the testimony of Mr. H. L. Russell, construction chief at a Red Indian school, as to the inhuman treatment of Red Indian boys at school. Mr. Russell's letter was placed before the Committee on Indian Affairs of the U. S. Senate, and part of it reads thus:

"I have seen Indian boys chained to their beds at night for punishment. I have seen them thrown in cellars under the building, which the superintendent called a gaol. I have seen their shoes taken away from them, and they then forced to walk through the snow to the barn to help milk. I have seen them whipped with a hemp rope, also a water hose, (and) forced to do servant's work for employees and superintendents without compensation, under the guise of industrial employment and education."

In short, says the correspondent, the Dotheboys Hall system is still alive and flourishing.

In 1926 the Red Indians in the United States numbered 349,964. Citizenship is supposed to have been conferred upon them. In reality, however, they are not only absolutely without any political power, but even civic rights are also withheld from them. The Federal Indian Bureau of the United States Government—which provides employment to nearly 5,000 salaried white men—has complete control of the property of all 'incompetent' Indians. The property of those directly under control of the Indian Bureau is valued at £300,000,000, of which the money and securities amount to £14,000,000. These 'incompetents' cannot take any legal step without the approval of the Indian Commissioner in Washington. 'They may not make a will, execute a lease, sell or give away their land unless he (the Commissioner) consents. They are permitted to retain counsel to represent them, but there are numerous complaints that their choice is limited to certain attorneys known to be amenable in general to the wishes of the federal authorities.' This last sentence, used recently by a New York correspondent, is once again reminiscent of Miss Mayo's observation that there are more ways than one of keeping the under-dog in its kennel.

This is the country from which Miss Mayo hails. For her to sit in judgment on us in the matter of the treatment of the 'depressed classes' is like the pot calling the kettle black. Yet the United States of America is considered to be the freest country in the world. Free indeed! Even now lynching of the Negroes goes on accompanied by unmentionable cruelties and barbarities worthy of the modern 'civilization.'

Miss Mayo and the Anglo-Indians pose as the friends of the 'depressed classes.' It pays the Britisher to play off Hindu against Muslim, Brahman against non-Brahman, high caste against low caste. It pays him to show a political sympathy for the depressed classes. But the moral hollowness of his pretensions is exposed when one remembers what treatment the coloured races are receiving at his hands throughout the world. Leave aside his wars of extermination in furtherance of the imperialistic cause, even then you have the Massacre of Amritsar and the 'crawling order.' In daily life the arrogance of the white man is seen wherever white and coloured people come together. The Britisher pretends he is the 'trustee' of the Kafir interests in Africa. The trustee deprives his ward of his freedom as well as his land. The ward drudges and the trustee enjoys the fruit of his toil. The trustee treats the ward in daily life much worse than the untouchable is treated in India. There is segregation not only in building houses but in everything in life. In many places the white man's roads and railway trains are closed to his ward. In India the colour arrogance in its more blatant forms is perhaps decreasing, but even now cases occur when Indians of culture and of the highest social standing are refused admittance into railway carriages by the arrogant whites.

Before I close this chapter I wish to guard against being understood to have produced all this evidence as a defence or in extenuation of untouchability. I condemn untouchability in the strongest terms possible as an absolutely indefensible, inhuman and barbarous institution, unworthy of Hinduism and the Hindus. It is a blot on what is otherwise one of the noblest of cultures—if not the noblest and most humane culture—the genius of man has evolved during the whole history of the race.

We have not included in this description the treatment that the Jewish citizens of several States even now get. The mere mention of the two words 'pogrom' and 'ghetto' is indictment enough.

We plead guilty to the charge that our social system developed caste enormities, and we are now trying to undo them as best as we can. But certainly it does not lie in the mouths of the white people to tell us that we are a ' world menace ' or that we treat a section of the humanity as ' less than men.' White imperialism is the greatest world menace known to history, and its racial arrogance rests on the assumption that those who are not ' white ' are ' less than men.' It has deprived vast populations of political and civic liberties, and is ruthlessly exploiting them for economic ends. It has perpetrated vandalistic enormities; amongst the more recent of such acts one may cite the bombardment of Damascus, Queen of the East, by the French. Unless it is promptly and effectively brought under check it promises not merely to bomb out non-white civilization, but even to end *all* civilization in a death dance—a dress rehearsal of which we have had in the World War of 1914—inspired by greed and jealousy.

What are the caste cruelties of India put by the side of what the white man has done to the non-white people?

Indians are asked to be proud of the British Empire, but are treated as helots in all parts of the Empire. In Australia, Canada, South Africa, they have suffered under all sorts of handicaps, and been subjected to all sorts of humiliation. They may not be allowed access to the white people's hotels, restaurants, cafés and other places.

But all this becomes a tame affair when one considers the treatment meted out to the African natives whose trustees the white people pretend to be. You require the pen of a Nevinson or a Morel to paint the horrible and blood-curdling picture. Mr. Morel who made a lifelong study of the subject was forced to the conclusion :*

" What the partial occupation of his soil by the white man has failed to do; what the mapping out of European political ' spheres of influence ' has failed to do; what the maxim and the rifle, the slave gang, labour in the bowels of the earth and the lash, have failed to do; what imported measles, smallpox and syphilis have failed to do; what even the oversea slave trade failed to do, the power of

* *The Black Man's Burden* (London : National Labour Press,. 1920), pp. 7-8.

modern capitalistic exploitation, assisted by modern engines of destruction, may yet succeed in accomplishing.

For, from the evils of the latter, scientifically applied and enforced, there is no escape for the African. Its destructive effects are not spasmodic : they are permanent. In its permanence resides its fatal consequences. It kills not the body merely, but the soul. It breaks the spirit. It attacks the African at every turn from every point of vantage. It wrecks his polity, uproots him from the land, invades his family life, destroys his natural pursuits and occupations, claims his whole time, enslaves him in his own home."

A history of this exploitation, or of the misery of the native under it, is beyond the scope of our book. But we may be permitted to give some incidents which will throw light on the 'humane' methods of white imperialism. Our selection will be confined to the rubber plantations of Africa. Speaking of the plantation system of the Congo, Mr. Morel says :*

" We have now to record the operations of a system which Conan Doyle has described as the 'greatest crime in all history'; Sir Sidney Olivier as 'an inversion of the old Slave-trade'; the British Primate as a matter 'far transcending all questions of contemporary politics'; and a British Foreign Secretary as 'bondage under the most

* *Ibid.*, p. 105.

barbarous and inhuman conditions, maintained for mercenary motives of the most selfish character'. These are quotations taken from a mass of similar utterances. It would be an easy matter to fill an entire volume with similar denunciations by men of many countries and of all classes and professions, which resounded in Legislative Chambers, from platform, pulpit, and throughout the world's Press for over a decade. And it is undeniable that all the misdeeds of Europeans in Africa since the abolition of the oversea slave trade pale into insignificance when compared with the tragedy of the Congo. Indeed, no comparison is possible as regards scale, motive, and duration of time alike."

Here is a comment on the 'humane' side of rubber made by an American missionary and quoted by Mr. Morel :†

" It is blood-curdling to see them (the soldiers) returning with hands of the slain, and to find the hands of young children amongst the bigger ones evidencing their bravery... The rubber from this district has cost hundreds of lives, and the scenes I have witnessed, while unable to help the oppressed, have been almost enough to make me wish I were dead... This rubber traffic is steeped in blood, and if the natives were to rise and sweep every white person on the Upper Congo into eternity, there would still be left a fearful balance to their credit."

† *Ibid.*, pp. 121-22.

This relates to the Belgian Congo. But the French Congo was no better. In 1908 an American missionary recorded the following :*

" Who is to blame for the annihilating conditions existing to-day in French Congo? Commerce is dead, towns, once prosperous and plentiful, are deserted and falling into decay, and whole tribes are being needlessly and ignominiously crushed for the aggrandizement of the few... Towns are sacked and plundered; fathers, brothers, husbands, are put in foul-smelling prisons until those at home can get together the taxes necessary to secure their relief. France has granted exclusive rights to concessionaires who claim everything upon, above, in or about any *hectare* of land described in their grant... To be hurled from active, prosperous freedom into inactive and enforced poverty would demoralize even a civilized country; how farther reaching, then, is it with the savage?... As the French say, the entire country is *bouleversé*, i.e., overthrown, in confusion, subverted, agitated, unsettled. And the French are right in so naming the result of their own misdeeds. All is desolation, demoralization, annihilation. Native customs are violated; native rights ignored... Great plains which not long since swarmed with the life and bustle of passing trade caravans are now silent and deserted. Ant-hills and arid grass and wind-swept paths are the only signs of life upon them."

* *Ibid.*, p. 145.

If one were to make a collection of the most revolting examples of human cruelty, one would do well to turn to Mr. Morel's *Red Rubber* and open the chapter headed, ' Deeds.' Some of the most horrible things I have ever read, I came across in that chapter. An English traveller, E. J. Glave, is quoted by Mr. Morel as having stated :*

" Up the Ikelemba away to Lake Mantumba, the State is perpetrating its fiendish policy in order to obtain profit... War has been waged all through the district of the Equator, and thousands of people have been killed and homes destroyed... Many women and children were taken, and twenty-one heads were brought to Stanley Falls, and have been used by Captain Rom as a decoration round a flower-bed in front of his house."

Campbell, a Presbyterian missionary is also quoted by Mr. Morel at great length.† We make the following extracts from his statement:

" Through the gross and wholesale immorality, and forcing of women and girls into lives of shame, African family life and its sanctities have been violated, and the seeds of disease sown broadcast over the Congo State are producing their harvest already. Formerly native conditions put restrictions on the spread of disease, and localized it to small areas. But the

* *Red Rubber*, (London : National Labour Press, 1919), p. 42.
† *Ibid.*, p. 44.

17,000 soldiers, moved hither and thither to districts removed from their wives and relations to suit Congo policy, must have women wherever they go, and these must be provided from the district natives. Native institutions, rights and customs, which one would think ought to be the basis of good government, are ignored."

Here is an incident of the 'ivory regime' narrated by Mr. Campbell:

" After that Katoro, another very large chief living near the apex of the western and eastern Lualaba, was attacked. The crowds were fired into promiscuously, and fifteen were killed, including four women and a babe on its mother's breast. The heads were cut off and brought to the officer in charge, who then sent men to cut off the hands also, and these were pierced, strung, and dried over the camp fire. The heads, with many others, I saw myself. The town, prosperous once, was burnt, and what they could not carry off was destroyed. Crowds of people were caught, mostly old women and young women, and three fresh rope gangs were added. These poor 'prisoner' gangs were mere skeletons of skin and bone, and their bodies cut frightfully with the *chicotte* when I saw them. Chiyombo's very large town was next attacked. A lot of people were killed, and heads and hands cut off and taken back to the officers... Shortly after the State caravans, with flags flying and bugles blowing, entered the mission station at Luanza, on Lake Mweru, where I was then alone, and I shall not soon forget the sickening sight of deep baskets of human heads. These baskets of 'war trophies were used...for a big war-dance, to which was added the State quota of powder and percussion-caps.' "

Before we close this part of our evidence which depicts white civilization in its true colours we must give a few extracts which relate to the events of the twentieth century. On April 10, 1900, the following confession was made by one, Lacroix, agent of the Anveroise Trust :*

"I am going to appear before the Judge for having killed 150 men, cut off 60 hands; for having crucified women and children, for having mutilated many men and hung their sexual remains on the village fence."

Mr. Morel relates many incidents about 1903-05, and even of later dates, but considerations of space rule these out. It must not, however, be inferred that these things are mere ancient history. During and after the War much fuss was made of German cruelty in the Colonies. But that was only propaganda carried on with the usual ethics of propaganda. For otherwise how do you account for the fact that unmentionable cruelties have been perpetrated even in the post-War years by the hypocritical mentors of Germany?

A well-known French writer, M. André Gide, recently went on a pleasure trip to Africa. His

*Ibid., p. 54.

Journal de Route was published by the *Nouvelle Revue Francaise*. M. Gide saw horrible things in the regions occupied by the rubber concessionary companies. Here is one of the choice bits which M. Gide culled from the diary of a white about the crimes of the French administrator, M. Pacha :*

" M. Pacha announces that he has finished his repressions of the Bayas in the environs of Bodo. He estimates (his own avowal) the number of killed at one thousand of all ages and both sexes. In order to prove the results of the battle, the guards and partisans were commanded to bring to the commander the ears and genitals of the victims. The date of this affair was the month of July.

" The cause of all this is the C. F. S. O. (*Compagnie Forestiene Sangha Oubangui*). With the monopoly of rubber and with the complicity of the local administration it reduces the natives to abject slavery."

The white exploiter combines callousness with resourcefulness. Against this formidable combination the poor native is absolutely helpless. There seems no exaggeration in Morel's conclusion that—†

" Thus the African is really helpless against the material gods of the white man, as embodied

---

* See *New Masses*, (New York), Jan., 1928.
† *Red Rubber*, p. 9.

in the trinity of imperialism, capitalistic exploitation, and militarism. If the white man retains these gods and if he insists upon making the African worship them as assiduously as he has done himself, the African will go the way of the Red Indian, the Amerindian, the Carib, the Guanche, the aboriginal Australian, and many more. And this would be at once a crime of enormous magnitude, and a world disaster."

Liberal opinion in the ' civilized ' world received a shock when, a short time ago, two British judges in the British Protectorate of Sierra Leone upheld the continuance of slavery under native chiefs. It is perhaps little realized that the native in Africa can be reduced to a virtual state of slavery even where slavery is said to be non-existent. In East Africa the British have set apart reserves of land for the Masai and other tribes which are not enough to support them. Further they have imposed taxes on them to find money for which they are forced to work on the white man's plantations on the white man's terms. To what helplessness this system reduces the native is a story that has been well told by Dr. Norman Leys, for long a British officer of health in East Africa, in his book, *Kenya*. It has more recently been related again also by a British engineer, McGreggor Ross.

The principle of native reservations is being introduced in South Africa as well. The Native Affairs Act promulgated by the Union Government last summer comes, as Dr. Norman Leys points out in a Press article, as ' the coping stone of the policy which is embodied in the Colour Bar Act that prohibits natives from engaging in certain skilled trades, and in the measure that deprives the natives of the Cape Province of the restricted franchise they have hitherto enjoyed.' Under the new South African Act the Governor-General may, ' whenever he deems it expedient in the general public interest, order the removal of any tribe or portion thereof or any native from any place to any other place within the Union upon such conditions as he may determine, provided that in case of a tribe objecting to such removal no such order shall be given unless a resolution approving it has been adopted by both Houses of Parliament.'

So the law has found a way of curbing the natives who had organised themselves into trade unions, and it may, if it is allowed to have its way, also find a way of depriving the natives of their lands. By what consequences to the native such deprivation may be followed, can be easily imagined.

CHAPTER XII

WOMAN IN INDIA : A RETROSPECT*

Vedic Period.† There can be no doubt that the position of woman in India has very much deteriorated since the Vedic times. There is a consensus of opinion that ' the position held by the Aryan woman in the Vedic Punjab was a most honourable, nay, an exalted one, which later influence and development changed by no means for the better, but rather, and very much, for the worse.'‡ The Vedic literature contains no discussion as to the relative positions of man and woman in an abstract sense. In the Rigveda woman is mentioned as maiden, wife, and mother, and her rights and obligations as such are very briefly alluded to. As a maiden she had the same rights of protection, maintenance and education as a boy had. In the choice of a mate she appears as free as the other sex. The Vedas presuppose some love-making on the part of boys and girls before marriage. There are many references to ' the love of the youth for the maiden ' and his seeking her, as also ' to their mutual affection.' In support of this, see Rv. X, 85, where Soma is supposed to

---

* The contents of this chapter are drawn from two articles by me which appeared in June and July, 1918 in *Young India*, a monthly Journal I was editing in New York.

† Vedic period, from 1500 B. C. backward. Epic period, 1500 B. C. to 500 B. C. Sutra period about 500 B. C.

‡ See Ragozin : *Vedic India* (Story of Nations), 1st edition.

have wooed Surya, the maiden daughter of the Sun-god, Savitar. Surya is called a 'willing bride' and immediately after marriage she is taken by the bridegroom in great ceremony to his home, where the marriage is consummated.

Verse 36 prescribes the marriage formula which is, to this day, repeated by every Hindu bride and groom at the marriage ceremony. 'By the right-hand, for happiness I take thee, that thou mayst reach old age with me, thy husband, *Aryaman, Bhaga, Savitar, Paramodi** gave thee to me, to rule our house together.'

On arrival at her husband's home, the bride is welcomed thus:

" Here may delight be thine, through wealth and progeny. Give this house thy watchful care. Live with thy husband, and in old age mayst thou still rule thy household. Here now remain nor ever part; enjoy the full measure of thy years; with sons and grandsons sporting, be glad in heart within thy house."

Then comes the final benediction, first by the husband and then by the rest of the assembly. Says the husband:

" Children and children's children may *Prajapati* gives us. May *Aryaman* bless us with wealth unto old age. Enter thy husband's homestead. Within the house may man and beast increase and thrive. Free from the evil eye, not lacking

* Names of Vedic deities.

wedded love, bring good luck even to the beasts;
*gentle of mind, bright of countenance, bearing
heroes, honouring the gods, dispensing joy.*"
[Italics are ours.]

Referring to this Mr. Ragozin* remarks:
' Might not the passage in italics be labelled for
all times ' The whole duty of woman?' He also
adds: ' How absolute the wife's and mother's
supremacy is here proclaimed and consecrated by
the husband... Even the popular life of modern
nations—especially the Slavs and Germans, where
the son's bride enters her husband's family in an
avowedly subordinate capacity, and becomes almost the bond slave of his parents, his sister's
servant and scapegoat—fall far short of the ideal
of domestic life set up by our so-called barbarian
ancestors,'—meaning thereby the Aryans who
composed the Vedic hymn referred to above.

The hymn presupposes a society in which—

(*a*) The parties to marriage were grown-up
persons competent to woo and be wooed, qualified
to give consent and make choice.

(*b*) The bridegroom was supposed to have a
home where his wife could be mistress, even in
case his parents and brothers and sisters, for some
reason, happened to live with him, thus giving her
the position of supremacy in the household.

(*c*) The object of marriage was the mutual
happiness of the parties, the raising of children,

* *Vedic India*, p. 372.

the service of the gods and the accumulation of all kinds of wealth.

It should be noted, that, unlike the Christian ceremony of marriage, the Hindu marriage rites do not require the wife to pledge obedience to the husband.

In this society, monogamy was the rule, though polygamy existed among the highest classes, as an exception;* on the other hand polyandry was not known to the Vedas.

Marital infidelity was, of course, disapproved, though cases of illegitimate love were not unknown, as they have never been in any age in any part of the world. The marriage ceremony was, in essence, the same as prevails throughout the length and breadth of India to-day.

There is little information about the rights the wife enjoyed in the property of her husband. As to the wife's right to her own property—the dowry and presents which she got from her parents and friends, etc.—there is nothing to indicate that she had not absolute control over it then as now. In this respect the position of the Hindu woman has always been much superior to that of her European sister. The poetical ideal of the family was decidedly high, and ' we have no reason to doubt,' remark Macdonnell and Keith, ' that it was often actually fulfilled.' The complete supremacy of the

* Ragozin's *Vedic India*, p. 373. *Vedic Index* by Macdonnell and Keith, p. 478.

wife as the mistress of the household has already been evidenced by the hymn quoted above. Moreover, we notice that the wife was a regular participator in the religious duties of her husband. No religious ceremony could be considered complete and efficacious unless both joined in it. The words, ' *pati* ' (master), ' *patni* ' (mistress) signify equality of position in the household. The widow had as much right to take another husband as the widower had to take another wife. Rigveda does not contemplate the custom of *suttee* anywhere*, though it is said that there is a reference to the custom in the Atharva Veda.

There is no trace of the seclusion of women in the Vedic literature, and the whole weight of evidence is in favour of supposing that women enjoyed full freedom of movement.

As regards the education of women, not only was there no restriction, but there is evidence to show that women attained positions of highest distinction, as scholars and teachers.

Epic Period. Coming to the Epic period we notice that the position of woman has not in any way deteriorated. There is the same freedom in the matter of marriage. Nay, even more; the Epic period expressly recognizes marriages of love contracted otherwise than with the consent of parents, for example, that of Arjuna and Subhadra, two of the principal characters in the

---

* Macdonnell and Keith : *Vedic Index*, p. 488.

story of the Mahabharata. The tendency of the Epic period seems to have been to confer the status of marriage on all permanent unions, however effected—permanent in the intention of the parties at the time of union. In fact forms of marriage are recognized which validate even irregular unions, so that the issue of such unions may not suffer from the stigma of illegitimacy. There are no caste restrictions at all. There is a clear development of the wife's right to, and power over her own property, called *stridhana*, though it would be wrong to say that either the Vedic or the Epic period contemplated the economic independence of woman as it is understood to-day, in the West. It is said that the custom of secluding the women originated in the Epic period, but this opinion is based on very slender data and ignores the weight of evidence on the other side. There are numerous references to women going to witness tournaments, accompanying their husbands in wars, on journeys, and otherwise moving about freely. Whatever authority there is to the contrary refers only to the warrior class. The Epics, it is admitted, have been freely added to, even during recent times, and the probability is that whatever references there are must be of later date, when seclusion of women had come to be looked upon as a mark of respectability.

In no other respect was the position of woman lowered in the Epic period. In fact, I am inclined to think that the position of woman in the Epic period was at its high-water mark in India. Since then it has declined steadily. Singing and dancing and dancing and riding were considered accomplishments and the sex relations were perhaps of the best kind.

Sutra Period. From the Epic period we come to the Sutra period. The Sutra period of Sanskrit literature, stands by itself. Sutra literally means string. The Sutra period literature is embodied in aphorisms. Religion, philosophy, law and science all were reduced to Sutras. This is the period to which most of the 'sacred laws of the Aryans' and the Smritis belong. Their groundwork was decidedly old, but the form belonged to a later day. These were evidently the first attempts of the Hindu Aryans at scientific codification and in their codes we notice a curious mixture of narrowness and liberalism, freedom and restriction in the rules concerning sex relations. It is difficult to fix the period of these laws. European scholars think that they are post-Buddhistic, i.e., subsequent to 500 B.C. Hindus claim a greater antiquity for them. The truth perhaps lies between the two extremes. The originals of these codes were pre-Buddhistic but the codes, as they stand to-day, are post-Buddhistic compilations, to which the compilers added many a rule of their liking or such as they found had already been adopted in practice. The outstanding features of these codes regarding the position of woman may be briefly stated—

(*a*) They lay emphasis on the necessity of a girl being married on the first signs of puberty becoming manifest or within three years of the event and look with approval on marriages even earlier.

(b) As such, any consent on the part of the parties becomes out of the question; nor is there any scope for love-making or wooing.

(c) But where guardians neglect the marriage of their female wards and let the three-year limit elapse, the girls are allowed to choose their own husbands, regardless of the consent or approval of their parents. The duty, however, of arranging the marriages of girls at an early age, is laid down in such stringent and awe-inspiring terms as to preclude the idea of parents daring to incur the penalties of neglect in this respect, so that the institution became ultimately universal.

We are not quite sure whether the institution was so universal as it afterwards became at the time when the Muhammadan dominance in India began, because instances of girls marrying at an advanced age and choosing their own husbands are not unknown in the first centuries of the Muhammadan rule. The daughters of Raja Dahir made captives in the eighth century A.D. were grown-up maidens, who, by a very ingenious stratagem revenged themselves on their captor. Samjogta, the princess of Kanauj, who chose Prithi Raj of Delhi as her husband in defiance of the wishes of her father, was also a grown-up maiden. These are by no means solitary instances, as the dramatic literature of the period immediately preceding Moslem invasion is full of instances of such grown-up girls falling in love with persons of their liking and marrying them by choice. Kalidasa, the greatest of Indian playwrights, flourished in the fifth century A.D. Śakuntala, the greatest of his creations, was a grown-up maiden who accepted the love of Dushyanta without waiting for the consent of her father. Her friends and companions were also grown-up maidens. Hiuen Tsang, the Chinese traveller, mentions a case of marriage between a grown-up Brahman young man and a girl with whom he at once began to live and who gave birth to a child of his after one year. This was in the sixth century. The eleventh century Moslem writer, Alberuni, says, 'the Hindus marry at a very young age; therefore the parents arrange the marriage for their sons.' We think it will be fair to conclude that the custom was in the making when the Moslem advent began, and that advent gave it a further point. The reason was that the Muhammadan religion prohibited the carrying away of married women as slaves.

To return to the provisions of the Sutras and the Smritis, the very conception of infant marriage pre-supposes the assumption of great powers on the part of the parents over the person of their sons and daughters. The Hindu law-givers had no difficulty in recognizing this power, but when they came to enunciate the principles which should guide men in their treatment of women, they found a strange conflict of views among the different strata of society. On one hand was the Aryan feeling of high respect for woman; on the other was a notion that she should never be independent. On one side we find Manu laying down that—*

" Women are to be honoured and adored by fathers and brothers, by husbands as also by brothers-in-law who desire much prosperity.

" Where women are honoured (or worshipped) there the gods rejoice; but when they are not honoured. then all rites are fruitless.

" Where women grieve, that family quickly perishes; but where they do not grieve that (family) ever prospers.

" Houses, which women, not honoured, curse, as if blighted by magic, perish utterly.

" Therefore, they are ever to be honoured at ceremonies and festivals, with ornaments, clothes, and food by men who desire wealth (or prosperity)."

Once more it is repeated that ' if the wife be happy all the house is happy and if she is not happy, all are unhappy.'†

Compare this with the following general disqualifications stated by Manu in chapter V:

" In her childhood (a girl) should be under the will of her father; in her youth of (her) husband;

---
* Manu, III, 55-59.
† Manu, V, 148-150.

WOMAN IN INDIA   161

her husband being dead, of her son; a woman should never have freedom of action.

" She must never wish separation of herself from her father, husband or sons, for by separation from them a woman would make both families contemptible.

" She must always be cheerful and clever in household businesses, with the furniture well cleaned and with a not free hand in expenditure."†

Again in chapter IX, verses 2 and 3 it is repeated that—

"Day and night they should be kept by the male members of the family in a state of dependence. The father guards them in childhood, the husband guards them in youth and in old age sons guard them."

In verse 7, the husband is enjoined to ' guard his wife with diligence as by guarding her he guards his posterity, his ancestral usages (*kula dharma*), his family, himself and his own duty (*dharma*).' The next two verses explain what is meant by ' guarding.' No man, it is said, can guard a woman by force or by secluding her; only those women are well-guarded, who guard themselves, through themselves, though some suggestions are offered as to how to keep them employed. In these laws the one point constantly kept in view is the purity of the offspring. It is to be

† *Ibid.*, III, 62.

secured (*a*) by a careful selection of the parties to the marriage, (*b*) by insisting on marriages within the caste, (*c*) by laying down a very high ideal of womanly fidelity, (*d*) by giving the husband full control over his wife, (*e*) by pointing out in strong language the evil consequences of marriage out of caste, and (*f*) by assigning a low social position to the issue of mixed marriages.

In the earlier literature, we notice an anxiety to legalize almost all permanent unions, whether the result of love, chance or caprice, in order to legitimize the offspring. It was expressly stated that in the case of marriages out of caste, the caste of the offspring shall be that of the father. The sons of maidens were declared to be legitimate sons of their fathers as well as the sons begotten on another's wife when such person had left the wife without her fault or when he was impotent or consumptive and so on. In the later literature the offspring of all unions out of caste are held as degraded; with a few exceptions the same fate is assigned to the issue of illicit intercourse. It will be interesting at this stage to enumerate the different kinds of marriages recognized by Hindu law.

Hindu law recognizes marriages of eight kinds. Of these four are approved, one is tolerated, the remaining three are disapproved. The fact, however, that they are acknowledged as marriages show that they were at one time legal. The approved forms are those in which the maiden is given away by her guardian, according to rites.

The tolerated one is the union of mutual love apparently without or against the consent of the guardian. The three disapproved ones are those (a) in which a price is demanded and taken by the father, (b) in which the maiden has been forcibly abducted, presumably against her will, (c) in which a man indulges in sexual intercourse with a woman when she is sleeping or otherwise unconscious. This was considered to be the basest act, but the act having been done, it was legalized in the interests of all concerned.*

Hindu Eugenics. Hindus had developed a high idea of the laws of eugenics, as is clear from the following rules which we take from the law books :

Says Narada : " The man must undergo an examination with regard to his virility; when the fact of his virility has been established beyond doubt, he shall obtain the maiden (but not otherwise).

" If his collar-bone, his knee, and his bones (in general) are strongly made; if his shoulders and his hair are (also) strongly made; if the nape of his neck is stout, and his thigh and his skin delicate; if his gait and his voice is vigorous... By these tokens may a virile man be known; and one not virile by the opposite characteristics."†

The fact that Narada lays emphasis on the competency of the man, and Manu on the

* See Narada, XII, 38-44.
† Narada, XII, 8-13.

eligibility of the woman, also shows what a change came about in the ideas of the Hindus from the days of Narada's book to the days of the code which is now extant by the name of Manu.

Says Manu : "Let him (the young man), who has completed his studies and is desirous of becoming a householder avoid for marriage ties these ten families : That by which rites are neglected, which has no males, which possess not the Vedas, the members of which are hairy or have piles; also families afflicted with consumption, dyspepsia (chronic), epilepsy and leprosy.

"Let him not marry a tawny maiden, or one with superfluous members, or a sickly (maiden), or one without hair or with excessive hair, or a chatterbox, or one red (-eyed), or one called after a star, a tree (or) a river; or one called after a bird, snake, or slave; or one with a terrifying name.

"Let him marry a woman not malformed, with a prosperous name, that walks like a *hans* (swan) or elephant, with slender hair locks, and teeth, (and) soft-bodied."

All the lawgivers are agreed that the most approved form of marriage is the one within the caste, though they allow a man of a superior caste to marry a woman of inferior caste. In the case of marriages out of caste but approved, the tendency of the earlier authorities is in favour of the issue getting the status of their fathers, but that of the later ones is against it. Such mixed marriages explain the numerous castes and sub-castes that are to be found among the Hindus to-day beyond the original four.

A careful study of all the provisions of the present code of Manu makes one think that at the time when this edition was compiled there was a strange conflict of opinion between jurists and lawyers about the rights and position of women. Some were in favour of maintaining the old ideals, while others were inclined to give to men a complete mastery over women.

So far we have considered the position of woman in general, or of woman as wife, but when we come to look into her position as mother we find that she is at once placed on a higher pedestal, a view in which all the authorities agree. In chapter II, 145, Manu lays down that the *acharya* (meaning a spiritual teacher) exceedeth ten *upadhyayas* (meaning an ordinary teacher) in the claim to honour; the father exceedeth a hundred *acharyas*; but the mother exceedeth a thousand fathers in the right to reverence and in the function of educator.' Motherhood, among the Hindus, is the most sacred function. They respect it all through nature. On her merits as a woman, every woman is a potential mother. So every woman, other than one's own wife, or one's own daughter or sister is addressed as mother. When talking to stranger women a Hindu always accosts them as 'mother,' sometimes even as 'sister' but more often the former than the latter. The mothers among the goddesses receive the highest homage and are sometimes placed even above the gods. Similarly, the native land is also worshipped as the motherland—*Matribhumi*—whence the ironical title of Miss Mayo's book.

The Hindus are generally very tender towards their children. There are, of course, exceptions to the rule. In the darkest period of Indian history certain customs sprang up, which though confined to certain sections of the population reflect the highest discredit on the originators and followers thereof; such as *suttee*, infanticide, the ill-treatment of widows, infant marriage, polygamy, the selling of girls and dedicating of girls to the services of the gods. Missionary zeal sometimes paints them thick, and gives them out as universal customs in India. They are sufficiently bad, and one at least, pretty general, namely, child marriage, but certainly not so bad or so general as they are represented to be. *Suttee* and infanticide were never general. They were confined mostly to royal families or the highest castes. *Suttee* was originally entirely voluntary. Some of these customs have already disappeared. Others are in the process of change and dissolution. All modern reforming agencies are pledged to the restoration of woman to her original high position in society.

Legal Status. Hindu law has always recognized the right of the wife to possess property of her own. In chapter IX, 194-195, Manu says:

" That which is given over the marriage fire, that which is given in the bridal procession, that (which is given over) for an act of love, and that (which is) received from brother, mother, father, (all this) is called the sixfold property of woman. That which is received as a gift (by a married woman) after her marriage from the family of her husband or of her connections, and that which has been given her by her beloved husband, shall become the property of her children should she die while her husband is alive."

In a joint Hindu family, no one, male or female, is entitled to a definite share of property. The property is managed by the head of the family, in the interests of all the members of the family, male and female. A daughter of the family remains a member of the family as long as she is not married, but when married she joins another family. In divided families, widows, mothers, daughters and sisters are recognized as heirs under certain circumstances. An unmarried daughter, according to some authorities, inherits a share of her father's property along with her brother. Ordinarily when sons survive they take the whole estate of the father, with a legal liability to maintain the women members of the family out of the father's estate. In case of their neglecting to do so and the property being sold, the right of the women members to be maintained out of that property is supposed to follow the property, whosoever may be in possession thereof. If no son survives, a widow inherits the property of her husband with full rights as to the use of the income thereof, but with restricted rights as to the alienation of it. She can only alienate for legal necessity or with the consent of the next heir. On her death the property goes to the daughters of the family with the same rights as were possessed by their mother. Similarly, the mother is also an heir in the absence of brothers.

The special property of a woman is inherited by her children (sons and daughters) in the first instance, or in their absence by the husband in certain cases, and by her father's family in certain others.

Rights of Adopting a Child. A Hindu woman has full rights of adoption. She can even adopt a son to her husband after his death, if he, in his lifetime, authorized her to do so for him, or if his blood relations consent.

Right to Guardianship of Children. In certain circumstances, a mother has the right of guardianship over her children of both sexes. She is also counted as one of the guardians for the purposes of giving away daughters in marriage.

Rights over Issue. Hindu law books contain very elaborate rules as to the raising of issue, and as to whom the issue should belong after birth. These rules will seem to be very curious to people brought up in conventional Christian theology, but when read in the light of modern advanced thought as to parentage and eugenics they will not be devoid of interest. Manu* likens woman

---

*Chapter IX, 32.

to land and man to seed. In some places the seed is the principal factor; in others, the womb of the woman; when both are good the offspring is considered the best. In a general comparison between seed and womb, the seed is called weightier, for the offspring of every created being is characterized by the characteristics of the seed. Whatever qualities the seed possesses, the same will be found in the produce. ' For (though) this earth is declared to be the eternal womb of created beings, (yet) the seed exhibits in the things produced from it, not a single one of the qualities of the womb. In the earth, even in one and the same (kind of) land, the seeds which spring up after being sown by husbandmen at the (proper) time are of various appearances, each according to its own natural qualities. Rice, *sali* (a kind of rice), *mudga*, sesame, beans, and barley sprout forth according to their seed, and so do leeks and sugar-canes. Hence a well-instructed man, aware of this law and understanding wisdom and science, should never sow seed in the wife of another man.'

Dissolution of Marriage. Marriage, according to the Hindu law, is a sacrament, and in theory, the tie is indissoluble. Once married always married, is the formula. This theory discountenances the remarriage of widows, though it has not in practice operated so strictly against the widowers. The earlier law books, however, show that in those days not only was the remarriage of widows common, but that in certain circumstances both the wife and the husband were allowed to remarry in the lifetime of their former mates. We shall revert to the question of widows in another chapter.

Remarriage. First, in the case of the woman. Says Narada :*

"When her husband is lost or dead, when he has become a religious ascetic, when he is impotent and when he has been expelled from caste—these are the five cases of legal necessity in which a woman may be justified in taking another husband."

Narada prescribes different periods of waiting for married women of different castes, in case of absent husbands, and says that no offence is imputed to a woman if she goes to live with another man after the fixed period has elapsed. To the males, presumably, Narada allows greater freedom. Starting with a general injunction that 'husband and wife must not lodge a plaint against one another, with their relations or the king, when a quarrel has arisen through passion, which has its root in the jealousy or scorn,' he adds that when husband and wife leave one another from mutual dislike they commit a sin.

Narada prescribes severe penalties for an adulteress but does not omit to say that "if a man leaves a wife who is obedient, pleasant of speech, skilful, virtuous, and the mother of issue, the king shall make him mindful of his duty by inflicting severe punishment on him.'

*Chapter XII, 97-101.

Manu lays down elaborate rules regulating the degree of guilt attachable to a husband in case of tarnsgression of marriage vows in different circumstances; for instance, it is laid down that ' the husband should wait one year for a wife who hates him; at the end of the year he should take away what (he) has given her and not live with her (any more).'* In the case of a wife taking to adultery, Manu excuses her if she hates the husband because he is crazy, degraded, castrated, impotent or afflicted with an evil disease, but not so if he only neglects her, or is a drunkard or troubled with an ordinary disease. Even in the latter case, the wife's guilt affords no ground for his setting her aside for good. She may be neglected for three months. Manu allows a man to ' over-marry in case his wife indulges in intoxicating liquors, or does sinful things, or (always) opposes her husband, or is diseased, or plagues her husband, or is always wasting his money. In the case of sterile women, however, a man has to wait for eight years. But if the wife is of a lovable disposition and endowed with virtue though sterile, the husband can only remarry with the permission of the former.

By the time of the present code of Manu, opinion had swung to condemn the rema:riage of widows. I do not think even the present code of Manu makes it illegal, but certainly it does not approve of it. The ideal of marriage set up by the present code of Manu is high from the ordinary conventional point of view, but rigid and illiberal

* Manu, IX, 77.

from the point of view of modern thought. In the
opinion of Manu, the whole duty, in brief, of husband and wife towards each other is that they cross
not each other, in thought, word or deed till death.
And the promise is that they, who righteously discharge this duty here, shall not be parted hereafter
even by the death of the body, but shall be
together in the world beyond.*

The idea was one of complete blending
of the two personalities into one. It is said
that ' as the quality of the husband is, such
becometh the quality of the faithful wife,
even as the quality of the waters of the
river becometh as the quality of the ocean
into which she merges'.† The husband here is
likened to an ocean and his superiority is presumed. In another place in the same chapter,‡
it is said that ' the man is not the man alone; he
is the man, the woman, and the progeny.' The
sages have declared that ' the husband is the same
as the woman,' as it is expressly stated elsewhere §
that ' if the wife be of noble soul and the husband
sinful and she determines to follow him in death
unwidowed, then, even as the strong snake hunter
grasps the serpent and drags it out to light from
the deepest crevice, even so shall her love and
sacrifice grip the husband's soul and drag it from
its depths of sin and darkness into the realms of

* Manu, IX, 101; V, 165.
† Manu, IX, 22.
‡ Ibid., IX, 45.
§ Ibid., IX, 23.

light above.' Here the love of the wife is assigned a higher position than the wisdom of the husband. The whole idea is poetically put in a book of mythology,* where it is said :

"He is Vishnu, she is Shri. She is language, he is thought. She is prudence, he is law. He is reason, she is sense. She is duty, he is right. He is author, she is work. He is patience, she is peace. He is will, and she is wish. He is pity, she is gift. He is chant, and she is note. She is fuel, he is fire She is glory, he is sun. She is orb, he is space. She is motion, he is wind. He is ocean, she is shore. He is owner, she is wealth. He is battle, she is might. He is lamp, she is light. He is day, and she is night. He is tree, and she is vine. He is music, she is words. He is justice, she is truth. He is channel, she is stream. He is flagstaff, she is flag. She is beauty, he is strength. She is body, he is soul."

It will be observed that in this description she is superior in certain respects and he in certain others. Both are 'equally important and indispensable and inseparable; that each has distinct psycho-physical attributes and functions which supplement each other; that both are present in each individual life; but that in certain epochs one with its set of forms and the other with its differentia and progress, in another set of forms.'†

* Vishnu Purana, I, 8. Vishnu Bhagavata, VI, 19.
† *The Science of Social Organization*, Bhagwan Das (Adyar : Theosophical Society), p. 222.

The English expression ' better half ' has an equivalent in Sanskrit (*ardhangini*) which means only 'one half of the body.' The idea is probably based on Manu I, 32, in which it is said that Brahma, the Creator, having divided his own body into two, became male by one half, and female by the other. So divided, a man and woman only become a perfect person when again joined in wedlock, and only as one perfected person can they perform effective religious ceremonies.

CHAPTER XIII

WOMAN AND THE NEW AGE

Miss Mayo has made some extremely revolting statements about the morals of Indian women, and their position in Indian society. She has very skilfully (from her point of view) but most dishonestly mixed up truth with untruth. The picture she has drawn is not only misleading and out of proportion, but a blatant and downright denial of the truth. If she had merely attacked the practice of child marriage and the ban on widow remarriage no one would have taken exception to her attitude. But she goes out of her way to damn Indian manhood and Indian womanhood in a most sweeping fashion by generalizations which are entirely untenable. I will take up the different questions dealt with by her one by one.

The general position of Indian women is deplorable enough in certain respects. The Indian woman is the victim of her environments. In a country where the political and social position of men is on the whole that of helots or slaves, the position of women could not be any better. The present position of Indian women as compared with that of the Western women is as bad as that of Indian men as compared with Western men. Miss Mayo's book gives you the impression that the position of Indian women has always been as bad as it is to-day. But that is not true. Our ' Retrospect' preceding this chapter must have made it clear to the reader how erroneous such a conclusion would be. During all periods of the history of real Hindu India woman enjoyed a better position in society than that enjoyed her European sister at any time before the mid-Victorian era.

In Vedic times the woman was an equal of man in all that matters. She chose her husband after she had attained the age of discretion and understood her interests. There were no restrictions to widow remarriage. This view is accepted by scholars like Sir Herbert Risley.* In certain respects the woman of Vedic India was freer than the European woman even of to-day.

In Europe the emancipation of woman is a very recent event. Not long ago nobody heard of 'votes for women.' Even 'souls for women' was at one time in Europe a heresy confined to a very few.

The most prosperous period of Europe before the advent of modern science was the one in which the Romans were at the helm of affairs. In the Europe of the Romans, woman was treated like chattel to be disposed of by man at his pleasure. Under Roman law the position of woman was in certain respects similar, in others inferior to that which was occupied by her in Medieval India. In India this status was the result of political de-

---

* Sir Herbert Risley was a pioneer in Indian Ethnography. His chief book on this subject is *The People of India* (Calcutta: Thacker, Spink). He served as Census Commissioner to the Indian Government.

generacy. In Europe it was so when the Romans were at the zenith of their political supremacy.

"Throughout her life," says a woman writer* discussing the position of her sex in the days of Rome's supremacy, "a woman was supposed to remain absolutely under the power of father, husband, or guardian, and to do nothing without their consent. In ancient times, indeed, this authority was so great that the father and husband could, after calling a family council, put the woman to death without public trial. That women were so subjected to guardianship was 'on account of their unsteadiness of character,' 'the weakness of the sex,' and their 'ignorance of legal matters.'"

About laws of marriage under the Romans we read in the same author's book :†

"As in all Southern countries where women mature early, the Roman girl usually married young; twelve years were required by custom for her to reach the marriageable age. In the earlier period a woman was acquired as wife in three different ways: (*i*) by *coemptio*—a mock sale to her husband; (*ii*) by *confarreatio*—a solemn marriage with peculiar sacred rites to qualify men and women and their children for certain priesthoods; (*iii*) by *usus*, or acquisition by prescription. A woman became a man's legal wife by *usus* if he had lived with her one full year and if, during

---

* Eugene A Hecker : *A Short History of Woman's Rights, with Special Reference to England and the United States* (Putnam, 1911), p. 2.

† *Ibid.*, pp. 8-9.

that time, she had not been absent from him for more than three successive nights."

A slight change came in the second century. A man could marry even if not present personally; a woman could not. The woman's parents or guardians were accustomed to arrange a match for her, as they still do in many parts of Europe. The consent of the daughter's marriage was also necessary, though his power to coerce his daughter was limited.*

Christian thought in Europe did not help in raising woman's status. According to *Genesis*, Miss Hecker points out, a woman is the cause of the fall of mankind.† St. Jerome held that all evils sprang from woman. St. Augustine argued that man was made in the image of God, but not so woman. He adds that ' a woman is not permitted to have dominion over her husband,' nor can she be a witness, nor give security, nor act in court.‡ The Fathers insist that marriage without the paternal parent's consent is fornication.

Among Germanic peoples marriage was always controlled by guardianship, the feeling of caste was very strong; a woman must marry below her station,§ and was never allowed to be independent. On marrying woman passed into

---

* *Ibid.*, p. 10.
† *Ibid.*, p. 53.
‡ *Ibid.*, pp. 58-59.
§ *Ibid.*, pp. 79, *et. seq.*

the power of her husband 'according to the sacred scriptures,' and the husband therefore acquired the lordship to all her property.*

Coming to England, Blackstone who wrote in 1763, says :

" The husband also, by the old law, might give his wife moderate correction. For, as he is to answer for her misbehaviour, the law thought it reasonable to intrust him with this power of restraining her, by domestic chastisement, apprentices or children, for whom the master or parent is also liable in some cases to answer..."†

This was about the time the Abbé Dubois was conducting his infamous researches in Hindu customs. Blackstone continues :

" The civil law in England gave the husband the same, or a larger. authority over his wife; allowing him for some misdemeanours *flagellis et fustibus acriter verberare uxorem* (to give his wife a severe beating with whips and clubs); for others, only *modicam castigationem adhibere* (to apply moderate correction)."

In the reign of of George III a woman guilty of murder was drawn and burnt alive.‡ 'The right of a husband to restrain a wife's liberty,' says Miss Hecker, 'may not be said to have become completely obsolete until the case of Reg. *v.*

---
* *Ibid.*, p. 84.
† Quoted by Miss Hecker, *op. cit.*, p. 125.
‡ Miss Hecker, *op. cit.*, p. 126.

Jackson in 1891.' 'Wife-beating is still a flagrantly common offence in England.'* This was in the year of grace 1911.

As to woman's rights of property, until about the third quarter of the nineteenth century, the wife during marriage had no power to alienate her land without her husband's concurrence. The widow was entitled to enjoy for her life, under the name of dower, one-third of any land of which the husband was seised in fee at any time during the marriage:

" Our law institutes no community, even of movables, between husband and wife. Whatever movables the wife has at the date of the marriage become the husband's and the husband is entitled to take possession of and thereby to make his own whatever movables she becomes entitled to during the marriage, and without her concurrence he can sue for all debts that are due her."†

During the marriage the wife could not contract on her own behalf. The Married Woman's Property Act, which finally abrogated the right of the husband to the full ownership of his wife's property, was passed in England only in 1882.‡

Even more worthy of note is what Miss Hecker says about the age of consent:

* *Ibid.*, p. 127.
† Pollock and Maitland, quoted by Miss Hecker, *op. cit.*, p. 129.
‡ Miss Hecker, *op. cit.*, p. 132.

"The saddest blot on a presumably Christian civilization connected with this matter is the so-called 'age of legal consent.' Under the older Common Law this was *ten* or *twelve*; in 1885 it was thirteen, at which period a girl was supposed to be at an age to know what she was doing. But in the year 1885 Mr. Stead told the London public very plainly those hideous truths about crimes against young girls which everybody knew very well had been going on for centuries, but which no one ever before had dared to assert. The result was that Parliament raised the 'age of legal consent' to sixteen, where it now stands."*

Higher education for women in England, as is well known, is distinctly a movement of the last half of the nineteenth century. The suffrage movement is all too recent a thing to require a discussion here.

In Miss Mayo's Country.

As late as 1880 there were in America people like Rev. Knox-Little, who said, speaking in a Philadelphia Church, that 'wifehood is the crowning glory of a woman... To her husband she owed the duty of *unqualified obedience*. There is no crime which a man can commit which justifies his wife in leaving him or applying for that monstrous thing, divorce.'† 'Lords on Earth,' in India or anywhere else, could not claim more.

---

* *Ibid.*, p. 138.
† *Ibid.*, p. 151.

Miss Mayo makes much of the speeches of some ultra-orthodox members of the Assembly on a *non-official* Bill to raise the Age of Consent. This Bill was introduced by a Hindu member, but was defeated because of opposition from the official benches. Another Bill fixing the minimum age for marriage, brought forward by R. B. Har Bilas Sarda, a Hindu member of the Legislative Assembly, was very strongly opposed by the official members. It is now in the Select Committee stage. What is significant is that the progressive element is gaining strength so rapidly in spite of opposition from the British Government. That there will always be opposition from some cnservative people goes without saying. This trait is by no means peculiar in India. In 1852 the British Parliament considered a Bill against the construction of the first railway! Napier opposed in the Commons the introduction of steam power in the navy. Scott denounced gas for lighting, Byron satirized it in verse. Miss Mayo's Boston beat all when (in the year of grace 1845) it passed a municipal ordinance declaring bath tubs illegal except under medical advice!

More relevant here is the following account of the history of the Age of Consent legislation in the United States, given by Miss Hecker :*

" In 1890 a bill was introduced in the New York Senate to lower the 'age of consent'—the age in which a girl may legally consent to sexual inter-

---

* *Ibid.*, pp. 155-56.

course, from 16 to 14. It failed. In 1892 the brothel keepers tried again in the Assembly. The bill was about to be carried by universal consent when the chairman of the measure, called for the individual yeas and nays. In order that the constituents of the representatives might know how their legislators voted. The bill thereupon collapsed. In 1889 a motion was made in the Kansas Senate to lower the age of consent from 18 to 12. But the public heard of it; protests flowed in and under the pressure of these the law was allowed to remain as it was."

American tourists who take stock of woman's disabilities in India would do well not to forget that in their own country woman's emancipation is such a recent thing. The American woman's movement became a force only towards the end of the last century. The first Women's Rights Convention in America was held at Seneca Falls, New York, in 1848, and was ridiculed by the American journals as a gathering organized by ' divorced wives, childless women, and some old maids.' Who has been in charge of affairs in India—the Indians or the British—during the time that the American woman has been getting her rights?

In no period of Hindu history has the position of Indian women been worse than, or inferior to the one held by the women in Europe and America up to the middle of the last century. We have already seen that in the Vedic period Indian woman occupied a position of equality with man. Her position began to deteriorate under Buddhism, but even then legally her position remained the same as before. It is curious that during the period of Hindu history parallel to the Roman in Europe the restrictions placed on woman's freedom were in certain respects similar. For example, a woman required a constant guardianship of her male relatives. But in India that was the opinion of only a few commentators and was never enforced. In no period of Hindu history was woman denied the right to make contracts, to dispose of her property, to inherit the property of her husband in certain contingencies (though on a life tenure), to be a guardian of her children and to inherit in certain contingencies as a mother, as a daughter and a sister. She had, and even now has, the first lien on her husband's estate for being maintained and housed according to her husband's station in life. Her right to receive education and take part in religious ceremonies was never denied.

The present position of woman in the West is entirely the growth of the last 75 years. Before that in Europe and America, legally, civilly, morally and socially, she was under handicaps greater than those of the Indian woman to-day. Had India been politically free during the same period the position of her women would have been no doubt much better to-day. If Miss Mayo were really a friend of her sex in other countries, the opposition by the officials to the private Bills to raise the age of consent and to fix the minimum marriageable age would be argument enough for her to refrain from eulogizing the present administration.

Under the present Indian constitution the members of the different legislatures have the right to extend the franchise to women. Though the right has been acquired only recently it has already been used by most of the major legislatures, so that women in many of the provinces are entitled to vote or seek election for the central and local legislatures. Miss Mayo is right when she says that we have not many women legislators; but may we know how many women there are on the American Senate? Woman's vote is a new thing and it will take time to work out its possibilities. The British House of Commons with its seven hundred members contains just four women M.P.'s. In India, however, some very high honours have been conferred on educated women. Dr. Muthulakshmi Reddi is the elected Deputy President of the Madras Legislature, and she is a woman. The Presidentship of the Indian National Congress is the highest distinction that unofficial India can confer on anybody—and women have not been precluded from it: the Congress counts two women among its ex-Presidents—Mrs. Annie Besant and Mrs. Sarojini Naidu. That is a sure indication of the progessive outlook of the Indian Nationalist on this question.

CHAPTER XIV

EARLY TO MARRY AND EARLY TO DIE

Child marriage is beyond doubt having pernicious effects on the physique of Indians. It is by no means an ancient institution in India. Messrs. Macdonnell and Keith, Sir Herbert Risley and other scholars, who have studied the question, all agree that the Hindus of the real Hindu India married not as children but as adults. It seems safe to say that child marriage was not common in India before the Mussulman invasion. Exactly how and when this evil system became prevalent may be uncertain, but there can be no doubt that it is to-day eating into the vitals of the nation.

However, it is one thing to admit child marriage to be one of the factors responsible for the material and spiritual ills of the present-day India and quite another to make its existence a pretext for ignoring the still more important factors. 'Give the dog a bad name and hang it' is a recognized maxim in political propaganda, and Miss Mayo's observations on early marriage in India do not ignore it.

Child marriage was prevalent among several of the peoples that produced great civilizations in antiquity. The Greeks, who still inspire models in the harmonious development of the whole man—physical, mental and moral—married very early. The Romans, who made good soldiers and administrators, married as children. So also did the Hebrews. In England, down to the time of the Stuarts, child marriage was common.

If child marriage were enough to make a nation effete, the Greeks and the Romans and the Hebrews would not have left such a lasting impress on history.

The fact is that a devastating factor like child marriage is seldom allowed by society to go altogether without counterbalancing safeguards. In India this safeguard is provided in many of the child-marrying castes by postponing the *consummation* of marriage till a considerable period after the marriage ceremony. Marriage thus becomes a sort of betrothal, and child marriage means only child betrothal.

Not all Hindus marry too early. The lower castes for the most part marry comparatively late. Among the higher castes too the system is not without safeguards in most cases. This fact of safeguards has been noticed by all competent observers, among them being Sir Herbert Risley and Sir Edward Gait, both of whom had ample opportunities of studying this question in their official capacity as Census Commissioners.

Observe Risley and Gait in the *Census Report* of 1901 (p. 433) :

" Nor one who has seen a Punjabi regiment march past, or has watched the sturdy Jat women lift their heavy water-jars at the village well is likely to have any misgivings as to the effect of their marriage system on the physique of the race."

Sir Denzil Ibbetson pointed out earlier in his *Report on the Punjab Census* that the Rajputs in the Punjab marry when about 16 years old and begin to co-habit immediately, the Jats on the other hand marry between 5 and 6 years generally —but the bride does not go to the groom's house for several years with the result that for all practical purposes the Jats begin married life sometimes even later than the Rajputs do.

Miss Mayo entirely ignores these facts, and with her usual 'courage' generalizes that every, or almost every, Indian girl becomes a mother soon after puberty. Says she on page 30 :

" The Indian girl, in common practice, looks for motherhood nine months after reaching puberty or anywhere between the age of fourteen and eight. The latter age is extreme, although in some sections not exceptional; the former is well above the average."

Miss Mayo produces no evidence in her support. On the other hand her conclusion has been challenged by a woman doctor of Bombay, M. I. Balfour, who, writing in the *Times of India*, the leading Anglo-Indian paper in Bombay, on October 11, 1927, says:

" I have notes of 304 Hindu mothers delivered of their first babies in Bombay hospitals. The average age was 18.7 years. 85.6 per cent. were 17 years or over, 14.4 per cent. were below 17. 14 was the youngest and there were 3 of that age.

" I have compared these figures with the reports of the Madras Maternity Hospital for the years 1922-24. 2,312 mothers were delivered of their first babies. The average age was 19.4 years. 86.2 per cent. were 17 years or over and 13.8 per cent. were below 17. 13 was the youngest age. There were 7 mothers aged 13 and 22 mothers aged 14. The Madras figures included not only Hindus but women of other communities also.

" I have reports of 3,964 cases of childbirth from other parts of India including the North. Of these only 10 were below 15 years of age. 13 was the youngest age."

Dr. Balfour concludes:

" There is no doubt that childbirth sometimes takes place too early in India and even more so that co-habitation commences too early. Legislation is badly needed. But...the figures I have given prove that the cases instanced by Miss Mayo do not in the least represent the common customs of the country."

It must also be remembered that for the Indian girl almost invariably sexual life commences after marriage. We shall revert to this subject in another chapter, and make a comparison with the conditions in the West.

If it is true, as is held by several scholars, that child marriage in India became prevalent during a period of foreign invasions, when the unmarried girls stood the risk of being enslaved by the invading hordes, it is reasonable to suppose that with the disappearance of those political conditions the marriage age ought again to go up. But this is prevented by artificial factors brought in by foreign rule. The natural inertia that helps a custom to linger on, even when it has outlived its utility, is helped in the present case by the super-imposed State, indirectly by its policies that prevent the spread of education and do not raise the standard of living, and directly by its opposition to the reformers in the legislature.

In Europe during recent centuries the marriage age has risen largely owing to the spread of education and the rise in the standard of living. There is no reason to suppose that in a free India the same factors would not help in banishing child marriage. That these factors, so far as they are allowed to operate, are working against child marriage is admitted in the census reports. The figures show clearly that in the educated class, particularly amongst the Hindus, the marriage age is going up. The Census Commissioners admit this fact. The spread of education on a nation-wide scale is not a problem to be satisfactorily tackled by private effort, and so it is stepmother Britain that by denying education to the masses is responsible for granting a fresh lease of life to the old and disappearing order of things.

The Indian reformers pressed for a higher age of consent, and legislation raising it from 10 to 12 was enacted because of their vigorous effort. Sir Hari Singh Gour's more recent Bill aims at raising it to 14 in the case of married girls and to 16 for others, but the officials in the Assembly are opposed to it. Mr. H. B. Sarda's Bill for minimum marriageable age for boys and girls was referred to a Select Committee at the summer session of the Legislative Assembly in 1927 in the teeth of official opposition. The measure still hangs fire. Several progressive Indian States—Baroda, Mysore, Kotah and a few others—the rulers of all of which are followers of orthodox Hinduism, have anticipated the Sarda Bill: Baroda first passed the law fixing the minimum marriage age more than two decades ago, but the authorities in British India are still hostile to such legislation.

CHAPTER XV

THE HINDU WIDOW

Prohibition of widow remarriage is also one of those evil customs which cannot be justified. The lot of the Hindu widow is bad indeed, but the wild statements made about the morality of the Hindu widows can only be described as products of an evil mind. In general Hindu widows lead a life of sacrifice and service. Their morality stands on a higher pedestal than Miss Mayo's mind can conceive of. In making her sweeping statements she has only shown her ignorance of the real condition and her readiness to generalize on very meagre data.

Firstly, the prohibition against widow remarriage is not universal. The vast majority of Hindus remarry their widows as a rule. This is the practice in all classes considered pastoral or military. This is also the practice among what are known as the low castes. " At the bottom of society, as understood by the average Hindu, we find a large group of castes and tribes practising adult marriage and widow marriage."* The restrictions are generally confined to people of higher castes whose number can in no case

---

* Risley, *op. cit.*, p. 178.

exceed 30 per cent. of the total Hindu population.*

Simply absurd is Miss Mayo's statement that remarriage in orthodox Hinduism is *impossible*. Why, there is orthodoxy and orthodoxy. I know of many orthodox Hindus who have allowed the remarriage of their widowed girls or daughters-in-law. The statement on page 86 of *Mother India* that the remarriage of a Hindu widowed wife is still held to be ' inconceivable ' is nothing short of a lie.

Secondly, the rules prescribed for a widow's life are not the same in all provinces or among all castes. I have never seen a Hindu widow's head

*" According to the Census Returns [in the Punjab] there were only 134,645 widows below 30 years of age, namely, 1,208 child-widows between 0 and 9; 6,778 between 10 and 14; 19,346 between 15 and 19; 41,686 between 20-24, and 65,627 between 25-29 (of these, at least three-fourths can remarry). There then remain those between 30 and 60 or upwards who have mostly grown-up children, and who practically preside over their households. The proportion, therefore, of marriageable widows is only 1 in 59.43 in a female population of 8,015,210 and, as not a fourth of these are condemned to celibacy, the hardship is not so universal as is alleged." *History of Indigenous Education in the Punjab* by G. W. Leitner, LL.D. (Calcutta : Govt. Press, 1882), p. 101, footnote.

Again in the same work :

"There were only 675 Hindu child-widows between 0-9 years of age and 4,070 between 10 and 14. Of these, at least two-thirds belong to the re-marrying castes. There were altogether 73,320 Hindu widows in 1881 below 30 years of age, of whom about a third are prevented from re-marrying. There were also 53,382 Muhammadan widows below thirty, most of whom will, no doubt, re-marry and only 8,035 Sikh widows of corresponding ages. Where is the country in Europe in which practically *more* widows have a better chance of re-marrying than in India?"

17

shaved anywhere in the N.-W. F. Province, or the
Punjab, or the U. P., or Rajputana.

Thirdly, hard as her lot is in the matter of
marriage, in other respects the Hindu widow's
life is not so hard as has been made out by Miss
Mayo. Professor Pratt, a New England gentleman from the United States takes a very judicious
view of the matter when he says :*

" The position and life of the Indian widow
varies, of course, with the personality of the
woman and with the family in which her lot is
cast. From writers like Dubois one would judge
that she is always an object of heartless persecution, a sad and unwilling drudge; while Sister
Nivedita and her school would have one suppose
that the Hindu widow is ever loved and fondly
cared for, and that she becomes a nun given over
to good works, which spring spontaneously from
her sorrow-crowned character. Both views are
doubtless true in their limited way, and neither
should be accepted without modification from the
other. Certainly the widow's lot is a sad one at
best; and stern Hindu theory believes that it
should be sad, that for the widow sadness is better
than joy. And doubtless those widows who
acquiesce in this judgment and give themselves
up willingly to a life of utter self-abnegation and
service shine at the end as gold purified by fire...
The widowed mother of the head of the house has
a position not only of respect and affection, but of

* *India and its Faiths* by J. B. Pratt (New York : Houghton
Mifflin, 1915), pp. 130-31.

authority and power. Younger widows, of course, have no such authority, but they have nearly as much work, and if the service be not willing much of it must be performed none the less, and for the young woman who has no ambition to be a martyr or a nun the fate of widowhood in India is very hard indeed.

" On the whole, the Indian home is a very narrow and limited place, but it may be a very sweet and holy place as well; and it has poduced a type of woman who knows how to love and how to suffer and be faithful and lose herself in those she loves : a type that has great limitations, but which is not without a certain lofty beauty—even though at the antipodes from that of the modern militant suffragette."

Fourthly, the Hindu widow, if she is a mother, is simply worshipped. " Perhaps nowhere in the world," says Mr. Pratt,* " is there more profound reverence for the mother than in India."

" The wife becomes regent," says Sister Nivedita,† " when a man dies during the minority of his son; and even if the latter be already of age, his ownership of an estate is by no means free and complete during the lifetime of his mother. The whole world would cry shame if he acted without her occasional advice, and, indeed, the Indian woman's reputation for business capacity is so like

---

* *Ibid.*, p. 130.
† *Web of Indian Life*, by the Sister Nivedita (Miss Margaret E. Noble), London : Heinemann, p 52.

the French that it is commonly said of encumbered property that it needs a widow's nursing."

Dr. G. W. Leitner, first Principal of the Lahore Government College, who studied the Punjab life during the last quarter of the last century very intimately, wrote thus of the lofty conception of marriage and of the state of widows among the Hindus :*

" The lot of a poor widow is sad enough in all countries to deserve sympathy, but it is minimized in India by the following considerations :

1. The widows of Muhammadans, of Sikhs, of most of the hill tribes, and of nearly all the lower Hindu castes *do* marry, and the widows of Jats are bound to marry their deceased husband's brother, for the protection of the inheritance.

2. The widows who have grown-up sons or whose age entitles them to have a voice in the management of the household, practically, and, in numerous cases admittedly, rule it.

3. There, therefore, only remains a comparatively small number of widows in the higher and middle Hindu castes, and among them only those are to be pitied who are poor or who have unfeeling or no relatives, a rare circumstance.

4. The misfortune of these, however, is alleviated—

* *History of Indigenous Education in the Punjab*, p. 100.

(a) by the ideal of the sacredness of the marriage tie; the hope of rejoining the husband and being made worthy of his regard in proportion to her, generally, self-inflicted privations, such as sleeping on the floor instead of on a *charpoy*. It is here where religion strengthens and raises the character of a noble-minded Hindu widow;

(b) the social consideration which is given to a widow who, by her acts, shows her underlying grief for her deceased husband;

(c) the sympathy of her own family to which she, in many instances, returns;

(d) the generally liberal provision for life that has been made for her on the thirteenth day, which relieves her, at any rate, from the most gnawing cares and allows her to address herself to the education of her children, if any."

This is a true account, as I can myself testify from my own personal experience of the numerous cases that have come to my notice privately, or in my professional capacity when I practised at the Bar. The following statement by Miss Mayo bristles with diabolic exaggeration :*

* *Mother India*, p. 84.

"An inmate of her husband's home at the time of his death, the widow, although she has no legal claim for protection, may be retained there on the terms above described, or she may be turned adrift. Then she must live by charity—or by prostitution, into which she not seldom falls. And her dingy, ragged figure, her bristly, shaven head, even though its stubble be white over the haggard face of unhappy age, is often to be seen in temple crowds or in the streets of pilgrimage cities, where sometimes niggard piety doles her a handful of rice."

Miss Mayo only shows her ignorance of Hindu law when she says that 'a widow has no legal claim for protection.' A widow has the first lien on a deceased Hindu's estate for her maintenance and housing. This has to be arranged according to the social position of her deceased husband.

CHAPTER XVI

THE DEVADASI

Another of the evils to which Miss Mayo draws attention is the existence of 'Devadasis.' This institution is a rotten one, no doubt. But even here Miss Mayo has supplied some details and explanations from her own fertile imagination. On pages 51 and 52 of her book we read:

" In some parts of the country, more particularly in the Presidency of Madras and in Orissa, a custom obtains among the Hindus whereby the parents, to persuade some favour from the gods, may vow their next born child, if it be a girl, to the gods. Or, a particularly lovely child, for one reason or another held superfluous in her natural surroundings, is presented to the temple. The little creature, accordingly is delivered to the temple women, her predecessors along the route, for teaching in dancing and singing. *Often by the age of five, when she is considered most desirable, she becomes the priest's own prostitute.*

" If she survives to later years she serves as a dancer and singer before the shrine in the daily temple worship; and in the houses around the temple she is held always ready, at a price, for the use of men pilgrims during their devotional sojourns in the temple precincts. She now goes beautifully attired, often loaded with the jewels of the gods, and leads an active life until her charms fade. Then stamped with the mark of the god under whose ægis she has lived, she is turned out upon the public, with a small allowance and with the acknowledged right to a beggar's livelihood. Her parents, who may be well-to-do persons of rank and caste, have lost no face at all by the manner of their disposal of her. Their proceeding, it is held, was entirely reputable. And she and her like form a sort of caste of their own, are called Devadasis, or 'prostitutes of the gods,' and are a recognized essential of temple equipment." [Italics are ours.]

We do not know if the institution of Devadasi was one of the subjects for personal research by Miss Mayo. Her researches did no doubt for the most part pertain to kindred subjects. But here the reader is referred to Sir James Frazer's *Golden Bough*.* Frazer's account, however, does not bear out all that Miss Mayo says. In his book we read:

" In India the dancing-girls dedicated to the service of the Tamil temples take the name of *deva-dasis*, ' servants of the gods,' but in common parlance they are spoken of simply as harlots. Every Tamil temple of note in Southern India has its troop of these sacred women. Their official duties are to dance twice a day, morning and evening, in the temple, to fan the idol with Tibetan ox-tails, to dance and sing before it when it is borne in procession and to carry the holy

---

*Vol. I, entitled, *Adonis, Attis, Osiris*, (Macmillan, 1914), pp. 61-65.

light called *kumbarti*. In order to obtain a safe delivery expectant mothers will often vow to dedicate their child if she should prove to be a girl to the service of God. Among the weavers of Tirukullikundram, a little town in the Madras Presidency, the eldest daughter of every family is devoted to the temple. Girls thus made over to the deity are formally married, sometimes to the idol, sometimes to a sword, before they enter on their duties; from which it appears that they are often, if not regularly, regarded as the wives of the god.

" Among the Kaikolans, a large caste of Tamil weavers who are spread all over Southern India at least one girl in every family should be dedicated to the temple service. The ritual, as it is observed at the initiation of one of these girls in Coimbatore, includes ' a form of nuptial ceremony.'

" In Travancore a dancing-girl attached to a temple is known as a ' servant of god.' The following account of her dedication and way of life deserves to be quoted because, while it ignores the baser side of her vocation, it brings clearly out the idea of her marriage to the deity. Marriage in the case of a Devaratial in its original import is a renunciation of ordinary family life and a consecration to the service of God. With a lady nurse at a hospital or a sister at a convent a Devadasi at a Hindu shrine, such as she probably was in the early ages of Hindu spirituality would have claimed favourable comparison. In the ceremonial of the dedication—marriage of the dasi, elements are not wanting which indicate a past quite the reverse of disreputable. The girl to be married is generally from six to eight years in age. The bridegroom is the presiding deity in the local temple. Thenceforth she becomes the wife of the deity in the sense that she formally and solemnly dedicates the rest of her life to his service with the same constancy and devotion that a faithful wife united in holy matrimony shows to her wedded lord. The life of a Devadasi bedecked with all the accomplishments that the muses could give was one of spotless purity. Even now she is maintained by the temple. She undertakes fasts in connection with the temple festivals, such as the seven days' fast for the *Apamaragam* ceremony. During the period of this fast, strict continence is enjoined : she is required to take only one meal, and that within the temple—in fact to live and behave at least for a term in the manner ordained for her throughout life. Some of her daily work seems interesting; she attends the *Diparadhana*, the waving of lighted lamps in front of deity at sunset every day; sings hymns in his praise, dances before his presence and goes round with him in processions with lights in hand. After the procession, she sings a song or two from Jayadeva's *Gitagovinda* and with a few lullaby hymns her work for the night is over. When she grows physically unfit for these duties she is formally invalidated by a special ceremony, i.e., *Totuvaikkuwa* (old mother), entitled only to a subsistence allowance. When she dies, the temple contributes to the funeral expenses. On her death-bed the priest attends and after a few ceremonies immediately after death, gets her bathed with saffron-powder."

Let the reader judge for himself if the version in *Golden Bough* is not at places materially different from that in *Mother India*.

The institution of Devadasi is a monstrous one and every South Indian must feel ashamed of it. But it must be remembered that the institution is unknown outside the Southern Presidency, and Miss Mayo's 'some parts of the country' is quite misleading. Even in the Southern Presidency large tracts like Malabar are unacquainted with it. The statement that 'by the age of five she becomes the priest's own prostitute' is obviously a gross exaggeration. The worst feature in the institution is of course the association of this class of women with the temples. Some temples in Southern India serve as brothels kept by priests. But it may be pointed out that some of the monasteries and churches in Europe used to be, and some perhaps even now are, no better.

In Dr. Sanger's *History of Prostitution* we read :

"Pope Clement II issued a bull that prostitutes would be tolerated if they paid a certain amount of their earnings to the church.

"Pope Sixtus IV was more practical; from one single brothel, which he himself had built, he received an income of 20,000 ducats."

Emma Goldman, the Russian-American revolutionist and feminist cites the above two sentences from Sanger's work and comments :*

" In modern times the church is a little more careful in that direction. At least she does not openly demand tribute from prostitutes. She finds it much more profitable to go in for real estate, like Trinity Church, for instance, to rent out death traps at an exorbitant price to those who live off and by prostitution."

At its worst the South Indian Devadasi prostitutes are no better and no worse than the class of prostitutes in Europe and America. In a subcontinent with 315,000,000 souls the presence of a microscopic class like Devadasis is surely no justification for condemning the morals of the entire nation.

Reform agencies are at work to abolish this vicious custom. It can be confidently hoped that if the Government does not take up cudgels to defend it, the elected members of the Madras Council will not allow it to survive very long. " Now, if it were asked," writes Miss Mayo, "how a responsible Government permits this custom to continue in the land, the answer is not far to seek." She finds it in the religious fierceness of the orthodox. Yet the action of the Mysore Government is there to disprove her contention. In this,

---

* Anarchism and Other Essays, p. 189.

as in so many other things—in introducing compulsory elementary education, in abolishing child marriages, etc.—the enlightened Indian States have forged ahead whilst the British Indian bureaucracy still tenaciously sticks to everything that is hideous.

CHAPTER XVII

' SCHOOLING, FREE OF CHARGE '

Miss Mayo should have known that in *schools* maintained by the State no tuition fee is charged in other countries. But in India they do charge a tuition fee from every pupil in every Government school.

On pages 129 and 130 of *Mother India* appears the following statement: " The rich men of India, as a whole, remain to-day still convinced at heart, that if indeed their daughters are to be schooled at all, the Government should give them schooling, free of charge.' This statement is on a par with other similar reckless statements made by Miss Mayo in her book. The difficulty is that in these general statements she never quotes her authority. I have before me the prospectuses of several schools and colleges for girls in Lahore and I am copying the scale of fees from them:

GOVERNMENT COLLEGE FOR WOMEN.

(Number of scholars about 69, out of which 30 are resident scholars.)

Intermediate classes, tuition fee ... Rs. 60 a year.
Entrance fee (Intermediate) ... Rs. 2
University Registration fees ... Rs. 5
Degree classes (tuition fee) ... Rs. 144 ,,

Entrance fee (B.A.) ... ... Rs. 2
University Special fee ... Rs. 3

These fees are for day scholars only. The resident students pay Rs. 22 a month in addition, i.e., Rs. 264 a year.

The Sacred Heart School.

School Department.

Boarding fees Rs. 40 a month, i.e., Rs. 480 a year.
Entrance fee for boarders Rs. 10.
Entrance fee for day scholars Rs. 5.
Tuition, Infant class, Rs. 8 p.m., i.e., Rs. 96 a year.
Primary class, Rs. 8 p.m., i.e., Rs. 96 a year.
Middle class, Rs. 8 p.m., i.e., Rs. 96 a year.
High class, Rs. 10 p.m., i.e., Rs. 120 a year.
School Car, Rs. 10 p.m., i.e., Rs. 120 a year.
Pianoforte, Rs. 10 p.m., i.e., Rs. 120 a year.
Lunch for day scholars, Rs. 5 p.m., i.e., Rs. 60 a year.

In this school, at the time of writing, there were 68 boarders and 300 day scholars.

In the College Department of this institution fees are up to Rs. 15 a month, and boarding fees up to Rs. 40 a month.

Queen Mary's College.

(A school called college by courtesy.)

Entrance fee ... Rs. 10
Boarding fees ... From Rs. 30 a month.

Day Scholars.

All classes below Middle ... Rs. 5 per month.
Middle and High classes ... Rs. 10 per month.

Equally high is the tuition fee in another college called the Kinnaird College where there are 130 resident scholars and 120 day scholars.

No one really knowing Indian conditions would be so perverse as to say that rich Indians want free schooling for their daughters and are not prepared to pay for their education. It is a gratuitously false charge.

On page 132, Miss Mayo puts the following sentence into the mouth of Miss Bose, Principal of the Victoria Girls' School, Lahore, which has, as Miss Mayo says, 500 students on its rolls :

" 'The tuition fees?' Merely nominal; we Indians will not pay for the education of our daughters. This school is maintained by government grant and *by private subscriptions from England.*" [Italics are ours.]

As to the last statement, the following letter from Dewan Bahadur K. B. Thapar, O.B.E., gives the truth :

My dear L. Lajpat Rai,

With regard to your enquiry about the Victoria Girls' School, Lahore, with which I was connected as Secretary from 1887 to 1914, when it was provincialized and taken over by government,

'SCHOOLING, FREE OF CHARGE'

I beg to state that during all this period the school was never in receipt of any monetary grant from England or any other country in Europe.

It was maintained by the Punjab Association with the help of an annual grant from provincial revenues and income derived from endowments which consisted of donations made by ruling chiefs and the gentry of the Province.

LAHORE :   Yours sincerely,
14-1-1928   (Sd.) K. B. THAPAR.

This nails another lie to the counter.

CHAPTER XVIII

THE SEX URGE IN THE WEST

Miss Mayo takes curious delight in dilating upon the imaginary sexual depravity of the Indians. All yellow journalists know what makes the story spicy. Their books are intended to form an accompaniment to chewing gum—the most saleable thing at many American bookstalls. Miss Mayo's 'personal researches' in India pertain mostly to the sexual side of life. Here official publications and statistics fail, and for the most part she has no reputable references—unless you call the Abbé Dubois a reputable authority. She has relied chiefly on hearsay—perhaps on her own imagination—and sometimes gives us old, insipid chestnuts. Yet she is a woman with ' courage '—as a sympathetic British reviewer of her book tells us—and so she does not hesitate to generalize about the morals of a nation. She cannot see mud, real or imaginary, without a strong impulse to wallow in it.

Yet this portion of Miss Mayo's work cannot be summarily dismissed, for it forms the most vital part of her argument, and interested persons are seriously using it in their propaganda of calumny against the Indian people.

Miss Mayo thinks it is the sexual depravity of the Indian that forms the ' rock-bottom ' physical base ' upon which rests the whole pyramid of his woes, material and spiritual.' To her the Indian's sex-life accounts 'for his slave mentality, his poverty, ignorance, political minority, melancholy, ineffectiveness,' etc., etc.*

To prove her contention Miss Mayo relies on hearsay and on hospital cases. But if hospital cases, the worst selected out of them, are to form the standard by which to judge, India is perhaps no better and no worse than countries in the West. Hearsay may give you interesting and sensational stories, but it cannot command credence with serious-minded people.

Imagine an utter stranger coming to a vast sub-continent like India inhabited by 300 million people with different usages in different parts, with languages not one of which is known to the stranger, who still goes about touring and does all the parts in a twelve-months' time, and then sits down to write of the most intimate side of the people's life, making sweeping generalizations against the whole nation, basing these for the most part on her own ' observation ' and 'frank' talks she had with people—does not that require ' courage ' indeed? Add to this the ' courage' to misquote most of the few people whose names are actually given in the story, and you will know how to evaluate Miss Mayo's statements.

We have not the least desire to slander the nations of the West. But Miss Mayo's generalizations about Indian sex morality invite a com-

* *Mother India*, p. 29.

parison with conditions in the West; and however unpleasant the task, it has to be undertaken. The only way to test the truth of Miss Mayo's statements about sex indulgence and sex depravity in India is a comparative survey of sex morality and usage in this country and the West. However, we shall refrain from making statements based on hearsay and shall leave the task to be done by scientific writers and competent observers of Europe.

At the outset we must admit, as we already have admitted in a previous chapter, that child marriage in India is a factor that does no doubt accentuate sex stimulus and cause physical deterioration. Miss Mayo's version is a gross and malicious exaggeration—we have examined it already—but the existence of this factor is undeniable.

Except for this one fact, we do not see anything in Indian customs and conditions that could make the social atmosphere over-charged with sex—as compared with conditions in the West. In fact, the boot is on the other leg. Modern industrial and housing conditions, the lust for cheap excitement which these breed, the big cities, and above all the organization of vice on a commercial scale so as to get dividends out of it—all these factors go to accentuate the sex stimulus in the Western countries beyond anything known here.

The opportunities for pre-marital and extra-marital sex indulgence in India are comparatively very rare. Too-early marriage may be unknown in the West, but not so too-early sex experience. In India child marriage seldom means *consummation* in childhood, while it also effectively excludes pre-marital indulgence. In the West, on the other hand, rightly or wrongly, radical sex thinkers now not only permit, but even command, some pre-marital experience. The custom, however, of ' free marriage unions ' is not confined to the radicals. These unions, says Havelock Ellis,* seem 'to be fairly common in many, or perhaps all, rural parts of England.' 'In some countries,' the same writer continues, ' it is said to be almost a universal practice for the women to have sexual relationship before legal marriage; sometimes she marries the first man whom she tries; sometimes she tries several before finding the man who suits her... Thus in some parts of Staffordshire it is the custom of women to have a child before marriage.' ' In Sweden,' Ellis states on the authority of Ellen Key, ' the majority of the population begin married life in this way.' The arrangement, we are told, is found to be beneficial, and ' marital fidelity is as great as pre-marital freedom is unbounded.' ' In Denmark, also, a large number of children are conceived before the unions of the parents are legalized.'

In fact, in all ' Teutonic lands, the custom of free unions is very ancient and well-established.' "In Germany," the same authority continues, "not only is the proportion of illegitimate births very

---

* *Sex in Relation to Society* (6th volume in the *Studies in the Psychology of Sex*), F. A. Davis, Philadelphia, 1921, p. 380.

high, since in Berlin it is 17 per cent., and in some towns very much higher, but ante-nuptial conceptions take place in nearly half the marriages, and sometimes in the majority. Thus in Berlin more than 40 per cent. of all legitimate first-born children are conceived before marriage, while in some rural provinces (where the proportion of illegitimate births is lower) the percentage of marriages following ante-nuptial conceptions is much higher than in Berlin. The conditions in rural Germany had been especially investigated by a committee of Lutheran pastors, and were set forth a few years ago in two volumes, *Die Geschlechtsittlich Verhaltnisse im Deutschen Reiche*, which are full of instruction concerning German sexual morality. In Hanover, it is said in this work, the majority of authorities state that intercourse before marriage is the rule. At the very least, a *probe*, or trial is regarded as a matter of course preliminary to a marriage, since no one wishes ' to buy a pig in a poke.'...In Saxony a German pastor was informed : " One does not buy even a penny pipe without trying it." ' The same story is told of other districts and states. 'The number of women who enter legal marriage still virgins is not large (this refers more especially to Britain).' But this state of things 'is found to be favourable to conjugal fidelity.'

Whether ' this state of things ' is something commendable or not, and whether the radical code is better than the conventional code are questions beyond our present purpose. What is relevant is to remember that whilst in India sex experience comes a considerable time after marriage, in the Western countries it comes considerably before it. In comparing the marriage age in this country with that in the West this fact must not be lost sight of it.

This conclusion is implicit in Ellis's observation that*—

" The gradual but steady rise in the age for entering on legal marriage also points in the same direction, though it indicates not merely an increase of free unions but an increase of all forms of normal and abnormal sexuality outside marriage."

Let him cast the first stone who is himself safe. Miss Mayo, if she had no propagandist axe to grind, could more usefully have given attention to the sex-life of American boys and girls. Things there as revealed by an earnest and ardent reformer, Ben Lindsey,† for 25 years Judge of a Juvenile Court, do not make very pleasant reading. Yet Judge Lindsey's conclusions are based not on hearsay but entirely on the facts with which he was himself confronted in his professional capacity.

Judge Lindsey's material is drawn from high-school boys and girls, for the most part of respectable, well-to-do families, and he is led to the

* Ellis, op. cit., p. 378.
† The Revolt of Modern Youth (New York : Boni and Liveright, 1925). See chapters 5-7.

conclusion that the type of American girl he had to deal with 'feels the urge of sex years before the mind has grown sufficiently mature to cope with it and control it.'

" The first item," says Judge Lindsey, " in the testimony of these high school students is that of all the youth who go to parties, attend dances and ride together in automobiles, more than 90 per cent. indulge in hugging and kissing... The testimony I receive regarding this estimated ninety per cent. is practically unanimous... Some girls insist on this kind of thing from boys they go with, and are as aggressive in a subtle way in their search for such thrills as are the boys themselves."

This hugging and kissing and dancing means a life of excessive stimulation and strain for the nerves. " These familiarities," says the Judge, " are responsible for much nervous trouble among young girls and for the prevalence of certain physical ailments which are peculiar to them.' The Judge then gives the opinion of eminent physicians ' that so far as the moral and physical results are concerned, the effect of such half-way improprieties on these young girls is just as dangerous as if they yielded themselves completely.'

But the kissing and hugging and dancing are only the beginning and not the end. ' At least fifty per cent. of those who begin with hugging and kissing do not restrict themselves to that, but go further and indulge in other sex liberties which by all the conventions are *outrageously improper.'* [Italics are ours.]

The ' whole-hoggers ' are by no means rare. ' Fifteen to twety-five per cent. of those who begin with hugging and kissing eventually go the limit.' This does not, in most cases, mean either promiscuity or frequency, but it happens. "I can only say," adds the Judge, " that the estimates come from high school students and that they are the most conservative estimates I have received from that source."

Judge Lindsey had a lot to do with girl-mothers, for he was consulted by them in his professional capacity, in all untoward situations. In 1920-21, the Juvenile Courts of Denver ' dealt with 769 delinquent girls of high school age... They ranged in age from 14 to 17 years.'

" At least 2,000 cases were directly involved in the cases of those 769 girls. For one thing, the boy had to be reckoned with. In addition the two of them always had a circle of intimates, many of whom were in on the secret and indulging in the same kind of experiences. So it goes, from one girl to other girls, and from one boy to other boys; and every time I have tried to follow up the many by-paths that present themselves for investigation it has been like exploring the endless passages of a dark cave, whose galleries and secrets lead one beyond the limits of endurance."

There are other facts which make Judge Lindsey infer that—

"For every case of sex delinquency discovered, a very large number completely escape detection. For instance, out of 495 girls of high school age—though not all of them were in high schools—who admitted to me that they had sex experiences with boys, only about 25 became pregnant. This is about 5 per cent., a ratio of 1 in 20. The others avoided pregnancy, some by luck, others because they had a knowledge of more or less effective contraceptive methods, a knowledge, by the way, which I find to be more common among them than is generally supposed.

"Now the point is this, first, that three-fourths of that list of nearly 500 girls came to me of their own accord for one reason or another. Some were pregnant, some were diseased, some were remorseful, some wanted counsel, and so on. Second, the thing that always brought them to me was their acute need for help of some kind. Had they not felt that need, they would not have come. For every girl who came for help there must have been a great many, a majority, who did not come because they did not want help and therefore kept their own counsel.

"In other words, that 500, covering a period of less than two years, represented a small group drawn from all levels of society...but a much larger group...didn't know the ropes and never came around at all. My own opinion is that for every girl who comes to me for help because she is pregnant or diseased, in need of comfort, there are many more who do not come because they escape scot-free of consequences or else because circumstances are such that they are able to meet the situation themselves. *Hundreds, for instance, resort to the abortionist. I don't guess this, I know it.*" [Italics are Judge Lindsey's.]

The Judge warns his reader, that he is not exaggerating and that the state of things described by him is not peculiar to Denver.

" I have no wish to run these estimates into the ground. Even the minimum figures are shocking. I handled about a hundred cases of illegitimate pregnancy last year (1924), taking care of most of the mothers and the babies, and in most cases adopting the babies out. With every one of these girls it was a touch and go whether to come to me and arrange to have the baby or to go to an abortionist and arrange not to have it."

" *And that among the girls of high school age, some in school and some out of school, in a city of 300,000 population!*" [Italics are Judge Lindsey's.]

The following again from Judge Lindsey's book gives telling figures about physical maturity among American school girls:

" We found that 265 of the 313 [girls] had come to physical maturity at 11 and 12 years, more of them maturing at 11 than at 12. Dividing the 313 girls into two groups we found that 285 of them matured at the ages of 11, 12, and 13; and that only 28 of them matured at 14, 15 and 16."

Havelock Ellis quotes from a report about East Germany :*

" With this inclination to sexual intercourse, it is not surprising that many believe that after sixteen *no* girl is a virgin."

This means that all girls in the European country referred to mature before 16 and a good many perhaps do so very considerably before that. In the case of American school girls a similar conclusion is arrived at by Judge Lindsey, as we have seen above.

With the atmosphere thus surcharged with sex, it is idle to expect virtue, in the conventional sense of conjugal fidelity, to flourish. Monogamy according to many European writers is no more than a myth. Says Ellis :†

" In no part of the world is polygyny so prevalent as in Christendom; in no part of the world is it so easy for a man to escape the obligations incurred by polygyny.' Schopenhauer expressed the same opinion.

Looked at superficially, marriage in the West may appear to be a happy, perfect system of love marriage. But a thinker like Max Nordau has described it as the ' lie of marriage.' Nordau thinks that not less than 75 per cent. of marriages are what are known as *mariages de convenance* and not real love marriages. George Hirth

* *Op. cit.*, p. 387. † *Op. cit.*, p. 493.

[quoted by Bloch] estimates this percentage to be even higher still.

No wonder, therefore, that we find Ellis saying on the authority of Professor Bruno Meyer, that ' far more than the half of sexual intercourse now takes place outside legal marriage.'*

Recognizing these facts, radical European thinkers are advocating unions of a lower degree than marriage, and other similar forms of sex relationships. One of the strongest arguments used by these thinkers is the increasing popularity of divorce in European and American countries.

" The voluntary, childless marriages of to-day," says Ellis,† " have served to show the possibility of such unions outside legal marriage, and such free unions are becoming, as Mrs. Parsons points out, a progressive substitute for marriage."

In the Western cities, vice has become a scientifically organized industry, and a most flourishing one too. M. Paul Bureau, a French writer, has described in a recent book, *Towards Moral Bankruptcy*,‡ the horrible ways and extent of this industry. Writing of Paris, he says :

" A short time before the War, an agency was established on the principle that every woman, whatever her condition, her surroundings, her

---
* Ellis, *op. cit.*, p. 377.
† *Op. cit.*, pp. 377-378. The reference to Dr. Elsie Clews Parsons is to her book, *The Family*, p. 351.
‡ *Towards Moral Bankruptcy*. Introduction by Dr. Mary Scharlieb (London : Constable, 1925), p 16.

fortune or her habitual moral conduct can in the long run be brought to accept the chance of a 'new experience;' while any man who wishes to enter into relations with *anyone* of the other sex has nothing to do but communicate with this agency, send twenty-five francs for expenses and state the amount of money he can offer to the person to be solicited. The agency transmits the request, and on receiving the reply informs the customer that he must abandon his plan 'at least in the meantime,' or on the contrary, that his application has been favourably received. I am assured that the double list of correspondents makes most instructive reading: all the social and financial world of Paris is creditably represented."

This traffic, M. Bureau assures us, goes on 'in broad daylight, under the official protection of the police and the municipal authority and with the tacit consent of a great number of honest (?) folks of all conditions and all opinions.'

In a footnote M. Bureau quotes from *Le Bilan de la Pornographie* a report presented to the Second National Congress against Immorality, held at Paris in March, 1912 :

" Alongside of this aristocratic way of keeping the business going, there are other cheaper and simpler ways. At X the performers at a cafechantant are put into a lottery; they themselves offer, in the hall, tickets at ten centimes each, the winner can keep the woman and her room for the night; the key is outside the bargain. At T, there is a kind of exhibition of the female personnel of the music-hall; the director, before a crowd of spectators, fixes the price for each of the artistes, by the month, day or night. It is a veritable market—the white slave-traffic."

During the War, says M. Bureau* in another footnote:

" The organization of ' war godmothers'—the ingenuous founders of that kindly institution never dreamt of such vice—was promptly utilized by systematized prostitution, the initiative coming at once from both clients and vendors. Several daily journals with a large circulation and notably two large illustrated papers, *Fantasio* and *Vie Parisienne* have found great profit in advertisements requesting or offering to provide these 'godmothers'; a single number of the *Vie Parisienne* at the beginning of 1917 had as many as 199 such offers advertised."

The kind of life that is confined in India to prostitutes and *devadasis* is said by competent authorities to be spread among a far wider portion of society in the West. The younger Dumas wrote thus in a classic passage defining the *demi-monde*:

" All these women have made a false step in their past; they have a small black spot upon their name and they go in company as much as possible so that the spot may be less conspicuous. They have the same origin, the same appearance, the same prejudices as good society, but they no

---

* *Op. cit.*, p. 15.

longer belong to it and they form that which we call the half-world (*demi-monde*), which floats like an island upon the ocean of Paris and draws towards itself, assumes, and recognizes, everything which falls from the firm land or which wanders out or runs away from the firm land... At the present day this irregular world is in full bloom and its bastard society is greatly loved by young men. For here love is less difficult than in circles above—and not so exepnsive as in circles below."

" To-day," comments Bloch,* " demi-mondaines are characterized by the fact that their price is high." " They are the prostitutes of the upper ten thousand. The modern half-world... forms a characteristic constituent of modern ' high life.' " About the ubiquity of the half-world in modern society Bloch says : " Whether this especially manifests itself on the race-course, at first nights at the theatre, in great charitable bazaars, at masked balls, at fashionable sea-side resorts, at Monte Carlo, at floral festivals and the like, there also we encounter the half-world, and its members, in respect of beauty, toilet, distinguished appearance, cultivation and conversation, are in no way to be distinguished from the ladies of high society." The half-world, says Bloch,† 'plays a great part in public life. The Parisian demi-mondaine maintains influential relationships with the new great power of our time—the power

* *Sexual Life of Our Time* (*English Translation*) London : Heinemann, 1914, p. 346.
† *Op. cit.*, p. 347.

of the Press. The journalists who are in the service of the demi-monde are by George Dahlen termed the *Presse-Fridoline*, because " their pens are paid, not with ducats but with more or less enviable hours of love in distinguished boudoirs." '

" To-day," says Mr. W. A. Coote of the National Vigilance Association, " London is an open-air cathedral compared with what it was forty years ago."*

But even then things are bad enough. " Women are distinctly abundant," says Flexner (1914), " in the streets radiating from and in the vicinity of, Trafalgar Square, Oxford Circus, Regent Street, and the various railway stations."†

"Brothels," the same authority tells us, " nowadays lead a stealthy, uneasy, transient life. In certain regions they are masked as massage establishments, baths, schools for teaching languages or elocution, and so on. The methods of attracting men are through the medium of small announcements in the daily, evening, and weekly papers."

These brothels are run under the guise of treatment establishments.‡ The employ several 'nurses' and 'assistants' on the premises during business hours, and if a customer is not pleased with the choice so afforded him, photographs of available girls are shown and the selected one

* *The Master Problem* by James Marchant (New York: Moffat and Yard, 1917), p. 186.
† *Ibid.*, p. 186.
‡ *Ibid.*, p. 188.

sent for. Veiled prostitution has become a great menace. *The Shop Assistant* drew pointed attention to the situation when it wrote :*

"What is the position of thousands of shop-girls working for a paltry pittance not sufficient to keep body and soul together? In the case of those who have good homes it means that their parents are subsidizing their employers, while the poor, friendless girl, left alone in the world to rely on her own resources and fight the battle of life, has to contend against this unfair competition, and is often driven to eke out a miserable existence by leading a life of shame. This is no exaggerated statement, but is only too true, as anyone who has been intimately connected with shop life in our big cities can testify."

Young girls run great risks and their employers incur a great responsibility because of the nefarious activities of those engaged in the White Slave Traffic. The British Government in 1913 gave emphatic official recognition to the fact when it caused an extraordinary warning to be issued to telephone girls against the devices of these traffickers. The circular was accompanied by the following leaflet which we copy *in extenso* from *The Master Problem* :†

WARNING TO GIRLS : FOREWARNED IS FOREARMED.

" Girls should never speak to strangers, either men or women, in the street, in shops, in stations,

* Quoted by Marchant, *op. cit.*, p. 188.
† pp. 195-196.

in trains, in lonely country roads, or in places of amusement.

Girls should never ask the way of any but officials on duty, such as policemen, railway officials, or postmen.

Girls should never loiter or stand about alone in the street, and if accosted by a stranger (whether man or woman) should walk as quickly as possible to the nearest policeman.

Girls should never stay to help a woman who apparently faints at their feet in the street, but should immediately call a policeman to her aid.

Girls should never accept an invitation to join Sunday School or Bible Class given them by strangers, even if they are wearing the dress of a sister or nun, or are in clerical dress.

Girls should never accept a lift offered by a stranger in a motor, or taxi-cab, or vehicle of any description.

Girls should never go to an address given them by a stranger, or enter any house, restaurant, or place of amusement on the invitation of a stranger.

Girls should never go with a stranger (even if dressed as a hospital nurse) or believe stories of their relatives having suffered from an accident or being suddenly taken ill, as this is a common device to kidnap girls.

Girls should never accept sweets, food, a glass of water, or smell flowers offered them by a stranger; neither should they buy scents or other articles at their door, as so many things may contain drugs.

Girls should never take a situation through an advertisement or a stranger registry office, either in England or abroad, without first making enquiries from the society to which they belong.

Girls should never go to London or any large town for even one night without knowing of some safe lodging."

This in the land which sends out 'saints' to our country!

A great authority on prostitution, Dr. Alfred Blaschko, after painstaking researches came to the conclusion :*

"Although prostitution has existed in all ages, it was left to the nineteenth century to develop it into a gigantic social institution. The development of industry with vast masses of people in the competitive market, the growth and congestion of large cities, the insecurity and uncertainty of employment, has given prostitution an impetus never dreamed of at any period in human history."

Public prostitution and the half-world apart, there is in modern cities 'a much more extensive *secret* prostitution.' Dr. Bloch gives an account of the various localities and types of this secret prostitution, which covers public-houses with 'women attendants,'—ball-rooms and dancing

---

*Quoted by Emma Goldman, *op. cit.*, p. 187.

saloons, variety theatres, low music-halls, cabarets. and academies of music. All of these are, for the most part, nothing less than brothels.

The sex stimulus provided by these semi-brothels is helped further by wide-spread and well-organized pornography. Says M. Paul Bureau :*
" These great establishments of luxury and debauchery have a most active auxiliary in pornographic literature, which is at once the preparation and the satisfaction of sensual appetites which ever grow more exacting." The obscene literature, picture cards, etc., are extensively advertised and boosted in journals because pornography is a very successful trade. Says M. Bureau :†

" The production of obscene pamphlets and books reaches in France proportions of which few people have any suspicion. Some of them have reached a circulation of 50,000 in the first edition and are now being sold in their sixteenth at 95 centimes. The price varies; so does the degree of licentiousness. Thus one can buy *Trois Nuits d'amour* for 30 c., *Les Péchés roses* for 25 c., *Les Adventures du roi Pauzole* or *Mariette* for 95 c., and for 3 fr. 50 c. *La Mort des Sexes, or Aphrodite, or Les Demi-Vierges* or the *Journal d'une Femme de Chambre*, or...the whole endless series of romances by well-known authors. To write a licentious book is counted no dishonour; still better if it runs into many editions; its success may lead to a chair in the Academy or at least to

* *Op. cit.*, p. 36. † *Op. cit.*, p. 39.

the Croix d'honneur. Sometimes the honourable author sits as a judge at the assizes or in the criminal court in cases of abortion or injury to those under age, but such, it seems are merely youthful sins, which a kindly judgment easily pardons and some questionable performances no more hinder a fine literary career than they compromise an advantageous political one..."

No wonder then, that M. Bureau's girl in Society [with a big S] had to remark, ' How tiresome it is : I can't find anything more to read that makes me blush.' M. Bureau continues :*

" The cheapness of these pamphlets and books puts them within everybody's reach, and the number of readers is enormous. Tobacconists' shops and newspaper kiosks, libraries and railway book-stalls, are fairly encumbered with them. Along with this licentious literature there is another, frankly obscene, and reserved for debauched exquisites and special collectors. ' The Lyons and Paris catalogues advertise, one 114 different works rising to 20 francs the volume, the other 229 works from 5 to 10 francs, of which I forbear to give the titles; there are copies at 60, 100 and 150 francs. The very abundant *Littérature Flagellante* includes 22 books by the same author... Among foreigners, Italy and Spain are the chief centres for the French output. One catalogue, " No 108," published at Madrid, advertises 298 works of the most obscene kind. It may be had for a franc. The price of the volumes

* *Op. cit.*, pp. 40-42.

varies from 10 to 15 francs. Another catalogue, from a Barcelona depôt, which must however be obtained from Turin, includes a hundred series still more varied and more obscene. The English works advertised in this list are represented by 113 various titles—a copy costs from 25 to 250 francs. There is one book in six volumes of which the price is a trifle of 1,875 francs".

" This obscene literature leads its readers on to still more revolting productions—obscene photographs—but here we enter on the indescribable, the unrelatable, and on whatever is most unclean...

" This trade is in possession of a powerful international organization which pushes the kind of goods sold, because photography shares with the other plastic arts the privilege of a free circulation on which diversity of language places no check. ' Portugal, Spain, Italy, Holland, Hungary, Germany, Belgium and Switzerland encircle France with their obscenities.' Perhaps our country is in this respect more threatened than threatening; the Paris houses are managed indiscriminately by Frenchmen and foreigners. One house alone in Amsterdam sells 6,000 different series, each containing 25 photographs; another at Turin puts out several series at 500, 2,000, 3,000 and even 7,000 fancs each... ' The Boche back is broad enough,' writes M. Pouresy, ' but truth obliges us to say that every week more than 300,000 copies of illustrated French papers, published in Paris by Frenchmen, commend to the public lists in which the most licentious series are advertised.'

"This clandestine trade, to which the police shut their eyes, occasions ravages, the gravity of which is not suspected by the public. 'These filthy photographs,' says M. Emile Poursey, 'produce an incredible disturbance of the senses, and tend to urge the unfortunate people who buy them to the most monstrous crimes'. Their disintegrating action upon boys and girls is fearful, and we have seen many colleges ruined morally and physically by their means. For girls there is no more powerfully destructive agent. We will say nothing of their effect upon rakes, libertines and old men, whom they lead quickly to sadism and satyrism."

These pornographic publications are no mere offence against prudery. They are the schools to instruct people in all sorts of perversions. Miss Mayo makes so much fuss about the nude sculpture in a few of the Saivite temples. The nude has never been absent from European paintings and sculpture, and a great artist like Leonardo da Vinci—perhaps the greatest figure thrown up by the Renaissance—is said to have painted the sexual embrace in one of his remarkable pictures. But the commercial and popular pornographic Press of these days has no artistic considerations to justify its existence. Bloch alludes to the motifs in the pornographic products and the centres of this industry :

"Side by side with these higher pornographic works,* there exists also a lower kind—obscene garbage writings and pornographic pictures of the

* Of these we shall speak presently.

worst possible kind, such as picture postcards, act-photographs, etc., in which all possible sexual perversities are represented either in printed matter or by pictures. [We omit the details; the curious may turn to Bloch's book.]... They are manufactured in France, Germany, Belgium and Spain (especially in Barcelona)."*

Another successful industry of a similar kind is the manufacture of 'fornicatory dolls,' 'Parisian rubber goods.' etc.

All these 'industries' spend a good deal on advertising. Miss May alludes to the advertisements of quacks in Indian papers as showing the conditions of the people here. But the advertisements that appear in the Press in the Western countries are something far less creditable. Dr. Bloch gives samples of these in his book :†

" The majority of matrimonial advertisements are inserted for mercenary or interested purposes, and really belong to the category of ' immoral advertisements ' which conceal themselves under all possible titles...

" A young widow, twenty seven years of age, desires friendly intercourse with a man of position, who will assist her with word and deed.

" A young stranger desires acquaintanceship [!] to relieve her of a temporary difficulty.

*Op. cit., pp. 736-737.
†Op. cit., pp. 723 et. seq.

"A merchant, a man of middle age, desires the acquaintanceship of a good-looking lady (a slender figure preferred), for the purpose of friendly intercourse.

"A young merchant, between twenty and thirty years of age, desires friendly intercourse with a young man of good family.

" A young vigorous [!] man, a Swiss, twenty-four years of age, well recommended, desires a situation with a gentlewoman living alone.

" A wealthy, talented uranian young man desires the patronage of a noble well-to-do urning.

" The numerous advertisements also in which young girls and women or widows desire 'position' as housekeepers, companions, etc., in the houses of ' well-to-do gentlemen ' ' living alone' have, as a rule, an immoral basis." Also often advertisements for teaching languages.

"*Advertisements of Rooms.*—Among these advertisements we find that of the ' convenient room ' or the room ' with separate entrance '—the ' storm free diggings ' of the student. Such rooms are usually offered to men; women must seek them for themselves...

" The advertisements regarding rooms to be let ' during the day ' mostly refer to opportunities for...('houses of accommodation').

"*Private Enquiries.*—Under this heading persons advertise in the newspapers that for an honorarium (usually a very high one) they will undertake to watch secretly any desired person—and almost invariably such watching relates to the sexual life and activity of the person under observation; when employed, they use all the methods of the most unscrupulous detective... A detective advertisement of this character is the following:

PRIVATE INQUIRY.

"Confidential! Enlightening! Unfailing! Truthful! Universal! Extraordinarily satisfactory conjugal inquiries; mode of life, family relationships, liaisons, peculiarities of character, occupations, present condition, past misconduct, future prospects, state of property, secret intercourse, etc., etc."

The 'higher' pornography to which Bloch refers in the passage quoted on page 234 is the pornography in literature, and the drama, etc. About the drama and the revue in France M. Bureau writes :*

"Who does not know, in France or among foreigners, how perseveringly our dramatic authors have devoted themselves, these last thirty years, to place on the stage all the most scandalous passages of adultery and free love, of licentious life and of divorce? Under the pretence of representing the manners of our time one would imagine that France had none but unfaithful

*Op. cit., pp. 43-45.

spouses, no husbands except boors and fools, and that women of the demi-monde have a monopoly of delicate and honourable sentiments. The manners of abandoned persons, the vilest passions, alone deserve the honours of the stage...

" At B, monologues and songs are grossly obscene; the tableux and dramatic scenes too, go so far as to picture the sexual relations. The audience—there are more than a thousand distinguished spectators (at least they appear so) —applaud frantically. At N, the little songs, the most obscene monologues and some gestures which are veritable public outrages on chastity are applauded by children and young people under the approving eyes of their parents. At L, a very numerous audienec calls five times the *cabotin* who ends his turns with the most lascivious little song imaginable.

" The revues in which there is even more intrigue are greatly appreciated, because they afford opportunity in every stanza for the greatest excess of filthiness."

Since the War this thing has been on the increase. The ' incest motif ' in particular appears to find special favour. In one of Mr. Noel Coward's dramas mother and son are represented in incestuous relationship. There are hordes of other people who have not the artistic qualities even of Mr. Coward, but who pander successfully to the depraved tastes. Mr. James Agate, British dramatic critic, in his book* published last year, tells us that Mr. Somerset Maugham's *Our Betters* has set a fashion for people without his talent to produce what he calls ' naughty plays.' The London stage just now is all but monopolized by these ' naughty plays'. Mr. Agate, however, feels sure that this is only a passing fashion and will not last long. Let us hope it will not.

The Government of India has appointed a Cinematograph Enquiry Committee because it wants to encourage British films as against American films. One of the charges against the American films is that they provide an exaggerated sex stimulus, and the Government is anxious to protect the Indian youth against it. Indian opinion is not in favour of this discrimination against America, for India with her present status has no cause to be grateful to Britain or the Empire. The talk of ' protecting the morals of the youth ' is mere cant. Censorship generally is cant. Who can forget the way this cant was exposed in one of Bernard Shaw's prefaces? The censorship, it seems, banned only the plays by authors with a sound moral view—Shaw, Tolstoi, Ibsen. Shaw's *Mrs. Warren's Profession* was banned and could not be brought on the stage for years. Shaw showed very successfully in his preface to the play that his book was not immoral enough to be permitted !

*

* *A Short View of the English Stage, 1900-26* (London: Herbert Jenkins).

Whether the radical code will solve these problems better than the conventional code which is honoured to-day more in the breach than in the observance, is yet problematic. What appears certain to competent observers is that in the modern western life sex stimulus is exaggerated beyond healthy limits. Says Bloch :*

" A great physician has said : ' We eat three times too much.' I might add, in amplification of this saying, not only do we eat three times too much, but we look for all other sensual pleasures in excess, and for this reason we love also three times too much, or rather, we indulge too often in sexual intercourse."

This ' oversexed ' life is leading to very pernicious psychological results. Bloch quotes approvingly the opinion of Willy Hellpach, ' one of our most talented psychologists ' :

" To the enormous majority of our young men sexual indulgence is a matter of course, like their card-parties, their evenings at the club, their glass of beer; and of the few who live otherwise, a considerable proportion do so simply from timidity, or from poverty of spirit."

A popular British author, ' A Gentleman with a Duster,' expresses the same opinion in one of his very popular books, *The Glass of Fashion* : †

* *Op. cit.*
† London : Mills and Boon, pp. 131-132.

"This atmosphere, which is now almost universal throughout society, I regard as fatal to the higher life of the human race. It makes passion one of the indecencies of life—a subject for grins and whispers, a theme for revue, an opportunity for gossip, a matter on all fours with a dirty story. It is a destructive atmosphere. It kills love as readily as an abortionist kills a future human being."

Sex indulgence is now becoming merely a means for 'killing time, the great modern disease,' as Bloch puts it. 'Killing time,' or having a 'good time' seems now to be nothing short of a malady. The author of *The Glass of Fashion** lays his finger unerringly when he puts down much of modern vice to a diseased craving for vacuous good time:

"The vice of our public streets has undergone a remarkable change. There is a new race of immoral women. They come from offices and shops. They are young, and the glamour of the summit has bewitched them. They desire the life of fashion, the life of indelicate clothes, gilded restaurants, the theatre, and the night-club.

"They are not vicious. They have none of the criminal instincts of those women who complain of their competition. Ask them what they want, and they will tell you 'a good time.' That is all. They want to see life. They have

* p. 142.

looked up to our highest, and in their own small way would copy them. So they sell first their modesty and then their virtue. It is the price they pay for 'a good time'."

*

Things do not stop here. This state of affairs leads to horrible crimes and a horrible prevalence of venereal disease. Miss Mayo speaks of the great prevalence of venereal disease among Indians. For her generalization she has no figures, no medical authority, no investigation to go upon. She merely gives some hospital cases, often without telling the reader where and how she got them, and then begins to generalize. There is good reason to suppose that venereal disease in India is not as wide-spread as it is in the West. It is a matter of history that in this respect Europe has proved a ' world-menace.' India along with other Asiatic countries got syphilis from the Portuguese and other European peoples four or five centuries ago, even as several primitive races in Africa are getting it to-day from their white civilizers. Indians call syphilis *frangi rog* or the ' Frankish disease ' because they got it from the ' Franks ' or Europeans. Dr. Iwan Bloch has gone into the matter thoroughly in his *History of Syphilis*, and shown conclusively that till the end of the fifteenth century this fell disease was unknown in the civilized world. This history is summed up by this eminent authority in these words :*

* *Op. cit.*, p. 355.

"Syphilis was first introduced into Spain in the years 1493 and 1494 by the crew of Columbus, who brought it from Central America, and more especially from the island of Hyati, from Spain it was carried by the army of Charles VIII to Italy, where it assumed an epidemic form; and after the army was disbanded the disease was transported by the soldiers to the other countries of Europe, and also was soon taken by the Portuguese to the Far East, to India, China and Japan.

In the sixteenth century in Europe, historians of this disease tell us, syphilis was almost pandemic, particularly amongst the well-to-do classes.

Dr. Bloch notices that syphilis in Europe has now become comparatively *mild*, for the white people have become to some extent immune from it because of its wide prevalence amongst their ancestors. "Our forefathers," says Bloch,* "carried out for us a great part of the campaign against syphilis,"—by themselves becoming victims of the disease. He quotes Albert Reimbayr as saying :

"During the last 400 years, every human being now living in Europe has had about 4,000 ancestors; of these, however disagreeable the fact may seem, a considerable number must have had to contend with syphilis."

Investigations carried out in different Western countries and cities about the spread of venereal

Op. cit., p. 384.

disease do not show a bright prospect. The Western Governments are spending a great deal on anti-syphilis campaigns and on popularizing prophylactic methods. The Indian Government has done but little in this direction. Still it is apparent in this matter that conditions in the West are much worse than in India.

Bloch gives results of an investigation carried out in Prussia in 1900, and quotes Kirchner who assumes that ' every day in Prussia more than 100,000 individuals are suffering from a transmissible venereal disease.' From Blasekka's inquiry, Bloch tells us : " It appears that, of the men who entered on marriage for the first time when above the age of thirty years, each one had, on the average, had gonorrhea twice, and about one in four or five had been infected with syphilis."*

The following based on Copenhagen figures is also taken from Bloch's authoritative work :†

" On the average, there are infected with venereal disease every year 16 to 20 per cent. of all young men between the ages of 20 and 30 years; with gonorrhea 1 in 8 are infected; with syphilis 1 in 55 are infected. In these last ten years, for every 100 young men living, there have been 119 infections during ten years; that is to say, on the average every one has been infected more than once."

* *Op. cit.*, pp. 394-395.
† *Op. cit.*, p. 393.

Yet conditions in Denmark are far better than in most other European countries. Says Bloch :*

"Denmark, Germany, German-Austria, and Switzerland show the most favourable conditions; next come Belgium, France, Spain, Portugal and North and Middle Italy. Worst of all are the conditions in Southern Italy, Greece, Turkey, Russia and England."

In Havelock Ellis's book we read :†

"In America a committee of the Medical Society of New York, appointed to investigate the question, reported as the result of exhaustive inquiry that in the city of New York not less than a quarter of a million of cases of venereal disease occurred every year, and a leading New York dermatologist has stated that among the better class families he knows intimately at least one-third of the sons have had syphilis. In Germany 800,000 cases of venereal disease are by one authority estimated to occur yearly, and in the larger universities 25 per cent. of the students are infected every term, venereal disease being, however, specially common among students. The yearly number of men invalided in the German army by venereal disease equals a third of the total number wounded in the Franco-Prussian war. Yet the German army stands fairly high as regards freedom from venereal disease when compared with the British army which is more syphilized than any other European army."

* *Op. cit.*, p. 392.
† *Sex in Relation to Society*, p. 327.

In a footnote to this Ellis adds :

"Even within the limits of the English army it is found in India (H. C. French, *Syphilis in the Army*, 1907) that venereal disease is ten times more frequent among British troops than among Native troops. Outside of national armies it is found, by admission to hospital and death rates, that the United States stands far away at the head for frequency of venereal disease, being followed by Great Britain, then France and Austria-Hungry, Russia and Germany."

Giving evidence before the Royal Commission for venereal diseases in 1914, Dr. Douglas White stated that, according to his estimate, there were every year 122,500 *fresh* cases of sexual disease in London alone and 800,000 in the United Kingdom; of these 114,000 would be cases of syphilis. From these figures he deduced that there must be in the United Kingdom some 3 million syphilitics.* Add to this figure the enormous number of those who have at some period of their life suffered from gonorrhea and then you will find that Miss Christabel Pankhurst's estimate of about 75 per cent. of the population having at some time or other suffered from venereal disease is not an overdrawn picture.

We shall conclude the section on venereal disease with two brief quotations about gonorrhea from Ellis :†

---

* *The Master Problem.*
† *Op. cit.*, pp. 330-33.

THE SEX URGE

"In America, Wood Ruggles has given (as had Noggerath previously, for New York), the prevalence of gonorrhea among adult males as from 75 to 80 per cent."

About England we read:

"In England, a writer in the *Lancet*, some years ago, found, as the result of experience and inquiries, that 75 per cent. adult males have had gonorrhea once, 40 per cent. twice, 15 per cent. three or more times."

India may or may not be a world-menace. But Europe has proved to be a world-menace in history by infecting the world with venereal disease. Even to-day it is infecting the primitive races whom it sets out to civilize, and even to-day it carries a menacing amount of this dangerous stock.*

*

*No country has been denounced more severely as a 'world-menace' than Soviet Russia,—and of course Russia *is* a menace to the interests represented by those who thus denounce her. However, it seems particular attention ought to be drawn to one fact : "Syphilis...has reached the proportions of a terrible plague; it is bad enough in the towns, but in the country there is not a village which has not been infected. There is not the least exaggeration in this statement, which is founded upon information given to me personally by Dr. Siemashko [Commissioner for Health] and upon official announcements made...in the Bolshevik newspapers... Syphilis, as we know, is very wide-spread, far more wide-spread than the average person supposes. But here we have a whole nation composed of 130 million souls stricken. One shrinks from imagining how awful must be the effects upon the race in the future; and upon the races with which it may be in contact." See p. 238 of *The Russian Revolution, 1917-1926* by Lancelot Lawton (Macmillan). This description, if true, might be some justification for calling Russia a world-menace.

In spite of the popularity of contraceptive methods in all strata of European society to-day abortion seems to be on the increase. M. Paul Bureau writes :*

" In 1905 Dr. Doleris submitted other figures to the Obstetrical Society. ' Seven years since, at the Boucicaut Hospital, the proportion of abortions to deliveries was 7 :7; it is now 17 :7.

And in a footnote he tells us :

" Yet M. Lucas Champonniere (surgeon) has challenged these figures as insufficient."

Again : †

" In his *Precis de medicine legale* Professor Lacassagne of Lyons, basing his estimate on very grave reports which it is impossible to reproduce here in detail, reckons the annual number of abortions committed at Lyons at 10,000. Now the population is about 550,000, and the annual birth-rate between 8,000 and 9,000. According to the same physician, one may estimate the annual abortions in France at half a million. i.e., two-thirds of the birth-rate. As to Paris, Dr. Robert Monin says : "We reckon 100,000 as the annual number of abortions, and we are pretty sure this is below the truth. Professor Bordin reckons at 500 a day, i.e., 182,500 a year, the number for the whole country. Dr. Paul Landroy, formerly President of the Societé de

---

* *Op. cit.*, p. 26.
† *Ibid.*, p. 28.

Medicine, maintains that there are nowadays more abortions than births. These estimates are far from agreeing with each other. If I may add my own opinion, I should say, without entering into the details on which it is grounded, that the number is, approximately, between 275,000 and 325,000, and this figure agrees with that reached in 1900 by the Societé Obstetricale de France, which reckoned that abortion destroys about one-third of the results of conception.

"According to Dr. Boissard (*Journal du Practicien, 1908*) there were at Lyons 150 midwives, of whom at least 100 were suspects. One of them acknowledged that she caused about three abortions a week—150 per annum. Taking the suspects' average at 100, one arrives at a total of 10,000 abortions for 550,000 inhabitants. There are, therefore, at Lyons more abortions than births."

In France, anyway, M. Bureau tells us that the crime of abortion 'no longer disturbs public opinion, therefore neither does it disturb the magistracy.' 'Without recourse to Parliament, custom has abolished law.' In such a state of affairs there is perhaps something to be said for the Soviet Russian practice of providing well-equipped state clinics for abortion, and granting easy licences for it. This frankly recognizes facts and makes the best of a bad bargain. Civilized Europeans express horror at the immorality of the Bolsheviks and at the large number of yearly abortions in Russia. But the Russians do not pass off their abortions as 'operations for appendicitis' as the Americans do.

From abortion to infanticide is but a step, and infanticide is by no means very rare. During the period that the custom of infanticide has been disappearing in India, for quite different reasons the practice of it has been increasing in some Western countries. Of France M. Bureau tells us :*

"In the wake of abortion come infanticide, incest, and crimes that outrage nature. There is nothing special to say about the first, except that the crime has become more frequent in spite of all facilities offered to unmarried mothers and of the extension of anti-conceptionist practices and abortion It no longer arouses the same reprobation among so-called 'respectable' people, and juries usually return a verdict of 'not guilty'."

The following two cases are cited by M. Bureau as showing the attitude of the French magistracy toward infanticide :†

"In February, 1918, the Court of Assize for the Loire district acquitted, in two separate affairs, two women guilty of infanticide, the girls F and D. The former had drowned her infant, though her relatives had offered to bring up the child, as they had done in the case of another to whom she had previously given birth. The girl D had

Ibid., p. 35.
† *Op. cit.*; p. 35, footnote.

strangled her baby and finished it by knocking its head against a wall.

" In March, 1918, the jury of the Seine even surpassed this, and acquitted a dancer at the La Scala, Maria M., age twenty-one, who had tried to tear out her infant's tongue, crushed its skull and cut its neck. She had then hidden the body in a cupboard. And this took place in March 1918, in the capital of France, on the eve of those bloody days when the flower of the country's youth went to face death that France might live."

Considering that this murder of infants is much more deliberate than that amongst people who commit it in deference to a rotten old usage, one should not be surprised to find it accompanied by callousness towards children, and 'offences against young persons'. But let that form the subject for a separate chapter.

The other and more horrible crimes in Europe and America, incest, bestiality, etc., would be too revolting reading, and those who want information about these may look into the authoritative books of Bloch, Kraft-Ebning and other medical authorities.

*

Miss Mayo has canonized Anglo-Indian officialdom. Their ranks, she says, contain many a saint. The 'saints' seem to be in their heart of hearts glad over her muck-raking, for it depicts their political opponents as blackguards and sexual perverts. We have no desire to slander their community, but it is only fair to point out to them that if an American tourist has used the tar brush in describing Indian morals, others may use, and in fact have used it, in describing Anglo-Indian character. Miss Mayo's English publishers, the house of Jonathan Cape, published only five years earlier a book by an Englishwoman, Barbara Wingfield-Stratford, who had spent perhaps more time in India than Miss Mayo did. In this book we read about the Anglo-Indian community :*

" For there never was a more Philistine community on this earth than the Anglo-Indian. Art, literature, music, practically do not exist for them. This craving for pleasure, and shirking of serious issues, was especially noticeable during the War. One was particularly struck by it on coming out, early in the War, straight from the gloom and stress of life in England to the sunny, thoughtless atmosphere of society in India. It was, indeed, hard to tell that there was a war on at all. Certainly there was some slight curtailment of the more formal and official type of festivity, such as large Civil Service and regimental balls (though some of these latter did take place), but still there was gaiety enough, dances at the club once or twice a week, race meetings, gymkhanas, official garden parties and plenty of private entertaining. No one seemed to bother much about what was happening at the Front, or to be very

---

India and the English (Foreword by the Rt. Hon. Srinivasa Sastri), 1923, p. 35.

interested in the war news, in fact one seldom heard any talk about the War at all."

Regarding the sexual morals of the Anglo-Indian community this Englishwoman observes:†

" The charge of having a lower moral standard than that usually maintained in England has often been brought against Anglo-Indian society, and as often fiercely denied by its defenders. Things are seen in a different perspective out there, and allowance has to be made for the fact that the transitory nature of station life encourages a certain degree of hedonism... Anyhow it is curious to see how Mrs. Smith, who, had fate settled her in a neat little house in Bromley or Pinner or West Hamstead, would have been a colourless, worthy, domesticated wife and mother, respectable to the point of dullness and with thoughts all for her children, her house, her little circle of lady acquaintances, will, just because she happens to live in India, be in actual fact a dashing mondaine whose only thoughts are of amusement and who has a different 'boy' every month. For in India nearly every woman under fifty has a 'boy', whom she rides and dances with, goes for walks with in the hills, and who is in constant attendance on her at the Club. He is in fact almost the *cavalier servante* so much advocated by Lord Byron. Of course these flirtation-friendships vary a great deal in intensity. Some are real friendships, and some serious love-affairs, but the majority of them are neither, but a sort of playing

† *Ibid.*, pp. 36-38.

at love, a titillation of jaded vanity, sentimental excursions by ladies who are generally horrified by any suggestion that they are not, with it all, devoted and constant wives..."

Here follow details which we refrain from reproducing. We have not the least desire to slander the British community in India, but if they begin to boost Miss Mayo's piffle, one may remind them that Barbara Wingfield-Stratford could with plausibility be expected to understand her cousins much better than Miss Mayo could understand Indians.

Miss Mayo in her sexual muck-raking deems it unnecessary to have even the doubtful authority of the Abbé Dubois in her support. Even the Abbé, as we have seen already, refuses to support her in her contention that Indian women cannot safely venture within reach of India's men. Her sole bit of evidence here is a discredited story about a marital law poster. She has dug the poster out from the Hunter Committee's report on Martial Law and the Disorders. The story was investigated by the Congress Enquiry Committee, including Mahatma Gandhi and the late Mr. C. R. Das as its members, and was completely refuted in its report. Miss Mayo makes no mention of that refutation. The fact is that in this respect the Indian standard is particularly high. Dr. Cornelius in his Current History article—extracts will be found in the Appendix—comments on Miss Mayo's libel, ' where women are not safe is by the side of forts and barracks in which British soldiers are quartered.' Miss Wingfield-

Stratford in her book, *India and the English*, remarks thus on this aspect of Indian character :*

"It has never been proved that a single Englishwoman was outraged during the Mutiny, and even at Cawnpore the soldiers stubbornly refused to murder the women and children, and Muhammadan butchers had to be called in from the bazar for the purpose. It is recorded that at the Barrackpore Mutiny in 1824 the leaders bound themselves by a solemn oath not to suffer any European lady or child to be injured or molested, whatever might happen. One English officer used to let his children go into the ranks and play with the soldiers up till the very day of the Mutiny, and no ladies troubled to leave the station till the guns were actually heard. 'For a good woman,' says Sir Andrew Fraser, ' whether European or Indian, they have a chivalrous respect and admiration'."

* Page 126.

CHAPTER XIX

A PRESENT TO MR. WINSTON CHURCHILL

Writing in the latest Hindu Annual, Col. J. C. Wedgwood tells us how Mr. Winston Churchill, British Chancellor of the Exchequer, passing him in the lobby of the House of Commons, wished to send him a presentation copy of *Mother India*. But the Colonel had already read the book, a copy of which had been received by him as a present. 'What! Read it already! Well, what do you think of your friends now?' enquired Mr. Churchill. And he added with righteous indignation : 'I could stand anything except these bloody outrages on children.'

Mr. Winston Churchill is horrified at the cases of outrages on children in India mentioned in Miss Mayo's book. Mr. Winston Churchill is a statesman of the type which, if it had its own way, there would be no peace in the world. Woe to an empire, the destinies of which are in such hands!

The basis of Miss Mayo's charge about outrages on young children is a memorial presented to the Legislative Assembly by the woman doctors practising in India in 1891. The list contains 13 cases of which Miss Mayo has picked out the worst 7. India is a country of 315 million human beings, inhabiting 2 millions of square miles of land. A dozen cases in such a country afford no basis for generalization. The fact that Miss Mayo had to disinter a document more than three decades old to show some evidence in support of her contention is significant. The following, however, from the pen of the very popular writer, 'A Gentleman with a Duster,' was written quite recently about Mr. Churchill's own country :*

" To realize the condition of modern childhood in our great cities, let your mind ponder the necessity for enactments concerning children under sixteen years of age and children *under fourteen years of age*. Where are the mothers of these children? And what have been the conditions of their home life? Is it unreasonable to ask questions of the womanhood of the country? Is it not folly to wander away into the side-issue of economic conditions?

"The novelist, Miss Clemence Dane, has lately taken up the question of cruelty to children, the awful and unspeakable cruelty which exists in all our great cities and towns, and which, for some unknown reason, is punished so lightly by the magistrates.

"She writes of ' that vilest of all cruelties, child assault'. I quote the following instances from her article :

" How these men guilty of unspeakable offences against children are too often dealt with

The Glass of Fashion (London : Mills and Boon), 1922, pp. 145-147.

in practice, the following random extracts from newspapers may show. *I omit the unprintable details.*

> For attempted assault on a child of four. Bound over on account of previous good character.
>
> For assault on a child of seven. Sentence: six months.
>
> For stealing leather from employers (same case): six months.
>
> For assault on a baby of four. Sentence: £2 fine.
>
> For assaulting and infecting a child of seven. Sentence: twelve months.
>
> For assaulting and infecting a child of seven. Bound over.
>
> For assaulting (on the same day) two little girls. Bound over.
>
> For assault on three small children—evidence unfit for publication. Sentence: £5 fine.
>
> For assault on a child of twelve (six previous convictions for the same offence). Sentence: three months."

" We are not reading of Siberia," ' A Gentleman with a Duster ' reminds his reader, " we are reading of the greatest country of the world and of the greatest cities in that country. Is it not folly to wander away into the side-issues of economic conditions? Women are becoming bad. There is a moral declension. It has nothing to do with economics. It is a spirit appearing in the richest and the poorest. Housing and education are no valid factors in this problem. In every circle of the community, and in all conditions, morality has lost its grip. The particular woman is everywhere an anachronism."

Mr. Winston Churchill is a member of the British Cabinet, and may be presumed to have read the report of the Departmental Committee on Sexual Offences against Young Persons presented to Parliament by command of His Majesty.* The report is dated the 2nd December, 1925. Three of its members were British women; also the Secretary was a woman. The Committee was originally appointed by the Labour Government on the 28th July, 1924, and confirmed by the Tory Government in February, 1925, by the appointment of a new Chairman in place of the old, who had died in the meantime. I make a present of the following passages and facts taken from the report of this Committee to Mr. Winston Churchill.

The report deals with cases *known to the Police and tried by Courts of Law*. The statistics

---

*Issued by His Majesty's Stationery Office, 1926. Cmd. 2561. Recently a deputation, headed by Lady Astor, waited on Sir William Joynson-Hicks asking him to give effect to the recommendations embodied in this report, and to raise the age of consent from 14 to 16.

21

are given in appendix III, tables A to E. Here
is an abstract of these tables :

	Annual Average 1909 to 1913.	Annual Average 1920 to 1924.
Unnatural offences	62	62
Attempts to commit unnatural offences	96	215
Indecency with males	132	176
Rape	165	120
Indecent assaults on females	1,129	1,515
Defilement of girls under 13	137	74
Defilement of girls under 16	214	184
Incest	56	89
Total	1,991	2,435

Analysed it means that in Great Britain
sexual offences against males (first three heads in
the table) *known to the Police* amounted to 290
every year during 1909-13 and to 453 during
1920-24. In 1924, the figures under the first three
heads were, 70; 265; and 185, giving a total of 520.
The figures for defilement of girls under 13 are
also important.

There is good reason to believe that the
number of ' cases known to the police ' fell short
of the actual number. The margin for undetected
and unpunished cases is particularly large here
because of certain inherent difficulties. In §16 of
the *Report* we read :

" *INCEST*.—The special relationship existing
between members of a family creates difficulties

which often prevent disclosure to the police when offence has been committed. A conviction for incest may deprive the family of the support of a father or brother for many years and there may be no source of income, other than Poor Relief, during the time he is in prison. It is therefore readily admitted by official and other witnesses that the number of incest cases reported to the police can only be a small proportion of those which actually occur."

In section 10 the Committee speak of the difficulties of getting convictions in cases involving young persons :

" The number of persons proceeded against is somewhat strikingly less than the number of offences known to the police. We are satisfied that this difference does not, as might be inferred, indicate of itself that proceedings are not readily taken, where possible, in respect of each offence reported to the police.

" The extreme difficulty of proof, the absence of corroboration, and the careful scrutiny which complaints receive before being brought into Court, also account for a certain proportion of offences known in which proceedings are not taken, and we have had reported to us cases in which proceedings were not taken for these reasons, although the perpetrator of the offence was known to the police.

" There are many reasons which in our view, account for the large number of acquittals, such, for example, as the strain on child witness and the difficulty of obtaining corroboration."

Yet another difficulty is that the ' Courts cannot act upon the unsworn evidence of children unless it is corroborated.' Not unoften Courts ' have declined to administer the oath to children of 10 or even 11 years of age.' The difficulties about corroboration are set forth in §68 of the *Report*.

" It is often impossible to obtain corroboration since those who perpetrate these offences generally take care not to do so in circumstances which may implicate them with the offence. It therefore happens that a serious crime may be committed on a child of tender years and for want of corroboration the man, who, the Court is convinced, is guilty has to be acquitted. We have had many such cases brought to our notice, and we have evidence of the reluctance of Courts to dismiss the case when, after receiving the unsworn evidence with great caution, they came to the conclusion that the child was speaking the truth. To give an example of a case in which a man was six times before the Court for indecently assaulting little children :

> *27th March, 1922.*—Indecent assault on a girl of five years—Withdrawn.
>
> *27th March, 1923.*—Indecent assault on a girl of seven years—Acquitted.

A PRESENT TO MR. WINSTON CHURCHILL

27th June, 1923.—Indecent assault on a girl of three years—Dismissed.

19th November, 1923.—Indecent assault on a girl of three-and-a-half years—Acquitted.

24th June, 1924.—Indecent assault on a girl of four years—12 months' hard labour.

" It is probable that, with such a record of alleged offences, and on different children, one at least of the previous acquittals may have been due to a lack of corroboration of the evidence of a child of tender years, and yet the man was legally entitled to go free until at last the assault was committed in circumstances which furnished corroboration."

Dealing with the ' Defilement of Girls between 13 and 16 ' (§17) the Committee seem to be of the opinion that the actual offences are far in excess of the number of cases known to the police and the courts :

" In this category there are cases in which both the girl and the man are concerned to keep the matter to themselves, and *the offence is only known if pregnancy results.* Many of these girls find their way to Rescue Homes or to Maternity Homes, and in a large majority of cases the police are never informed that an offence has been committed.

" The Ministry of Health assisted us by making inquiries from 72 'Mother and Baby' Homes as to the number of girls admitted during the year ended June 1, 1925, who became pregnant under 16 years of age. Thirty-five Homes reported that they had admitted no such cases in the year. Thirty-seven Homes reported a total admission of 78 girls who were pregnant under 16 years of age. Of these 78 girls it was reported that no proceedings had been instituted in 44 cases. Thus there were no proceedings in respect of 56 per cent. of offences known to have been committed.

" It should be remembered that *with young girls under 16 pregnancy results in only a small proportion of cases* in which the full offence has been committed. The criminal statistics show that some 200 offences of carnal knowledge of a girl under 16 are reported annually to the police, and among these 200 offences are included some 'attempts' to commit the offence. Since thirty-seven Homes for unmarried mothers alone report 78 offences and there are 101 'Mother and Baby' Homes (as well as all the Poor Law Institutions, Hospitals, and other Maternity Homes which also receive cases), it is clear that the official figures for cases of carnal knowledge of a girl between 13 and 16 would be very much higher than 200, if every offence was reported to the police. Those in charge of Homes hesitate, perhaps, to report these offences because the girl is not in good health, and they may also have been discouraged by the failure of prosecutions. Of 5 cases under 16 in one Home all were reported to the police; in two the police could but advise proceedings; in two others the prosecution failed; in the last the man was convicted at Assizes, but his conviction was quashed on appeal. In another Home which had admitted 11 girls under 16, three cases were taken into Court, and the prosecution failed in all of them." [Italics are ours.]

The general conclusions of the Committee as to the prevalence of the offences within their scope of investigation are summed up thus in §18 :

" We have now considered official statistics, local statistics and general evidence as to the prevalence of sexual offences against young persons, and we have come to the following conclusions :

1. That there are many more sexual offences committed against young persons than are reported.

We hope that one result of this enquiry will be a greater readiness on the part of the public to report these very serious offences to the police in every case which is discovered.

2. That when proceedings are taken the proportion of acquittals is high.

3. That there is a considerable decrease in sexual crimes accompanied by violence.

4. That there is a distinct increase in indecent assaults on boys and on girls under 16 as shown in the criminal statistics.

We have received conflicting evidence as to how far this increase in the official figures denotes a genuine increase in the occurrence of the offence. We consider, after weighing all the evidence, that *there is an increase in the number of indecent assaults on young persons.*

5. That owing to the practice of reducing charges, mainly in the interests of the child or young person, the statistics of indecent assaults now include a proportion of more serious sexual offences, and this is an additional ground for viewing their increase with concern."

Many witnesses recommended to the Committee that an offence between uncle and niece should be made punishable under the Punishment of Incest Act. The Committee have had to make special recommendations to cover cases of indecent assault by father on daughter!

Full five paragraphs (84-88) are filled in the *Report* by 'Elderly Offences,'—i.e., indecent assaults on young persons by aged people. In §84 we read:

" We have had brought to our attention the cases of old men who commit indecent assaults on children, and the difficulty that there is in dealing with them, especially when the offence is due to some physiological or psychological cause. We consider that where an elderly man has been guilty of an isolated offence of this nature, the best method of dealing with him is, where he has relations willing to be responsible, to place him on probation under supervision, or to bind over with sureties on condition that he consents to live with his relatives.

"We have had evidence of men over 80 years of age, otherwise respectable, who had been to prison repeatedly for indecent offences. We consider that for such cases detention in a non-penal institution is the best solution."

The concluding paragraph on 'Elderly Offences' gives 'only a few examples of the cases which have been reported to us.' But these few cases ought to make Mayos and Churchills pause when they grin over hospital and criminal court cases in India. Says the *Report:*

"We have come to the conclusion, however, after bearing in mind the representations made to us, that in certain cases the sentence was very inadequate, having regard to the nature of the offence. Several of the cases have called for comment in Parliament and there can be no doubt the comment has been justified. For instance, we have had reported to us the case of two indecent assaults by a father on his daughter, which were punished with one month's imprisonment. In another case two indecent assaults of a very grave character were committed by one offender on two little girls, and he was punished by two terms of four months to run concurrently. We have also had brought to our notice particulars of a man placed on probation for an indecent assault who, during the term of his probation, committed another indecent assault, and was then dealt with by an extension of his period of probation. In another case tried at Assizes a man of 24, lodging in the house, was convicted of carnal knowledge of a girl of 14 who was childish for her age and in poor health and the girl became pregnant. At the trial the man pleaded guilty and stated that he had taken precautions to prevent anything happening. He received 4 months' imprisonment."

Dr. Bloch,* the great authority on European sexual life, speaks of a 'mania for defloration', which flourished in England in the eighties, and which meant such a hardship for children.

Before concluding, it is perhaps necessary to point out one particular factor which is reponsible for a considerable number of these indecent assaults on children,—i.e., the superstition in several civilized European countries that intercourse with children is a cure for venereal disease! Dr. Bloch† cites 'a gross case' in which 'a peasant affected with venereal ulcers, having been advised that a cure could only be obtained by intercourse with a pure virgin, had sexual intercourse with his own daughter, and was cured!!'

The British Committee from whose report we have quoted copiously also had to come across this superstition. Speaking of the cases of gonorrhea and syphilis in children between 1 and 5 years, and between 5 and 14 years, they say:

Op. cit.
† *Ibid.*

"We are of opinion, from the evidence of legal and medical witnesses, that a certain number of cases of gonorrhea in these young girls is due to the superstition that connection with a virgin will cure a man."

The Committee hope that at no distant date this superstition will be entirely dispelled. We say a most sincere ' Amen !' to this.

*

In her *Liberty* article to which we had occasion to refer in our *Introduction*, Miss Mayo reverts to her charges to which the present chapter is a reply. Mahatma Gandhi who so appropriately dubbed *Mother India* a ' Drain Inspector's Report ' had argued :

" If I open out all the stench exuded from the drains of London and say, ' Behold London,' my facts will be incapable of challenge, but my judgment will be rightly condemned as a travesty of truth. Miss Mayo's book is nothing better, nothing else."

To this Miss Mayo replies by quoting the New York *Outlook's* ' Yankee comment, terse and sufficient' :

" Perhaps. But no one has ever shown that in London they imprison little girls in the drains."

Chicago and New York, of all places, to indulge in such cant! But perhaps this hypocrisy is characteristic of these crime centres of the World. The authentic evidence we have put together in this chapter does not make out London's drains to be very pleasant for children. Those of American cities are certainly no better. We have not before us, at the time of writing, American documents of the kind of the official British report we have drawn upon in this chapter. To put the New York and Chicago daily muck-rakers in the witness-box would not be fair to America. But in passing we may mention that it was an American State, Nevada, that had to devise the novel and 'scientific' punishment of electric sterilisation to deal with its incorrigible people indulging in sexual offences against young persons. And this novel punishment had soon after to be taken off the statute-book because the incorrigible Yankees refused to acknowledge the punishment as a punishment at all!

CHAPTER XX

MUCK-RAKERS WHOM WE KNOW

No one who wants to acquaint himself with the methods of American journalists, the tribe to which Miss Mayo belongs, can do better than turn to Upton Sinclair's classic study, *The Brass Check*. As a boy Upton Sinclair had occasion once to hear a candidate for district attorney, who was busy carrying on a whirlwind campaign. The orator waxed eloquent in his wrath over the system of prostitution which was paying its millions to the city police every year. He pictured rooms in which a man would make his selection out of women kept for inspection, pay his three or five dollars to the cashier at the door and receive a ' brass check.' The man would then go upstairs and pay the ' check ' to the woman upon receipt of her favours. The orator suddenly drew forth from his pocket a bit of metal, and cried ' Behold! the price of a woman's honour.' Since he heard that speech, the brass check has been to Sinclair the symbol of ' the most monstrous wickedness in the world.' And as he found this ' most monstrous wickedness ' in such abundant measure in American journalism, he called his book giving glimpses of it, *The Brass Check.**

***The Brass Check: A Study of American Journalism* by Upton Sinclair (Pasadena, California), 1920.

There are of course noble exceptions even in American journalism. But it is highly significant that so many of America's greatest writers to-day are writers of protest—H. L. Mencken, Upton Sinclair, Jack London, Sinclair Lewis. The best, that is, the most honest and independent American journals—The Nation, New Republic, American Mercury, New Masses—are likewise pre-eminently journals of protest. But in dealing with *Mother India* we have not to deal with the noble exceptions.

One of Sinclair's chapters is entitled, ' The Scandal Bureau,' and the American Press is a veritable Scandal Bureau. Some of the American cities are recognized leading world-centres of crime. But in spite of that, the Scandal Bureau know full well, the most effective method of discrediting a man in America is to circulate a scandalous sex story about him. The hypocritical puritanism is always anxious to be shocked. Besides, the story becomes spicy, and spicy, salacious stuff is ever in demand.

Upton Sinclair has had often to suffer at the hands of the Scandal Bureau. At one time in fact his life was made so miserable by the muck-rakers that he had to leave America with the intention of never coming back. Besides, he has often found that when he happens to be particularly active against the vested interests that control the Press, the Scandal Bureau become particularly active against him. He started a socialist colony, and the Bureau dubbed it ' Sinclair's Love Nest,' and cir-

culated all sorts of scandals against it. He went
to help the workers in a strike at Denver, and again
the same tactics were adopted. When Gorki
went to America after the Russo-Japanese War,
the American capitalist Press adopted its usual
tactics and successfully defeated his mission of
getting money for the Russian Revolution. It
happened that Gorki's marriage had not taken
place in the official Christian way, so the Bureau
cried from the house-tops that the woman that
passed for Mme. Gorki was a disreputable mistress
of a libertine. Gorki was denounced as a moral
leper in the Press, on the platform and the pulpit.
We have in a previous chapter had occasion to
speak of Judge Lindsey. The Judge is an ardent
radical reformer, and so he has always received
special attention at the hands of the Bureau. In
Lindsey's case the Bureau adopted very extreme
methods indeed. Lindsey's Juvenile Court served
for the Bureau as a basis for grave charges against
him. Upton Sinclair tells us that the Scandal
Bureau hired perjured affidavits and even organised a fake reform organisation to lend authority to
the scandals.

Miss Mayo has adopted the usual tactics of
the Scandal Bureau against a whole nation to discredit it in the eyes of the Americans. She has
attributed to them all the vices and enormities
that can stir up the puritanical conscience against
a people.

In American newspaper-offices reports of
events are called 'news stories,' or even more

generally, simply stories. Interviews are also called 'stories,'—and for the most part they give not facts but stories. Miss Mayo has adopted the same style in her 'stories' in *Mother India*. But some of her stories are so silly that judged even by American newspaper standards they make a very large draft on human gullibility.

The place of honour in these 'stories' must be given to the stale yarn, which is now no better than an insipid chestnut, about the prince who is alleged to have bragged that 'if the British left India, in three months' time there would not be a virgin or a rupee left in the land.'

'Ditcher' (the late Mr. Pat Lovett) writing in the *Capital*, Calcutta, observed :

"Miss Katherine Mayo is seemingly conscious of her limitations, for she shows a fondness for smoking-room stories to eke out her mess of stale kail. Those who told them to her pulled her leg egregiously. Take the following, for instance :

'Here is a story from the lips of one whose veracity has never, I believe, been questioned. The time was the stormy period in 1920 when the new Reforms Act was casting doubt over the land and giving rise to the persistent rumour that Britain was about to quit India. My informant, an American of long Indian experience, was visiting one of the more important of the princes—a man of great charm, cultivation and force, whose work for his State was of the first order. The

Prince's Dewan was also present and the three gentlemen had been talking at ease, as became the old friends that they were.

"'His Highness does not believe,' said the Dewan, 'that Britain is going to leave India. But still, under this new regime in England, they may be so ill-advised. So, His Highness is getting his troops in shape, accumulating munitions and coining silver. And if the English do go, three months afterwards not a rupee or a virgin will be left in all Bengal.'

"To this His Highness sitting in his capital, distant from Bengal by half the breadth of India, cordially agreed. His ancestors through the ages had been predatory Mahratta chiefs."

I heard the original of that story much better and more racily told more than forty years ago. The actors were Lord Dufferin and Sir Partab Singh, the gallant Rajput who so often acted as Regent of Jodhpur.

'What would happen if the British left India?' asked the Viceroy.

'What would happen,' replied the Rajput warrior, 'I would call to my Jawans to boot and saddle and in a month there would not be a virgin or a rupee left in Bengal.'

I knew Sir Partab well, and at the Curzonian durbar I asked him if this conversation had ever taken place. 'Lie, my friend, a damned lie,' he answered fiercely. 'We Rajputs never offend the inoffensive. When we insult our foes we give them the chance to retaliate with the sword.' I am tempted to quote Sydney Smith on American gullibility, but why libel a nation for the rantings of an eccentric woman?"

Chapter XXIV of *Mother India* is headed 'Firebrands to Straw.' In this chapter Miss Mayo gives the too familiar one-sided version of the disturbances during the Non-co-operation days. She makes no attempt to notice, or even to mention, the reply given to those allegations by the Non-co-operators. On page 294, her careless chronology places Chauri-Chaura before the Moplah Revolt, and she says: " Less than six months before the Moplah affair began, occurred the Chauri-Chaura incident in the United Provinces, far away from Malabar." This statement is untrue. On page 295 she says: " In the Punjab during the disorders of 1919, anti-Government workers launched a special propaganda for the violation of foreign women." The sole evidence in support of this monstrous allegation is the copy of a placard which was emphatically repudiated by the leaders of the Punjab as soon as it was brought to their notice. It was supposed to be the work of an *agent provocateur*. Mr. Gandhi also commented on it in his report. Miss Mayo takes no notice of these repudiations.

Take another story (pages 273-74):

" In the same line, a well-informed New York journalist, in the winter of 1926-27, asked certain Indians who had been publicly talking in the city:

MUCK-RAKERS WHOM WE KNOW

'Why do you make such egregiously false allegation about conditions in India?' 'Because,' said one of them, speaking for the rest, ' you Americans know nothing of India. And your missionaries, when they come back for more money, tell too much truth, and hurt our pride. So we have to tell lies, to balance up'."

The name of the New York journalist is not given—nor that of the man to whom the absurd statement is ascribed.

Take yet another story (pages 305-6) :

" More usual is the spirit illustrated in another incident, which occurred in February, 1926. An old Muhammadan assistant engineer who had long served in the Irrigation Department under a British superior, suddenly found himself taking orders from a Hindu. This young man, just out of college and full of new ideas, set himself to worry his senior, baiting and pin-pricking till his victim could bear no more. So, accompanied by his son, the old Muslim sought out a major British official, asking for counsel. ' Sahib, can't you help my father? Surely it is a shame, after all his years of service, to treat him so!' exclaimed the son, at the end of his story. But the Briton could not resist his opportunity. 'Mahmoud,' said he, ' you have always wanted Swaraj. You see, in this, what Swaraj does to you. How do you feel about it?' 'Aha!' replied the youngster. ' But I have got a Deputy Collectorship now. I take office shortly, and when I do, God help the Hindus I get my hands on'."

No names are given. Miss Mayo does not give the source of her information. It could not be the major British official nor the Muslim Deputy Collector. Can any one in his senses believe that an educated Muhammadan already appointed a Deputy Collector, could have made such a statement to a British official, thereby running the risk of having his remarks reported to his superiors and imperilling his appointment and his future prospects? Or are we to suppose that high British officials encourage this kind of outbursts on the part of the subordinate Indian staff?

The credulous may turn sceptic when they read on page 204 of *Mother India*:

"One orthodox Prince, at least, when going into European society, used always to wear gloves. But it is told of him that, at a certain London dinner party, when he had removed his gloves, the lady beside him chanced to observe a ring that he wore. 'What a beautiful stone, your Highness!' she remarked. May I look at it?' 'Certainly,' said he, and, removing the ring from his finger, laid it by her plate. The lady, a person of rank, turned the jewel this way and that, held it up to the light, admired it as it deserved, and with thanks, laid it beside the plate of the owner. The latter, then, by a sidewise glance indicated the ring to his own attendant who stood behind his chair. 'Wash it,' ordered the Prince, and, undisturbed, resumed his conversation."

Who was the Prince? When did this London incident take place, and what is Miss Mayo's authority for the statement? Of course these questions are unanswered. Miss Mayo ignores the obvious fact that an orthodox prince of this style will not attend ' a London dinner party'. The whole story is a concoction on the face of it. It has evidently been supplied to her by a story-teller.

CHAPTER XXI

THE HYGIENE OF THE HINDUS

Yet another of the false impressions left by a perusal of Miss Mayo's book is about the unhygienic, unclean habits of the Hindus. Now, in fairness to Miss Mayo, it must be admitted that this is the first impression that is produced on the mind of a foreign visitor to Indian cities and villages. Such a visitor knows nothing of the inner life of the people, nor can he make any distinction between the different communities of the Indian population or the different parts of this subcontinent. The impression once made remains and no amount of explanations can modify it. Yet it is a fact that no other people in the world (except the Japanese) regard cleanliness to be so absolutely an essential qualification for a good man as the Hindus do. It is a binding part of their religion, and as Professor Lowes Dickinson of Cambridge has remarked in his book, *Appearances*, that India is perhaps the only part of the world where religion is a real live thing which matters.

Cleanliness is of several kinds: of person, of environments and of clothing. In provinces where the Hindus form the great bulk of the population, one finds absolute cleanliness of

THE HYGIENE OF THE HINDUS 279

person, combined with a modicum of the other varieties. In other provinces where the cold is bitter and poverty great, one comes across a different state of things. Cleanliness of clothing in cold climates is necessarily a question of money. A person who cannot find money enough to get two meals a day can hardly be expected to find money for clean dresses. Clean environments are more a concern of national and local administration than of the individual. In the Deccan, south of the Vindhyachal, where there is no winter, or at least not a severe winter, you find Hindus of all classes keeping their persons and homes scrupulously clean. Their environments are as neat as they can be under a system of government foreign in its methods and foreign in its aims and objects. In Northern India, on the other hand, where six months of the year are cold (in some places like the Punjab, Oudh, Bihar and Assam, the cold is rather severe) the condition of things is different and yet all Hindus, everywhere, even of the lowest classes, have scrupulously clean habits, so far as cleanliness of person goes.

In this respect it will be useful to refer to the religious books of the Hindus to show the background of their ideas of public and private hygiene. The Hindu religious as well as medical books lay down standards of cleanliness very rare in the ancient world among any other class of people. His Highness the Thakore Saheb of Gondal (who is an M.D. of London, and also an A.D.C.L., F.R.C.P.E., etc.) has discussed the subject in a chapter of his excellent *History of*

Aryan Medical Science. About the religious duty of bathing we read in the Thakore Saheb's work :*

"Among the Hindus, bathing is included as part of their religious duty. Manu's ordinance is: 'Early in the morning, let him void faeces, bathe, decorate his body, clean his teeth, apply collyrium to his eyes, and worship the gods' (iv, 203). Yajnavalkya also recommends ablution as one of the required religious observances (iii, 314)."

Nor is the injunction a dead letter. As a rule every Hindu in normal health bathes at least once daily. As the Thakore Saheb says: "As a rule, bathing is a pre-requisite to the morning meal, though not a few of the higher classes perform ablution before taking their evening meal also, as well as after touching any unclean thing." It is because of these habits that the Hindus boast that they are the most cleanly nation in the world.

Long before the European nations knew anything of hygiene, and long before they realized the value of tooth-brush, and a daily bath, the Hindus were, as a rule, given to both. Only twenty years ago, the London houses had no bath-tubs and the tooth-brush was a luxury. Both in Great Britain and America, the Hindus used to be complimented on their clean teeth.† Even now with all their scientific advance, Europeans have much to learn

---

* A Short History of Aryan Medical Science (Macmillan, 1896), p. 62.

† Mr. Colgate, a well-known British tooth paste manufacturer, who visited India in the cold weather of 1927-28, was struck by the clean beautiful teeth he saw in this country.

THE HYGIENE OF THE HINDUS

about personal cleanliness from the Hindus. The European methods of toilet are absolutely unscientific and unclean. The bath-tub and the wash-basin are the repositories of germs of disease and dirt. The Hindu methods of toilet, wash and bath, are the cleanliest. A Hindu who does not use water for toilet, and does not bathe and clean his teeth every day is a rare being—unless he is an anglicised person who has taken to European mode of life.

Hindu books of medicine lay down elaborate rules for *dincharya*, (i.e. the outline of daily duties). These include early rising and cleaning the teeth with paste or powder with the aid of a fresh twig. The Thakore Saheb, quoting ancient Hindu books, says :*

" It is good for a healthy man to rise early in the morning, that is, about an hour before sunrise. He should then answer the calls of nature... Then he should clean his teeth with a tooth-paste or powder. The substances generally used for the purpose are powdered tobacco, salt, or burnt betelnut, or some compound preparation of drugs such as pepper, dry-ginger, long-pepper and jijbal (*Xanthoxylum rhetsa*). The most common toothbrush is a tender twig of Bavala (*Acacia arabica*); but the medical works recommend other twigs. Persons suffering from certain diseases are prohibited from using the tooth-brush. After cleaning the teeth, the tongue is polished by means

* *Op. cit.*, pp. 57 *et. seq.*

of a scraper, which may be of gold, silver, or copper, or even of a split twig ten fingers long. Then the mouth is rinsed with cold water several times and the face washed. This process keeps the mouth free from disease. The washing of the mouth with cold water is a necessary adjutant to remedies for aphthæ, pimples, dryness of, and burning sensation in the mouth. Washing with lukewarm water removes phlegm and wind, and keeps the mouth moist. The nose is preserved from disease by dropping into it a little rape-seed oil every day. This tends to keep the mouth sweet, improves the voice, and prevents the hair turning gray. White antimony applied to the conjunctiva with a lead or zinc pencil, besides making the eyes beautiful, ensures acute vision. Black antimony of the Sindhu mountain can be used even in its unrefined state. It removes the irritation, burning, hypersecretion of mucus and painful lachrymation, renders the eyes beautiful, and enables them to stand the glare and the wind... The nails, beard, and hair are to be kept clean and trimmed, and are to be cut every fifth day. This promotes strength, health, cleanliness, and beauty... Regular exercise should be taken every day. It makes the body light and active, the limbs strong and well-developed, and the gastral fire increases so much that any kind of food is soon digested. Physical exercise is the surest means of getting rid of sluggishness... Exercise after dinner or after sexual intercourse is injurious. It is not recommended at all for one suffering from asthma, consumption, and chest diseases. Over-exertion is deprecated. There are various kinds of physical exercises, indoor and outdoor...

" When the bath is over, the body is to be carefully rubbed dry with a towel and properly dressed... "

Detailed instructions are given about diet. Only two meals a day are recommended for adults. Then it is said : "Gormandizing is to be avoided... One must study the nature of the food before eating it, for the food one eats, has much to do with the development of the mind, and it is the mind that makes a man either good, bad, stupid, or wicked."

" It is not proper," says the Thakore Saheb, " to peep into the privacy of a bedchamber. But the ancient writers on Medicine and Religion have not omitted to prescribe rules of conduct to be observed even there." Thus he cites Sushruta, the great Hindu physician, laying down instructions about sexual intercourse.* Nor did the religious lawgivers like Manu† neglect this important domain. They took good care to emphasize the evils of over-indulgence. Anyone who turns to Hindu literature will easily see how false Miss Mayo's contention is when she says that nobody ever preached continence to the Hindu. The fact

---

* "Again Sushruta is of opinion that the carnal desire may be gratified at the interval of a fortnight in summer, and at the interval of not less than three days in other seasons. Those who have eaten a heavy meal, are hungry, thirsty, impatient, boyish, old, with aching limbs and pressed with the calls of nature, should abstain from the indulgence." *Ibid.*, p. 77.

† *Ibid.*, pp. 76-77.

is that continence was preached even to the limit of asceticism.

The Thakore Saheb quotes* the injunction prohibiting the use of ' shoes, clothes and garlands used by others,' and comments: " This advice shows that the Hindus were not blind to the risk of contagion."

In personal cleanliness the Hindu ideal has always been, and to this day is, an exceptionally high one. The cleanly habits of the Hindus impelled Sir William Hunter who had long experience of them in the latter half of the last century to remark:

" It is needless to say that the Indian Hindus ...stand out as examples of bodily cleanliness among Asiatic races, and, we may add, among the races of the world. The ablutions of the Hindu have passed into a proverb. His religion demands them, and the custom of ages has made them a prime necessity of his daily life."

Nor were the Hindus deficient in a sense of *public* hygiene. Their political treatises recognized a separate department of state, which insisted on the purity of water supplies, on the cleanliness of roads, streets and other places of public utility and which made offences against public hygiene punishable. Lord Ampthill, Governor of Madras, when declaring open the King Institute of Pre-

---

* *Ibid.*, p. 72.

ventive Medicine, Madras, in February, 1905, dwelt at length on this topic :*

"Now we are beginning to find out," said Lord Ampthill, " that the Hindu Shastras also contain a sanitary code no less correct in principle, and that the great lawgiver, Manu, was one of the greatest sanitary reformers the world has ever seen."

Of the achievements of the Hindus in this field His Excellency remarked :

"When we undertake municipal water-supply schemes, with filter beds and hydraulic pressure, when we build hospitals and establish medical schools, when we promulgate regulations to check the spread of plague, or when we impose on local bodies the duty of watching over the health of the people, we are not introducing any modern innovations or European fads, but merely doing that which was done centuries ago, and again centuries before that, but which has long since been forgotten by all except the historian and the archæologist. The study of these questions brings out the truth of the old saying that there is nothing new in the world. Now, this saying is even true as regards preventive medicine, which we are all apt to regard as one of most recent discoveries of modern science. Colonel King gives clear proof that the ancient caste injunctions of the Hindus were based on a belief in the existence of transmis-

* Extracts from the speech will be found in Mr. Har Bilas Sarda's *Hindu Superiority*, pp. 253 *et. seq.*

sible agents of disease, and that both the Hindus and Muhammadans used inoculation by small-pox virus as a protection against small-pox; and certain it is that long before Jenner's great discovery, or to be more correct, *re-discovery of vaccination*, this art of inoculation was used for a while in Europe, where it had been imported from Constantinople; and knowledge of medicine which flourished in the Near East at the commencement of the Christian era, *emanated, as I have already shown you, from India.*"

His Excellency then added : " It is also very probable, so Colonel King assures me, that ancient India used animal vaccination secured by transmission of the small-pox virus through the cow, and he bases this interesting theory on a quotation from a writing by Dhanvantari, the greatest of the ancient Hindu physicians, which is so striking and so appropriate to the present occasion... Take the fluid of the pock on the udder of the cow or on the arm between the shoulder and elbow of a human subject on the point of a lancet, and lance with it the arms between the shoulders and elbows until the blood appears : then mixing the fluid with the blood, the fever of the small-pox will be produced. *This is vaccination, pure and simple.* It would seem from it that *Jenner's great discovery was actually forestalled by the ancient Hindus.*'

His Excellency further said : " I cannot refrain from mentioning yet another of Colonel King's interesting discoveries, which is that the modern plague policy of evacuation and disinfection is not a bit different from that enjoined in the ancient Hindu Shastras."

Of the history of medical lore Lord Ampthill spoke thus :

"The people of India should be grateful to him (Col. King) for having pointed out to them that they can lay claim to have been acquainted with the main principles of curative and preventive medicine at a time when Europe was still immersed in ignorant savagery. I am not sure whether it is generally known that the *science of medicine originated in India*, but this is the case, and *the science was first exported from India to Arabia and thence to Europe*. Down to the close of the seventeenth century, European physicians learnt the science from the works of Arabic doctors; while the Arabic doctors many centuries before had obtained their knowledge from the works of great Indian physicians such as Dhanwantari, Charaka, and Sushruta."

Disease and bad sanitation in the present-day India are to be traced very largely to the poverty of the masses. They cannot spend adequately on clean surroundings, and their dwindled vitality due to impoverishment makes them easy victims of epidemics. If India is becoming a 'world-menace' the blame must largely rest on the government's niggardly policy in spending on education and public health. The new conditions from which India cannot get the prosperity they have brought about in self-governing lands have very much aggravated the disease problem in India. Railways have made it easier for epidemics to spread and therefore made it very imperative for the government to spend money on combating them. The irrigation systems have contributed largely to the spread of malaria, but effective anti-malaria measures, like those adopted in the Panama Canal area and elsewhere, remain yet to be adopted by the government.

The importance which the Government of India have attached to the health of the people of India, can best be judged by the amount they have been spending on the Health Department from the Central and Provincial revenues. In a letter from the Government of India. Department of Health and Education, dated the 9th January, 1928, I have been informed that ' up to the year 1916-17, Public Health expenditure was included under the head "Medical." ' If India is the land of illiteracy and disease, it is only reasonable that the Government should spend more money on education and public health than do the States, where literacy is common, education in all respects general, and people fully conscious of the benefits of a hygienic life. But what are the actual facts? In the letter referred to I am informed that up till 1916-17, the total expenditure of the Government, both from Central and Provincial revenues for this work was Rs. 1,29,86,498 (i.e., less than one million sterling) yearly. In 1918-19 when India lost six million lives from influenza alone, it was Rs. 1,66,43,053. The latest figures available are for 1924-25. The total expenditure

during that year from Central funds was
Rs. 26,07,271 (i.e., less than two hundred thousand
sterling) and from Provincial funds, Rs. 3,04,20,169
(i.e., about £2,250,000). The improvement began
with the introduction of the Reforms scheme in
1919-20, i e., with the coming of Indian ministers.

CHAPTER XXII

WHY THE COW STARVES

Chapters XVII to XX of Miss Mayo's book are devoted to the Cow. Chapter XVII is called *The Sin of the Salvation Army*, but has really nothing to say about the Army, except what is contained in a footnote at the end. There is besides a passing reference to it in a *Young India* quotation, to which we shall refer shortly. The burden of this chapter is that the Hindus raise ' food for themselves, but they will not raise food for their mother, the cow. So the cow starves.'

The only mention of the Salvation Army in the text of the Salvation Army chapter is on page 206, where one of the correspondents of Mahatma Gandhi, Mr. Desai, is quoted as saying: "In ancient times, and even during the Mussalman period, cattle enjoyed the benefit of common pastures and had also the free run of the forests. The maintenance of the cattle cost their owners practically nothing. But the British Government cast a greedy eye upon this time-honoured property of the cattle, which could not speak for themeslves and which had none else to speak on their behalf, and confiscated it, sometimes with an increase in the land revenue in view, and at other times in order to oblige their friends, such as the missionaries." "This writer," adds Miss Mayo, "then supports his last quoted phrase by the statement that the Salvation Army was once allowed by the Government to take up 560 acres of public grazing ground in Gujarat for farm purposes."

Comparing India with the United States, Miss Mayo remarks :

" We have, it is true, great grazing areas—but we rotate them and protect them from overgrazing—a matter unconceived by the Indian. And even in the section where this area is widest, our semi-arid and arid western range country, we devote three-fifths of our total cultivated ground to raising feed for our cattle. Our cotton belt gives 53 per cent. of its crop area to live-stock feed, as corn, cow-peas, beans, peanuts, against 10 per cent. used to grow food for man; our corn and winter wheat belt uses 75 per cent. of its cultivated land to grow similar forage for its cattle, our corn belt gives 84 per cent. of its crop land to forage growing, and only 16 per cent. to man's food, and the North and East devote about 70 per cent. of their crops to fodder. Seven-tenths of our total crop is devoted to harvested forage. We have 257,000,000 acres in crops for human food, and we have one milching cow to every family of five."

Speaking of the Hindu's respect for the cow, Miss Mayo quotes from the Abbé Dubois to the effect that 'very holy men drink it [the cow's urine] daily '—a statement which is a lie. I do not know whether it was true or not of some people in Madras at the end of the eighteenth century; but in my life [I am now 63] I have never come across a single holy man who drank cow's urine. However, Miss Mayo's comment on the Abbé's statement is, " Orthodox India, in these fundamentals, has changed not a whit since the Abbé's time.' This at any rate makes the proposition preposterous.

In taunting the Hindu with the neglect of his cattle by omitting to raise feed for them, Miss Mayo shows her ignorance of the agricultural conditions of India as compared with those of the United States. Firstly, the United States have almost double the area of India while their population is only about one-third of the latter. Secondly, there is no such thing as a system of ' annual land revenue ' there. Thirdly, the United States ranchers have the support of their Government, as cattle-raising is a regular industry which is necessitated by the conditions of land and the sparseness of its population. Fourthly, the people are not so poor as to be compelled to raise ' better paying crops ' for the payment of land revenue to the government and keeping their families alive. In India every acre of cultivated land is taxed.

There is no analogy between India and the United States in this respect. There are hundreds of thousands of acres in the United States where nothing can be grown except forage. Miss Mayo knows that a large number of cattle is raised in the United States for the meat industry. Millions of cattle, including cows, are slaughtered for that industry.

However, I am free to confess that throughout Europe and America milching cows are better looked after than in India. In India, the cow is rather neglected for various reasons, primarily economic. All governments in the world have actively and seriously handled the question of the milk supply. Milk, good milk, is a necessity for the healthy growth of children and the health of the nation. Governments have therefore enacted laws to see that the cow is well protected and the milk supply is ample, good and cheap. The Government of India have practically done nothing in this line for the simple reason that for them the Army and the European Services are more important than the health of the children and the people of the country. For the Government of India, the health of the people is at best only a secondary concern. In the United States of America it is a primary concern of the government (Federal, State or City). Throughout her book, Miss Mayo has ignored this vital point, and my contention is that she has ignored it out of dishonest and partisan motives.

On page 210 Miss Mayo remarks: " Mr. Gandhi's correspondent has shown us in the cow's hunger one of the evil effects of British rule. And British rule is indeed largely responsible for the present disastrous condition." She explains what she means by the responsibility of the British Government in this matter :

" Upon this order [the old order] broke the British with their self-elected commitment, first of all, to stop banditry, warfare and destruction, and to establish peace. The task was precisely the same that America set for herself in the Philippines. As we achieved it in the Philippines so did the British achieve it in India—in a greater interval of time commensurate with the greater area and population to be pacified. About fifty years ago, Britain's work in this respect until then all-absorbing, stood at last almost accomplished. Life and property, under her controlling hand, had now become as nearly safe as is, perhaps, possible. Epidemics were also checked and famine largely forestalled. So that, shielded from enemies which had before kept down their numbers, men and cattle alike multiplied. And men must be fed. Therefore Government leased them land in quantity according to their necessities, that they might raise for themselves and not die."

What all this has to do either with the cow or the Salvation Army one fails to understand. But this brief paragraph is characteristically full of misstatements—(1) '*Self-elected commitment.*' Who implored them to commit themselves to the pacification of India? Who invited them? They came for their gain and they remain for their gain. (2) 'About 50 years ago, Britain's work...stood accomplished.' Miss Mayo ought to have known that the last annexation was that of 1849, more than 75 years ago, and the settlements of land revenue which devastated Bengal, Bihar and the U. P. were made before that time. (3) Life and property is even now not safe under British control. (See the accounts of Frontier wars and raids and riots, etc.) (4) Devastating epidemics are still there in the country, and famines are everyday occurrences. Epidemics have increased both in frequency and intensity because of the railways and poverty. The poverty and ignorance of the masses feed epidemics and bring about famines as is to a certain extent corroborated by Miss Mayo's chapter, ' The World Menace.'

The best reply to these foolish comments of Miss Mayo is the one given by Mr. Arnold Lupton. Discussing the food supply of India, Mr. Lupton observes :*

" On the other hand there must be deducted from these figures the amount of grain consumed by the cattle, of which there are nearly as many as human beings—that is to say, about 209,000,000 altogether, large and small, equivalent to about 170,000.000 oxen. This is without counting poultry, etc. There can be no doubt that these animals require some richer food additional to the fodder crops, to grass, leaves, straw, corn stalks, roots, cotton seeds, rape seeds, husks, chaff, etc.

" There can be little doubt that in addition they get a great deal of that grain, which I have calculated as being sufficient for the human population, and it is probable that it is the need of giving this grain to the cattle which is one of the

* *Happy India*, Arnold Lupton (London : George Allen and Unwin, 1922), pp. 144-8.

chief causes of the insufficient supplies of food to the working population. The richer people, who own horses and who desire a good supply of milk from their cows and good work from their oxen, will buy corn for those purposes, thus raising the price and diminishing the supply of corn for their poorer neighbours...

" Some portion of grain, bran or meal is generally set down as part of the daily ration of a cow or a working ox or horse, so I am forced to the conclusion that in the densely populated parts of the Ganges Valley and the Punjab, and elsewhere the cattle eat a considerable proportion of grain which is required for human consumption, and for that reason many of the poorer people are half starved...

" If the production was increased 50 per cent. it would add very greatly to the health and well-being and efficiency of the cattle, and that again would help the people, for whom the labour of the cattle is so essential and the milk so valuable, to say nothing of the supply of meat to those whose principles and pockets will allow them to eat flesh food."

Mr. Lupton does not, like Miss Mayo, protest again and again that he has no politics to actuate his study, but he does try to present 'test facts' of present-day India in an impartial way. He does not connive at the evils that exist here but looks at them from a practical helpful point of view. His remarks quoted above sum up the

WHY THE COW STARVES 297

position regarding the question under comment so correctly that one need not labour the point any further.

In this statement Mr. Lupton does not consider the evil effects of a policy of free export of food grains even in years of famine. The exports are a source of profit to the landlords, but they are as much causes of the Indian masses being starved and insufficiently fed as the Indian cattle in the opinion of Mr. Lupton are.

And yet it would not do to say, as superficial critics have sometimes actually suggested, that half the cattle of India should be exterminated. Compare the number of cattle per acre of cultivable land in India with that in other countries, and you will get the reply. The cattle in India have not increased proportionately to the increase in population, and the present number is not enough to till the available land in order to feed the present population.*

These economic factors explain why the cow starves in the land in which it is venerated. It must, however, be admitted that there is a good deal of callousness about the treatment the cattle receive at the hands of the ignorantly selfish *gowalas* (cowherds and dairymen) in India. The Indian can easily ask Miss Mayo to spare him the sermon on his flaying goats alive when she knows

---

* *The Condition of Cattle in India* by N. Chatterjee (Foreword by Sir John Woodroffe, Calcutta All-India Cow Conference Association, 1926), p. 14.

that in her own country and in the European countries infinitely more callous things are done for the sake of feathers and furs for ladies. But that reply does not absolve Indian *gowalas* from the sin of the abominable practices like *phooka*. It must in fairness be pointed out, however, that cow slaughter on a large scale is a new factor in India. The interests of the government of foreign exploiters appear to conflict with those of the nation. For the sake of the meat and hides export industry foreigners from Brazil and other countries are allowed a free hand by the government. The post-War cattle famine in the West has wrought havoc among Indian milch cattle. The foreign buyers come as a disturbing factor, tempting the *gowalas* to make milch cattle unfit for milking after one or two lactations by practices like *phooka*, for the sake of a little commercial gain. As a recent authority, Mr. N. Chatterjee, points out in a foot-note in his carefully written and well-documented volume already referred to :*

"In countries where people are accustomed to flesh-eating, they raise a particular type of cattle for meat purposes... They never brook the idea of slaughtering their milch cattle. But here we have no such provision, and the ' best milkers are being sent to the towns...and are being slaughtered in large numbers'."

Mr. Chatterjee in his book complains: "Taking advantage of the poverty and ignorance

---

*Chatterjee, *op. cit.*, p. 27. In the last sentence Mr. Chatterjee is quoting Sir John Woodroffe.

of the native cattle owner the exporters usually purchase the best cattle ' at a price which hardly represents half their economic value'."*

Miss Mayo complains that the care of cattle has unwisely been included in the schedule of ' transferred subjects ' administered by Indian ministers under the new Reforms Act, and therefore deprived of the Briton's solicitude for it. But have cattle in India prospered under British rule? Mr. Chatterjee says :†

" The animals all over India have considerably deteriorated. Open the pages of any District Gazetteer, official or non-official report on cattle, and you will find that the common complaint is that cattle have grown stunted in size, poorer in milk-producing capacity and weaker for agricultural or draught purposes."

Again :‡

" Their quality is fast deteriorating—deteriorating in strength as well as their milk-producing capacity. During Akbar's time ' many cows at Delhi gave 20 quarts of milk each and were seldom sold for more than 10 rupees.'

" They would walk faster than horses and could fight with tigers and elephants.§ Only 25

---

* Chatterjee, *op. cit.*, p. 38. In the last sentence Mr. Chatterjee is quoting from the *Proceedings of the Board of Agriculture, 1916.*

† Chatterjee, *op. cit.*, p. 41.

‡ *Ibid.*, p. 12.

§ Bernier, quoted by Chatterjee.

years ago Bengal cattle used to yield from 3 to 5 seers of milk per head on an average, but now the yield has dwindled down to one seer only per head per day.* And this figure applies generally to all milch cattle in India."†

The ' quality of mercy ' is not altogether independent of economic factors and of governmental action and inaction.

* Blackwood : '*A Survey and Census of Cattle of Bengal,*' in the Calcutta *Englishman*; quoted by Chatterjee.
† Sir John Woodroffe, quoted by Chatterjee.

CHAPTER XXIII

INDIA—HOME OF PLENTY*

To the author of *Mother India* this country not only is, but has always been, the 'home of stark want.' She contends so in all seriousness, and even makes a pretence of basing her conclusion on historical research. But her ignorance of history is matched only by her rashness in generalization. Her superficial history lets her down when she naively speaks of the 'Sikh Rebellion in 1845' (page 259). Mr. Edward Thomson pertinently asks, "Against whom did the Sikhs rebel? The English had not yet annexed their territory; did they rebel against their own authority?" That perhaps is not a very important matter in itself; but it does mean that the reader need not take Miss Mayo's knowledge of Indian history seriously.

It is only a courageous—i.e., rash and ignorant—generalizer that could contend that India never developed a system of village government. "It is well to observe," says Miss Mayo "that north or south, a history made up of endless wars and changes of dynasty developed no municipal institutions, no free cities, no republics, no political consciousness in the people." Other similar generalizations, unsupported and insupportable by

---

*The material for this chapter is mainly extracted from my book, *England's Debt to India*.

historical data, abound in Miss Mayo's story of the 'Home of Stark Want.' Thus on page 251 we read: "A very few bridges and such roads as are made by the plodding of bullocks' feet through dust and mud comprised the communication lines of the land." Miss Mayo's own table of contents could effectively refute the lie about roads. A section of it is called, 'The Grand Trunk Road.' If she is at all aware of what the Grand Trunk Road is she must be aware that it is neither bullock-made nor Briton-made. Some of the pre-British roads of India in fact number their miles in four figures, and in the pre-steam era kept travellers busy for months on end before they could traverse their whole length.

In her picture of the 'Home of Stark Want' Miss Mayo has made it a point to include accounts given by travellers who happened to find famine conditions in some part or other of this vast sub-continent. But that is hardly a fair way of giving a true historical retrospect. India may not have been wealthy according to twentieth century American standards; but, judged by standards appropriate to past ages, India undoubtedly was a land of plenty and prosperity.

The part of India included in the Empire of Darius was, according to Mr. V. A. Smith,* the richest province of all his dominions. Thornton's *History of British India* tells us in the opening paragraphs:

* *Early History of India*, 3rd edition, p. 33.

" Ere yet the Pyramids looked down upon the valley of the Nile,—when Greece and Italy, those cradles of European civilization, nursed only the tenants of a wilderness,—India was the seat of wealth and grandeur. A busy population had covered the land with the marks of its industry; rich crops of the most coveted productions of Nature annually rewarded the toil of husbandmen; skilful artisans converted the rude produce of the soil into fabrics of unrivalled delicacy and beauty; and architects and sculptors joined in constructing works, the solidity of which has not, in some instances, been overcome by the evolution of thousands of years... The ancient state of India must have been one of extraordinary magnificence."

Says Rhys Davids about the India of Buddha's day :*

" There was security; there was independence, —there were no landlords and no paupers." The mass of the people " held it a degradation to which only dire misfortune would drive them, to work for hire."

But perhaps Miss Mayo has no patience with such remote antiquity. So we shall confine our citations to the Mussalman period and the period immediately preceding British rule in India.

In the *India Reform Pamphlet,' No. 9* issued by the India Reform Society, which had 37 Members of Parliament on its Committee, we read :

* *Buddhist India* (London, 1903), p. 49.

"We found the people of India, it is said, abject, degraded, false to the very core... The most indolent and selfish of our own governors have been models of benevolence and beneficence when compared with the greatest of the native sovereigns. The luxurious selfishness of the Moghul Emperors depressed and enfeebled the people. Their predecessors were either unscrupulous tyrants or indolent debauchees... Having the command of the public press in this country and the sympathy of the public mind with us, it is an easy task thus to exalt ourselves at the expense of our predecessors. We tell our own story and our testimony is unimpeachable; but if we find anything favourable related of those who have preceded us, the accounts we pronounce to be suspicious. We contrast the Moghul conquest of the fourteenth century with the ' victorious, mild and merciful progress of the British arms in the East in the nineteenth.' But if our object was a fair one, we should contrast the Mussalman invasion of Hindusthan with the contemporaneous Norman invasion of England—the characters of the Mussalman sovereigns with their contemporaries in the West—their Indian wars of the fourteenth century with our French wars or with the Crusades—the effect of the Muhummadan conquest upon the character of the Hindu with the effect of the Norman conquest upon the Anglo-Saxon when ' to be called an Englishman was considered as a reproach—when those who were appointed to administer justice were the fountain of all iniquity—when magistrates whose duty it was to pronounce righteous judgments were the most cruel tyrants and greater plunderers than common thieves and robbers;' when the great men were inflamed with such a rage of money that they cared not by what means it was acquired—when licentiousness was so great that a princess of Scotland found it ' necessary to wear a religious habit in order to preserve her person from violation!' (Henry of Huntington, *Anglo-Saxon Chronicle and Edmon*.)

" The history of Muhammadan dynasty in India is full, it is said, of lamentable instances of cruelty and rapacity of the early conquerors, not without precedent in the contemporary Christian history; for when Jerusalem was taken by the first Crusaders, at the end of the eleventh century, the garrison, consisting of 40,000 men, ' was put to the sword without distinction; arms protected not the brave, nor submission the timid; no age or sex received mercy; infants perished by the same sword that pierced their mothers. The streets of Jerusalem were covered with heaps of slain, and the shrieks of agony and despair resounded from every house.' When Louis the Seventh of France, in the twelfth century, ' made himself master of the town of Vitri, he ordered it to be set on fire.' In England, at the same time, under our Stephen, war ' was carried on with so much fury, that the land was left uncultivated, and the instruments of husbandry were left or abandoned,'—and the result of our French wars in the fourteenth century, was a state of things ' more horrible and destructive than was ever experienced in any age or country.' The insatiable cruelty of the Muhammadan conquerors, it is said, stands recorded upon more undeniable authority than the insatiable benevolence of the Muhammadan conquerors. We have abundant testimony of cruelty of contemporary Christian conquerors,—have we any evidence of their benevolence?

" As attempts are thus systematically made, in bulky volumes, to run down the character of native Governments and Sovereigns, in order that we may have a fair pretext for seizing upon their possessions, it becomes necessary to show that we have a Christian Roland for every native Oliver; that if the Muhammadan conquerors of India were cruel and rapacious, they were matched by their Christian contemporaries. It is much our fashion to compare India in the fifteenth and sixteenth centuries with England in the nineteenth, and to pique ourselves upon the result. 'When we compare other countries with England,' said a sagacious observer, ' we usually speak of England as she now is—we scarcely ever think of going back beyond the Reformation—and we are apt to regard every foreign country as ignorant and uncivilized whose state of improvement does not in some degree approximate to our own, even though it should be higher than our own was at no distant period.' It would be almost as fair to compare India in the sixteenth with England in the nineteenth century, as it would be to compare the two countries in the first centuries of the Christian era, when India was at the top of civilization, and England at the bottom."

Mr. W. M. Torrens, M.P., writing in the last century, observed :*

"There never was an error more groundless than that which represented the ancient systems of Indian rule as decrepit or degrading despotisms, untempered by public opinion. It accords too well with the arrogance of national self-love and seems too easily to lull the conscience of aggression to pretend that those whom it has wronged were superstitious slaves, and that they must have so remained but for the disinterested violence of foreign civilization introduced by it, sword in hand. This pretentious theory is confuted by the admissions of men whose knowledge cannot be disputed and whose authority cannot be denied."

As to the so-called usurpations, infamies and fanaticism of Indian monarchs, Mr. Torrens asks his readers to compare them with the deeds and practices of the Borgias, Louis XI, Philip II, Richard III, Mary Tudor and the last of the Stuarts, and to ' look back at the family picture of misrule ' in Europe, from Catherine de Medici to Louis le Grand,—from Philip the Cruel to Ferdinand the Fool,—from John the Faithless to Charles the False,—not forgetting the parricide Peter of Muscovy and the Neapolitan Bourbons! "It is no more true," he concludes, " of Southern Asia than of Western Europe to say that the everyday habits of supreme or subordinate rule were semi-barbarous, venal, sanguinary or rapacious."

*Empire in Asia, London, p. 100.

Again we read in the *Reform Pamphlet, No. 9:*

" Writers, both Hindu and Mussalman, unite in bearing testimony to the state of prosperity in which India was found at the time of the first Muhammadan conquest. They dwell with admiration on the extent and magnificence of the capital of the Kingdom of Canauj, and of the inexhaustible riches of the temple of Somnath."

Let us put the British administrator and historian, Elphinstone, in the witness-box :*

" The condition of the people in ordinary times does not appear to have borne the marks of oppression. The historian of Feroz Shah (A.D. 1351-94) expatiates on the happy state of the ryots, the goodness of their houses and furniture, and the general use of gold and silver ornaments by their women."

Elphinstone went through the records left by other historians and travellers. We summarize below the verdict of some of his authorities :

" The general state of the country must no doubt have been flourishing. Nicolo de Conti, who travelled about 1420 A.D., speaks highly of what he saw in Guzerat, and found the banks of the Ganges covered with towns amidst beautiful gardens and orchards, and passed four famous cities before he reached Maarazia, which he describes as a powerful city filled with gold, silver

---

* Elphinstone, vol. II, p. 203.

and precious stones. His accounts are corroborated by those of Barbora and Bartema, who travelled in the early part of the sixteenth century."

Cæsar Frederic gives a similar account of Gujrat, and Ibn Batuta, who travelled during the anarchy and oppression of Muhammad Tughlak's reign, in the middle of the fifteenth century, when insurrections were raging in most parts of the country, enumerates the large and populous towns and cities, and gives a high impression of the state the country must have been in before it fell into disorder.

In the account of Moghul India we read in the *Reform Pamphlet:**

" Abdurizag, an ambassador from the grandson of Tamerlane, visited the south of India in 1442, and concurs with other observers in giving the impression of a prosperous country. The kingdom of Kandeish was at this time in a high state of prosperity under its own kings; the numerous stone embankments by which the streams were rendered applicable to irrigation are equal to anything in India as works of industry and ability."

" Baber speaks of Hindusthan as ' a rich and noble country', and expresses his astonishment at the swarming population and the innumerable workmen of every kind and description."

* Page 10.

The following again from Elphinstone effectively refutes Miss Mayo's statement about roads in pre-British India :*

"[Sher Shah] made a high road extending for four months' journey from Bengal to Western Rohtas near the Indus with caravanserais at every stage and wells at every mile and a half... The road was planted with rows of trees for shade, and in many places was in the state described when the author saw it, after it had stood for 82 years."

Amongst the authorities quoted in the *Reform Pamphlet* is the Italian traveller, Pietro del Valle, who, writing in 1623, says :†

"Generally all live much after a genteel way and they do it securely, as well because the King does not persecute his subjects with false accusations, nor deprive them of anything when he sees them live splendidly and with the appearance of riches!"

And about Aurangzeb we read :‡

"Notwithstanding the misgovernment of Aurangzeb and the reign of a series of weak and wicked princes, together with the invasion of Nadir Shah, who carried away enormous wealth when he quitted Delhi in 1739, the country was still in a comparatively prosperous condition."

---

*Elphinstone, vol. II, p. 151; *Reform Pamphlet*, pp. 10 and 11.

† *Reform Pamphlet*, p. 12.
‡ *Ibid.*, p. 16.

We shall cite a few more testimonies about the economic condition of the different provinces of India in the pre-British days. James Mill, father of the philosopher, writing of Oude and Karnatic says :*

"Under their dependence upon the British Government, it has been seen that the people of Oude and Karnatic, two of the noblest provinces of India, were, by misgovernment, plunged into a state of wretchedness with which no other part of India—hardly any part of earth,—had anything to compare."

Col. Fullarton's *View of the Interests of India* contains an estimate of the character of Hyder Ali of Mysore and of conditions during his reign. The writer of the *Reform Pamphlet* remarks :

"Manufacturer and merchant prospered... cultivation increased, new manufactures were established, wealth flowed into the kingdom...the slightest defalcation by the officers of revenue was summarily punished..."

The following is the substance of Moore's estimate of Tipu's administration : †

"When a person, travelling through a strange country, finds it well cultivated, populous with industrious habitants, cities newly founded, commerce extending, towns increasing and every-

---

* Mill : *History of British India*, Bk. VI, pp. 51-2.

† Moore's *Narrative of the War with Tipu Sultan*, p. 201, quoted in the *Reform Pamphlet*.

thing flourishing so as to indicate happiness, he naturally concludes the form of government congenial to the people. This is a picture of Tipu's government."

All this prosperity was not created entirely by Hyder or his son, whose sway did not last half a century. For the foundations of this flourishing condition, we must look to the rulers of the ancient Hindu dynasty—they were the constructors of those magnificent canals which intersect Mysore and insure the people prodigal returns from the fertile soil.

Howell, writing in his *Tracts upon India*, says of Bengal :*

" Here the property, as well as the liberty, of the people, are inviolate. The traveller, with or without merchandise, becomes the immediate care of the government, which allots him guards, without any expense, to conduct him from stage to stage... If...a bag of money or valuables is lost in this district, the person who finds it hangs it on a tree and gives notice to the nearest guard..."

About Dacca we read :†

" The rich province of Dacca was cultivated in every part...justice was administered impartially... Jeswant Roy...had been educated in purity, integrity and indefatigable attention to business, and studied to render the government of

---

* *Reform Pamphlet*, p. 21.

† Stewart : *History of Bengal*, p. 430; *Reform Pamphlet*, p. 22.

his province conducive to the general ease and happiness of his people—he abolished all monopolies and the imposts upon grain."

Here is another passage about Bengal immediately before the British assumed charge of it :*

"Such was the state of Bengal when Alivardy Khan...assumed its government. Under his rule ...the country was improved; merit and good conduct were the only passports to his favour. He placed Hindus on an equality with Mussalmans, in choosing ministers, and nominating them to high military and civil command. The revenues, instead of being drawn to the distant treasury of Delhi were spent on the spot."

Miss Mayo has given a good chit to the East India Company. Here is what Macaulay said about Bengal under the Company's rule :†

"Accordingly, the five years which followed the departure of Clive from Bengal, saw the misgovernment of the English carried to such a point as seemed incompatible with the existence of society. The Roman proconsul, who, in a year or two, squeezed out of a province the means of rearing marble palaces and baths on the shores of Campania, of drinking from amber and feasting on singing-birds, of exhibiting armies of gladiators and flocks of camelopards; the Spanish Viceroy, who, leaving behind him the curses of Mexico or

---

* Stewart quoted in *Reform Pamphlet*, p. 22.
† Macaulay : *Essay on Clive*.

Lima, entered Madrid with a long train of gilded coaches and sumpter horses trapped and shod with silver, were now outdone. The servants of the Company obtained for themselves a monopoly of almost the whole internal trade. They forced the natives to buy dear and sell cheap. They insulted with impunity the tribunals, the police and fiscal authorities...every servant of a British factor was armed with all the power of the Company...Enormous fortunes were thus rapidly accumulated at Calcutta, while thirty millions of human beings were reduced to an extremity of wretchedness... Under their old masters,...when evil became insupportable, the people rose and pulled down the government. But the English Government was not to be shaken off. That Government, oppressive as the most oppresive form of barbarian despotism, was strong with all the strength of civilisation."

Writing of the Company's methods, even Warren Hastings had to use strong language. Said he:*

" I fear that our encroaching spirit, and the insolence with which it has been exerted, has caused our alliance to be as much dreaded by all the powers of Hindusthan as our arms. Our encroaching spirit, and the uncontrolled and even protected licentiousness of individuals, has done injury to our national reputation... Every person in India dreads a connection with us."

*Gleig : *Life of Hastings*, vol. II, quoted in *Reform Pamphlet*, p. 20.

The extent of the salaries, pensions and encroachments of the company's service, civil and military, upon the Nawab's revenues and authority, says Warren Hastings, "have become an intolerable burden and exposed us to the enmity, and resentment of the whole country, by excluding the native servants and adherents of the Vizier from the rewards of their service and attachments. I am afraid few men would understand me were I to ask by what right or policy we levied a tax on the Nawab Vizier for the benefit of patronized individuals, and fewer still, if I questioned the right or policy of imposing upon him an army for his protection, which he could not pay, which he does not want; with what expression could I tell him to his face, ' You do not want it, but you shall pay for it!'... Every Englishman in Oude was possessed of an independent and sovereign authority. They learned...to claim the revenue of lacs as their right, though they could gamble away more than two lacs (I allude to a known fact) at a sitting."*

Now about the Mahratta territory. The traveller, Anquetil du Perron, writing in his ' Brief Account of a Voyage to India,' published in the *Gentleman's Magazine* (1762) writes :

" From Surat, I passed the Ghats,...about ten in the morning, and when I entered the country of the Mahrattas, I thought myself in the midst of the simplicity and happiness of the golden age, where nature was yet unchanged, and war and

---

* *Life of Hastings*, vol. II, p. 458; *Reform Pamphlet*, p. 26.

misery were unknown. The people were cheerful, vigorous and in high health, and unbounded hospitality was an universal virtue; every door was open, and friends, neighbours and strangers were alike welcome to whatever they found."

This is how Sir John Malcolm expressed himself about the Mahratta administrator, Nana Furnawese :*

" It has not happened to me ever to see countries better cultivated, and more abounding in all the produce of the soil as well as in commercial wealth, than the Southern Mahratta districts. ... Poonah, the capital of the Peishwah, was a very wealthy and thriving commercial town and there was as much cultivation in the Deccan as it was possible, and an arid and unfruitful country could admit...

" With respect to Malwa, I saw it in a state of ruin, caused by the occupancy...of the predatory hordes of India. Yet, even at that period, I was surprised...to find that dealings in money up to large amounts had continually taken place between cities, where bankers were in a flourishing state, and goods to a great extent continually passed through the province...the insurance offices which exist through all parts of India...had never stopped their operations... I do not believe that in Malwa the introduction of our direct rule could have contributed more, nor indeed so much, to the prosperity of the commercial and agricultural

* *Reform Pamphlet*, pp. 28-9.

interests, as the re-establishment of the efficient rule of its former princes and chiefs. With respect to the Southern Mahratta districts, of whose prosperity I have before spoken...I do not think either their commercial or agricutural interests are likely to be improved under our rule. Their system of administration is, on the whole, mild and paternal. I refer their prosperity to be due... to the knowledge and almost devotion of the Hindus to agricultural pursuit; to their better understanding, or better practice than us...in raising towns and villages to prosperity, from the encouragement given to moneyed men, and the introduction of capital...but above all causes which promote prosperity, is the invariable support given to the village and other native institutions, and to the employment, far beyond what our system permits, of all classes of population."

Regarding Oudh we get glimpses in Bishop Heber's *Journal*. About Bharatpur the Bishop wrote :*

" This country...is one of the best cultivated and watered tracts which I have seen in India. The crops of corn on the ground were really beautiful; that of cotton...a very good one. What is a sure proof of wealth, I saw several sugar-mills, and large pieces of ground where the cane had just been cleared... The population did not seem great, but the villages were in good condition and repair, and the whole afforded so pleasing a picture of industry, and was so much superior to

* *Journal*, vol. II, quoted in *Reform Pamphlet*.

anything I had been led to expect in Rajputana, which I had seen in the Company's territories... that I was led to suppose that either the Raja of Bhurtpore was an extremely exemplary and parental governor, or that the system of management adopted in the British provinces was less favourable to the improvement and happiness of the country than in some of the native states."

Governor-General Lord Hastings declared in 1827 (*Parliamentary Papers*, page 157):

" A new progeny has grown up under our hand; and the principal features of a generation thus formed beneath the shade of our regulation, are, a spirit of litigation, which our judicial establishments cannot meet, and a morality certainly deteriorated."

About Clive himself a recent British historian says :*

" Clive had no sense of responsibility for the good government of Bengal. His sole desire was to preserve the Company's political ascendency by playing upon the weaknesses of the Nabob and his subjects." But in the language of Brooks Adams, " the takings of Clive either for himself or for the government were nothing compared to the wholesale spoliation which followed his departure, when Bengal was surrendered a helpless prey to a myriad of greedy officials who ' were irresponsible and rapacious and who emptied the private hoards.' "

* Muir : *Making of British India* (Manchester, 1915), p. 82.

CHAPTER XXIV

INDIA—' HOME OF STARK WANT '

India will not remain and ought not to remain content to be a hewer of wood and a drawer of water for the rest of the Empire.

J. AUSTEN CHAMBERLAIN,
Secretary of State for India,
London *Times*, March 30, 1917.

The above quotation very pithily embodies the economic position of India in the British Empire. India has been the making of wealthy Great Britain, and the latter has been the economic unmaking of India. The tale has been told in many books on the subject by competent English and Indian authorities. I have condensed it in my book, *England's Debt to India*. The present chapter is practically extracted from that book.

That India played a very definite part in the success of the British Industrial Revolution, is a fact almost universally acknowledged; yet how great a part India played in making for the industrial and economic prosperity of Great Britain is known to very few.

Let us consider first the respective economic positions of India and England at the time when the Industrial Revolution was brought about by the invention of the steam engine and of mechanical contrivances for the spinning and weaving of cloth.

We have already given the reader an idea of the economic prosperity of India in pre-British days. In the seventeenth and eighteenth centuries India had enormous wealth; the treasuries of her rulers were full of money, bullion and precious stones of fabulous value; her industries and manufactures flourished, and she exported large quantities of goods in return for payment in gold and silver. Her trade with Asia, Europe and Africa was extensive, and she made enormous profits from the sale of her manufactured goods. Her cotton muslins, manufactured silks, woollen shawls, brass and bronzes had made her famous throughout Asia and Europe.

For more than a century and a half the English trade in India consisted mainly of the export of cotton and silk goods, indigo and spices in return for bullion. During this period India imported practically nothing. Bruce says that 'on the average of ten years, from 1747 to 1757, £552,423 bullion was exported to India, but after that year bullion was no longer exported there.'*

How the East India Company made enormous profits from this trade is told by all the historians of the time. Macaulay says:

* *Plans for British India* by J. Bruce, p. 316.

"The Company enjoyed, during the greater part of the reign of Charles II, a prosperity to which the history of trade scarcely furnished any parallel, and which excited the wonder, the cupidity and the envious animosity of the whole capital (London)... During the twenty-three years that followed the Restoration the value of the annual imports from that rich and popular district (the Delta of the Ganges) increased from £8,000 to £300,000." And he adds that 'the gains of the body (i.e., the Company) were almost incredible... the profits were such that in 1676 every proprietor received as a bonus a quantity of stock equal to that which he held. On the capital thus doubled were paid, during five years, dividends amounting to an average of 20 per cent. annually.'*

In 1677 the price of the stock was 245 for every one hundred. In 1681 it rose to 300 and later on to 360 and 500. The only limitations to the profits of the Company were the exactions of the English Crown, the demands of the English Exchequer, and the dishonesty of its servants.

At that time the balance of trade was entirely in favour of India. The British historian, Orme, in his *Historical Fragments* says that the manufacture of cotton goods was almost universal throughout India. The rupee which now sells for 1s. 6d. was then worth 2s. 8d. Such was the economic condition of India.

Let us now consider the economic condition of England. "In the sixteenth century," says

* Macaulay's *History of England*, vol. V, p. 2094.

Robertson, "England was a backward country; and capitalists seeking investments looked towards it from all the monetary centres."

"Early in the seventeenth century," says Mill, "the English, whose country, oppressed by misgovernment or scourged by civil war, afforded little capital to extend trade, or protect it, were unequal competitors of the Dutch."

By the end of the seventeenth century, conditions had become alarmingly acute, not only in England, but throughout Europe, as has been shown by Brooks Adams. Adams says that towards the close of the seventeenth century Europe appeared to be on the brink of a contraction of money, due partly to the constant drain to Asia and the increasing demands of commerce. From the reign of Augustus commerce between Europe and Asia had usually favoured Asia. The lack of money led to a considerable depreciation of currency in England.

Speaking of the time of the Revolution, Ruding says:

"At that time the diminution of the value of money and counterfeiting had been so excessive that what was good silver was worth scarcely one-half of the current value, and a great part of the coins was only iron, brass, or copper plated, and some no more than washed over."

In the decade between 1710 and 1720 the actual export of bullion by the East India Company averaged £4,344,000.

The story of how England supplied her needs at this time is one of the most dramatic pages of history. As Jevons has observed, 'Asia is the great reservoir and sink of the precious metals.' From time immemorial the Oriental custom has been to hoard, and from the Moghul blazing with the diamonds of Golconda, to the peasant starving on his wretched pittance, every Hindu had, in former days, a treasure stored away against a day of trouble:

"*These hoards, the savings of millions of human beings for centuries, the English seized and took to London*, as the Romans had taken the spoils of Greece and Pontus to Italy. *What the value of the treasure was, no man can estimate, but it must have been many millions of pounds—a vast sum in proportion to the stock of the precious metals then owned by Europeans*."* [Italics are ours.]

We have already pointed out on the authority of Bruce that the last export of bullion from England to India took place in 1757, the year in which the battle of Plassey was fought. After that, bullion was no longer exported to India. 'From this period on, the export of bullion to China very considerably decreased and it was only sent occasionally after the supply from India failed. This circumstance was explained in every letter sent by the Directors to their servants at Madras and Bengal, which contained instructions

* Brooks Adams in *The Law of Civilization and Decay*, p. 305.

to them to collect as much bullion as they could, to be ready for ships which would come out from Madras and China, and by the answers to the letters specifying the quantity sent by the different vessels.'*

The circumstances in India at that time were very favourable to the collection of bullion by the servants of the East India Company. In the words of Macaulay, ' Treasure flowed to England in oceans; and what was lacking in England to make the fullest possible use of the mechanical inventions made by Watt and others was supplied by India. The influx of Indian treasure added considerably to England's cash capital.'

It is clear then that the 'Industrial Revolution,' the foundation on which England's economic prosperity was built up, was made possible only by the influx of Indian treasure, and that but for this capital, not loaned but taken, and bearing no interest, the ascendency of the steam engine and mechanical appliances for mass production might have remained unutilized. England's gain was India's loss—a loss of treasure more than enough to starve her industries and retard the progress of agriculture. No country, however, rich or resourceful, could bear such a drain unharmed.'

As an example of how the East India Company carried on its trade operations we will quote what Sergeant Brago wrote :

* J. Bruce : *Plans for British India*, pp. 314-15.

"A gentleman sends a *gomastah* here to buy
or sell; he immediately looks upon himself as
sufficient to force every inhabitant either to buy
his goods or sell him theirs; and on refusal (in
case of non-capacity) a flogging or confinement
immediately ensues. This is not sufficient even
when willing, but a second force is made use of,
which is to engross the different branches of trade
to themselves and not to suffer any person to buy
or sell the articles they trade in; and if the country
people do it, then a repetition of their authority
is put in practice; and again, what things they
purchase, they think the least they can do is to
take them for a considerable deal less than another
merchant and often-times refuse paying that; and
my interfering occasions an immediate complaint.
These and many other oppressions, more than can
be related, which are daily used by the Bengal
gomastahs, are the reasons that this place
(Backergunj, a prosperous Bengal district) is growing destitute of inhabitants; every day numbers
leave the town to seek a residence more safe,
and the very markets, which before afforded
plenty, do hardly now produce anything of use,
their peons being allowed to force poor people;
and if the zemindar offers to prevent it, he is
threatened to be used in the same manner. Before,
justice was given in the public *catcheree* (court),
but now every *gomastah* is become a judge, and
every one's house a *catcheree;* they even pass
sentences on the zemindars themselves and draw
money from them by pretended injuries, such as
a quarrel with some of the peons, or their having,

as they assert, stole something, which is more likely to have been taken by their own people."*

William Bolts, an English merchant, thus narrated this part of this sad story:

"It may with truth be now said that the whole inland trade of the country, as at present conducted, and that of the Company's investment for Europe in a more peculiar degree, has been one continued scene of oppression; the baneful effects of which are severely felt by every weaver and manufacturer in the country, every article produced being made a monopoly; in which the English, with their *banyas* and black *gomastahs*, arbitrarily decide what quantities of goods each manufacturer shall deliver, and the prices he shall receive for them... Upon the *gomastah's* arrival at the *aurung*, or manufacturing town he fixes upon a habitation which he calls his *catchery*; to which, by his peons and *hircarahs*, he summons the brokers, called *dallals* and *pykars*, together with the weavers, whom, after receipt of the money despatched by his masters, he makes to sign a bond for the delivery of a certain quantity of goods at a certain time and price, and pays them a certain part of the money in advance. The assent of the poor weaver is in general not deemed necessary; for the *gomastahs*, when employed on the Company's investment, frequently make them sign what they please; and upon the weavers refusing to take the money

* Quoted by Romesh Dutt in *India Under Early British Rule*, pp. 23-24.

offered, it has been known they have had it tied in their girdles and they have been sent away with a flogging... A number of these weavers are generally also registered in the books of the Company's *gomastahs* and not permitted to work for any others, being transferred from one to another as so many slaves, subject to the tyranny and roguery of each succeeding *gomastah*... The roguery practised in this department is beyond imagination; but all terminates in the defrauding of the poor weaver; for the prices which the Company's *gomastahs* and, in confederacy with them, the *jachendars* (examiners of fabrics) fix upon the goods, are in all places at least 15 per cent. and some even 40 per cent. less than the goods so manufactured would sell in the public bazar or market upon free sale... Weavers also, upon their inability to perform such agreements as have been forced upon them by the Company's agents, universally known in Bengal by the name of *mutchulcahs*, have had their goods seized and sold on the spot to make good the deficiency; and the winders of raw silk, called *negoads*, have been treated also with such injustice, that instances have been known of their cutting off their thumbs to prevent their being forced to wind silk."

Even Lord Clive wrote a graphic and strongly-worded letter to the Directors at Home.* But of Clive's own gains, Macaulay says :

"As to Clive, their was no limit to his acquisitions but his own moderation. The

---

* Malcolm : *Life of Clive*, p. 379.

treasury of Bengal was thrown open to him. There were, well piled up, after the usage of the Indian princes, immense masses of coin among which might not seldom be detected the florins and byzants with which, before any European ship had turned the Cape of Good Hope, the Venetians purchased the stuffs and spices of the East. Clive walked between heaps of gold and silver crowned with rubies and diamonds and was at liberty to help himself."

What followed Clive's departure was thus summed up by the same authority :

" Enormous fortunes were thus rapidly accumulated at Calcutta while thirty millions of human beings were reduced to the extremity of wretchedness. The misgovernment of the English was carried to such a point as seems hardly compatible with the very existence of society."

During the five years following Lord Clive's retirement from the service of the East India Company the servants of the latter left nothing undone to wring out as much money as they could, by every means, from the rulers and natives of Bengal. The ' trade oppression ' practised during this period may better be described in the words of William Bolts, a servant of the Company, from his *Considerations on Indian Affairs*, published in 1772, a description which Professor Muir pronounces as ' substantially true.'*

---

* Muir : *The Making of British India*, p. 89.

Says Mr. Bolts on page 73 of his book :

"Inconceivable oppressions and hardships have been practised towards the poor manufacturers and workmen of the country, who are, in fact, monopolized by the Company as so many slaves... Various and innumerable are the methods of oppressing the poor weavers, which are duly practised by the Company's agents and *gomastahs* in the country; such as by fines, imprisonments, floggings, forcing bonds from them, etc., by which the number of weavers in the country has been greatly decreased. The natural consequences whereof have been the scarcity, dearness and debasement of the manufactures as well as a great diminution of the revenues; and the provision of the Company's investment has thereby now become a monopoly, to the almost entire exclusion of all others, excepting the servants of the Company highest in station, who having the management of the investment, provide as much as their consciences will let them for the Company, themselves and their favourites; excepting also the foreign companies, who are permitted to make some small investments, to prevent clamours in Europe..."

In this way, the servants of the Company ruined the trade of the country, and by coercion and oppression established their monopoly.

The whole matter was clearly put by Burke in the report of the select committee of the House of Commons appointed later on to enquire into the affairs of the East India Company :

" This new system of trade, carried on through the medium of power and public revenue, very soon produced its natural effects. The loudest complaints arose among the natives and among all the foreigners who traded in Bengal. It must have unquestionably thrown the whole mercantile system of the country into the greatest confusion. With regard to the natives, no expedient was proposed for their relief. The case was serious with respect to European Powers. The Presidency plainly represented to the Directors that some agreement should be made with the foreign nations for providing their investment to a certain amount or that the deficiencies then subsisting must terminate in an open rupture with France."*

" Notwithstanding the famine in 1770, which wasted Bengal in a manner dreadful beyond all example, the investment by a variety of successive expedients, many of them of the most dangerous nature and tendency, was forcibly kept up; and even in that forced and unnatural state it gathered strength almost every year. The debts contracted in the infancy of the system were gradually reduced and the advances to contractors and manufacturers were regularly made; so that the goods from Bengal, purchased from the territorial revenues, from the sale of European goods, and from the produce of the monopolies for the four years which ended with 1780, when the investment from the surplus revenues finally

* *Ninth Report*, p. 47; Burke : *Collected Works*, vol. III, quoted by Digby, p. 28.

closed, were never less than a million sterling, and commonly nearer twelve hundred thousand pounds. This million is the lowest value of the goods sent to Europe for which no satisfaction is made."* (The sale, to the amount of the hundred thousand pounds annually, of the export from Great Britain ought to be deducted from this million).

" In all other countries, the revenue, following the natural course and order of things, arises out of their commerce. Here, by a mischievous inversion of that order, the whole foreign maritime trade, whether English, French, Dutch or Danish, arises from the revenues. These are carried out of the country without producing anything to compensate so heavy a loss."†

This is one part of the story.

Drain.

The question whether India pays tribute to England, or ever has paid it, has been and still is the subject of bitter controversy among English publicists. One party asserts that India has been paying an enormous tribute to England and still pays it; that there has been going on a regular ' drain of India's wealth to England ever since British connection with India began; that under the direct administration of India by the crown

---

* *Ibid.*, pp. 47-48.
† *Ibid.*, p. 50.

since 1858 that drain not only has not ceased but has actually increased; and that this drain has impoverished India beyond description. The other party holds that India has never paid any tribute to England; that there is no drain from India to England; that what has been paid by India has been received by England in lieu of services rendered or capital loaned for her improvement; and that under British rule India has attained a prosperity which she had never known before in her history. Miss Mayo agrees with the latter party and has adopted their point of view.

In the preceding section we have shown how England stood economically for more than two centuries immediately preceding the battle of Plassey and thereabout; also how Indian treasure flowed to England and changed the whole economic outlook there. We do not know of a single publicist, English or Indian, who denies or questions the facts upon which the theory of drain is based. All parties are agreed that at least for thirty years, from 1757 to 1787, Bengal was 'plundered' by the servants of the East India Company.

In a letter of July 2, 1901, published in the *Morning Post*, London, the late Mr. H. M. Hyndman, the great Socialist leader, said:

"More than twenty years ago the late Sir Louis Mallet (I presume with the knowledge and consent of Lord Cranbrook, then Secretary of State for India, and of my friend the late Edward Stanhope, then Under-Secretary) put at my disposal the confidential documents in the India Office, from Indian finance ministers and others, bearing on this question of the drain from India to England and its effects. The situation is, to my mind, so desperate that I consider I am entitled to call on Lord George Hamilton to submit the confidential memoranda on this subject, up to and after the year 1880, for the consideration of the House of Commons. I venture to assert that the public will be astonished to read the names of those who (privately) are at one with me on this matter. As to remedy, there is but one, and it is almost too late for that; the stanching of the drain and the steady substitution of native rule, under light English supervision for our present ruinous system."

On page 208 of his *Prosperous British India* Mr. William Digby gives the photographic reproduction of two pages from an Indian Blue Book containing admission about the drain:

" Great Britain, in addition to the tribute she makes India pay her through the customs, derives benefit from the savings of the service at the three presidencies being spent in England instead of in India; and in addition to these savings, which probably amount to near a million, she derives benefit from the fortunes realized by the European mercantile community which are all remitted to England."*

The following extracts are made from the *Reports of the Committees of the House of Com-*

* *Parl. Papers, 1853* (445-11), p. 580.

mons (vol. V, 1781-82, printed 1804). Comparing Indian rule with the rule of the East India Company, Mr. Philip Francis, once a member of the Bengal Council, wrote:

" It must give pain to an Englishman to have reason to think that since the accession of the Company to the Divanee, the condition of the people of this country has been worse than it was before; and yet I am afraid the fact is undoubted; and I believe has proceeded from the following causes: the mode of providing the Company's investment; the exportation of specie, instead of importing large sums annually; the strictness that has been observed in the collections; the endeavours of all concerned to gain credit by an increase of revenue during the time of their being in station, without sufficiently attending to what future consequences might be expected from such a measure; the errors that subsist in the manner of making collections, particularly by the employment of *aumils*. These appear to me the principal causes why this fine country, which flourished under the most despotic and arbitrary government, is verging towards its ruin while the English have really so great a share in the administration."

Ten years later, says Mr. Digby,* Charles Grant of the India House, the greatest panegyrist of British rule in India—and at the same time himself the worst disparager of the Indian people known in British-Indian literature—was cons-

---

* *Prosperous British India*, p. 215.

trained to admit: "We apply a large portion of their annual produce to the use of Great Britain."

The Honourable F. J. Shore, once a Bengal administrator, says in his *Notes on Indian Affairs* :*

"More than seventeen years have elapsed since I first landed in this country; but on my arrival and during my residence of about a year in Calcutta, I well recollect the quiet comfortable and settled conviction which in those days existed in the minds of the English population, of the blessings conferred on the natives of India by the establishment of the English rule...

"I was thus gradually led to an inquiry into the principles and practice of British-Indian administration. Proceeding in this, I soon found myself at no loss to understand the feelings of the people both towards the government and to ourselves. It would have been astonishing indeed had it been otherwise. *The fundamental principle of the English had been to make the whole Indian nation subservient, in every possible way, to the interests and benefits of themselves. They have been taxed to the utmost limit; every successive province, as it has fallen into our possession, has been made a field for higher exaction; and it has always been our boast how greatly we have raised the revenue above that which the native rulers were able to extort. The Indians have been excluded from every honour, dignity, or office*

*London, 1837, vol. II, p. 516.

which the lowest Englishman could be prevailed upon to accept." (Italics are ours.)

And elsewhere he writes:

"The halcyon days of India are over; she has been drained of a large proportion of the wealth she once possessed; and her energies have been cramped by a sordid system of misrule to which the interests of millions have been sacrificed for the benefit of the few."*

John Sullivan, also an eminent English administrator, who served in India from 1804 to 1841 and was examined by the Select Committee of the House of Commons when the question of the renewal of the charter of the East India Company came up in 1853, said:

"*Q.*—Do you suppose that they (the people of India) have traditions among them which tell them that the economic condition of the population was better in former times under their native rulers than it is now?

"*A.*—I think, generally speaking, history tells us that it was; they have been in a state of the greatest prosperity from the earliest times as far as history tells us.

"*Q.*—How do you account for the superior economic state of the people, and for their ability to lay out the money which they did in canals and irrigation and tanks, if they were wasting more wealth and sacrificing more lives in war, than we

---

* *Ibid.*, p. 28.

do now, especially seeing that the wars were carried on very much upon their own territories, instead of being beyond their limits?

"*A.*—We have an expensive element which they were free from, which is the European element, civil and military, which swallows up so much of the revenue; from that cause our administration is so much more expensive; that, I think, is the great reason."

John Sullivan did not shrink from the logical conclusion of his opinions, when he was asked if he would restore British territory to native rule, keeping the military control of the Empire in British hands.

"You would restore a great deal of territory to native rulers upon principles of justice?"

"Yes."

"Because we have become possessed of them by violence or by other means without any just right or title?"

"I would do so upon principles of justice and upon principles of financial economy."*

He also said:

"As to the complaints which the people of India have to make of the present fiscal system, I do not conceive that it is the amount altogether that they have to complain of. I think they have rather to complain of the application of that

* *Third Report of the Select Committee, 1853,* pp. 19-20.

amount. Under their own dynasties, all the revenue that was collected in the country was spent in the country; but under our rule, a large proportion of the revenue is annually drained away, and without any return being made for it; *this drain has been going on now for sixty or seventy years, and it is rather increasing than the reverse...* Our system acts very much like a sponge, drawing up all the good things from the banks of the Ganges, and squeezing them down on the banks of the Thames..." [Italics are ours.]

Sir John Malcolm, Governor of Bombay in 1827 (one of the makers of the British Empire in India) was examined before the Select Committee of the House of Commons in 1832:

"In your opinion, was the substitution of our government for the misrule of the native princes the cause of greater prosperity of the agricultural and commercial part of the population?"

"I cannot answer this in every province of India, but I shall, as far as my experience enables me. I do not think the change has benefited or could benefit either the commercial, the monied, or the agricultural classes of many of the Native States, though it may be of others. It has not happened to me ever to see countries better cultivated and so abounding in all the produce of the soil as well as commercial wealth than the southern Mahratta districts when I accompanied the present Duke of Wellington to that country in the year 1803...

"With respect to Malwa... And I do not believe that the introduction of our direct rule could have contributed more, nor indeed so much, to the prosperity of the commercial and agricultural interests as the establishment of the efficient rule of its former princes and chiefs...

"With respect to the southern Mahratta districts of whose prosperity I have before spoken... I must unhesitatingly state that the provinces belonging to the family of Putwarden and some other chiefs on the banks of the Krishna present a greater agricultural and commercial prosperity than almost any I know in India... Above all causes which promote prosperity is the invariable support given to the village and other native institutions, and to the employment far beyond what our system admits of all classes of the population."*

Sir George Wingate, who had held high posts in the Government of Bombay, recorded the following observations for the consideration of his countrymen when the administration of the Empire passed to the Crown in 1858 :

"If, then we have governed India not merely for the natives of India but for ourselves, we are clearly blamable in the sight of God and man for having contributed nothing towards defraying the cost of that government...

* *Minutes of Evidence taken before the Select Committee,* 1832, vol. VI, pp. 30-31.

"With reference to its economic effects upon the condition of India, the tribute paid to Great Britain is by far the most objectionable feature in our existing policy. Taxes spent in the country from which they are raised are totally different in their effects from taxes raised in one country and spent in another...

"The Indian tribute, whether weighed in the scales of justice or viewed in the light of our true interest, will be found to be at variance with humanity, with common sense, and with the received maxims of economical science."

Again :

"Were India to be relieved of this *cruel burden of tribute* and the whole of the taxes raised in India to be spent in India, the revenue of that country would soon acquire a degree of elasticity of which we have at present no expectation."*

On page 126 of his book, *India in the Victorian Age*, Dutt quotes the opinion of Colonel Sykes, a distinguished Director of the East Indian Company, who ' spoke of the economic drain from India of £3,300,000 to £3,700,000 a year,' and remarked that ' it is only by the excess of exports over imports that India can bear this tribute.'

Henry St. John Tucker, Chairman of the East India Company (quoted by Dutt), said that this economic drain was an increasing quantity.

---

* *Our Financial Relations with India* by Major Wingate, (London : 1859), pp. 56-64, quoted by Dutt : *Early British Rule*, pp. 618-20. [Italics are ours.]

'because our home charge is perpetually increasing,' a prophecy which has been more than amply fulfilled.

Similarly another East Indian merchant quoted in the *Parliamentary Report of 1853*, said :

" I may say generally that up to 1847, the imports (of India) were about £6,000,000 and the exports about £9,500,000. *The difference is the tribute* which the Company received from the country which amounts to about £4,000,000.*

Mr. Montgomery Martin, an historian of the British colonies and dependencies, wrote in 1838 :

" So constant and accumulating a drain, even on England, would soon impoverish her; how severe then, must be the effect on India, where the wage of a labourer is from twopence to threepence a day."†

Professor H. H. Wilson, author of History of India, says of the annual drain of wealth :

" Its transference to England is an abstraction of Indian capital for which no equivalent is given; it is an exhausting drain upon the country, the issue of which is replaced by no reflux; it is an extraction of the life-blood from the veins of national industry which no subsequent introduction of nourishment is furnished to restore."

Mr. A. J. Wilson in an article in the *Fortnightly Review* of March, 1884, wrote :

* *First Report, 1853.*
† *History, etc. of Eastern India*, vol. II, p. 12. See also Dutt : *Early British Rule*, p. 609.

"In one form or another we draw fully £30,000,000 a year from that unhappy country (India), and there the average wage of the natives is about £5 per annum, less rather than more in many parts. Our Indian tribute, therefore, represents the entire earnings of upwards of six millions heads of families—say of 30,000,000 of the people. It means the abstraction of more than one-tenth of the entire sustenance of India every year."

In 1875 Lord Salisbury, the great English statesman, spoke of India as a country from which 'much of the revenue' was 'exported without a direct equivalent.'

Dr. J. T. Sunderland, a Unitarian minister of the United States, in his pamphlet, *The Causes of Famine in India* (page 22), refers to the heavy drain of wealth that is going on as 'the greatest of all the causes of the impoverishment of the Indian people.'

This synopsis of opinions about the 'tribute' which India pays, and has been paying for more than a century and a half to England, or about the 'drain' of India's wealth to England, is by no means exhaustive. In fact, one could fill a volume with such extracts. Besides, we have scrupulously kept back the opinions of those British statesmen (several of them very eminent Anglo-Indian administrators like Sir Henry Cotton, late Chief Commissioner of Assam, and once an M.P.; Sir William Wedderburn, retired member of the Bombay Council and once an

M.P.; Mr. W. S. Caine, late M.P.; Mr. A. O. Hume, once a Secretary to the Government of India; and many others), who have openly and actively identified themselves in one way or other with the cause of Indian nationalism. Similarly, we have made no mention of the opinions of Indians themselves.

It is clear that the amount of the treasure transferred from India to England during the century from 1757 to 1857 or to the present is not correctly represented by the excess of exports over imports; for, to this excess should be added the amount of public debt that the East India Company contracted during this period, as also the treasure that was transferred in the shape of gold, silver and precious stones which entered into no account.

The beauty of the English conquest of India lies in the fact that from the first to the last not one single penny was spent by the British on the conquest. India was conquered by the British with Indian money and Indian blood. Further, almost all kinds of expenses incurred by the British in Asia, for the conquest of territories for the expansion of trade, for research and inquiry, were borne by the Indian exchequer. The profits almost went into the pockets of the Britishers. The expenses and losses were debited to India.

R. C. Dutt points out how the total revenues of India have always been in excess of total expenditure incurred in India.

" The whole of the public debt of India, built up in a century of the Company's rule was created by debiting India with the expenses incurred in England."

The total Indian debt, bearing interest, was a little over 7 million in 1792. It had risen to 10 millions in 1799. Then came Lord Wellesley's wars and the Indian debt rose to 21 millions in 1805. In 1807 it was 27 millions. By 1829 it had risen to 30 millions. The total debt of India (registered debt *plus* treasury notes and deposits *plus* home bond debt) on April 30, 1836 was £33,355,536.* By 1844-45 the total debt of India had reached the figure of $43\frac{1}{2}$ million pounds. This included the enormous expense of the Afghan War to which England contributed only a small part of the 15 millions expended, although, in the words of John Bright, the whole of this expenditure ' ought to have been thrown on the taxation of the people of England, because it was a war commanded by the English Cabinet, for objects supposed to be English.'

The annexation of Sind, and the Punjab wars undertaken by Hardinge and Dalhousie, raised the debt to 55 million pounds by 1850-51. Then came the great Mutiny in 1857 and the public debt was increased by 10 million sterling. On April 30, 1858, the public debt of India stood at $69\frac{1}{2}$ million pounds sterling.

About the expenses incurred in putting down the Mutiny, it is interesting to note the following opinions of Englishmen :

*R. C. Dutt: *India in the Victorian Age*, pp. 215-16 and footnote.

"If ever there was a case of justifiable rebellion in the world," says an impartial historian,* "it was the rebellion of Hindu and Mussalman soldiers in India against the abomination of cartridges greased with the fat of the cow and the pig. The blunder was made by British administrators, but India paid the cost.

Before this the Indian Army had been employed in China and in Afghanistan; and the East India Company had received no payments for the service of Indian troops outside the frontiers of their dominions. But when British troops were sent to India to suppress the mutiny, England exacted the cost with almost unexampled rigour.

"The entire cost of the Colonial Office, or in other words, of the Home Government of all British colonies and dependencies except India, as well as of their military and naval expenses is defrayed from the revenues of the United Kingdom; and it seems to be a natural inference that similar charges should be borne by this country in the case of India. But what is the fact? Not a shilling from the revenues of Britain has ever been expended on the military defence of our Indian Empire.

"How strange that a nation ordinarily liberal to extravagance in aiding colonial dependencies and foreign States with money in their time of need, should with unwonted and incomprehensible

* Lecky: *Map of Life*, quoted by R. C. Dutt.

penuriousness refuse to help its own great Indian Empire in its extremity of financial distress.

"The worst, however, is not yet told; for it would appear that, when extra regiments are despatched to India, as happened during the late disturbances there, *the pay of such troops for six months previous to sailing is charged against the Indian revenues* and recovered as a debt due by the Government of India to the British army pay-office. In the crisis of the Indian Mutiny then, and with the Indian finances reduced to an almost desperate condition, Great Britain has not only required India to pay for the whole of the extra regiments sent to that country from the date of their leaving these shores but has demanded back the money disbursed on account of these regiments for the last six months' service in this country previous to sailing for India."* [Italics are ours.]

But a far greater man than Sir George Wingate spoke on the subject of the Mutiny expenditure in his own frank and fearless manner.

"I think," said John Bright, "that the forty millions which the revolt will cost is a grievous burden to place upon the people of India. It has come from the mismanagement of the Parliament and the people of England. If every man had what was just, no doubt that forty millions would have to be paid out of the taxes levied upon the people of this country."†

* *Our Financial Relations with India* by Major Wingate (London, 1859).
† John Bright's Speech on the East India Loan, March 1859.

Surely very little of this debt, if any, represented British investments in public works as there were no railways in India before 1850. When the Empire was transferred to the Crown it was provided that the dividend on the capital stock of the East India Company and other debts of the Company in Great Britain, and all the territorial and other debts of the Company were to be 'charged and chargeable upon the revenues of India alone.' Thus the annual interest which India had till then paid on the capital of the Company was made permanent. Is there anything parallel to this in the history of the world?

By 1860 the public debt of India had risen to over 100 million pounds. Since then it has gone upward by leaps and bounds. In 1913-14 the total liabilities of the Government of India stood at £307,391,121. The argument that the whole of this debt is a commercial transaction, from which India got a return in the shape of productive works, is on the face of it untenable. It is a pity that eminent Englishmen, when dealing with the question of 'drain,' should ignore this phase of the question, and always harp on the misleading statement that the interest paid in England represents interest on capital invested in India on productive works for which India got a fair return in the shape of materials supplied by England. Productive works indeed! The stock of the East India Company and the expenses of wars in India and outside were all productive works! The *Imperial Gazetteer* makes the bald statement that out of the total Home Charges amounting to $17\frac{3}{4}$

millions (of what year it is not stated) nearly 11 millions ' consist of payments on account of capital and materials supplied by England.' As to the total amount ' drained ' various authorities have made various estimates. Mr. Digby estimated the drain up to the end of the nineteenth century at £6,080 million.* To this should be added the figures for the last 27 years. Mr. Hyndman fixed the amount in 1906 at £40 million per annum. Mr. A. J. Wilson fixed it at £35 million per annum.† Sir Theodore Morison, the official apologist, fixed the amount of what he calls ' potential drain ' at £21 million a year. Computed in rupees the figures would look enormous.

Mr. K. T. Shah has made a very careful analysis of the total wealth that goes out of India. Here is a summary of his conclusions :

	Rs.	
Political deduction or Home Charges	50.00	crores.
Interest on foreign capital registered in India	60.00	,,
Freight and passenger carriage paid to foreign companies ...	41.63	,,
Payment on account of banking commissions	15.00	,,
Profits, etc., of foreign business and professional men in India	53.25	,,
Total ...	219.88	,,

or a total first charge of 220 crores in round figures.

* *Prosperous British India*, p. 230.
† *An Empire in Pawn* by A. J. Wilson (London, 1911), pp. 64-65.

Mr. Shah then discusses trade figures over a long period, and states his conclusion with regard to the present situation in these words :*

" At the present time (1923-24) the situation is this. Including and allowing for foreign payments the trade balance in favour of India may be taken at 150 crores against which the claims upon India aggregate 178 crores. *India thus remains a debtor on the whole of some 30 crores per annum.* The debt, however, is apparently not collected, but the amount is reinvested in the country thereby adding still further to the permanent mortgage on Indian resources."

* *Wealth and Taxable Capacity of India*, p. 236.

CHAPTER XXV

POVERTY—THE ROCK-BOTTOM PHYSICAL BASE OF INDIA'S ILLS

" *Even as we look on, India is becoming feebler and feebler. The very life-blood of the great multitude under our rule is slowly, yet ever faster, ebbing away.*"

—H. M. HYNDMAN in *Bankruptcy of India*, page 152.

Says Mr. W. S. Lilly in his book on *India and its Probelms* (pages 284-5):

" The test of a people's prosperity is not the extension of exports, the multiplication of manufactures, or other industries, the construction of cities. No. A prosperous country is one in which the great mass of the inhabitants are able to produce with moderate toil, what is necessary for living *human* lives, lives of frugal and assured comfort. Judged by this criterion, can India be called prosperous?

" Comfort, of course, is a relative term. In a tropical country like India, the standard is very low. Little clothing is required; simple diet suffices. An unfailing well full of water, a plot of land, and a bit of orchard—these will satisfy his desire. If needed, you add the cattle needful to him. Such is the ryot's ideal—very few realize it. Millions of peasants in India are struggling to live on half an acre. Their existence is a constant struggle with starvation, ending too often in defeat. Their difficulty is not to live human lives, lives up to the level of their poor standard of comfort, but to live at all, and not die. We may well say that in India, except in the irrigated tracts, famine is chronic—endemic."

The people of India are the poorest on earth. If there existed such poverty in any other country in Europe or America, the government would have been turned out of office. "The foremost and most important fact about the Indian people," says Mr. Arnold Lupton,* "is this; out of every hundred, seventy-two are engaged in agriculture."

Thus engaged he tell us :†

"It is quite easy to see why the Indian peasant is now excessively poor in most parts of India. It is simply this : the condition of the soil is too poor, it does not yield enough; it does not yield one-half of what the British soil yields. What would be the condition of the British farmer and the British labourer if for all their labour they only got one-half of their present produce per acre? Yet the Indian labourer works very hard, and he and his family give minute and particular care, working often from morn till dark, and yet the produce per acre is not more than one-half of the British produce per acre. When one considers that out of this half he has to pay rent, he

* *Happy India*, p. 39.
† *Ibid.*, pp. 36-37.

has to pay a salt tax and some other taxes, it is not surprising that his economic condition is extremely bad; the only wonder is that he can exist at all; and he exists simply because he has learnt to live in an exceedingly cheap manner.

"His mansion is a mud hut with a roof of sticks and palm-leaves; his bedstead, if he has one, consists of twisted sticks which raise his mattress, if he has one, six inches from the ground. He has no door or windows to his hut. He has a little fireplace and cooking place outside. The sofa upon which he can recline in leisure moments is made of mud outside his sleeping chamber. He has one garment round his loins and he has no other garment that he can wear whilst he is washing that one garment. He neither smokes nor drinks nor reads the newspaper; he goes to no entertainments. His religion teaches him humility and contentment, and so he lives contentedly until starvation lays him on his back."

On the poverty of Indian masses the evidence is so overwhelming that only a special apologist of the type of Miss Mayo could ignore it. A recent book which created quite as much sensation as *Mother India* is *The Lost Dominion* written by a retired member of the Indian Civil Service under the *nom de plume,* ' Al. Carthill.'

Al. Carthill's description of the Indian villager is so relevant to our enquiry that we make no apology for quoting it :*

***The Lost Dominion* (London : Blackwood, 1924), pp. 305-6.

THE ROCK-BOTTOM PHYSICAL BASE 353

"The whole of India is divided into villages. There are hundreds of thousands of them. A cluster of mud huts, a temple or two, some old trees, a well; an open space in the centre is the nucleus. Round about lie the arable pasture and waste of the village. Here lives and dies the peasant. The real Indian nation is here, that hardy patient folk whose labour pays the taxes, and whose blood has built up the Empire and kept the gates."

Mr. Arnold Lupton, to whose book, *Happy India*, we have already referred, quotes 'an English nobleman of great experience as the Governor of a great Indian Presidency,' who, speaking in the early part of 1922, remarked of Indian cultivators that 'they do not live, they only exist.'*

Sir William Hunter, one of the most candid writers and a distinguished historian of India, Director-General of Indian Statistics for many years, declared that 40,000,000 of the people of India were seldom or never able to satisfy their hunger.

Says Mr. J. S. Cotton: †

"If the security of British rule has allowed the people to increase, it does not follow that it has promoted the general prosperity. That could only

---

* *Happy India*, p. 182.

† *Colonies and Dependencies*, 1853, p. 68. For the citations that follow I have used the material in my book, *England's Debt to India*.

27

be done in one of two ways—either by producing a distinct rise in the standard of living among the lowest classes or by diverting a considerable section of the people from the sole occupation of agriculture... Neither of these things has been done. Competent authorities indeed are of opinion that the condition of the lowest classes has become worse under the British rule."

Mr. A. O. Hume, Secretary to the Government of India in the Agricultural Department, wrote in 1880 : " Except in very good seasons, multitudes for months every year cannot get sufficient food for themselves and family."

Sir Auckland Colvin, once a Finance Minister in India, describes the tax-paying community as made up in the main of ' men whose income at best is barely sufficient to afford them the sustenance necessary to support life, living as they do upon bare necessities.'

Sir Charles Elliott, once Chief Commissioner of Assam, wrote in 1888 : " I do not hesitate to say that half the agricultural population do not know, from one year's end to another, what it is to have a full meal."

The *Indian Witness*, a Christian paper, once remarked : " It is safe to assume that 100,000,000 of the population of India have an annual income of not more than $5.00 a head."

An American missionary wrote from Southern India in 1902 :

" The most trying experience I ever had was a three weeks' tour in September of last year (1901). My tent was surrounded day and night, and one sentence dinned perpetually into my ears : ' We are dying of lack of food.' People are living on one meal every two or three days. I once carefully examined the earnings of a congregation of three hundred, and found the average amounted to less than one farthing a head per day. They did not live, they eked out an existence. I have been in huts where the people were living on carrion. Yet in all these cases, there was *no recognized famine!* In Heaven's name, if this is not famine, what is it? The extreme poverty of the poorer classes of India offers conditions altogether extraordinary. Life is the narrowest and hardest conceivable, with no prospect of any improvement. For a family of six persons, many an outfit, including house, utensils, furniture, clothing and all, is worth less than $10.00. The average income for such a family will not exceed 50 cents per head a month, and is frequently little over half that. It may therefore be surmised that not much of this income is spent upon cultivation of the mind, sanitation, or the appearance of the dwelling."*

The following observation was made in the *Moral and Material Progress of India for 1874-75* (Parliamentary Blue Book) :

" The Calcutta Missionary Conference dwelt on the miserable, abject condition of the Bengal

* Digby : *Condition of the People of India, 1902,* pp. 14-15.

ryots, and there is evidence that they suffer many things, and are often in want of absolute necessities... In the North-Western Provinces, the wages of agricultural labourers have hardly varied at all since the beginning of this century; and after the payment of the rent, the margin left for the cultivator's subsistence is less than the value of the labour he has expended......many live on a coarse grain, which is most unwholesome, and produces loin palsy... This extreme poverty among the agricultural population is one of the reasons which makes any improvement in farming and cultivation so difficult."

Says Mr. H. M. Hyndman in his *Bankruptcy of India*, page 74:

" That the people India are growing poorer and poorer; that taxation is not only actually, but relatively, far heavier; that each successive scarcity widens the area of impoverishment; that famines are more frequent; that most of the trade is but an index to the poverty and crushing overtaxation of the people; that a highly organized foreign rule constitutes by itself a most terrible drain upon the country."

Said Sir William Hunter, former member of the Viceroy's Council, in a speech in 1875:

" The Government assessment does not leave enough food to the cultivator to support himself and family throughout the year."

The *Pioneer*, the semi-official Allahabad daily of the British Indian Government, wrote in an article in 1877:

THE ROCK-BOTTOM PHYSICAL BASE 357

"Worried by the revenue survey, for heavily enhanced public payments......the Deccan ryot accepted, for a third of a century *the yoke of British mismanagement*... Report upon report has been written upon him; shelf upon shelf in the public offices groaned under the story of his wrongs. If anyone doubts the naked accuracy of these words, let him dip into the pages of Appendix A. (*Papers on the Indebtedness of the Agricultural Classes in Bombay.*) *A more damning indictment was never recorded against a civilized government.*" [Italics are ours.]

Mr. Wilfred Scawen Blunt, in his *India under Ripon*, pages 236-38, observes :

" No one accustomed to Eastern travel can fail to see how poor the Indian peasant is. Travelling by either of the great lines of railways which bisect the continent, one need hardly leave one's carriage to be aware of this... In every village which I visited I heard of complaints...of over-taxation of the country, of increase and inequalities of assessment...complaints of the forest laws, of the decrease of the stock of working cattle, of their deterioration through the price of salt, of universal debt to the usurers..."

Says the same writer, earlier in his work, page 232 :

"India's famines have been severer and frequent; its agricultural poverty has deepened, its rural population has become more hopelessly in debt, their despair more desperate. The system of constantly enhancing the land-values has not been altered. The salt tax, though slightly lowered, still robs the very poor. Hunger, and those pestilences which are the result of hunger, are spread over an increasing, not diminishing area. The Deccan ryot is still the poorest peasant in the world. Nothing of the system of finance is changed, nothing in the economy which favours English trade and English speculation, at the expense of India's native industries. *What was bad twenty-five years ago, is worse now.* At any rate, there is the same drain of India's food to alien mouths. Endemic famines and endemic plagues are facts no official statistics can explain away." [Italics are ours.]

In 1888 a confidential enquiry into the economic condition of the people of India was made by Lord Dufferin. The results of the enquiry have never been made public, but extracts from the reports of the United Provinces of Agra and Oudh, and the Punjab, have been published by Mr. Digby in his monumental work. These reports are well worth the attention of the student of economic conditions in India. We can only refer to them briefly. One of the most interesting documents is the report of Mr. A. H. Harrington, Commissioner, of April 4, 1888. Mr. Harrington quotes Mr. Bennett, the compiler of the *Oudh Gazetteer*, an officer whom he calls ' wholly free from pessimism,' as to the condition of the lowest castes of Oudh.

' The lowest depths of misery and degradation are reached by the Koris and Chamars,' whom he describes as ' always on the verge of starvation.'

These represent from 10 to 11 per cent. of the population of Oudh. Mr. Harrington then quotes from papers he himself contributed to *The Pioneer* in 1876, under the heading, ' Oudh Affairs' :

" It has been calculated that about 60 per cent. of the entire native population...are sunk in such abject poverty that, unless the small earnings of child labour are added to the scanty stock by which the family is kept alive, some members would starve."

As to whether the impression that the greater number of the people of India suffer from a daily insufficiency of food is true or untrue, he adds :

" My own belief, after a great deal of study of *the closely connected questions of agricultural indebtedness, is that the impression is perfectly true as regards a varying but always considerable number throughout the greater part of India.*"

Mr. A. J. Lawrence, then Commissioner, Allahabad Division, who retired in 1891, reports :

" I believe there is very little between poorer classes of the people and semi-starvation, but where is the remedy?"

Of Shahjahanpur, another district of the United Provinces, it is stated : " The landless labourer's condition is by no means all that could be desired. The combined earnings of a man, his wife and two children cannot be put at more than Rs. 3 a month (less than a dollar in American money). *When prices of food grains are low or moderate, work regular and the health of house-*

hold good, this income will enable the family to have one fairly good meal a day, to keep a thatched roof over their heads, to buy cheap clothing and occasionally a thin blanket. Cold and rain undoubtedly entail considerable suffering, as the people are insufficiently clothed, and cannot afford fires. A few twigs or dried sticks constitute the height of their ambition, and these, owing to the increased value and scarcity of wood, are more and more difficult for the poor man to obtain." [Italics are in the original.]

Mr. White, Collector of Banda, states :

" A large number of the lower classes clearly demonstrate by their physique, either that they are habitually starved, or have been exposed in early years to the severity of famine; if any young creature be starved while growing, no amount of subsequent fattening will make up for the injury sustained."

Mr. Rose, Collector of Ghazipur, says :

" Where the holding is of average size, and the tenant unecumbered with debt, when his rent is not excessive and there is an average outturn of produce; when in fact, conditions are favourable, the position of the agriculturist is, on the whole, fairly comfortable. But unfortunately these conditions do not always exist. As a rule, a very large proportion are in debt."

Of the Jhansi Division, Mr. Ward, Commissioner, says :

THE ROCK-BOTTOM PHYSICAL BASE   361

"A very small proportion in this Division are habitually underfed."

Mr. Bays, Officiating Commissioner for Sitapur Division, records particulars obtained from twenty families taken at random:

"Nineteen shillings, twopence or less than five dollars per annum for each adult.

"Nine shillings, sixpence, or less than two and a half dollars per annum for each child."

He is of the opinion that this is sufficient to keep them in good health, and adds: "For some reasons, it is not desirable at present that the standard of comfort should be very materially raised."

Mr. Irwin, Deputy Commissioner of Rai Bareli, says:

"The mass of the agricultural population, in ordinary times, and the elite always, get enough to eat; but there is a considerable minority in bad seasons who feel the pinch of hunger, and a small minority...' suffer from chronic hunger,' except just at harvest time when grain is plentiful, and easily to be had. I do not understand that the indigent town population are intended to be included in this enquiry. There can be no doubt that they suffer much more than the agricultural classes for want of food, especially the unfortunate *purdahnashin* women, and indeed. men too, of good and impoverished families, who have sunk in the world, who are ashamed to beg, and live on the remnants of their property, and whom every rise in prices hits cruelly hard. For such people dear grain means starvation, while to the producer, it of course means increased value of the produce."

Mr. Toynbee, C.S.I., former Member of the Viceroy's Council and Senior Member of the Board of Revenue, said:

"The conclusion to be drawn is that, of the agricultural population, 40 per cent. are insufficiently fed, to say nothing of clothing and housing. They have enough food to support life and enable them to work, but they have to undergo long fasts, having for a considerable part of the year to satisfy themselves with one full meal a day."

In Grierson's statistics, as summed up in the *Pioneer*, in 1893, we have:

"Briefly, it is that all persons of the labouring classes, and 10 per cent. of the cultivating and artisan classes, or 45 per cent. of the total population, are insufficiently fed, or housed, or both. It follows that nearly one hundred millions of people in British India are living in extreme poverty."

The Punjab is supposed to be one of the most prosperous provinces of India. Mr. Thorburn, Member of the Punjab Commission, one time Financial Commissioner, says of the agriculturists of that province in his book entitled *The Punjab in Peace and War:**

* Page 175.

"It is worthy of note that the whole revenue of the Punjab, from the largest item, land revenue, to the smallest, stamps, £10,000, are practically drawn from the producing masses, whilst the literate and commercial classes, whom the new regime was to benefit at the expense of those masses, escape almost untaxed."

Again :[*]

"Since the Mutiny, there have been in all seven years of famine, namely, 1860-61, 1876-78, 1896-97, 1899-1901; in addition, scarcities from short droughts in semi-dependent tracts, have been frequent. During the earlier famines, four years in all, out of the annual land revenue demand, apart from water rates and canal irrigated lands, hardly, two per cent. were suspended, and the fraction ultimately remitted or written off as recoverable, was infinitesimal. Since 1896 the destitution of a large part of the cultivators having been officially proved, the Government has been less niggardly in granting suspensions and remissions. Unfortunately the relief given, coming too late, fails to reach the classes who most require it—the poorest of the peasant proprietary—and only saves the pockets of the capitalist mortgagees and purchasers of holdings...

"If it be remembered that the average daily income per head of the Indian population is less than three halfpence, and that fully 25 per cent. of that population never attain that average, the

Ibid., pp. 242-3.

hand to mouth existence of the Punjab peasantry, even in normal years, will be realized. If so, their general inability to pay, without borrowing, the land revenue, or to even avoid death from starvation whenever a scarcity from drought occurs, let alone a famine period, requires no demonstration."

Says Mr. Manohar Lal, late Minto Professor of Economics at the University of Calcutta, in the course of an article in the *Indian Journal of Economics*, for July 1916 :

"Poverty, grinding poverty, is a tremendous fact of our economic, and therefore national, position, and it is to the mind of the present writer an immeasurably more potent fact than even the ignorance and illiteracy that prevails among our masses. This poverty exposes us to the havoc of disease and pestilence, famine and plague and it makes advance at every step difficult..."

"It is a picture of literal starvation mentally, and all but so physically; it can represent the life of no unit of civilized humanity."

Mr. Manohar Lal is now a Member of the Punjab Government having been appointed to that office by the Governor of the province.

On January 11, 1917, Mr. S. P. Patro, an investigator into economic conditions in the Madras Presidency, read a paper in a meeting presided over by His Excellency the Governor of Madras. We make the following extracts from the Press report of his paper :

"Mr. Patro found that in a particular village the budget of the ryot showed a deficit of Rs. 22-9 every year and it was not possible to obtain a full meal every day. Dealing similarly with a typical village in the Chicacole division, Mr. Patro found that the annual income of the family of a typical zemindar, who had wet and dry lands, was Rs. 129-8-0, and that the expenditure, including cost of rice, oil, clothing, etc., was Rs. 181-8, leaving a deficit of Rs. 52 a year. For marriage and litigation the head of the family raised a loan of Rs. 380 in 1907, and discharged the same in 1913 by the sale of rice and by living on inferior corn and the profits of rice-pounding. The family had full meals only from January to the month of May according to the statement of the ryot. In a zemindari village the annual income of a typical family was Rs. 316 and the expenditure Rs. 321-6-0, and there was a debt outstanding against the family. In another zemindari village the income of a typical family was Rs. 786 and the expenditure Rs. 698-4-0, leaving a balance of Rs. 68 to the credit of the family, whose affairs were conducted in a most economic way. That was not a profit, but it represented the wages which the members of the family earned for their personal labour on the land at Rs. 14 a head per year."

*

According to official estimates, the average annual income per head of the people of India till some time back was Rs. 30. Lord Cromer, then Finance Minister for India, made the first estimate in 1882, placing the average at Rs. 27; Lord Curzon, the late Viceroy, estimated the income of the agricultural population—85 per cent. of the whole—to be Rs. 30 per year. In his budget speech for 1901, Lord George Hamilton, then Secretary of State for India, said that the average income was Rs. 30 (£2); Mr. William Digby, C.I.E., after a full and exhaustive study of the condition of the people, financially and industrially, furnishes overwhelming evidence to show that the average annual income of the people of India is not over Rs. 17-8 (about six dollars). Considering the value of the rupee, which is equivalent to about 33 cents in American money, we have the startling condition of millions of people subsisting on from $6.00 to $10.00 per year, or about two cents a day—this according to official estimate.

The Rev. Dr. Sunderland cites these facts and figures in support of his observations on Indian famines:

" The truth is, the poverty of India is something we can have little conception of, unless we have actually seen it, as alas, I have... Is it any wonder that the Indian peasant can lay up nothing for time of need...? The extreme destitution of the people is principally responsible for the devastations of plague; the loss of life from this terrible scourge is startling. It reached 272,000 in 1901; 500,000 in 1902; 800,000 in 1903; and over 1,000,000 in 1904. It still continues unchecked. The vitality of the people has been reduced by long semi-starvation. So long as the present destitution of India continues, there is small ground for hope that the plague can be overcome... The real cause of famines in India is not lack of rain; it is not over-population; it is the extreme, the abject, the awful poverty of the people."

One of the more recent investigators is Mr. Arnold Lupton, who thrashed out the whole subject in his book, *Happy India*, to which we have already referred.

Mr. Lupton tries to compute the national income of India and concludes :*

"Adding [the] manufacturing value to the agricultural value, I get a total production of £1,900,000,000 worth, or adopting the figures in Table VII, £1,902,936,000 worth, for the work of the population of 247,000,000 people who are under the direct British Government. This gives a value per head of about £7-6s. or £7-12s. a year, or five pence a day for every day in the year, for every man, woman and child.

"Taking the wealth production in the United Kingdom in the year 1920 as £2,500,000,000 and the population as 47,000,000, that would give for that year a production per head of about £53, or nearly eight times as much as the Indian income per head."

The following table taken from Professor K. T. Shah's authoritative book, *The Wealth and*

* *Op. cit.*, p. 98.

Taxable Capacity of India* (Bombay, 1924) summarizes the different estimates of *per capita* income :

Estimated by	Relating to year	Income per head
		Rs.
Dadabhoy Naoroji	c. 1870	20
Baring-Barbour	1882	27
Digby	1898-99	18.9
Lord Curzon	c. 1900	30
Digby	c. 1900	17.4
Mr. Findlay Shirras	1911	50
The Hon'ble Sir B. N. Sarma†	1911	86
Professor Shah	1921-22	46

An important index of the poverty of India is the total number of persons who pay the income-tax. In reply to a question put in the Legislative Assembly on March 8, 1924, the Finance Member gave the total number of assessees in 1922-23 as 238,242 out of a population of about 240 millions. The minimum taxable annual income is Rs. 2,000. Agriculturists pay land revenue and not income tax.

Miss Mayo's economic conclusions are based on evidence of a queer description. Thus, speaking of the economic condition of the masses, she says on page 375 of her book :

" As general circumstantial evidence of increased means, one sees the consumption by the

*Page 68.
† Quoted in the Council of State, March 6, 1921.

peasants of non-essentials, once beyond their dreams. Thus, at the fair at Aligarh, in February, 1926, the turnover of cheap boots in one week amounted to £1,000, netting a profit of 20 per cent. Boots, to the sort of people who snapped these up and put them on their own feet, were, twenty years ago, an unheard-of luxury. Big stocks of umbrellas, lamps, and gaily painted steel trunks were sold out and renewed over and over again, on the same occasion, the buyers being the ordinary cultivators. Tea, cigarettes, matches, lanterns, buttons, pocket-knives, mirrors. gramophones, are articles of commerce with people who, fifteen years ago, bought nothing of the sort. The heavy third-class passenger traffic by rail is another evidence of money in hand. For, railway travel to the Indian peasant takes the place that the movie fills in America. In 1924-25, 581,804,000 third-class railway travellers as against 1,246,000 of the first-class, proved the presence of money to spare in the peasants' possession. 'Where are they all going?' I repeatedly asked, watching the crowds packing into the third-class carriages.

" 'Anywhere. Visiting, marriage parties, little business trips—just " there and back," mostly for the excitement of going,' was the answer."

Who supplied Miss Mayo with the information about 'boots'? ' Boots ' in India means Western footwear. The villagers of India and the masses do not use them. Who told her about the conditions that existed twenty years before, to institute the comparison? The British officers, of course. This is the language of official apologists. Her 'glimpses through the economic lens' are only distortions through the official lens. The railways have driven out old conveyances, but the poor people certainly cannot afford to keep moving about merely for the fun of 'just there and back.'

Speaking of the miserable economic condition of the peasantry in the Bombay Presidency, Dr. Harold Mann, the retiring Director of Agriculture in that province, in the course of an interview given to a representative of the *Times of India* in October 1927 remarked:

" He had no hesitation in saying that although the standard of living of the agriculturists had undoubtedly improved, he could not say that the majority of the people were living up to that standard. His enquiries had shown, in fact, that fully 75 per cent. of the people in the famine tracts were living so much below their own standard that their economic position had to be reckoned as unsound, whilst even in the areas which were looked upon as reasonably prosperous, there was only 66 per cent. of the people in a sound economic position. He admitted that it was most difficult to make any detailed observations on this point because there was so little data to compare notes, but his candid opinion, after twenty years' careful investigation and observation, was that in those two decades the standard of life in the villages had improved but the actual relationship of the bulk of the people towards that standard had not improved."

After putting forward Dr. Mann's suggestions for possible improvements in agriculture that the villagers themselves could bring about without any large expenditure of money, the report about the interview continues:

" But little could be done on an extensive scale even along these lines, said Dr. Mann, until the Government and the social reformers recognized that *the secret of the whole prosperity of the agricultural population was the filling of their stomachs.* The empty stomach was the greatest obstacle to progress in India, and he wished to emphasize before he left the country that all efforts should ultimately concentrate on filling the stomachs of the people. When asked what measures he would suggest for this great work of filling the empty stomachs of the people, Dr. Mann said that much could be done by the people themselves. They must put themselves to work, for no country could ever hope to be prosperous if the majority of its population were idle for six months in the year. The people must be given some work, no matter how small the income derived therefrom, during the dry season, and Dr. Mann said that no matter in what other way Mr. Gandhi had gone astray, he had penetrated into the secret of the poverty of India when he advocated the spinning wheel, no matter if it did produce only a few annas a day. Dr. Mann therefore thought Government should pay the closest attention to this phase of the problem if they ever hoped to have a prosperous countryside, and he expressed bewilderment that so long a period had elapsed before Government had tackled the problem in right earnest."

Dr. Mann's last message to the people of the country was given in the following words:

" Dr. Mann said that he had the greatest hopes of the Bombay Presidency reaching a very high standard of economic prosperity in which the ryots would participate, *but no endeavour towards such better state could be made, said Dr. Mann, by a people with empty bellies*, and so his last message to the people of this land, to all social workers, and to those in charge of the administration was to devise means whereby the cultivators might be given sufficient food."

The crux of the matter has been given by Dr. Mann in the words italicized above. This is the language of an Englishman who has been in intimate touch with village life for the last twenty years and has been a member of the bureaucracy which rules the country. This is not the language of any ' cursed ' Swarajist or Home Ruler or fire-eater, but of a high-placed official.

CHAPTER XXVI

SOME ASPECTS OF THE DRAIN TO-DAY

Miss Mayo's avowed purpose in writing *Mother India* was to supply 'test facts' about India to the American citizen. One would think that the American citizen would very much like to be enlightened about the economic situation and the economic potentialities of India. It ought certainly to be of interest to the American to know that with greater purchasing power India could become a very great customer. Miss Mayo, however, is a hopeless guide in the economic field. Her knowledge of economic principles is of the crudest order, and she has absolutely failed to grasp factors in the Indian economic situation. She seems never to have heard of the work of Indian economists: Dadabhai Naoroji, Ranade, Joshi, Wacha. None of these names, regarded as classics in Indian economics, occurs in her index. Eminent living economists like Professor K. T. Shah have also been entirely ignored by her. She has quoted some of my books, but I do not find my *England's Debt to India* referred to even once in her book.

With such wide gaps in her knowledge of economic conditions in India, it was the height of impudence for her to write a book about India for the benefit of the American reader who is above all interested in economic facts. The fact, for instance, that the British Government to-day is thinking of adopting measures to hit the American film manufacturer in the Indian market, in order that his otherwise incompetent English competitor may thrive, is of greater importance to Americans than all the ignorant sexual and religious bunkum to which Miss Mayo treats her reader. The American manufacturer must naturally be curious to know why it is that India purchases more than half her requirements in Great Britain, whilst only six per cent. of her import trade falls to the lot of the United States; and also how it happens that India's carrying trade is almost entirely confined to British bottoms. ' We raise great crops of tea, and almost the whole is swept out of India—another exhausting drain upon the country,' she makes the Indian economist complain; and in reply she asks, ' Do you sell your tea, or give it away?' To this the imaginary Indian economist murmurs, ' Ah, yes—but the *tea*, you perceive, is *gone*.' We ask what Indian economist could put the matter so crudely—and, excepting Miss Mayo, who could refute in such a naive fashion?

Military expenditure.

Miss Mayo's discussion of the **military expenditure** is no better than it could be expected to be with her knowledge of economics. She states the case and demolishes it in this summary fashion (pages 351-2):

" ' The army is too big,' says the politician.

'Is it too big for the work it has to do in keeping your safety and peace?'

'I don't know. I have not looked into that,' is the usual reply. 'But anyway it costs an outrageous percentage of India's revenue'."

It may be a passable story stuff; but as economic criticism it is hopeless. There are many who have 'looked into that'; why did not Miss Mayo examine the case presented by them?

Amongst the more recent of such examinations is that by Mr. K. T. Shah, Professor of Political Economy in the Bombay University, in one of his standard works, *Wealth and Taxable Capacity of India.** Mr. Shah had also prepared a minute for the Inchcape Committee (1923), which he summarises in his book.

First of all, is it sound economics to say that the expenditure on defence bears no relation to the taxable capacity of the country? The expenditure on defence, as on other things has to keep in view the capacity of the national purse. The following table compiled by Professor Shah from the *Statesman's Year Book* (1922) throws interesting light on this question.

A far more important point to be noted is that India regards the military expenditure as a 'drain' not merely because it is unbearably heavy but also because such a large part of it is spent on British soldiers and *in Britain*. Of the

*London : P. S. King & Sons, 1924.

1		2	3	4	5	6
Country		Total Revenue	Total Expenditure	Defence Expenditure	Per cent. of (2) to (3)	Per cent. of (2) to (4)
		Figures in Millions.				
India	Rs.	1332.2	1423.9	919.0	70.7	63.8
United Kingdom	£	1426.9	1195.4	642.0	45.0	53.7
Australia	£	61.78	64.60	31.20	50.0	48.3
Canada	£	89.38	74.19	17.9	20.0	24.2
South Africa	£	29.67	25.69	13.4	4.5	5.2
Spain	Pesetas	1976.66	2550.79	450.36	22.8	17.6
France	Francs	22450.9	24932.0	5027.4	22.4	20.0
Italy	Lire	17603.0	20454.8	3553.77	20.0	17.3
United States	Dollars	3345.18	3143.41	1201.44	35.9	38.2
Japan	Yen	1319.20	1399.29	646.40	49.0	49

* In the case of Canada the figure includes half the total debt charge. The French figures include the Ordinary and Extraordinary and Naval Budgets, but do not include the Debt Charge, which would make the total to be 17,553 million francs or 38 per cent. and 70 per cent., respectively.

total military services, expenditure in England amounted to—

>Rs. 18.16 crores in 1922-23
>Rs. 18.20 ,, ,, 1923-24
>Rs. 15.03 ,, ,, 1924-25

The Esher Committee on military affairs wrote in a covering letter of their report :

" We cannot consider the administration of the Army in India otherwise than as part of the total armed forces of the Empire. Novel political machinery created by the peace treaty has enhanced the importance of the Army in India relatively to the military forces in other parts of the Empire and more particularly to those of the British Isles."

But if the Army is to be used for Empire purposes, in fairness the Empire should share the expenditure also. At present Britain calls the tune for the delectation of the Empire, and India pays the piper—who again generally is the Britisher himself. Even if sometimes part of the Indian Army that serves beyond the Indian frontiers to save the Empire be temporarily financed by Britain or the Empire, it must not be forgotten that no part of the permanent expenditure is shared by the Empire. Says Professor Shah :

" If the annexation of the frontier territories be an object of the Indian Army; if the maintenance of the balance of power in Asia is desirable—

these are objects imposed upon us by imperial considerations, which are, to say the least, as beneficial to England as to India. Of the total military strength of the British Empire, India has supplied the largest proportion and borne the largest share of such expenditure, after England. The advantage of such armies is common to the Empire, though its greatest benefit is to England. Why then should England not bear a share of such increased expenditure on the army maintained in Imperial interests?...

" Geographically and politically India is so situated that we cannot conceive of India needing naval assistance from Britain for the exclusive benefit and defence of this country. Should she chance—against all probabilities—to attract enemies from across the seas, she has a seaboard so effectually dominated by the ghats and protected by the deserts, that she need not apprehend any serious danger on that score. And as for her maritime commerce, though considerable, it is not entirely to her own benefit. The customers of India are more interested in keeping open the commerce of India than she herself. There is thus no ground to regard the military expenditure as in any way a substitute for, or set-off against, the absence of a naval budget in India."

Miss Mayo of course had no time and no inclination to go into these facts. But it is well to remember that in the Great War India sent no

SOME ASPECTS OF THE DRAIN TO-DAY

less than 1,338,620 men* to the different theatres of war, and that her *direct* money contribution has been officially put down at £146.2 million, besides indirect money help and immense help in material. What sacrifice has Britain ever made in the interests of India that can be put alongside of these figures?

Britain keeps in India one British soldier for every two Indian soldiers. The British soldier is expensive and adds to the drain.

De-Europeanization of the Army has been a plank of Indian politicians, Liberal as well as Nationalist, for a long time past. A few years ago the Government appointed a committee presided over by an eminent British soldier, Sir Andrew Skeen, to consider some important questions in this connection. The unanimous recommendations of this committee, appointed on Government's initiative with a personnel of Government's own choice and with an eminent British soldier as president, contemplated Indianization at what the Nationalists regard at a decidedly slow pace. But even these recommendations have been treated with scant respect.

Britain as a buyer of Indian raw produce.

That India is industrially backward is a commonplace of Indian life. Agriculture is Inida's chief industry. The subject has been discussed in detail in Mr. Lupton's book, *Happy*

---

* *India's Contribution to the Great War* (published by authority of the Government of India, 1923), pp. 98 and 160.

India, referred to already. In my book, *England's Debt to India*, I traced the history of the land policy of the British Government from the earliest days of the East India Company up to the time of writing that book. I quoted therein figures about the raw produce of India exported to England from 1903-04 up to 1913-14. In 1913-14, the United Kingdom commanded 23.4 per cent. of India's total exports. No other country took more than 10 per cent In 1924-25, the figure for the United Kingdom rose to 25.5 per cent., next in order coming Japan with 14.3 per cent. In 1913-14 the United Kingdom supplied 64.1 per cent. of the total purchases of India. In 1924-25 it supplied 54.1 per cent. From the figures given in my *England's Debt to India*, I deduced the following conclusions with regard to some important articles of produce:

Jute.—The United Kingdom is the largest importer of raw jute from India.

Wool.—The United Kingdom is not only the largest importer of raw wool, but practically the whole of the raw wool exported by India goes to the United Kingdom. Out of a total of £1,756,448 worth of raw wool exported in 1912-13, the United Kingdom took £1,704,785 worth.

Wheat.—The United Kingdom is not only the largest buyer of wheat from India but in some years takes practically the whole of the total quantity exported. That was so until 1908-09. In 1909 and 1910, she took more than £7,000,000 worth out of a total of almost £8,500,000 worth exported. In 1911-12 she took £6,741,190 worth of wheat out of a total of £8,898,972 exported and in 1912-13 £8,380,422 worth out of a total of £11,795,816.

Barley and Seeds.—The United Kingdom is the greatest consumer of Indian barley. In seeds, again, we find that the United Kingdom heads the list of importers from India.

Tea.—More than two-thirds of the tea exported from India goes to the United Kingdom.

Skins and Hides.—Similarly, the United Kingdom gets the largest quantity of raw skins, dressed or tanned hides.

This shows the hollowness of Miss Mayo's laboured plea that Great Britain gets no benefit from her connection with India.

CHAPTER XXVII

SOME ASPECTS OF THE DRAIN TO-DAY—*concld*.

Cheap capital for railways.

That India has to-day nearly 40,000 miles of railways is a fact. But the story how these railways were built, financed and worked is nothing short of a scandal. Indian railway policy has never shown much regard for India's interests. Its chief concern has been Britain's strategical or commercial advantage. The Indian railways were built or worked by British companies who ran no risk whatever, but who fleeced the Indian taxpayer of crores of rupees. With all this their treatment of Indian passengers has in the past been full of contempt and insolence. Third class passengers, from whom they derived the bulk of their receipts, were always treated most shabbily. Some of these companies who fed fat on the third-class traffic, contemptuously dubbed it the ' coolie class'.

Miss Mayo asks us to be thankful to London for having given us capital for railways at such wonderfully cheap rates. " India," she says, " borrowed from her cheapest market, London,... paying from 2.5 to 5 per cent., with an average of 3.5 per cent. on the loans—the lowest rates that the world knows.' But there was no borrowing here in the ordinary sense of the word. What

Miss Mayo is referring to is what they called the 'guarantee system.' Under this system the Government of India guaranteed the railway companies a *minimum* rate of interest; it did not get the 'cheap' capital and build and own the railways itself. Nor did it prevent the companies from earning very high rates. The guaranteed rate was merely the lower limit.

The companies ran no risks whatever. For all their extravagance and inefficiency the Indian tax-payer had to suffer. Besides the companies enjoyed several privileges in the shape of free land, etc. By several petty devices they managed to squeeze more money from India than was due to them. Thus, when the company had fat days in the first half of the year with a prospect of lean days ahead, it could put off all expenses till the lean days—so that it would get good 'surplus profits' during the first half, while the losses enhanced by the postponed expenditure were shifted on to the Indian revenues. Then there is the fact that the British Secretary of State for India could always so manipulate exchange as to allow his fellow-Britishers financing Indian railways in actual fact a much higher guaranteed minimum than that provided for in the contract.

As a concrete example of this 'cheap loans' system take the G. I. P. Railway. From 1849 to 1900 this railway was worked under the guarantee system. In 1901 the Government bought up the railway, but, curiously enough, handed it over again to the same company to work as agents in its behalf. So the company controlled huge properties without owning a mile of railway. It has been calculated that during the guarantee period the working results of the G. I. P. Railway showed a nett loss of 14.91 crores. Interest on that loss calculated at 4 per cent. per annum works out at Rs. 93,20,37,781 from 1852 to 1924. During the agency period the nett loss from 1901 to 1923 was 1.73 crores. The company came into existence in 1849. It was working at a loss but in 1855 its £20 share was sold at a premium of 25 to 30.62 per cent. The extravagance under the guarantee system for which India had to pay may be gauged from the fact that up to the year 1880 the capital cost per mile on the G. I. P. Railway was Rs. 1,95,945, while the neighbouring lines, the Nagpur-Chhatisgarh and the Dhond-Manmad State Railways cost only Rs. 57,315 and Rs. 71,756 per mile, respectively.*

Such in brief is the story of cheap capital. No wonder the companies that invested at such philanthropic rates, and were supposed to be working at a loss, could still sell their shares at handsome premia.

Mr. Thornton, giving evidence before the Parliamentary Committee of 1872 said :

"I do believe unguaranteed capital would have gone into India for the construction of railways had it not been for the guarantee. Considering how this country is always growing in wealth,

* See an article by Mr. C. P. Tewari, author of *Indian Railways*, in *The People*, Lahore, for November 29, 1925.

and that an immense amount of capital is seeking investment which it cannot find in England and goes to South America and other countries abroad, I cannot conceive that it would presistently have neglected India."*

Says the Parsi economist, Mr. D. E. Wacha, who in politics is supposed to be a henchman of the Government:

" As a matter of fact it is recorded in black and white in one of the important appendices to the report of the Royal Commission on Indian expenditure (1896-97), generally called the Welby Commission, that from 1848 to 1895, the whole system of Indian railways cost to the State, that is the tax-payer, fully 55 crore rupees; and though since that date there have been gains, still in the railway ledger of the Government of India there is a debit balance against railways of as many as 30 crore rupees.

" It is since 1899-1900 that Indian railways have turned the corner and earned something for the tax-payer on his colossal capital recorded in the administration report for 1910 at 430 crore rupees! The average gain since 1904-05 has come to 3 crore rupees per annum. There are no doubt paying railways; but there are also losing ones and these 3 crores are the net balance of gain after writing out the losses. The large gains of the earning railways are absorbed by the losing ones, as could be easily discovered on a reference to

* Quoted by R. C. Dutt in his *India in the Victorian Age*, p. 354.

appendix IX of the annual administration report which gives the financial operations of each system of railways."

Mr. Wacha sums up his analysis in these words: " *It is a dismal tale, the history of Indian railway finance, from first to last.*"

Regarding the indifference of the railway management to the needs of the Indian travelling public, Mr. Wacha says :

" The worst and most inexcusable feature of Indian railway policy is the supreme indifference and neglect of the authorities to the crying wants and wishes of the Indian public—those vast millions of the population who travel about 36 miles in a year and who now contribute the largest portion of the coaching traffic amounting to 13 crore rupees per annum. The interests of the European mercantile community are deemed of paramount importance while those of the Indian population at large have been uniformly held of secondary importance, if at all. At the beck and nod of the former, with their screaming organs of opinion behind, the Government readily spend millions like water on railways without an ultimate thought of the tax-payers and the return such capital would give. It is the greatest blot on Indian railway administration that it ignores the interests of the permanent population and is eager to satisfy first the cry of the interested and migratory European merchant. No private railway enterprise would spend such enormous sums of money and no proprietary body, however rich and influential, would tolerate in any part of the civilized world the loans after loans, ranging from 15 to 20 crores, which are annually borrowed and expended without let or hindrance, save for a kind of official control, which is no control at all."

Regarding railway finance, the following opinion expressed by the Inchcape Committee on Retrenchment is also significant:

" We are of opinion that the country cannot afford to subsidize the railways and that steps should be taken to curtail working expenses in order to ensure that not only will the railways as a whole be on a self-supporting basis, but that an adequate return should be obtained for the last capital expenditure which has been incurred by the State. We consider that, with economic working, it should be possible for the railways in India to earn sufficient net receipts to yield an average return of at least $5\frac{1}{2}$ per cent. on the total capital at charge. The average return to the State during the three years prior to the War was 5 per cent., and, in view of the fact that large amounts of additional capital are being raised at 6 per cent. or over, we think a return of $5\frac{1}{2}$ per cent. cannot be regarded as excessive."

'Cheap' capital was awarded in yet another way. We refer to the fact that the purchase of stores was made in England even when it was not 'India's cheapest market.' Thus says the Retrenchment Committee :*

* Part IV, para. 52.

"The High Commissioner has drawn our attention to the fact that indentors frequently tie his hands by restricting him, in spite of his protests, to a particular manufacturer or sources of supply. This inevitably connotes the payment of higher prices than would otherwise be necessary, and the High Commissioner has furnished us with several instances where large sums of money have been lost both to the central and provincial Governments as the result of such restrictions, and also by indentors conducting initial negotiations with the representatives of particular firms. These practices are greatly to be deprecated, and we recommend that orders should be passed strictly prohibiting them. Private communications between indentors and suppliers should also not be permitted."

To those acquainted with the customary reticence of official language, this cannot but sound as severe censure; and the practices must be far more questionable than the letter of the remarks would imply. Every year, even now, the guardians or spokesmen of the Indian commercial interests have to draw the attention of the government departments concerned to discrepancies between the tenders received and the orders for stores actually placed; and government explanations often merely explain away things.

The story of railway finance in the early 'cheap loans' phase was told among others by A. J. Wilson in his book, *An Empire in Pawn;* by Digby in his *Prosperous British India*, and by Naoroji, Gokhale and Wacha and others before the Royal Commissions of 1880 and 1897. Mr. A. K. Connell wrote thus on this question :*

"The truth about the capital expenditure is as follows : Of the guaranteed railways capital of £96,794,226, spent up to the end of 1880-81, £46,918,177 were withdrawn in England and £49,876,049 in India, while the charge for interest, amounting, as shown above, to about £28,000,000, was almost entirely remitted to England... Indeed, there was a deficit on the whole transaction of £8,000,000. So far, then, from this investment of foreign capital leading to an 'outlay of a larger sum than the interest sent away,' it actually led to the outlay of a smaller sum than would have been spent in the country if no guaranteed railways had ever been built.

"Of the £32,000,000 odd raised for State railways, 24 millions have been appropriated in India, and 7½ millions in England, while the charge for interest, between 2 and 3 millions to be added to the capital account, has also gone to England."

Mr. Connell discussed also the question whether or not India was the better off because of the railways. His conclusions in his own words are :†

"To sum up, the joint results of railways and free trade may be briefly stated in this way : India used to clothe itself, now England sends clothes, and Indian weavers have lost an enor-

*The Economic Revolution of India, 1883, p. 31.
† Ibid., p. 53.

mous source of income, with the gain to the country of the difference in price between English and Indian goods. But to pay for these goods India has to export vast quantities of food, and those who sell this food make larger profits than before. Therefore a certain portion of the community gain by cheaper cotton goods and higher prices for grain. But in order to attain this result they have had to pay the sums before mentioned to build the railways. Besides that, they have to support in years of scarcity a gigantic system of outdoor relief. Is it not obvious that, taking the economic changes as a whole, the country has lost an enormous source of wealth? If the import of cotton to India and the export of grain from India ceased to-morrow, the Indian people would be the gainers, though the Indian Government would be at its wit's end. In fact, the interests of the two are not identical. The Indian Government is now doing its best to stimulate export of wheat in order to lessen its 'loss by exchange'; but this will only result in higher food prices in India. We now see the explanation of Mr. Hunter's assertion that two-fifths of the people of British India enjoy a prosperity unknown under native rule; another two-fifths earn a fair, but diminishing subsistence; but the remaining fifth, or forty millions, go through life on insufficient food. And in ten years, according to Mr. Caird, there will be twenty millions more people to feed. Can it, then, be maintained that the condition of India has been improved by the enormous outlay on railways?

" But you forget, replies the opponent of these heretical views, that in time of famine the railway brings food to starving districts. What would have become of the people of Madras, Bombay, and the North-West Province during the last famine if it had not been for the railways? My reply is: What did become of them? It is true, the railways brought grain; yet they had previously taken it away, and they brought it back at a quadrupled price, and the Government had to spend millions of pounds to enable the peasants to buy it, and even then could not prevent frightful mortality.

" What has been the native's custom from time immemorial of providing against bad years? Why, the simple method of Joseph in Egypt—that of storing grain. This is what the official report on the Mysore famine tells us: ' The country had suffered in former years from deficient rainfall, but actual famine had been staved off by the consumption of the surplus ragi, a coarse millet, stored in underground pits, from which it is withdrawn in times of scarcity, as the grain will keep sound and good for forty and fifty years. Only two of the Famine Commissioners, Messrs. Caird and Sullivan, seem to have recognized the importance of this custom...

" Since the introduction of railways there is reason to believe that the ryot, tempted by immediate gain, or forced by taxation to sell his grain, is beginning to store rupees instead of food; but, as he cannot eat his rupees or jewellery, and cannot buy fuel so as to keep the manure for the land, and has, according to the Famine Commissioners, to give in famine times a quadrupled price for his food, it is very doubtful whether he gains in the long run. Anyhow, the landless labourer, who has no produce to exchange for rupees, finds the market price in time of scarcity utterly beyond his means. Then the Government comes to the rescue with relief works, the railways make roaring profits—in fact, famine and war, both exhausting for the country, are perfect godsends to the foreign investor—and the Indian Government complacently holds up its Public Works policy to an admiring and interested English public. It wholly omits to mention that in time past nearly £30,000,000 of taxation have been squeezed out of the country to pay interest charges, and that, if that sum had been left in the agriculturist's pockets, he might himself have been better able to face bad times and have helped the labourer to do the same. But Sir John Strachey utterly ignores this aspect of the question; he is quite content with pointing to the relief works, and then insists on the necessity of constructing more railways to meet the next famine cycle. One would suppose that railways proceeded as a free gift out of the benevolent bosoms of British capitalists, instead of being paid for out of the hungry bellies of the Hindu ryots. The sum of £30,000,000, represents the amount which India has had to pay out of taxation to get its railways built, and then it has paid £15,000,000 (part of which went to the railway shareholders) to keep the people alive, and after all has lost about five millions of human beings."

Public Services.

A few facts and figures about public services may fittingly close this chapter. There is no country on the face of the globe than India where superior public servants are paid so lavishly, and where the bulk of the savings of the public servants goes out of the country.

The British Government in India is generally called 'bureaucracy.' A certain element of bureaucracy is of course unavoidable in all forms of Government. But in India the public services constitute the steel frame—to use Lloyd George's phrase—of Britain's domination. The 'I.C.S.' and other bureaucrats do not merely carry out administrative policies, they very largely formulate them.

The Indian superior services are therefore very largely manned by Britishers. This means fine careers for British 'lads'—and a heavy drain on India's public revenue. Merely to benefit the British lads the cost of administration has been made to increase exorbitantly. New jobs for young British bureaucrats are being created every now and then; and their emoluments are far beyond the capacity of Indian revenues. The services are a 'drain' in the real sense of the word. They are so expensive, and such a large portion of their income is spent outside India. The heavy amount remitted as pensions is a dead loss to the country.

In April 1913, the proportion of Indians and Britishers including Anglo-Indians in different departments of State service was as under:*

Total number of posts worth
Rs. 200 per mensem or
over 11,064

Of these Englishmen and
Anglo-Indians held ... 6,491 or 59 per cent.

Whilst Indians held ... 4,573 or 41 per cent.

A further analysis of this expenditure, as given by Professor K. T. Shah in a table, which we are reproducing on the next page, will be of interest to the reader :

*Sixty Years of Indian Finance, K. T. Shah, 2nd edition, p. 121.

SOME ASPECTS OF THE DRAIN TO-DAY

Of posts carrying Rs. 200—300, Englishmen held 12%, Indians held 64%, Anglo-Indians held 24%
,, ,, ,, 300—400 ,, 19% ,, 62% ,, 19%
,, ,, ,, 400—500 ,, 36% ,, 49% ,, 15%
,, ,, ,, 500—600 ,, 58% ,, 31% ,, 11%
,, ,, ,, 600—700 ,, 54% ,, 36% ,, 10%
,, ,, ,, 700—800 ,, 78% ,, 14% ,, 8%
,, ,, ,, 800—900 ,, 73% ,, 21% ,, 6%
,, ,, ,, 900—1,000 ,, 92% ,, 4% ,, 4%

The Indian National Congress almost from its very start had been protesting against this deliberate exclusion of Indians from the superior services of their own country. The Congressmen pressed for simultaneous examinations (in India and England) for recruitment to the Imperial services. In 1893 Parliament accepted this principle, but no steps were taken to enforce it. The Montagu-Chelmsford report declared that the success of the new policy of progressive responsible government ' must very largely depend on the extent to which it is found possible to introduce Indians into every branch of the administration.' At once a hue and cry was raised by the British ' lads.' And now the actual policy of the government has been found out in the acceptance of the proposals of the Lee Commission over the head of the legislature.

The salaries and allowances of the public services had been very considerably increased in the decade 1914-24, with further advantages in the shape of more liberal pension rules, and passage allowances. According to the Inchcape Committee of 1922-23, the total staff paid from the Central revenues (excluding railway staff), had increased in number from 474,966 in 1913-14 to 520,762 in 1922-23—an increase of nearly 10 per cent. The table on the next page will throw further light on this question :

SOME ASPECTS OF THE DRAIN TO-DAY

(000 omitted.)

	Military Services			Civil Services		
	1913-14	1922-23	Increase	1913-14	1922-23	Increase
	Rs.	Rs.	Rs.	Rs.	Rs.	Rs.
Pay proper ...	12,13,75	23,67,91	11,54,16	5,85,37	11,97,60	6,12,23
Special pay or Duty allowance	84,63	1,19,29	34,66	4,22	16,25	12,03
Compensatory or Local allowance	1,44	1,40	0	13,51	29,93	16,42
House rent ...	8	1,76	1,68	5,42	14,98	9,56
Travelling allowance	30,59	70,01	39,42	35,09	69,97	34,88
Other allowances ...	15,05	1,39,35	1,24,30	31,51	46,49	14,98
Total ...	13,45,54	26,99,72	13,54,18	67,512	13,75,22	7,00,10

Note specially the increased expenditure under special allowances, etc. As if this were not enough the Lee Commission made further proposals for an all round increment.

The total increase for the *first year* of the Lee regime has been estimated thus:

Pay and remittance concession			
	I.C.S.	18.6	lakhs.
	I.P.S.	12.7	,,
	I.M.S. (Civil)	7.0	,,
	I.E.S. (Men)	3.3	,,
	I.F.S.	3.4	,,
	I.S.E.	10.9	,,
	I.A.S.	.8	,,
	I.V.S.	.4	,,
	Total	57.1	,,

Other services (approximately) 13.0 to 15.0 lakhs.
Pensions—Uncovenanted service ... 1.2 ,,
I.C.S. officers holding high posts ... .18 ,,
Passages ... ... 25.0 ,,

Grand Total (First Year)   96.21 to 98.21 ,,

This additional annual expenditure of a crore will no doubt strengthen the ' steel frame ' but at the same time it must prove a heavy drain on India's resources.

CHAPTER XXVIII

'DIVIDE ET IMPERA'

Miss Mayo chuckles over the Hindu-Muslim riots of recent years. It is true that the Hindus and the Mussalmans have been fighting almost ferociously for the last 5 years. The position may briefly be stated thus:

In 1919, during the agitation over the Rowlatt Act, the Hindus and Mussalmans made a united stand against the government. One of the counts in the indictment of the Punjab leaders in the Maritial Law summary trial courts was the promotion of unity. They were charged with having brought about unity in order to overthrow the British Government! In 1920 and 1921, Hindus and Muslims all over India united in the Non-co-operation Movement. This was an eye-sore to the foreign bureaucracy. Various steps were taken to kill the Non-co-operation movement by destroying Hindu-Muslim unity. In this the government was substantially helped by the institution of separate Hindu and Muslim electorates for the elective bodies. To the separate electorates they had added a policy of communal preferment in the public services also. It was particularly the Hindus who were to be suppressed and made to feel the iron heel.

The policy of divide and rule is the sheet-anchor of all Imperial governments. British rule in India has been persistently following that policy. The evidence of British official records is conclusive on this point. In the earlier phase the slogan was 'Mussalmans must be suppressed'—to-day it is, 'They must be won over and pitted against the Nationalists.' This would be clear from the citations that follow.*

Writing to the Duke of Wellington from Simla on October 4, 1842, after the fall of Kabul and Ghazni, Lord Ellenborough, then Governor-General of India observed :

"I could not have credited the extent to which the Muhammadans desired our failure in Afghanistan, unless I had heard here circumstances which prove that the feeling pervaded even those entirely dependent upon us.

" ...... The Hindus, on the other hand, are delighted. It seems to me most unwise, when we are sure of the hostility of one-tenth, not to secure the enthusiastic support of the nine-tenths which are faithful."

Again Ellenborough to Wellington on January 18, 1843 :

"I cannot close my eyes to the belief, that that race (Muslims) is fundamentally hostile to us and therefore our true policy is to conciliate the Hindus."

---

* The reader will do well to refer to Dr. J. T. Sunderland's article on 'Hindu and Muhammadan Riots' in the *Modern Review* (Calcutta) for January 1928, and to Major B. D. Basu's article, 'Muhammadanism Must be Suppressed' in the same journal for September 1925.

Why the Muhammadans incurred the wrath of Englishmen was explained in a pamphlet published in 1858 and written by a retired member of the Bengal Civil Service, named Henry Harrington Thomas :*

" I have stated that the Hindus were not the contrivers or the primary movers of the (1857) rebellion; and I now shall attempt to show that it was the result of a Muhammadan conspiracy, which had been in agitation for a longer period than was generally suspected, though it was developed somewhat sooner than its authors had intended... But the question is, Who planned and organized this combined movement for the murder of every Christian man, woman, and child throughout the country? Left to their own will and to their own resources, the Hindus never would, or could, have compassed such an undertaking... No; it is amongst the Muhammadans not the Hindus, that we must look for the real originators of this terrible plot !...... But, in order to comprehend in their full force the motives which induced the Muhammadans, more particularly than our other Indian subjects, to lay their plot for our extermination, it will be necessary to consider the character and tenets of the Muhammadans in general. They have been uniformly the same from the times of the first Caliphs to the present day, proud, intolerant and cruel, ever aiming at Muhammadan supremacy by

*The Late Rebellion in India and Our Future Policy, pp. 13-17. Quoted by Basu.

whatever means and ever fostering a deep hatred of Christians. They cannot be good subjects of any government which professes another religion : the precepts of the Koran will not suffer it. They deem themselves placed in a false position under any but a Muhammadan dynasty. For this reason, no favours or honours can conciliate them, but they can dissimulate to perfection, until their opportunity presents itself; and then their true character becomes manifest... But in India the Muhammadans had other motives for seeking our destruction, besides their rooted anti-Christian feeling. They could not forget that they had been the masters of the country for many generations, and they never ceased to persuade themselves, that if the British power were thoroughly destroyed they would recover their lost position, and once more lord it over the Hindus. They perceived the disaffection which had been spreading among the native regiments and fanned the flame by their intrigues. Well aware that no decisive blow could be struck without the co-operation of the Hindu troops, and that the surest means of urging them to desperate measures was to convince the Brahmans, in the first place that their religion was in danger, the Muhammadans artfully circulated a report which was echoed by the Brahmans, that the British Government was undermining the Hindu faith, with the covert intention of converting the Hindus to Christianity ... In their determined character, their education and mental capacity, the Muhammadans are vastly superior to the Hindus, who comparatively speaking are mere children in their hands. The

Muhammadans, moreover, on account of their higher qualification for business, have been more generally taken into public employ, which afforded them facilities for becoming acquainted with the measures of government and gave weight and importance to their assertions... the Muhammadans planned and organized this rebellion (or rather revolution) for their own aggrandizement alone, and that the Hindu Sepoys of the Bengal Army were their dupes and instruments."

For yet another reason, this writer refers to the impossibility of converting the Muhammadans to Christianity :*

" The missionary seldom convinces a Muhammadan; the very fact of his Christianity militates against his success. In general the Muhammadan avoids discussion with the missionaries and he listens with impatience to their arguments, if he does not wholly turn a deaf ear to them. Of a nature less stern and obdurate, the Hindus are frequently touched by the preachings of the missionaries."

As early as 1821, a British officer, signing himself 'Carnaticus' wrote in the *Asiatic Journal*:†

" *Divide et Impera* should be the motto of our Indian administration, whether political, civil or military."

* *Op. cit.*, p. 26.
† Quoted by Basu in his *Consolidation of the Christian Power in India*, pp. 74-5.

The same thing was put in as outspoken a language by Lt.-Col. John Coke, Commandant at Moradabad, who, about the time of what the British historians have called the 'Sepoy Mutiny' of 1857, wrote :*

"OUR ENDEAVOURS SHOULD BE TO UPHOLD IN FULL FORCE THE (FOR US FORTUNATE) SEPARATION WHICH EXISTS BETWEEN THE DIFFERENT RELIGIONS AND RACES, NOT TO ENDEAVOUR TO AMALGAMATE THEM. *DIVIDE ET IMPERA* SHOULD BE THE PRINCIPLE OF INDIAN GOVERNMENT."

Lord Elphinstone, Governor of Bombay, in a minute, dated May 14, 1859, wrote :† '*DIVIDE ET IMPERA* WAS THE OLD ROMAN MOTTO AND IT SHOULD BE OURS.'

Sir John Strachey, an eminent British Indian Civilian and writer on India, said : " The existence, side by side, of hostile creeds among the Indian people, is one of the strong points in our political position in India."‡

Contrast with this unimpeachable evidence the assertion of Miss Mayo that during the 'first half-century of Crown rule' 'government was operated by British officers of the Civil Service, both in the administrative and in the judicial branches. These officers, in the performance of

---

* Quoted by Basu, *op. cit.*
† See Basu, *op. cit.*
‡ Basu, *op. cit.*

their duties, made no difference between Hindu and Muhammadan, holding the general interests in an equal hand'!!

During that half-century, as to-day, *divide et impera* formed the corner-stone of British policy in India.

The only difference is that in the first phase the Muslims were to be 'suppressed,' now they are to be patted on the back and won over by favours.

We have given some citations from British records about the earlier phase. But soon after the British found that the Hindu majority, once aroused from its slumber, would mean the surest death of foreign domination. As a make-weight the foreigners were to enlist the friendship of the Muslim minority. The last two decades of the last century witnessed this swing of the pendulum. The Civilian, H. H. Thomas, as we have seen above, had concluded that the Muslims ' cannot be good subjects of any government which professes another religion: the precepts of the Koran will not suffer it.' But why not make another effort with the precepts of the Koran? So Hunter discussed anew the question whether Muslims could remain good Muslims and yet be good subjects of Queen Victoria—and he came to a different conclusion!

The *divide et impera* jack-boot is still there—only it is now on the other leg.

Some of the quotations in this chapter are disparaging to the Islam and Muslims. We have given them not because we share these opinions but because we want the world to know what kind of opinions the early British rulers of India held about the Muslims, in order that it may appraise correctly the opinions which they sometimes now propagate about the Hindus.

" In 1900," says Miss Mayo, " the wind switched to a stormy quarter." She is referring to the Minto-Morley Reform Act, which for the first time introduced communal electorates.

" India owes to Lord Minto the system of communal representation," said Sir Surendra Nath Banerjea.* Those who think that Lord Minto had merely to concede what was thrust upon him by the Muslims would do well to ponder over the words of the prominent Muslim leader, Mr. Muhammad Ali, who in his address at the Cocanada session (1923) of the National Congress said :

" Some months previously a Muslim deputation had waited at Simla on the Viceroy, Lord Minto, to place before him and his Government a statement of the Muslim demands in connection with the Minto-Morley Reforms then foreshadowed. To follow the fashion of British journalists, during the War, ' there is no harm *now* in saying ' that the deputation's was a ' command ' performance ! It was clear that

---

* A Nation in Making (Oxford University Press), p. 283.

government could no longer resist the demands of educated Indians, and, as usual, it was about to dole out to them a morsel that would keep them gagged for some years. Hitherto the Mussalmans had acted very much like the Irish prisoner in the dock who, in reply to the judge's enquiry whether he had any counsel to represent him in the trial, had frankly replied that he had certainly not engaged counsel, but that he had ' friends in the jury!' But now the Muslims' ' friends in the jury,' had themselves privately urged that the accused should engage duly qualified counsel like all others."

Lord Morley, joint author of the Minto-Morley reforms evidently took the same view. ' I won't follow you again into your Mahometan dispute,'—said he in a letter* to Minto—' I respectfully remind you once more that it was *your* early speech about their extra claims that first started the M. [Muslim] hare.'

The ' extra claims ' rested partly on the Muslim loyalty to British rule!

The dissension-creating device of the communal electorate has come in very handy to the British administrator, and it has not a little to do with the recent riots—as is clear even from Miss Mayo's account.

No wonder, therefore, that when Montagu and Chelmsford—and later on the Parliamentary

* Morley : *Recollections*, vol. II, p. 325.

Committees—sat down to shape the 1919 Reforms, ' the very idea of *India* vanished from the Bill, to be replaced by the disunited communities of Hindu, Muslim, Sikh, Mahratta, Brahmin, non-Brahmin, Indian Christian, Anglo-Indian and English.'*

It is because the Britishers are thoroughly aware of what to them are the helpful effects of communal electorate that the *Times* and other Tory and anti-Indian papers of London so vehemently defend communal representation.

The *bona fides* of the bureaucracy in India has been suspected by responsible British statesmen. Mr. Ramsay MacDonald, late and future Premier of Britain, speaks of the wide-spread suspicion :

" Sinister influences have been, and are, at work on the part of the Government; that Muhammadan leaders have been and are inspired by certain British officials, and that these officials have pulled, and continue to pull, wires at Simla and in London, and of malice afore-thought sow discord between the Muhammadans and Hindu communities, by showing to the Muhammadans special favours."†

In a recent article contributed to the *Foreign Affairs*, London, Sir John Maynard, a retired

---

*Josiah C. Wedgwood, M.P., in *The People* (Lahore), May 1, 1927.
† *Awakening of India*, p. 283.

senior Member of the Executive Council of the Punjab says:

"It is, of course, true that British authority could not have established and could not now maintain itself but for a fissiparous tendency, of which the Hindu-Muslim antagonism is one manifestation. It is also true that the mass rivalry of the two communities began under British rule. Persecuting rulers made their appearance from time to time in the pre-British era, levying tribute on unbelievers or punishing with fanatical zeal the slaying of kine. But the Hindu and Muslim masses—before they had eaten of the tree of knowledge and become religion-conscious—worshipped peacefully side by side at the same shrines."

Sir Bampfylde Fuller, late Governor of the Curzon-created Province of 'East Bengal,' in an oft-quoted address picturesquely referred to the British Government in India as having two wives, Hindu and Muslim, of which the Muslim was the 'favourite' wife.

Writing only last year in the London *Times*, Lord Olivier, Secretary of State for India in the Ramsay Macdonald Government, observed:

"No one with a close acquaintance with Indian affairs will be prepared to deny that on the whole there is a predominant bias in British officialdom in favour of the Muslim community, partly on the ground of closer sympathy but more largely as a make-weight against Hindu nationalism."

This confession from high authority again reminded people of the ' favourite wife ' figure of Sir Bampfylde.

CHAPTER XXIX

'THE SONS OF THE PROPHET'

Miss Mayo's book gives an impression that the 'Sons of the Prophet' are hostile to the political advancement of India and that they are entirely loyal to the British Government, so much so that they hate the Hindus for their political activities. Hence her general admiration of the Muslims and scrupulous avoidance of any criticism of them. She has largely quoted from the speeches of anti-Hindu Muslim leaders. The Hindu-Muslim differences are the great sheet-anchor of British policy in India. They are the foundation of British rule. But the statement that the Muslims as a community are opposed to the emancipation of India is such a gross libel on their intelligence and patriotism that we make no apology for giving long extracts from the speeches of representative Mussalmans made in the different conferences and congresses held in the month of December, 1927.

Mr. Muhammad Ali Jinnah is a leading Muslim patriot. He was appointed by government a member of the Muddiman Committee which was asked to go into and report on the working of the Reforms in 1924. He was again appointed by the government a member of the Skeen Committee to which was entrusted the task of reporting on the question of the Indianization of the officers of the Army. He thus enjoys official recognition as a Muslim leader of influence. Yet in the Assembly, as outside of it, his attitude has been as firm against foreign rule as that of any Hindu nationalist.

On page 307 of her book, Miss Mayo observes that she talked with many ' leading ' men of the North-Western Frontier Province. One wonders in what language she talked because there are very few ' leading ' men in that province who can talk in English. However, that is only a trifle. She says, " All seemed of one mind in the matter. The whole province is satisfied now and desires no change." The All-India Muslim League, however, passes a resolution every year demanding a reformed government in the Frontier Province. A resolution of the same kind was moved in the Legislative Assembly in 1926 and carried. The ' representative ' whom Miss Mayo professes to quote in her book is also said to have remarked: ' If the British withdraw...immediate hell will follow, in the first days of which the Bengali and all his tribe will be removed from the earth.' No such statement could have been made by any sensible man as the ' Bengali and his tribe ' had been in India for thousands of years before the British came. This talk concludes with the following gem: " But without the British, no Hindus will remain in India except such as we keep for slaves." Of course, it never occurred to Miss Mayo to enquire from her informant, if one such exists or existed in flesh and blood,—no names are given,—as to how the Hindus managed to live free men for ages, before the British came. What is even more pertinent is, how did they manage to conquer and rule not only the areas now covered by the North-Western Frontier Province, but also Kabul and Kandhar which are wholly Mussalman and are included in the territory of the King of Afghanistan? At the time of the annexation of the Punjab in 1849, all these provinces were under the rule of the Sikhs. Several important towns in the provinces bear Sikh names, Haripur being one of them, named after Hari Singh, who spread terror among the entire Afghan population in that part of India. We are certain the whole statement is a figment of Miss Mayo's brain or was passed on to her by a British officer to pull her leg or to prove that everybody in India except the Hindu was in love with British rule.

*

Sir Ibrahim Rahimtoolla is a Muslim leader of Bombay. He is a great business man and has been the President of the Bombay Legislative Council for a number of years. At first he was nominated by the government, but when the rule of electing the president came into operation, he was unanimously elected to that office. Presiding over the last session of the All-India Industrial and Commercial Congress, held at Madras in the last week of December, 1927, he examined Britain's claim of being a ' trustee for the people of India ' and said :

" In view of this claim, it becomes desirable to examine how the ' trustees ' have discharged their duty by India during the century and a half they have been in supreme control of this country... If Britain was a disinterested 'trustee' animated by an earnest desire to do her best for the people of India, it would redound to her great credit. If, as a result of her long trusteeship, there had been a happy and contented India, her association with this country would undoubtedly be regarded as providential. The question is whether Britain has proved a disinterested trustee, and whether the long association of this country with her in the economic sphere has made the people of India happy and contented. To anyone who has taken any interest in the public life of the country, there is only one answer, and that answer is that *Britain has throughout been primarily concerned with maintaining the Indian market for her manufactures. Her political power has been used for the promotion of this object.* The small band of merchant adventurers who came out to India, we are told, intended only to carry on a lucrative trade. The political power which they acquired was used by the East India Company for this purpose. It is true that in the year 1858 the Crown of Britain took over the direct control of the administration of India. The question is whether in the economic sphere any change took place from the assumption of responsibility by the Crown. The power which was centred in the Directors of the East India Company, was transferred to the British Parliament in theory, but in practice the Secretary of State for India in Council has merely taken the place of the Board of Directors of the East India

Company. *This Board, now called the Secretary of State in Council, still controls the fiscal policy, and the British officials who are carrying on the administration of the country are required to carry out the orders of the Board.* A glaring instance of the real state of things has been recently furnished. Sir Basil Blackett, the Finance Member of the Government of India, with his high financial reputation, was obliged to go to England personally to place before the ' Board of Directors ' his views with regard to the Reserve Bank controversy. The Government of India were unable, even by means of elaborate use of telegraphic wires, to persuade the Board to accede to the constitution of a Reserve Bank for India as suited to the requirements of the people of India. What usually happens in cases of a board of directors of joint-stock companies located in London with overseas factories, has happened in the case of a vast country like India. The overseas manager is called to headquarters to satisfy the board and the shareholders, who in this case are the British bankers, that the policy recommended is the best in the interests of the company. *Can anything show more conclusively that the claim of a ' sacred trust ' is a mere eye wash, and that British bankers and manufacturing interests are predominant in determining the policy which is pursued in this country?*"

Sir Ibrahim is as strong a critic of Britain's economic policy in India as the Bengali and his tribe. He very aptly points out—

"Agriculture, industry, transport, currency and exchange, and the fiscal policy should all form the subject of one or simultaneous enquiry having as its aim and object the economic growth of India. You will observe that, except in one solitary instance, all the commissions appointed by government have been constituted on the basis of a European chairman and a European majority. The policy suitable to be applied to the economic problems of India is not determined by Indians but by Britishers, and it is but natural that, with the training they have received, they should visualize each problem from the point of view as to how it will affect Britain."

The only exception where an Indian was appointed as chairman of an economic commission, was that of Sir Ibrahim himself. Discussing India's capacity to bear taxation, Sir Ibrahim observes :

"It has been argued that, since the advent of the British, India has grown more prosperous and that it has more money now than it possessed before. Assuming it is a fact that India is better off, so far as the amount of money is concerned, it is to be remembered that the cost of living has substantially increased, that the purchasing power of money has depreciated, that there are no appreciable accumulations of wealth as a result of savings, and that the masses are steeped in poverty. The average consumption of piece-goods, one of the necessities of life, was 18 yards per head of population before the War and it is now reduced to 10 yards per head. If the position were different the state of diminishing returns on the present scale of taxation would not have been reached. Is there then any wonder that there is a persistent demand for retrenchment in the State expenditure? I admit that efforts have been made in that direction but they have not been sufficiently far-reaching. In considering the question of retrenchment we are confronted with the stock argument that administrative machinery must be maintained at a high pitch of efficiency, the test of efficiency being determined by the authorities themselves. A great deal of harm has resulted from this slogan of efficiency. It must be obvious that a country can get only such efficiency as it can afford to pay for. The question, therefore, arises whether India's economic resources permit the maintenance of the standard of efficiency imposed upon it. No one can force for any length of time a standard of efficiency which is beyond a country's means. The essential duty of a civilized government is to develop the economic resources of the country in order to increase the tax-bearing capacity of the people and the supply of capital for its further progress."

Sir Ibrahim concludes his frank outspoken address with the following appeal to the British:

"Britishers do not come to India on a mission of philanthropy or for the benefit of their health. I will ask them to drop the pretence of holding India as a 'sacred trust' and boldly to acknowledge the fact that they are here for promoting their trade interests. I would appeal to Lord Irwin to visualize the Indian economic problem in the same spirit in which he, with Lord Lloyd, has done for Birtain in the 'Great Opportunity,' and to lay down a policy for India consistent with the views he has pressed therein. I would ask him to call together the best brains of commercial India, to state the real object of Britain's control of India's destiny, and jointly to evolve measures for the prosperity of India."

It would be thus seen that there is not much difference between the Hindu view of British rule in India and that of an enlightened educated moderate Muslim leader like Sir Ibrahim Rahimtoolla.

The attitude of the Muslims towards the Simon Commission, which has been recently appointed by the British Government to enquire into the working of the Reforms of 1919, is also a fair index of their attitude towards the British Government. Almost all the all-India Muslim leaders who count in the public life of the country have joined hands with Hindu leaders in boycotting the Simon Commission. The All-India Muslim League, which held its session in Calcutta on December 30, 1927, passed a resolution to that effect with only two dissentient votes. The session was presided over by Maulvi Muhammad Yaqub, the Deputy President of the Legislative Assembly, who made a strong speech against the policy of appointing an exclusively British commission.

A rival meeting was held at Lahore on the same dates, professing to be an annual session of the All-India Muslim League. It was presided over by Sir Muhammad Shafi of Lahore. In this meeting the resolution objecting to the boycott of the Commission was declared passed by a narrow majority, but the minority demanded a recounting of votes, which was disallowed. The leaders of the alleged minority, Messrs. Muhammad Alam, M.L.C., Abdul Qadir (President, Punjab Khilafat Committee), Afzal Haq, M.L.C., Mazhar Ali Azhar, and Muhammad Sharif, issued a statement to the Press, in which they complained of the high-handedness of the President and made out a case to prove that the votes were almost equal. But even this reactionary and loyalist President said in his address :

" The existing control of the Secretary of State in the departments dealing with internal affairs was not conducive to the best interests of the administration. He suggested the Government of India be relieved of the *irksome chains with which they were bound in this respect.* Detailing his suggestions for immediate reforms in the central and provincial machineries, he urged *inter alia* that the Foreign and Political Department in the Government be placed in charge of one member; an additional civilian member for the army be appointed to take his place within the Indian Cabinet; and membership of the Viceroy's Executive Council be increased to eight, four of whom would be Indians. He also opined that in the central Government a member or members of Transferred Subjects be selected from among the elected representatives of the people in the central legislature and should be made responsible to it for their administration. As for dyarchy in the provinces, Sir Muhammad remarked that that interesting experiment should now be abandoned and they should revert to the principle of unitary provincial government."

This ought to be quite sufficient to break Miss Mayo's heart who thought that the Muslims were good boys and wanted no changes in the existing machinery of the administration. We shall now give a few opinions regarding the much talked-about and advertised Hindu-Muslim quarrels. Speaking as President of the All-India Muslim League, Maulvi Muhammad Yaqub, the Deputy President of the Legislative Assembly said :

" Dealing with Hindu-Muslim quarrels he did not wish to apportion blame, but their Prophet had left for them guidance. The action of His Holiness in making a settlement with the Jews of Medina in a spirit of give and take should regulate their conduct. Unity would not mean absorption of the community by another. They should, like a joint Hindu family, sit at home and mutually divide property. Such an action would win for them the respect of the outside world but if they took recourse to litigation and decision by a third party the world would condemn them for casting a blot on the fair name of their ancestors. (Applause.) He opined that the Madras Congress settlement would be acceptable to 90 per cent. of the enlightened and educated Muhammadans."

The views of another Muslim leader, Sir Ali Imam, an ex-Member of the British Indian

Cabinet, on the subject of boycott, as expressed at the annual meeting of the Muslim League may be gathered from the following report:

" Sir Ali Imam (Bihar) then, on behalf of the Subjects Committee, moved the boycott resolution, which the President declared as the principal resolution of the morning. It ran: ' The All-India Muslim League emphatically declares that the Statutory Commission and the procedure as announced are unacceptable to the people of India. It, therefore, resolves that Mussalmans throughout the country should have nothing to do with the Commission at any stage or in any form.'

" Sir Ali Imam said: ' The Simon Commission had become the subject of deep concern and anxiety to the people of India. The procedure was already known and did not require a detailed exposition. It was clear, firstly, that Indians were excluded from the Commission; and secondly, the procedure reduced them to a position of witnesses. The resolution dealt with both these points

" ' Sectarian interests were next trotted out for the exclusion. He did not believe that British statesmanship and intellectuality, which stood at such a high water mark, could not find representative Indians. The British Cabinet could have taken the simple step of asking the provincial and central legislatures to elect finally from among their members or non-members, of whom five could be selected, two Hindus, one Muslim, one European non-official and one High Court Judge, but all of these must first be elected by the popular legislature. The British Government would then have been absolved from any criticism about Indian representatives.

" ' As regards the accusation of prepossessions there was no individual in the world without prepossessions. But if there were prepossessions, once the oath of office was taken by a man, be he British or Indian, he entered upon the discharge of duties as an official who had got to be dispossessed of his prepossessions. Sir Ali ventured to think that there were many Indians who would act on that Commission with a sense of responsibility and not allow their prepossessions to come in just like any Britisher. (Applause.) Has a single Indian Judge of the High Courts been found to show communal bias and not dispense impartial justice? Was membership of the Commission more honourable and onerous than High Court judgeship?

" ' Are you going to submit to this indignity?' (Voices, ' No, no'). I am a moderate of moderates; I was called a sundried bureaucrat; but my conscience finds it impossible to accept this Commission.' (Applause.) ' The opposition', said Sir Ali Imam, ' was not merely sentimental. He would not stand out on that ground alone. The real issue was: What was the relationship between India and England?' "

Continuing, Sir Ali said :

" ' *Our position is that of serfs who would gratefully pick up crumbs falling from the table of*

British statesmanship. It was another relationship to which we were lavishly treated during the War. We were called partners. We were told of a change in the angle of vision. We were told to hold together. Our blood had mixed in the battlefield of Flanders.

" ' I frankly tell you I fully believed that there was a change in the angle of vision, but have been disillusioned. We are now told we are not fit to sit at the same table. Are you going to go down? No, no.). I, for one, an ex-sundried bureaucrat, refuse to take the insult lying down'." (Loud applause.)

The very plain fact is that whatever Muslim politicians may think of their communal claims, they cannot be friends of the foreign government in India. A time was when they permitted themselves to become the ready tools of the foreign ruler. But the humiliation of that position has now dawned upon them. Disillusionment has come, as it was bound to.

That there is a change in the Hindu-Muslim relations, will be seen from the following quotations from the presidential address to the Indian National Congress which was this year presided over by a great Muslim, Dr. M. A. Ansari :

" All schools of political thought in India are agreed that the goal of our activities is a free, a self-governing India, offering equal opportunities to all, and recognizing and guaranteeing the just and legitimate rights of all sections and classes at peace within herself and friendly with the rest of the world. Indians do not claim anything more or less than that they shall occupy the same position and enjoy the same rights in their country as free people do in their own. If this can be achieved within the Empire, they have no desire to break away from it, but if the Imperial connection stands in the way of our reaching the goal we should not hesitate to sever that connection. Our motto in the words of Mahatma Gandhi, should be, ' Within the Empire if possible, without if necessary.'

" I do not minimize the difficulties in our path. They are many; but none so fomidable as the one arising out of the aggressiveness of Imperialism and the greed of High Finance, the two most fruitful sources of trouble and misery in the world to-day. Empires are carved and nations are deprived of their liberties to satisfy the imperialist ambition and to monopolize resources in raw materials to feed the factories in Europe and to secure exclusive markets for their output...

" Politicians and statesmen wax eloquent over the ' mission of civilization ' and the ' white man's burden,' but none has exposed the hollowness of these professions better than Cecil Rhodes, the great pioneer of imperialism in South Africa, when he said ' Pure philanthropy is very well in its own way, but philanthropy *plus* five per cent. is a good deal better.' Joseph Chamberlain, the High Priest of Imperialism, was more outspoken. ' The Empire,' he said, ' is commerce '—and India, he was frank enough to add, was ' by far the greatest and the most valuable of all the customers we have or ever shall have.' The history of this philanthropic burglary on the part of Europe is written in blood and suffering from Congo to Canton. The steel frame theory of government, the arrogant claims to trusteeship of dumb millions and the newly invented illusion to cloak the pre-War Concert of Europe, known as the League of Nations, are but different manifestations of the same spirit. So long as these dangerous doctrines are pursued, the sources of human misery shall endure. India holds in her hands the remedy for this universal misfortune, for she is the keystone of the arch of imperialism. Once India is free, the whole edifice will collapse. The best guarantee for the freedom of Asia and the peace of the world is a free self-governing India..."

In what respect does the attitude of the Hindu politician towards British rule differ from this, as expressed by a great Muslim leader, Dr. M. A. Ansari?

CHAPTER XXX
BRITISHERS ON BRITISH RULE

Political propaganda is the beginning and the end of Miss Mayo's book. Every chapter has something to say about the excellence of Great Britain's work in India, and of the popularity of the British officer. Every chapter contains reflections on the Indian, showering ridicule and contempt on his life and aspirations. Read the book from cover to cover and you will not find one word of praise for Indians as a class and not one of blame for the British. The book is unique in this respect. Britishers have written numerous books on India, but there is not one which is so sweepingly anti-Indian, and so sweepingly pro-British. Their books generally justify British policy in India, admitting its foibles and faults here and there. But for Miss Mayo British rule in India is perfect, and yet India is a hell of a country which is a menace to the world. The fault is wholly that of Indians and not in the least of the Government or the Britisher. She has out-heroded Herod. She has outdone the most shameless apologist of British rule. A perfect, efficient, honest, humanitarian administration; and a thoroughly corrupt, immoral, dirty, inefficient. diseased, debased, and ignorance and poverty-ridden people—that is Miss Mayo's picture of India. Never for a moment does it enter into her head that the two things are entirely incompatible.

All foreign rule, whether of a democracy or of a bureaucracy, is immoral, unnatural and demoralizing. From the very nature of things, it cannot be anything else. The English may be a highly moral people but they are after all *men*, and even the best of men cannot rule over others for the good of the latter. That is why people condemn the monarchical system of government. But if a monarchical government, though national in its character, is bad and does not always lead to happiness and prosperity of the people, the rule of a foreign democracy or autocracy (as the author of *The Lost Dominion* calls the British system in India) can hardly be better. The best of Englishmen have admitted that English rule in India is no exception to the general rule. Professor J. Seeley, in his *Expansion of England* has expressed grave doubts about the beneficent nature of English rule in India. He very significantly remarks ' subjection for a long time to a foreign yoke is one of the most potent causes of national deterioration.' In the Montagu-Chelmsford Report of 1918, the joint authors described the then Government of India as a ' benevolent despotism,' but according to Mr. Ramsay Macdonald, the Imperialist leader of the British Labour Party, in all attempts to govern a country by a ' benevolent despotism,' the governed are crushed down. ' They become subjects who obey, not citizens who act. Their literature, their art, their spiritual expression go.'*

* *Awakening of India*, p. 213.

But instead of advancing our own arguments and opinions on this matter it would be better to put together the testimony of British writers and administrators who, in any case, knew India and and the Government ruling it better than the presumptuous Miss Mayo does.*

Mr. G. Lowes Dickinson, well-known English thinker and author, discusses the question of the competency of the British people to rule India in his *Essay on the Civilization of India, China and Japan*, which he wrote after his Eastern tour. Here is his conclusion in his own words:

" Of all the Western nations the English are the least capable of appreciating the qualities of Indian civilization. Of all the races they are the least assimilable. They carry to India all their own habits and ways of life; squatting, as it were, in armed camps; spending as in exile twenty or twenty-five years; and returning, sending out new men to take their place, equally imbued with English ideals and habits, equally unassimilable. Facility of communication has only emphasized and strengthened this attitude. The Englishman sends his children home to be educated; commonly his wife will spend at least half her time at home; he himself returns every few years: his centre is not India, but England. Between him and the Indian the gulf is impassable."†

---

* For part of the material used in this chapter I am indebted to Rev. J. T. Sunderland's article entitled, 'Are the British (or any other Foreigners) Fit to Rule India?' which appeared in the *Modern Review* (Calcutta) for December, 1927.

† *Essay on the Civilization of India, China and Japan* (London : Dent & Sons), pp. 18-19.

In his *Studies of Indian Life and Sentiment*, Sir Bampfylde Fuller, the Lieutenant-Governor of Eastern Bengal who resigned when Lord Morley was the Secretary of State, says:

" Young British officials go out to India most imperfectly equipped for their responsibilities. They learn no law worth the name, little Indian history, no political economy, and gain a smattering of one Indian vernacular. In regard to other branches of the service, matters are still more unsatisfactory. Young men, who are to be police officers, are sent out with no training whatever, though for the proper discharge of their duties an intimate acquaintance with Indian life and ideas is essential. They land in India in absolute ignorance of the language. So also with forest officers, medical officers, engineers, and (still more surprising) educational officers... It is hardly too much to say that this is an insult to the intelligence of the country."

Mr. H. M. Hyndman, the well-known British Socialist who always took a keen interest in Indian affairs, wrote:

" The British who come to India to rule it have been brought up and educated in accordance with methods as remote from, and as irreconcilable with, Asiatic ideas as it is possible for them to be. In their work and in their pleasure they keep as aloof as possible from the people they govern. The head of the government, who himself is brought out fresh from Europe and entirely ignorant of India, does not remain in office more than five years (thus leaving as soon as he begins to get a little knowledge). His subordinates return ' home ' frequently for their holidays, and go back to England permanently, to live on a considerable pension paid by India after their term of service is completed. The longer this reign of well-meaning but unsympathetic carpet-baggers continues, the less intimate do their general relations with the Indian people become. The colour and race prejudices which were only slight at the beginning of English dominance, now become stronger and stronger every year. In India itself, men of ancient lineage, beside which the descent of the oldest European aristocracy is a mushroom growth, are considered in the leading cities, as well as on the railways, unfit to associate on equal terms with the young white bureaucrats just arrived in the country."*

Mr. Hyndman quotes a prominent British official in India as saying :

" It is sadly true that the Englishmen in India live totally estranged from the people. This estrangement is partly unavoidable, being the result of national customs, language and caste, and largely it is contempt, growing out of ignorance. This tendency to aloofness is increasing."

Speaking of the ignorance of India seen in many government officials, Mr. Ramsay Macdonald says :

*"*The Truth About India,*"* New York, Series I, p. 10.

"I have met men in the Indian Civil Service who had been there for a score of years. They knew few Indians, they had rarely discussed public affairs with them, they could not answer accurately some of the most elementary questions about Indian life, their opinions on current affairs were obviously the parrot repetitions of the club talk or newspaper statements. In fact, they were as separate from India as I am at home in London, and took their opinions of India in an even more second-hand way than I had taken mine before I ever set foot on Indian soil."*

Mr. Macdonald quotes Lord Curzon as saying that in former days the assumption of everybody who went to India to take part in the government was that he must learn what languages were necessary to enable him to speak with the people:

"But the arrogance of these modern days assumes that that is quite unnecessary. The number of officers now who speak the vernaculars with any facility is much smaller than fifty or even twenty-five years ago, and the number devoting themselves to anything like a serious study of the literature of the country is diminishing year by year."†

In *The Bookman* of February, 1926, an Englishman of letters (Mr. Aldous Huxley) gives the following description of the arrogance and egotism of his countrymen who are ruling India:

* *Awakening of India*, p. 261.
† *The Awakening of India*, p. 236.

"A young man goes out from a London suburb to take up a clerkship in the Indian Civil Service. He finds himself a member of a small ruling community; he has slavish servants to order about, dark-skinned subordinates to whom it is right and proper to be rude. Three hundred and twenty million Indians surround him; he feels incomparably superior to them all, from the coolie to the Maharaja, from the untouchable to the thoroughbred Brahman, from the illiterate peasant to the holders of half a dozen degrees from European universities. He may be ill-bred, stupid, poorly educated; no matter. His skin is white. Superiority in India is a question of epidermis."

Mr. George Lansbury, late Editor of the London *Daily Herald,* said in a speech in Essex Hall, December 11, 1920 :

"There are more than three hundred million people in India; there are forty million of us English in the British Isles. We claim to know what is good for those people better than they do themselves. Was there ever impudence more colossal? Because our skin happens to be white we claim more brains than those whose skin has been browned by the sun. Whenever I look at Indians I feel ashamed of myself. How can I know more about India than they do?"

The Rt. Hon. Edwin S. Montagu, Secretary of State for India, said in a speech in the House of Commons in July, 1917 :

"The Government of India is too wooden, too iron, too inelastic, too antediluvian, to be of any use for modern purposes. The Indian Government is indefensible."

On the whole, the people of India regard the government under which they are compelled to live to-day as little, if any, better than that which was condemned so severely by Mr. Montagu in 1917.

Sir Louis Mallet, when Under-Secretary of State for India, was reported as saying:

"Nothing but the fact that the present system of government in India is almost secure from all independent and intelligent criticism has enabled it so long to survive."

Even the Viceroys, as a rule, know no Indian language when they come to India, and seldom during their stay do they acquire anything more than the merest smattering of any. Such contact with the people as they have is mostly second-hand, through English subordinates or through Indians who speak English.

Said John Bright in a speech in Parliament:

"The Governor-General of India (the Viceroy) goes out knowing little or nothing of India. I know exactly what he does when he is appointed. He shuts himself up to study the first volumes of Mr. Mill's *History of India*, and reads through this laborious work without nearly so much effect in making him a good Governor-General as a man might ignorantly suppose. He goes to India, a land of twenty nations, speaking twenty languages. He knows nothing of these nations, and he has not a glimmer of the grammar and pronunciation or meaning of these languages... He knows nothing of the country or the people. He is surrounded by an official circle, he breathes an official air, and everything is dim and dark beyond it. You lay duties upon him which are utterly beyond the mental and bodily strength of any man who ever existed, and which he therefore cannot perform... He has a power omnipotent to crush everything that is good. If he so wishes, he can overbear and overrule whatever is proposed for the welfare of India, while as to doing anything that is good, I could show that with regard to the vast countries over which he rules, he is really almost powerless to effect anything that those countries require... I do not know at this moment, and never have known, a man competent to govern India; and if any man says he is competent, he sets himself up as of much higher value than those who are acquainted with him are likely to set him."

This from John Bright, a man as careful in his speech and as just in his judgments as England ever knew.

Dr. Sunderland illustrates Bright's conclusion by quoting from a letter which Col. Josiah C. Wedgwood, M.P., wrote to me (and this was printed in my Lahore weekly, *The People*), about Lord Irwin when he was appointed Viceroy of India. Says Col. Wedgwood:

" He will be very uncomfortable in India—an obvious martyr to duty. It is a grave drawback to him that he knows nothing whatever of India, and is therefore all the more helpless in the hands of the bureaucratic experts... I do not remember him ever even being present at an Indian debate."*

Think of a man who can be thus described by a distinguished Member of Parliament being appointed Viceroy to govern the vast Indian nation.

Premier Asquith declared in 1909 that there were great numbers of Indians who were well-qualified to fill high official positions in India. He also called attention to the low and inadequate qualifications that were thought sufficient to fit Englishmen for those positions; and he affirmed that if high places were given to Indians half as unfit as were many Englishmen who occupy them, it would be regarded as a public scandal.†

In his recent book, *Modern India: its Problems and their Solution*‡ (p. 161), Dr. V. H. Rutherford examines the character and results of British efficiency, and pronounces it ' one of the chief causes of India's poverty.' He declares that the British Government in India is efficient only on behalf of *British* interests, only in carrying on the government and managing the affairs of the

---

* *The People*, December 25, 1925.

† See *India* (London weekly), April 9, 1909, p. 209. Quoted by Sunderland, *op. cit.*

‡ Labour Publishing Co., 1926 .

country for the benefit of Great Britain. As regards promoting the welfare of India and the Indian people, he declares it to be strikingly and shamefully inefficient; in proof of which he cites the Government's :

" Neglect of education of the masses; neglect of sanitation and medical services in the villages; neglect to keep order; neglect of housing of the poor; neglect to protect the peasants from the money-lenders; neglect to provide agricultural banks; comparative neglect to improve and develop agriculture; neglect to foster Indian industries; neglect to prevent British profiteers from capturing the tramways, electric lighting and other public services; and neglect to prevent the manipulation of Indian currency in the interests of London."

In the light of these facts can we wonder at the words of Dr. Rutherford ?—

" British rule, as it is carried on in India, is the lowest and most immoral system of government in the world—the exploitation of one nation by another."*

Mr. Edward Thompson in his book, *The Other Side of the Medal*,† says :

" We (British) would repudiate the suggestion that our Indian Empire is a rule of masters over slaves. Yet we judge as slave-drivers would, and

* *Modern India*, p. 77.
† Page 118.

we assess the virtues of our (Indian) fellow-citizens as a hunter assesses the virtues of dogs."

Some years ago, at the time of the Congo atrocities, an Irish author wrote :*

" The English people love liberty for themselves. They hate all acts of injustice, except those which they themselves commit. They are such liberty-loving people that they interfere in the Congo and cry, ' Shame!' to the Belgians. But they forget that *their heels are on the neck of India.*"

In his book, *Secret History of the English Occupation of Egypt*, Mr. Wilfrid Scawen Blunt gives some strong and important testimony regarding British rule in India as seen close at hand and under the most favourable light. He was an intimate personal friend of Lord Lytton, who at that time was the Viceroy of India. Mr. Blunt came to India to make a study of the condition of things here. He belonged to the Conservative party in British politics, and expected to find the British conduct of affairs in India worthy of the warmest approval. Moreover, he was taken charge of by the Viceroy and the highest officials, and was shown everything from their standpoint. What was the result? In spite of his prejudices in favour of the British—his own countrymen—and in spite of the pains taken to insure that he should see India as fully as possible from the English side, he was soon disillusioned. He found that British rule in India,

* See Sunderland, *op. cit.*

instead of being a blessing, was working India's ruin. Of the British imperial system in general he writes :*

" It is one of the evils of the English Imperial system that it cannot meddle anywhere among free peoples, even with quite innocent intentions, without in the end doing evil. There are too many selfish interests always at work not to turn the best beginnings into ill endings."

Of India he writes :

" I am disappointed with India, which seems just as ill-governed as the rest of Asia, only with good intentions instead of bad ones or none at all. There is just the same heavy taxation, government by foreign officials, and waste of money, that one sees in Turkey. The result is the same, and I don't see much difference between making the starving Hindus pay for a cathedral at Calcutta and taxing Bulgarians for a palace on the Bosphorus... In India the 'natives,' as they call them, are a race of slaves, frightened, unhappy, terribly thin. Though myself a good Conservative and a member of the London Carlton Club, I own to being shocked at the bondage in which they are held, and my faith in British institutions and the blessings of English rule has received a severe blow. I have been studying the mysteries of Indian finance under the 'best masters,' government secretaries, commissioners, and the rest, and have come to the conclusion

* Page 47.

that, if we go on developing the country at the present rate, the inhabitants will have sooner or later, to resort to cannibalism, for there will be nothing but each other left to eat."

Mr. C. F. Andrews in his recent book, *India's Claim for Independence*, says :

" We see in the Italy and Austria of last century a signal instance of the fallacy of imperialism—of foreign rule. The Austrian Empire, with its Italian appendage—with Italy held in subjection by force—was a monstrosity. It could produce only hate, ever deepening hate, between two nations which ought to have been friends. The British Empire to-day with its Indian appendage—with India held in subjection by force—is also a monstrosity. It can produce only bitterness, ever-increasing bitterness, and estrangement, between India and England, two peoples that ought to be friends."

Concludes Dr. Sunderland :

" There is not a myth on the earth more baseless or more cruel than the claim put forth to the world that England is ruling great, distant India well, or that she can by any possibility rule it well, or without constant blunders and injustices of the most serious and tragic nature."

But Miss Mayo knows India much better than Macaulay or Fuller did, or than Macdonald, or Rutherford or Dickinson or Sunderland do. Evidently she is the most competent and the most truthful observer of Indian conditions that the world has produced in the last two centuries! Vanity, thy name is Katherine Mayo!

CHAPTER XXXI

THE STORY OF THE REFORMS

Miss Mayo devotes one whole chapter to the reforms introduced in the Indian system of Government by the India Government Parliamentary Statute of 1919. She is evidently of opinion that it was a mistake to have introduced these so-called reforms, and that the Indian system of government prior to 1919 was perfect and needed no changes.

That seems to be her general thesis, but reading the chapter through, it is difficult to say what she exactly means. It is full of inconsistent and unintelligible statements. The only thing consistent and intelligible is her unqualified hatred of the Indian Nationalist and her desire to paint him as black, absurd, untruthful, ignorant and petulant as she can. In the opening sentence we are told, ' the roots of the form of government *now gradually working out in British India ramify into past centuries and are visible through continuous growth* '—[italics are ours]. A little later in the same chapter ' the scheme in its shape of to-day,' is criticized as lacking the ' stability of the slow-growing oak.' It is condemned as ' a hothouse exotic, weedy, a stranger in its soil, forced forward beyond its strength by the heat of a generous and hasty emotion.'*

* Page 265.

THE STORY OF THE REFORMS 441

Then on page 268 'without presuming to offer a criticism of the Reforms Act,' she ventures the criticism that the 'chief obstacle lies deeper in the roots of things than any enmity can reach. The whole structure of the reforms is planned to rest on the foundation of a general electorate... And the difficulty is that, while the structure hangs waiting in mid-air, the foundation designed to sustain it yet lingers in the blue-print stage— does not in fact exist.'

The whole chapter is a jumble of rambling statements and ideas, which have no sequence, no relation to one another, no clarity of thought, except that there is to be found therein the unqualified praise of the British official and a merciless condemnation of the Hindu Nationalist. Stories and descriptions are interposed which are only the products of imagination, and from them are made deductions, sweeping and absurd on their very face. Dialogues with anonymous persons cannot be verified. But most of those reported by Miss Mayo expects a good deal of gullibility in the reader. Again and again she tells the reader that the Indian Nationalist does not mean what he says. One day, she tells us on page 267, she took the matter up with a notable anti-British member of the Legislative Assembly, and asked him if his fellow-legislators, who 'make terrible accusations against the good faith of Government', really meant what they said. 'How could they?' he replied. 'Not a man in the House believes anything of the sort.' But if the members of the Assembly were really such hardened hypocrites they would surely not so frankly own up before a foreign tourist unknown or almost unknown to them. Again, on page 266 is a statement which none but those utterly devoid of a sense of proportion could make :

" A village headman [nine to ten he is illiterate] knows and feels infinitely more than do these elected ' representatives ' as to the duties and responsibilities of government."!!

In the circumstances, it is best to leave Miss Mayo alone and to give as briefly as possible a connected story of the Reforms—their genesis, and their working. The space at our disposal here forbids our tracing the history of British rule in India, the different evolutionary stages through which it has passed, eventually culminating in the Reforms of 1919. That story has been told by me in my books, *Young India* and *The Political Future of India*, both originally published in the United States of America, the former in 1916 and the latter in 1919.*

Before the Great War started in 1914, parts of India were honeycombed with revolutionary societies. India as a whole was very much agitated over her political status. During the War the pronouncements of the statesmen of the allied countries and of President Wilson as to the aims and objects of the War, raised hopes in the minds of the Indian Nationalists of justice being done to India in case the Allies came out

---

* Both published by B. W. Huebsch, New York. *Young India* has recently been reprinted by the Servants of the People Society, Lahore.

victorious. In 1916 when the War was at its worst fury, the Indian National Congress and the All-India Muslim League prepared a joint scheme of such political reforms as they wanted to be immediately introduced into their country. Along with this, they gave their unstinted support to the British Government in its war projects. Mahatma Gandhi went about recruiting soldiers for the British Army and organizing ambulance corps, etc. India was literally 'bled white' in order to win the War. But for Indian support in men and money and arms and supplies, Britain would have terribly suffered in prestige, and the Allies might have been unable to check the German advance to Paris.

"With regard to her troops," the admission will be found in the official publication, *India's Contribution to the Great War*, " the Indian Corps reached France in the nick of time and helped to stem the great German thrust towards Ypres and the Channel Ports during the autumn of 1914. These were the only trained reinforcements immediately available in any part of the British Empire and right worthily they played their part.

" In Egypt and Palestine, in Mesopotamia, Persia, East and West Africa and in subsidiary theatres they shared with their British and Dominion comrades the attainment of final victory."*

In April 1916 came the disaster in Lower Mesopotamia, the responsibility for which was

* Page 221.

thrown on the Government of India. After a careful and rapid enquiry the Commission appointed to investigate into it pronounced that the 'Mespot muddle' was due to the inefficiency of the Government of India. When a debate was raised in the House of Commons on this report, Mr. S. E. Montagu, who was then the Minister of Munitions, made a trenchant speech in the course of which he declared :

" The Government of India is too wooden, too iron, too inelastic, too antediluvian, to be of any use for the modern purposes we have in view. I do not believe that anybody could ever support the Government of India from the point of view of modern requirements. But it would do. Nothing serious had happened since the Indian Mutiny, the public was not interested in Indian affairs, and it required a crisis to direct attention to the fact that the Indian Government is an indefensible system of government."

Further on he added :

" I tell this House that the statutory organization of the India Office produces an apotheosis of circumlocution and red tape beyond the dreams of any ordinary citizen."

The red tape had been there all the time, but, as Disraeli pointed out long ago, it requires a disaster to attract the attention of England.

In the speech from which we have quoted above Mr. Montagu went on to say :

" But whatever be the object of your rule in India, the universal demand of those Indians whom I have met and corresponded with is that you should state it. Having stated it, you should give some instalment to show that you are in real earnest, some beginning of the new plan which you intend to pursue : that gives you the opportunity of giving greater representative institutions in some form or other to the people of India...

" But I am positive of this, that your great claim to continue the illogical system of government by which we have governed India in the past is that it was efficient. It has been proved to be not sufficient. It has been proved to be not sufficiently elastic to express the will of the Indian people; to make them into a warring nation as they wanted to be. The history of this war shows that you can rely upon the loyalty of the Indian people to the British Empire—if you ever before doubted it. If you want to use that loyalty, you must take advantage of that love of country which is a religion in India, and you must give them that bigger opportunity of controlling their own destinies, not merely by Councils which cannot act, but by control...of the Executive itself. Then in your next war—if we ever have war—in your next crisis, through times of peace, you will have a contented India, an India equipped to help. Believe me, Mr. Speaker, it is not a question of expediency, it is not a question of desirability. Unless you are prepared to remodel in the light of modern experience this century-old and cumbrous machine, then, I believe, I verily believe, that you will lose your right to control the destinies of the Indian Empire."

In the meantime the war was taking a grave turn. Russia was on the verge of collapse. It was apparent that unless India's man power and material power was tapped, the Allies might lose the war. Mr. Lloyd George decided what to do. He put Mr. Montagu in charge of the India office and authorized him to make the famous announcement of August 20, 1917, which ran thus:

" The policy of His Majesty's Government with which the Government of India are in complete accord, is that of the increasing association of Indians in every branch of the administration and the gradual development of self-governing institutions with a view to the progressive realization of responsible government in India as an integral part of the British Empire. They have decided that substantial steps in this direction should be taken as soon as possible, and that it is of the highest importance, as a preliminary to considering what these steps should be, that there should be a free and informal exchange of opinion between those in authority at home and in India. His Majesty's Government have accordingly decided, with His Majesty's approval that I should accept the Viceroy's invitation to proceed to India to discuss these matters with the Viceroy and the Government of India, to consider with the Viceroy the views of local Governments, and to receive with him the suggestions of representative bodies and others.

"I would add that progress in this policy can only be achieved by successive stages. The British Government and the Government of India, on whom the responsibility lies for the welfare and advancement of the Indian people, must be judges of the time and measure of each advance, and they must be guided by the co-operation received from those upon whom new opportunities of service will thus be conferred, and by the extent to which it is found that confidence can be reposed in their sense of responsibility."

Whatever may have been inside the crooked mind of the British Premier, it is evident that the announcement was not the result of 'a hasty and generous emotion.' It was a calculated step considered necessary and expedient in the interests of England and the Empire. If there was 'hasty generosity' in the transaction anywhere it was on the Indian side. The Indian leaders took the promises of British statesmen at face value, little knowing that the 'art of lying' had not yet decayed, and little anticipating that one day Anglophils of the Katherine Mayo type would jeer at their 'outburst of loyalty.' Indians did not take to the policy of the Irish Nationalists, whose motto had always been 'England's difficulty is Ireland's opportunity.' They stood by England in her hour of need. Britain in inaugurating the Reforms was only yielding an inch lest an ell be wrested, and her statesmen were giving a good appearance to things because they needed Indian co-operation so badly. As far as Mr. Montagu was concerned, he was in all probability sincere.

The announcement of 1917 had its effect in India. The politically-minded Indians were not satisfied with its language and reservations and they made no secret of their dissatisfaction, but they decided to accept it as a proof of England's desire to do justice to their claims for being masters of their own house, just as the Canadians were in Canada, the Australians in Australia, and the South-Africans in South Africa.

To translate his promise into action, Mr. Montagu visited India, and, jointly with the then Viceroy, Lord Chelmsford, wrote the report which is associated with their joint names. Commenting on this announcement and report, in my book, *The Political Future of India*, in the early part of 1919 I observed :*

" It is obvious that the content of the second sentence of paragraph two in the above announcement is in fundamental opposition to the right of every nation to self-determination, a principle now admitted to be of general application (including, according to the British Premier, even the black races inhabiting the colonies that were occupied by Germany before the War, within its purview). The people of India are not on a level with these races. Even if it be assumed that they are not yet in a position to exercise that right fully and properly, it is neither right nor just to assume that they shall never be in that position even hereafter. Besides the qualifications implied in that sentence are quite needless and

---

* Page 9, *et. seq.*

superfluous. As long as India remains 'an integral part of the British Empire' she cannot draft a constitution which does not meet with the approval of the British Parliament and the British Sovereign. It is to be regretted that the British statesmen could not rise equal to the spirit of the times and make an announcement free from that spirit of autocratic bluster and racial swagger which was entirely out of place at a time when they were making impassioned appeals to Indian manhood to share the burdens of Empire by contributing ungrudgingly in men and money for its defence. This attitude is somewhat inconsistent with the statements in paragraph 179 of the Montagu-Chelmsford Report, wherein, after referring to the natural evolution of 'the desire for self-determination,' the distinguished authors of the Report concede that 'the demand that now meets us from the educated classes of India is no more than the right and natural outcome of the work of a hundred years.'

"In spite of this uncalled for reservation in the announcement, it is perfectly true that 'the announcement marks the end of one epoch and the beginning of a new one.' What, however, makes the announcement 'momentous,' is not the language used, as even more high-sounding phrases have been used before by eminent British statesmen of the position of Warren Hastings, Macaulay, Munro, Metcalfe and others, but the fact that the statement has been made by the Secretary of State for India, as representing the Crown and the Cabinet, who, in their turn, are the constitutional representatives of the people of Great Britain and Ireland."

Further on, I emphasized :

" What differentiates this announcement from the statutory declarations of the Act of 1833 and the Royal Proclamation of 1858 is not the language used but the step or steps taken to ascertain Indian opinion, to understand and interpret it in accordance with the spirit of the times and the frankness and fairness with which the whole problem is stated in the joint report of the two statesmen, who are the present official heads of the Government of India. Nor can it be denied that the announcement and the report have received the cordial appreciation of the Indian leaders."

We have made these lengthy excerpts to give the reader an adequate idea as to how we, Indian Nationalists, received the announcement *at the time it was made.*

Even the Anglo-Indian official world put a liberal interpretation on the action of the Secretary of State. One of their chief and trusted spokesmen, Sir Harcourt Butler, the then Lieutenant-Governor of the United Provinces of Agra and Oudh, emphasized the need for a new order of things. ' Nothing will ever be the same,' philosophized Sir Harcourt, and went on to orate :

" This much is certain, that we shall have to shake off all our old ideals and begin afresh...we have crossed the watershed and are looking down on new plains. The old oracles are dumb. The old shibboleths are no more heard. Ideals, constitutions, rooted ideas are being shovelled away without argument or comment or memorial..."

Like Mr. Montagu he realized the too wooden, too inelastic, too antediluvian character of the old machine. In his own words :

" Our administrative machine belongs to another age. It is top-heavy. Its movements are cumbrous, slow, deliberate. It rejoices in delay. It grew up when time was not the object, when no one wanted change, when financial economy was the ruling passion of Governments, imperial and provincial. Now there are the stirrings of young national life, and economic springtime, a calling for despatch, quick response, bold experiment."

Speaking of red tape, Sir Harcourt recalled the remarks of an ecclesiast who had told him ' that Rome had, by centuries of experience, reduced delay to a science; he used to think her mistress of postponement and procrastination, but the Government of India beat Rome every time.'

On this utterance I made the following comment,* which was typical of the mood then prevailing :

" Coming, as it does, from a member of the Anglo-Indian bureaucracy, this statement means much more to the Indian people than even the

* *Ibid.*, pp. 13-14.

words of the British Premier. If this statement is not a mere camouflage, but represents a genuine change of heart on the part of the British bureaucracy in India, then it is all the more inexplicable to us why the new scheme of the Secretary of State for India and the Viceroy should breathe so much distrust of the educated classes of India. Anyway, we have nothing but praise for the spirit of frankness and fairness which generally characterizes the report. However we might disagree with the conclusions arrived at, it is but right to acknowledge that the analysis of the problem and its constituting elements is quite masterly, and the attempt to find a solution which will meet the needs of the situation, as understood by them, absolutely sincere and genuine. This fact makes it all the more necessary that Indian Nationalists of all classes and all shades of opinion should give their best thought to the consideration of the problem in a spirit of construction and co-operation as distinguished from mere fault-finding."

All this happened in the early part of 1919, before the Rowlatt Bills had become law, and before Mr. Gandhi had launched his passive resistance movement. Even then there was a section of the bureaucracy gnashing its teeth and swearing at Montagu, and fully determined to undo even the little the Secretary of State was doing. This class was represented by Sir Michael O'Dwyer and General Dyer. The former manufactured a rebellion, and the latter proceeded to place the Indians where, according to his idea, they belonged. The massacre of Amritsar and the Martial Law atrocities were the outcome of that mentality.

But even then the Congress held at Amritsar (December, 1919), although holding that the Reforms were inadequate, unsatisfactory and disappointing, resolved to work them for what they were worth. They had, however, counted without their hosts. In a moment of 'hasty and generous emotion' they had believed that the announcement of August, 1917, was honest and sincere, and that the British meant to stand by their word. They deliberately chose to ignore the lessons of British dealings with the Colonies and Ireland, and in their attitude towards Great Britain they credulously gave the first place to hope and trust. They forgot that gratitude was a word unknown in the dictionary of imperialism, and that vested interests were yet strong enough to defeat them at every step. The hour of need was now over. New codes for new times. The War had been won, the Empire was safe, so the British were once more free to manipulate things in such a way as to nullify even the meagre reform that Montagu had been permitted to introduce. They wanted to continue the policy of exploitation. The British Government in India was more or less an impersonal machine, wooden as Montagu said, and soulless, exacting and cruel, and it was only waiting for an opportunity to renew the old policy for which Sir George Chesney pleaded in his book, *India under Experiment*.*
The closing words of that book reveal the real

---

* Published by John Murray, London, 1919.

Anglo-Indian mind, and are a crushing reply to
that part of Miss Mayo's book wherein she tries to
prove that Britain derives no material benefits
from her rule in India.

To Sir George 'there is a certain sense of
futility' in all talk of constitutional reform, all
'suggestions of improvement or palliatives', as he
calls it, for the 'main question', in his words,
is, 'Whose is to be the rule?' Sir George puts
Britain's foreign policy ever since the days of
Napoleon in the witness-box and exclaims:

"A singular situation it would be if the
British power in India, which has outridden so
many emergencies, which before it was securely
established found itself confronted with the ambitions of Bonaparte, which within present memories
was cheerfully bracing itself to meet the
apparently inevitable onset of the Muscovite—if
this power should be discovered to have been
surrendered away in a fit of national absent-
mindedness."

As a last word Sir George entreats the British
public 'to dismiss for once confused politico-
moral ideas as to natural rights, self determination, and what not, and to look at the matter from
the point of view of *its own* interests.' This does
not sound as philanthropic as Miss Mayo would
make out British rule to be. The question of
philanthropic motives is discussed by Sir George
in such unambiguous and outspoken a manner
that no apology is needed for the lengthy quotation
from his book that follows:

"India cannot serve two masters, and if Britain stands aside she will have to cleave to the men on the spot. She will not like it, but the election will not be hers, it will have been forced upon her by the people of England, who therefore should surely weigh well the consequences of the innocent-looking step that they are invited to take. That they are indifferent to the subject can scarcely be believed, seeing that the preservation of India against the Russian menace was the pivoting point of our foreign policy from the middle of the nineteenth century to its close, seeing even at the present moment what costly and distracting efforts are imposed upon Britain's sorely taxed energies by the necessity of preserving her dominion in Asia. What other meaning has the campaign in Mesopotamia except that of a precaution to keep the enemy's influence at a safe distance from India? It would seem, therefore, that after all we are very much of the same conviction as those before us who judged that NO SACRIFICE OR EXERTION OR PERSONAL HAZARD WAS TOO GREAT IF THEY HELPED THEIR COUNTRY TO WIN THIS GREAT PRIZE AND TO HOLD IT AGAINST THE ENVY OF THE WORLD. But if in these last days the democratic mind has become insensible to the appeal of national prestige, THE MERELY MATERIAL CONSEQUENCES THAT WOULD FOLLOW TO EVERY HOUSEHOLD IN THE COUNTRY FROM ALLOWING INDIA TO SLIP OUT OF OUR KEEPING SHOULD BE WELL APPRECIATED. They cannot, of course, be tabled out in advance, but their general effect could not fail to be immense.

"CONSIDERING THE ARRAY OF VESTED INTERESTS INVOLVED, THE CAPITAL SUNK, THE NUMBERS DEPENDENT ON ITS RETURNS, THE IMPORTANCE OF INDIAN PRODUCTS TO BRITISH INDUSTRY, THE NUMBERS OF BRITISH EMPLOYED IN THE COUNTRY EITHER OFFICIALLY OR COMMERCIALLY, THE ARMY OF PERSONS ON THIS SIDE—MERCHANTS, SHIPPERS, DISTRIBUTORS, PRODUCERS, AND CONSUMERS—WHOSE PROSPERITY AND CONVENIENCE ARE MORE OR LESS BOUND UP WITH THE INDIAN CONNECTION, IS IT NOT PLAIN THAT THE EFFECT UPON THEM, AND BY CONSEQUENCE UPON THE WHOLE PEOPLE OF THIS COUNTRY, OF ANY RUPTURE OF THE TIE WOULD AMOUNT TO A SOCIAL DISASTER OF THE FIRST MAGNITUDE? THE INSTALMENT OF A HINDU GOVERNMENT IN INDIA, WHETHER IT LED UP TO INTERNAL CHAOS OR TO INTERNAL PASSIVITY WITH EXCLUSIVENESS AGAINST THE OUTER WORLD, WOULD IN FACT BE THE BEGINNING OF A REVOLUTION IN THE MATERIAL CONDITION OF THE ENGLISH PEOPLE." [Capitals are ours.]

Some time ago, Sir William Joynson-Hicks, Home Minister in the Baldwin Government, dismissed 'philanthrophic' motives in quite as outspoken a language as this. Here is the relevant passage from his speech :

" We did not conquer India for the benefit of the Indians. I know it is said in missionary meetings that we conquered India to raise the level of the Indians. That is cant. We conquered India as the outlet for the goods of Great Britain. We conquered India by the sword and by the sword we should hold it... I AM NOT SUCH A HYPOCRITE AS TO SAY WE HOLD INDIA FOR THE INDIANS. WE HOLD IT AS THE FINEST OUTLET FOR BRITISH GOODS in general, and for the Lancashire cotton goods in particular."

We maintain, and most of the Nationalists are of the same opinion, that besides the inherent defects in the Reforms, they have not been worked in the spirit in which they were inaugurated. From the very outset, the British Government in England and in India have been trying to wriggle out of the dilemma in which they were placed by the Reforms. Even the letter of the law has not been always observed. The whole history of the working of the Reformed Governments, whether in the provinces or in the national sphere, betrays an anxiety to prove (*a*) that it was a mistake to have given the Reforms, (*b*) that the Reforms have failed, (*c*) that there was not only no case for an advance, but that there were reasons for taking back what had been conceded. In any event, it is clear that the high hopes raised by the Reforms in the national mind, and even in the mind of genuine internationalists interested in the peace and progress of the world, have not been realized.

When the Reforms were being shaped I was in the United States. The impression left upon me by the Montagu-Chelmsford Report was reflected in the last book I published in the United States under the title, *The Political Future of India*. In that treatise I discussed the bearing of the proposed reforms on the polity of India in all its aspects. I have also stated how in spite of the Punjab wrongs the Indian National Congress held at Amritsar reconciled itself to the Reforms. The Amritsar resolution was a compromise between those who wanted to boycott the Reforms because they were ' unsatisfactory, inadequate and disappointing', and those who wanted to work them notwithstanding their defects. The resolution was a personal triumph of Mahatma Gandhi. The late Lokamanya Tilak and the late Mr. C. R. Das had favoured the idea of rejecting the Reforms and fought for their view rather strenuously.

1920 changed the situation almost completely. The Hunter Committee's report on the Punjab atrocities, and the parliamentary debate and the action of the Government thereon gave us the first indication of the change that had already begun in the mentality of the British rulers of India. In September 1920 the Congress at its special session held in Calcutta passed by a large majority the famous Non-co-operation resolution by which it resolved to boycott the Councils and the Reforms. This again was a personal triumph for Mahatma Gandhi. Lokamanya Tilak was dead, but before he breathed his last he was said to have given an indication of his mind to the effect that he was opposed to the boycott of the Councils. Mr. C. R. Das, Babu Bepin Chandra Pal, and all those who had till then been prominent in the political world of India were opposed to it. Pandit Motilal Nehru was with the Mahatma. The resolution reflected the mass mind rather than the ' balanced ' political mind.

The last elections under the Reforms took place in November 1920. No Congressman sought election. The Liberals, till then known as Moderates, went into the Assembly and the Councils in large numbers. They were till then the favourites of British statesmen. Lord Morley had left a legacy in their favour. The Government still believed in them, and many of their leaders were appointed as Ministers and Executive Councillors in the various provincial Governments. One of them was even appointed as the Law Member of the Government of India. Thus the Reforms were inaugurated in 1921 in an atmosphere of hope on the part of the Moderate politicians of India, and of suspicion on the part of the Congress Nationalists. Non-co-operation was at its height in 1921. Towards the end of 1921 it culminated in the imprisonment of about 40,000 Nationalists, including most of the topmost leaders of Northern India. Mahatma Gandhi himself was put out of the way in March 1922. The Liberal leaders, Ministers and Executive Councillors, were still with the Government, and generally speaking supported the latter in all the measures which they adopted to repress and suppress the Non-co-operation movement. This is not the place to discuss the why and wherefore of the Non-co-operation movement and what it did. But there is no denying the fact that it created an unprecedented political awakening in the country, accompanied by an unprecedented bitterness against, and mis-trust of, the British. If the Liberals had joined the Non-co-operation movement the Government would surely have collapsed and capitulated. But throughout the struggle they backed the Government.

The first Reformed Administration lasted for three years, 1920-23, and whatever success it achieved, was mainly due to the wholehearted co-operation of the Liberals. In the general elections of 1923, Liberals were defeated by Congressmen. In their own words it was more a rout than a defeat. But curiously enough, it was just then that the Government also began to desert them and to replace them with men who had till this period little or no part in the political life of the country and who were known for their reactionary views.

This started the downward march of the Reforms. The Non-co-operation movement had by this time weakened. The Hindu-Muslim tension, manufactured and nurtured by the political moves of the Government and the deliberate efforts of officials and interested people, was increasing. The bureaucracy was recovering its lost or dwindled influence. It was just at this juncture that the authorities contracted an unholy liaison with the reactionary forces, and began to utilize them as ready and willing tools for a policy of backsliding. After that the Reforms became synonymous with reaction, and decisions were taken that not only reduced the Reforms to a farce but gave a clear indication of the future intentions of British statesmen with regard to the demand of Indians for Home Rule. Considerations of space forbid our giving a detailed account of these reactionary measures. We can only refer to them by merely stating them in general terms.

The first in importance and time may be mentioned the decision of the Government on the report of the Lee Commission on Public Services. This decision has involved the country in an additional annual expenditure of one crore of rupees. But that is not the worst of it. It has strengthened the ' steel frame ' of British rule in India. Mr. Lloyd George was still at the head of the government in Great Britain when this happened and his speech was the most pronounced evidence of what was in the mind of the British people. He has a reputation for brazen-faced opportunism—which is sometimes only a polite word for hypocrisy—and for pharisaism of the worst kind. He has no use for a conscience nor does he care for the sanctity of promises and pledges. His own colleagues consider him to be unreliable.

But in this matter what he expressed was really the imperial mind of Great Britain. The action taken by the Government on the Lee Commission Report has tightened the chains around India for decades to come, and no Indian can ignore it. There can be no Home Rule in

India, no advance towards real self-government as long as the superior services are manned by the British. On this point even Al. Carthill, the anti-Indian author of *The Lost Dominion*, holds the same view as Indians do.

Then, again, the finance and the Military departments are the key-stones of an administration. The Reformed Government has made itself notorious for its maladministration of Indian finance and a deliberate misuse of its statutory powers. The Governor-General has restored taxation proposals turned down by the Legislative Assembly. He has sanctioned expenditure disallowed by the popular and representative chamber. Moreover, the Government has manipulated exchange, and by clever handling of the currency fleeced the Indian taxpayer of billions of pounds. It has treated the decision of the Assembly and the intelligent non-official opinion of the country with supreme contempt.

India's carrying trade is done mostly in British bottoms. The policy of the British Government towards efforts at encouraging Indian navigating companies has always been one of opposition. The British vessels do not care for the interests of the Indian manufacturer, and yet India is not allowed to organize a mercantile marine of her own. The recommendations of the Indian Mercantile Marine Committee of 1924 have been quietly shelved.

The policy underlying this attitude is still in the ascendant. The Government holds tight the reins of railway administration, and manages tariffs in such a way as to help British trade and retard the progress of industrial development in India. The railway administration is completely in the hands of Europeans, and the refusal to appoint even one Indian member to the Railway Board, on the monstrous plea that throughout the length and breadth of this country there is not one Indian who is qualified for the job, has further convinced Indians that the Government is not sincere in its profession of sympathy for Home Rule for India.

The new feature of the tariff policy is that preference for British and Empire goods is being introduced by back-parlour methods. Although the British officials were so nice and hospitable to the author of *Mother India*, the greatest slanderer of this country, they are hypocritically telling us that the American films sometimes depict Indian life in an offensive way and that therefore India should accord preference to British films. This is being preached merely because the British film manufacturer is on his merits no match for his American competitor.

Turning from the Finance deparment to the Military we find that while on the one hand we are charged with inability to defend India and told that that is a ground for the continuance of the British in India, on the other hand, we are, deliberately and persistently denied the opportunities of qualifying for that task. The Military department is sacrosanct. Its expenditure is non-votable and its higher ranks are guarded against

Indians. From a population of 315 millions only nine cadets are taken every year for the King's Commission.

In 1925, on the persistent demand of the Assembly, the Government appointed a committee of officials and non-officials, of Military experts and representative Indians, to go into the question of Indianizing the Army. The committee was presided over by one of their own officers. This committee made a unanimous report on which orders were delayed for over a year, and eventually the chief recommendations of the committee have been turned down by Whitehall. Indians are denied all opportunities in the artillery and air forces.

The culminating point of the policy of reaction is the appointment of an exclusively British Statutory Commission to enquire into the working of the Reforms and to recommend a constitution for India. Is it any wonder then that Indians have lost all trust in the good faith of the British, and that they often express their lack of faith in bitter words at the meetings of the central legislature?

CHAPTER XXXII

'CUMBROUS, COMPLEX, CONFUSED SYSTEM'

We have seen that the Reforms associated with the names of Montagu and Chelmsford did not spring from a 'hasty and generous emotion'. Even so, the reader will like to know how they have worked. Indians are sometimes accused of being perverse obstructionists who would not co-operate in inaugurating a democratic regime by working the 'democratic' reform measure. Such judgment is very misleading. The plain fact is that the Reforms Act is not a democratic measure —it enfranchises barely 2 per cent. of the population; and it does not create a workable constitutional machinery. The little that there was of the progressive spirit in it has been whittled down by the illiberal Anglo-Indian officialdom and by the India Office. Even those who were enthusiastic over the Reforms have found them to be unworkable. That was the burden of the evidence given by many of the Indian ministers and ex-ministers before the Reforms Enquiry Committee of 1924 presided over by Sir Alexander Muddiman. Even British administrators had been driven to that conclusion from their experience of it. Sir Henry Wheeler, Governor of Bihar and Orissa, expressed himself thus about the Montagu-Chelmsford dyarchical system: "Whatever defects exist are inherent in the system itself... It is workable now, though creakily." The Governor's European executive councillor, Sir Hugh McPherson, concurred in this view.

Sir William Marris, Governor of Agra and Oudh, who was associated with the reforms from their very inception as the Reforms Secretary, described dyarchy as ' obviously a cumbrous, complex, confused system.'

Eminent Indians associated with working the dyarchic machine have expressed themselves in no unambiguous terms about it. Sir Muhammad Fakhruddin, senior minister in Bihar and Orissa, said about a year ago in the Patna Council :

" The classification of transferred subjects is seriously defective. There is no reason why you should give the minister Agriculture without Irrigation. Why should you give him the administration of the spending department without any control over finance? Without a purse others consider me simply a clerk to prepare a certain scheme, and after the scheme is ready the Finance Department is entitled to knock it down on the ground of want of funds."

Sir K. V. Reddi, when he was yet a minister in Madras, the province in which it used to be said the reforms were being worked in the best spirit, said in 1923 :

" I am Minister of Development *minus* Forests, and you all know that development depends a good deal on forests. I am Minister of Industries without Factories, which are a reserved subject, and industries without factories are unimaginable. I am Minister of Agriculture *minus* Irrigation. You can understand what that means. How agriculture can be carried on extensively without irrigation, in the hands of those who are responsible for it, is hard to realize. I am also Minister of Industries without Electricity, which is also a reserved subject. The subjects of Labour and Boilers are also reserved."

The minister rightly concluded by saying: " But these, after all, are some only of the defects of the Reform scheme."

Sir K. V. Reddi's sentences quoted above furnish a good commentary on the story of the ' transferred ' departments. The ' responsible ' ministers are not quite responsible. Besides, as Mr. Sachchidananda Sinha, who himself belonged to the ' reserved ' half of the Bihar and Orissa Government, points out that 'the newest executive councillor is senior to the oldest minister.'* In the ' executive ' or reserved half it is the European member that dominates. In one case we are told, though an Indian executive councillor was labelled the ' Home Member,' the main work of the Appointment Department was entrusted by the Governor not to him but to his Civilian colleague. When the point was raised in the legislature, the answer was given that the transac-

* See his paper on '*Dyarchy in Indian Provinces in Theory and Practice*' read last year before the East India Association, London. Some of the material used in this chapter is taken from that paper.

tion of official business was a domestic concern of the Government!

The transferred departments are very often controlled not by the Indian ministers, but by their permanent Secretaries who are generally European I.C.S. men. Says Sir Ali Imam who has held the highest judicial and executive offices under the Crown :

" The transferred departments are in the hands of ministers who are supposed to be responsible to the House. But, while all the appearance of democracy is there, it is a shell without the kernel. The minister has to run his departments, but he must have a permanent secretary over whom he has no control. If the minister wants anything to be done, the secretary can go beyond him to the Governor, and the latter can overrule the minister. The result is that although the minister is said to be responsible to the House, he has to carry out the orders of the Governor. The danger lies in this that a form has been given to the constitution but without the substance."

Mr. E. Villiers, who twice represented Bengal Europeans in the legislature, in his manifesto declining to seek re-election in the last general election, said :

" I hold them [the reforms] to be wrong in practice, since, if we are going to carry out the policy of teaching India how to rule herself with the maximum of efficiency and at the minimum of cost, if we are to teach her a sense of ' political responsibility,' we are going the wrong way to do it. Instead of teaching her responsibility we are teaching her irresponsibility. In these circumstances, then, feeling as I do strongly on the question, I do not think that I can any longer serve your interests or the interests of the provinces to advantage."

Prominent British statesmen have expressed their misgivings about the workability of the dyarchical system. Lord Curzon, in the Lords' Debate on the reforms, accepted the decision of the House, but did not fail to remark that personally he abominated the system. Lord Ronaldshay, former Governor of Bengal, has recorded about this system that it is a 'complicated constitutional machine.' Even Lord Birkenhead has said that he was 'very distrustful of the dyarchial principle.' He pronounced it to be 'pedantic and hide-bound.'

Why blame Indians when they endorse this verdict about the system they are asked to work?

CHAPTER XXXIII

INDIA—A WORLD-MENACE

Towards the conclusion of her book Miss Mayo declares that, being the home and the source of epidemics, India is a world-menace. We agree that India is a world-menace. Only we look at it in a different way. We have proved from facts and figures given in this book that the responsibility for such a state of things rests with the British, who hold India in a state of political subjection and who use their political dominance for the economic exploitation of India. Unless, therefore, India's political helplessness is removed and she is given the freedom which is enjoyed by other self-governing nations, India must continue to be a danger to the world from both the health and the peace points of view. India is the pivot of the British Empire; and India and China between them hold the key of world peace. From time immemorial India has been the goal of empire-builders' ambitions. Whoever holds India holds the key to world dominance and prosperity, particularly in modern times. Before Great Britain acquired India she was rather a poor country without very notable resources and without any empire. Indian wealth enabled her to bring about the industrial revolution and to amass wealth. Indian gold and Indian troops enabled her to conquer the world. Almost every bit of territory she holds in Asia and Africa was acquired after she had secured the mastery of India. India has been, and is, the base of the empire in the orient. This is a fact which no amount of verbal jugglery can change. Most of Britain's wars with the other Powers of Europe or Asia were directly or indirectly connected with her rule in India. Ever since she established her rule in India she has been quarelling with Russia. For over a century the Russia of the Czars was on the brains of British diplomats and journalists, just as Soviet Russia is to-day. This opinion is shared by many competent observers—among them Mr. Herbert Adams Gibbons, an American writer of repute. His book, *The New Map of Asia** opens with this thesis. According to Mr. Gibbons, all through the nineteenth century—as in the twentieth—Britain's foreign policy was governed by considerations of the safety of the British Empire in India. The different phases of British foreign policy fully bear out this contention. Mr. Gibbons has admirably summed up and explained these phases in the opening chapter of his book. We prefer to let the story be narrated by this American author:

" None can understand the foreign policy of Great Britain, which has inspired military and diplomatic activities from the Napoleonic wars to the present day, who does not interpret wars, diplomatic conflicts, treaties and alliances, territorial annexations, extensions of protectorates, with the fact of India constantly in mind.

* Century Co., New York, 1919.

"It was for India that the British fought Napoleon in the Mediterranean, Egypt, and Syria. At the Congress of Vienna, Great Britain asked for nothing in Europe. Her reward was the confirmation of her conquest of Malta, the Cape of Good Hope, Mauritius, the Seychelles, and Ceylon. After 1815, Great Britain became champion of the integrity of the Ottoman Empire in order to bar to any other Power the land route to India. When Muhammad Ali, starting from Egypt, sent his armies to overthrow the Ottoman Empire, he found a British fleet and army in Syria, just as Napoleon had found them. Against the natural instinct of the British people, the Foreign Office consistently opposed the affranchisement of the Balkan States, and condoned the massacres of Christians by Moslems. The Crimean War was fought to protect Turkey, and if the treaty of San Stefano had not been renounced, Lord Beaconsfield would have started another war with Russia in 1877. The British Government opposed the piercing of the Isthmus of Suez. But when the canal was an accomplished fact, control by the Suez Company was acquired. The British then did, themselves, what they would have fought any other European nation for trying to do. They made the first breach in the integrity of the Ottoman Empire by the Cyprus convention and the occupation of Egypt. With Egypt safely in British hands, the Foreign Office did not hesitate to change its Balkan policy. The incorporation of eastern Rumelia in Bulgaria was supported in 1885. Eight years before, British statesmen would not have hesitated to plunge

Europe into a bloody war to prevent the formation of a large Bulgaria.

"The occupation of Egypt was to have been provisional. The British Government solemnly declared to the other Powers that it had no intention of settling permanently on the Nile, and that it would evacuate Egypt ' at an early moment.' The occupation dragged on. There was always a good reason for not leaving. At the end of the nineteenth century, the British reconquered the Sudan to assure their position in Egypt and the Red Sea, and fought the Boer War to prevent South Africa from passing out of their hands. The idea of the Cape-to-Cairo Railway—' all British '—was launched. By pushing up the Nile, the British came into contact with the French at Fashoda. If the French had thought it possible, or if they had had allies to help them, they would have declared war against Great Britain. Instead of fighting, the statesmen of the two countries came to an understanding on all colonial questions. This was not hard to accomplish. because the French had set their hearts on Morocco and did not claim any of the approaches to India. On May 8, 1904, an agreement was signed between Great Britain and France, settling their disputes throughout the world. The basis of the compromise was mutual disinterestedness in Egypt and Morocco. The principal factor which led Great Britain into the *entente cordiale* was a desire to get rid of French intrigue in Egypt. This was necessary to hold permanently the route to India by the Suez Canal...

"To protect India by sea, the British decided to control the Arabian Sea on the west, the Gulf of Bengal on the east, and all the passages from the Indian Ocean to these waters. In the mind of the British Foreign Office, unquestioned supremacy of the seas meant the occupation of islands, and supremacy of the straits leading to the Arabian Sea and the Gulf of Siam, the occupation of the mainlands bordering them. Later, the policy of control was extended to include the littoral of the Arabian Sea and the Gulf of Siam. Then, it was evident that the littoral could be made secure only by occupation of the hinterland! From London and Liverpool to Hongkong, the control of the sea could not be maintained by a fleet alone. The result? Gibralter, Malta, Cyprus, Egypt, Aden, Perim, the Sudan on the route to India from the west; Sokotra the Seychelles, and other islands guarding the Arabian Sea, the Bahrein Islands dominating the Persian Gulf, Ceylon at the tip of India; the islands and mainland of the Gulf of Bengal; Singapore and the Malay Peninsula, and the northern side of Borneo on the route to India from the east."

Turning to land, the same authority continues :

"On land, India is surrounded by Baluchistan; Afghanistan; the Russian provinces of Bokhara and Turkestan; the Chinese provinces of Sinkiang and Tibet; Nepal; Bhutan; and Burma. Since the Government of India annexed Baluchistan and Burma, Persia, the Szechuan and Yunnan provinces of China, French Indo-China, and Siam have had common boundaries with India.

" The sovereignty of British India was extended over Baluchistan from 1875 to 1903, and over Burma from 1879 to 1909. Because Baluchistan and Burma were on the sea coast, the British were satisfied with nothing less than actual political control and effective military occupation. But, once started, there is no limit to ' safeguards.' The appetite grows in eating. When the recent war broke out, Great Britain was ensconcing herself in southern Persia, not with the consent of the Persians, but by reason of an agreement with Russia. Afghanistan was forced to accept British control. In Egypt, not the consent of the Egyptians, but an agreement with France, gave Great Britain what she considered her ' rights ' on the Nile, and those rights were never satisfied until the head-waters of the Nile were reached.

" As the control of southern Persia followed logically the incorporation of Baluchistan into India, expansion at the expense of Siam followed the absorption of Burma. In 1909, Great Britain achieved command of the coast of the Gulf of Bengal by wresting from Siam the tributary states of Kelantan, Trengganu, and Keda. To protect India on the land side, military occupation has followed the sending of punitive expeditions to punish tribesmen for raiding protected states. New territories occupied became in turn protected, and so the process continued until the great mountain frontiers were reached.

"On the confines of India only three independent states remain, Nepal, Bhutan, and Afghanistan. But these states are not independent in fact. They are bound hand and foot to the Government of India. There has been a British Resident in Nepal for a hundred years. The British are allowed to recruit freely for the Indian Army from among the splendid dominant race of Gurkhas, and the Prime Minister, who is all-powerful, holds the rank of Lieutenant-General in the British Army. The rulers of Afghanistan and Bhutan receive, large subsidies on condition of 'good behaviour,' which means doing always what the Government of India says, and treating with the outside world only through the Government of India.* Part of Bhutan was annexed to Bengal in 1864, and the country has received a British subsidy since 1865. In 1907, the dual control of clergy and laity, which had been in force ever since the British began to occupy India, was done away with in Bhutan. The difficulties in Tibet were a warning that could not be disregarded. A Maharaja was elected, and this gave the British the opportunity to get effective control of the country without conquering it. In consideration of doubling the subsidy, the Bhutan Government surrendered control of foreign relations to the British in 1910, and allowed them to occupy two strong positions inside the Bhutan frontier. Judging from the

*The position regarding Afghanistan has now altogether changed.

history of the formation of British India, unless we are on the threshold of a radical change in international relations, one is safe in predicting that both Nepal and Bhutan will become integral parts of India in the near future."

"The situation in regard to Afghanistan," continues Mr. Gibbons, "has been different. The treaty of 1893, which followed long and costly wars, gave the Btirish predominance in Afghanistan. But Russia, in her Asiatic expansion, was not disposed to allow Afghanistan to become British without a struggle. Russian imperialism turned against British imperialism its own argument... After penetrating Mongolia, the Russians desired to extend their influence over Tibet—and, for exactly the same reason as the British, had been following out their own imperialistic policy. In the minds of British statesmen, Afghanistan and Tibet became the two shields of India. During the first decade of the twentieth century, these two countries, as well as Persia, became—to the Government of India and the British Foreign Office —'safeguards' which must be added to the British Empire. War with Russia was avoided because of the Convention of 1907. In the same decade Germany became a menace to India through the Bagdad Railway conception. Great Britain had determined to allow neither Russia nor Germany to reach the Persian Gulf. Having compounded colonial rivalries with France and Russia, she had no way of arriving at a diplomatic understanding with Germany. The Bagdad Railway question was decided on battlefields from Flanders to Mesopotamia."

The statement of facts and events in the sequence in which they have been put by Mr. Gibbons, is based on history which cannot be contested. The Great War has not ended wars. At one time it was claimed that it would. Europe is even now sitting on the crest of a volcano and a war in the near future is certain. India, being a huge source of British wealth and British man-power, is looked upon with great suspicion and distrust by all the Powers of Europe and Asia. The Orient is in revolt against the authority of Europe. The Soviet is busy trying to alienate from Great Britain the European working-man and the Asiatic Nationalists of different countries. India is also ablaze with the fire of a spirit of independence. In the circumstances much political sagacity is not required to predict that India cannot very long be held in bondage as it has been for the last 150 years. Even British interests require that the British should come to an agreement with India as to the future relations of Britain and India. China is already ablaze. Afghanistan has become independent. Persia is organizing herslf into an efficient nation. Russia is almost on the borders of Afghanistan. In these circumstances, it is for Great Britain to see what the consequences of a discontented and unhappy India can possibly be to her political future. Britain's imperial rivals are interested in inflaming Indian Nationalists. They will leave no stone unturned to make India unsafe for England in the next war. England is popular nowhere in the world, and, although we hear so much of *ententes* and treaties and understandings, they are not worth the paper on which they are written. The history of the past 200 years has shown that treaties have been treated like scraps of paper whenever they stood in the way of imperial ambitions of any great Power. The League of Nations, really speaking, commands no influence. It is completely under the thumb of the two or three great Powers of the world. It is abundantly clear that even these two or three Powers are not quite happy with each other, much less so are those who either stand out or have to get compensation for past wrongs. India will thus be always an object of solicitude, a field for intrigue to Britain's enemies. But a contented India may safely keep out of all wars between the European Powers. England's military arrogance against other countries is very much dictated, or at least influenced, by her resources in India. Once those resources are gone or decreased or placed out of reach, Britain will become a chastened nation and treat with other people on terms of justice and fair play. As long as she can count upon India, India's material resources and her man-power, she is bound to maintain her present aggressive attitude, which is often reflected in the speeches of her statesmen like Lord Birkenhead and Mr. Winston Churchill. An aggressive, defiant, insolent Great Britain, with India at her beck and call, is a danger to world peace. With India self-governing that danger will disappear. The point is so clear that one need not labour it any further.

It is also abundantly clear that, as long as India does not become free, she cannot very much improve those departments of her national life that could secure for her freedom from disease. Diseases and epidemics, as we have already shown, are the product of ignorance and poverty. And ignorance and poverty are bound to continue as long as Britain holds India in the hollow of her palms, and as long as Britain's fiscal policy is determined by British interests—imperial, military and economic. It is too much to expect that England will forego any fraction of them. The fact, that in this intoxication of power the British Cabinet and the British Parliament should be defying Indian public opinion in the matter of the constitution of the Statutory Commission, also gives support to the same view. We may here fittingly quote another American authority who hails from New York. Reverend Dr. Charles Cuthbert Hall, late President of the Union Theological Seminary of New York, and Burrows Leturer on the Orient, remarks:

" There is no denying the fact that England is administering India for England's benefit and not India's. It is hard for me to say this, because until I went to India my sympathies were all on the English side. My early education was much in England and I have many dear personal friends there. But what I am saying now is the truth, and the truth must be told...

" The obvious fact stares us in the face that there is at no time, in no year, any shortage of foodstuffs in India. The trouble is that, the taxes imposed by the British Government being fifty per cent. of the produce, the Indian starves that England's annual revenue may not be diminished by a dollar. Eighty per cent. of the whole population has been thrown back upon the soil because England's discriminating duties have ruined practically every branch of native manufacture; and these tillers of the soil, when they have sold themselves for the last time to the money-lender, when they have over and over again mortgaged their crops and their bit of land, are sold by the tax-collector to wander about until they drop of starvation... We send shiploads of grain to India, but there is plenty of grain in India. The trouble is the people have been ground down until they are too poor to buy it. Famine is chronic there now, though the same shipments of food-stuffs are made annually to England, the same drainage of millions of dollars goes on every year...."*

Dr. Paul S. Reinsch, who served as an American Minister in China, observes in his book called the *Intellectual and Political Currents in the Far East*:

" The present situation in India illustrates some of the unfortunate results of the political dependence of a civilized people. Not only politically but also in economic matters, India is kept in a state of dependence on the metropole. But the most hopeless feature of the situation is that the men who would naturally be leaders in government and enterprises find themselves excluded from opportunities for exercising legitimate power in their own country. Such a decapitation of an entire people is a great sacrifice to impose, even in return

*From a speech in the Bar Association Club House, New York, quoted in *The Public*, Novemebr 20, 1908.

for the blessings of peace and an efficient policing of the country. The continuance of this policy would mean either the total destruction and degradation of Indian national life, or the end of the British Raj."

It may be argued that in order to protect herself from foreign aggression, India cannot do without British help. This is again an unwarranted assumption. Here is the testimony of General Sir Ian Hamilton about the military possibilities of a free India:

" There is material in the north of India, sufficient and fit, under good leadership, to shake the artificial society of Europe to its foundation once it dares to tamper with that militarism which now alone supplies it with any higher ideal than money and the luxury which that money can purchase. It is heroism, self-sacrifice and chivalry which redeem war and build up national character. What part do these heroic qualities find in the ignoble struggle between nations for commercial supremacy, with stock exchanges and wheat-pits for their battle-fields? If then it is a question of finding leaders, a gradual diffusion of knowledge will produce those leaders, and once they have been found, how can England hope to retain under the British crown this vast empire permanently—unless the Indians are exactly in the same position of independence as Canadians and Australians to-day occupy?"*

The possibility of India being conquered by any other Power also may be dismissed without

* See *Japan's Foreign Policy*, by A. M. Pooley.

much discussion. The world situation would not allow any other Power taking possession of India. The European Powers may not feel any danger from India if she is self-governing. But any attempt on the part of any other Power to take possession will be resented and resisted by the Powers of Europe in their own interests and for reasons that have already been stated in the opening part of this chapter. Of course, if India remains within the Empire, as she at present might be contented to be, she may be a source of strength to Great Britain as against her enemies. But if she is compelled to leave the Empire, then one source of danger to the peace of the world would be removed.

In the post-War world a keen struggle has been going on between the principles of imperialism and socialism. The War has produced a revolution in Russia, the like of which has never been known in history. The Russian revolution has been opposed and the Soviet has been attacked in many ways by the capitalistic empires of Europe. We have been from time to time told that Russia's dissolution was imminent, yet it has survived all those attacks and is very much alive, so much so that British diplomacy and even British Foreign Office have to take note of the influence of Russia, both political and economic, in Asia and in Europe. We may or may not agree with Bolshevik ideas, but it is certain that the experiment that is being tried in Soviet Russia is going to influence the life of the world in a great measure. There is no doubt from what one can observe in Europe and America that the tide against imperialism is rising. A struggle between imperialism and socialism, or say, between capitalism and socialism will take some time, but by all portents eventually the new spirit is bound to triumph. The only way to meet Bolshevism is to concede rights to the different peoples of the earth—India among them—now being bled and exploited by the imperial races. Otherwise the discontented and exploited countries of the world will be the breeding centres for it. India must come into her own, else not even the Himalayas can effectually bar the entry of Bolshevism into India.

Then, again, let us look at the question from the commercial point of view. By its geographical situation India is a connecting link between the Near East and the Far East, and a clearing house for the trade of the world. Racially it holds the balance between the European Aryans and the yellow races. In any military conflict between the white and the yellow races the people of India will be a decisive factor. In peace they will be a harmonizing element. Racially they are related to Europeans. Religiously and culturally they are nearer to the Chinese and Japanese.

Yet another aspect of it: With 70 millions of Moslems, India is the most important centre of Islamic sentiment. At present the British Government is trying to keep the Moslems contented and on its side, by raising up the Hindu-Muslim conflict in various forms, and by doles of favour, but this policy is eventually bound to fail because the

pan-Islamic element is growing stronger. Among
the Moslem population of India a large number of
Indian Moslems are alive to the importance of
India to the cause of Islam in the world. The
freedom of Islamic Powers, so to speak, depends
upon the freedom of India. The present temporary tension between the Hindus and Mussalmans is bound to end some day—at least when the
fact dawns on the millions of Indian Moslems that
Islam cannot be revived or strengthened or made
independent of European influence until India is
again free. Islam is not dead. It cannot and will
not die. The only way to make it a force of
harmony and peace is to recognize its potentialities and to respect its susceptibilities. The
political independence of Islamic countries is a
basic foundation for such a state, and India is
destined to play a very important part in the
future developments of Islam.

 Looking at the progress of humanity, it cannot
be ignored that India, inhabited by one-fifth of the
human race, and China, with its even greater
population, are the greatest stumbling-blocks in
the way of rapid human progress. Both the
countries are alive to that fact. Both the great
populations are conscious of their present disabilities—and also of their immense potentialities.
They are at present spokes in the wheel of
progress. But a self-governing India will be a
great help to the advance of human progress.
With a republican China in the north-east, an
independent and progressive Persia in the background, and a Bolshevik Russia on the north up

across the Hindu Kush, it is extremely foolish to attempt to rule India despotically. Not even the gods could do so for a considerable length of time. It would not be possible even if the British Parliament and the Indian legislatures were to devote all their sittings to the drafting and passing of a hundred coercive Acts. The peace of the world, international harmony and goodwill, the reputation of the English nation, the progress of mankind and the economic welfare of the world, all demand the peaceful introduction and development of the democratic form of government in India, and the sooner the English realize that patent fact the better it will be for all concerned.

APPENDIX I

SOME OPINIONS ABOUT 'MOTHER INDIA'

The following is the full text of the letter written by Dr. Rabindranath Tagore from Bali to the *Manchester Guardian Weekly* for October 14, 1927 :

"May I appeal to your sense of justice and claim a place in your paper for this letter of mine, which I am compelled to write in vindication of my position as a representative of India against a most unjustifiable attack?

"While travelling in this island of Bali I have just chanced upon a copy of the *New Statesman* of July 16, containing the review of a book on India written by a tourist from America. The reviewer, while supporting with an unctuous virulence all the calumnies heaped upon our people by the authoress, and while calling repeated attention to the common Hindu vice of untruthfulness even amongst the greatest of us, has made public a malicious piece of fabrication, not as one of the specimens picked up from a show-case of wholesale abuse displayed in this or some other book, but as a gratuitous information about the truth of which the writer tacitly insinuates his own personal testimony. It runs as thus : 'The poet Sir Rabindranath Tagore expresses in print his conviction that marriage should be consummated before puberty in order to avert the vagaries of female sexual desire.'

"We have become painfully familiar with deliberate circulation of hideous lies in the West against enemy countries, but a similar propaganda against individuals, whose countrymen have obviously offended the writer by their political aspirations, has come to me as a surprise. If the people of the United States had ever made themselves politically obnoxious to England, it is imaginable how an English writer of this type would take a gloating delight in proving, with profuse helps from the news columns in the American journals, their criminal propensity and quote for his support their constant indulgence in vicarious enjoyment of crimes through cinema pictures. But would he, in the fiercest frenzy of his rhetoric running amok, dare to make the monstrous accusation, let us say, against the late President Wilson, for ever having expressed his pious conviction that the lynching of the Negroes was a moral necessity in a superior civilization for cultivating Christian virtues? Or would he venture to ascribe to Professor Dewey the theory that centuries of witch-burning have developed in the Western peoples the quick moral sensitiveness that helps them in judging and condemning others whom they do not know or understand or like and about whose culpability they are never in lack of conclusive evidence? But has it been made so easily possible in my case, such a deliberately untruthful irresponsibility in this writer, condoned by the editor, by the fact that the victim was no better than a British subject who by accident of his birth has happened to be a Hindu and not belonging to the Muslim community, which, according to the writer, is specially favoured by his people and our Government?

" May I point out in this connection that selected documents of facts generalized into an unqualified statement affecting a whole large population may become in the hands of the tourist from across the sea a poison-tipped arrow of the most heinous form of untruth to which the British nation itself may afford a broadly easy target? It is a cunning lie against a community which the writer has used when she describes the Hindus as cow-dung eaters. It is just as outrageous as to introduce Englishmen to those who know them imperfectly as addicted to the cocaine habit because cocaine is commonly used in their dentistry. In Hindu India only in rare cases an exceedingly small quantity of cow-dung is used not as an ingredient in their meals but as a part of the performance of expiatory rites for some violation of social convention. One who has no special interest or pleasure in creating ill-feeling towards the Europeans will, if he is honest, hesitate in describing them, though seemingly with a greater justice than in the other case, as eaters of live creatures or of rotten food, mentioning oyster and cheese for illustration. It is the subtlest method of falsehood, this placing of exaggerated emphasis upon insignificant details, giving to the exception the appearance of the rule.

" The instances of moral perversity when observed in alien surroundings naturally loom large to us, because the positive power of sanitation which works from within and the counteracting forces that keep up social balance are not evident to a stranger, especially to one who has the craving for an intemperate luxury of moral indignation which very often is the sign of the same morbid pathology seen from behind. When such a critic comes to the East not for truth but for the chuckling enjoyment of an exaggerated self-complacency, and when he underlines some social aberrations with his exultant red pencil, glaringly emphasising them out of their context, he goads our own young critics to play the identical unholy game. They also, with the help of the numerous guide-books supplied by unimpeachable agency for the good of humanity, explore the dark recesses of Western society, the breeding-grounds of nauseous habits and moral filthiness, some of which have a dangerous cover of a respectable exterior; they also select their choice specimens of rottenness with the same pious zeal and sanctimonious pleasure as their foreign models have in besmearing the name of a whole nation with the mud from ditches that may represent an undoubted fact yet not the complete truth.

" And thus is generated the endless vicious circle of mutual recrimination and ever-accumulating misunderstandings that are perilous for the peace of the world. Of course our young critic in the East is under a disadvantage. For the Western peoples have an enormously magnifying organ of a sound that goes deep and reaches far, either when they malign others or defend themselves against accusations which touch them to the quick, whereas our own mortified critic struggles with his unaided lungs that can whisper and sigh but not shout. But is it not known that our inarticulate emotions become highly inflammable when crowded, in the underground cellars of our mind, darkly silent? The whole of the Eastern continent is daily being helped in the storage of such explosives by the critics of the West, who, with a delicious sense of duty done, are ever ready to give vent to their blind prejudices while tenderly nourishing a comfortable conscience that lulls them into forgetting that they also have their Western analogies in moral licence, only in different garbs made in their fashionable establishments or in their slums. However, let me strongly assure my English and other Western readers that neither I, nor my indignant Indian friends whom I have with me, have ever had the least shadow of intimation of what has been described in this book and quoted with a grin of conviction by this writer as the usual practice in the training of sexual extravagance. I hope such Western readers will understand my difficulty in giving an absolute denial to certain facts alleged when they remember the occasional startling disclosures in their own society in Europe and America, allowing to the unsuspecting public a sudden glimpse of systematic orgies of sexual abnormality in an environment which is supposed not to represent ' sub-human ' civilization.

"The writer in the *New Statesman* has suggested for the good of the world that the people in India condemned by the tourist for malpractices should never be assisted by the benevolent British soldiers safely to preserve their existence and continue their race. He evidently chooses to ignore the fact that these people have maintained their life and culture without the help of the British soldiers for a longer series of centuries than his own people has. However that may be, I shrink from borrowing my wisdom from this source and make a similarly annihilating suggestion for this kind of writers, who spread about the malignant contagion of race-hatred; because, in spite of provocations, we should have a patient faith in human nature for its unlimited capacity for improvement, and let us hope to be rid of the lurking persistence of barbarism in man, not through elimination of the noxious elements by physical destruction but through the education of mind and a discipline of true culture."

RABINDRANATH TAGORE.

Moendock, Bali, Sept. 6, 1927.

*

"Ditcher"—to his friends, the late Mr. Pat Lovett—who had 40 years' journalistic experience in India, and edited the leading Anglo-Indian commercial weekly, *Capital* of Calcutta, wrote in his paper on September 8, 1927:

"It was not until the end of last week that I got a loan of a copy, which I read through as a matter of duty, but with increasing disgust. In the first place it confirmed the opinion of one of the greatest of living essayists, that a ' best seller ' nowadays is not, in nine cases out of ten, a good book; in the next place the intellectual dishonesty of *La grosse Americaine* was appalling; and in the last place her ghoulish propensity of frequenting hospitals to discover inhuman cruelties to indict a whole people borders on stark pornography. The book is devoid of literary merit. It is the crudest form of transpontine journalism. It sold like hot cakes partly because of its morbid sensationalism, but mostly because it was unscrupulous propaganda against the claim of India for Home Rule published at the ' psychological moment'."

*

Mr. A. H. Clark, an American missionary in India, writes to the *Indian Social Reformer* of Bombay about the missionary feeling regarding *Mother India:*

" I hope that you will give me space for a brief reply to a communication from Mr. S. Veerabhadra published in the *Reformer* of November 26th. In this communication the author, while acknowledging that some American missionaries in India have condemned Miss Mayo's book, asserts that some share her point of view. Personally I doubt whether there are American missionaries in India who really share Miss Mayo's point of view or fully endorse her repulsive charges. In general we Americans have probably been at fault in the matter of making public in India our attitude to this book, confining our efforts too largely to counteracting its effect in America.

"The very day on which I first had opportunity to read *Mother India*, I sent to America a brief review of it, which has just been published, in which I said, among other things, that I was ashamed that a fellow-American should write a book whose picture of India was a 'slimy caricature.' All of us Americans on the Executive Committee of the National Christian Council, except Bishop Robinson, whose objection I understand to have been largely technical, approved the statement condemning *Mother India* issued by the secretaries of the Council. I myself had 400 copies of this statement struck off and am sending them to a wide constituency in America. A group of American missionaries from all over India is issuing a statement, repudiating *Mother India* and sending it broadcast to the American Press. I have myself gathered what seems to me to be conclusive evidence against many of Miss Mayo's worst mis-statements and have sent it to Miss Mayo in the form of a letter, with an appeal to her, in the name of truth and goodwill, to withdraw the book. Mr. K. T. Paul happened to see a copy of this letter and urged me to let him print it in *The Young Men of India*, but I had previously put in into the hands of a representative in America for publication there, if, as I fear may be the case, Miss Mayo's reply is unfavourable. To my personal knowledge a stream of articles and letters designed to offset the effect of *Mother India* is going to America from the American missionaries in India.

APPENDIX I

"It is hard for me to believe that any such warped and hideous presentation of India as Miss Mayo's can long have much influence for evil in the world. It is bound to lead to reaction in which the great gifts of India for world civilization will again have emphasis. I share the hope of Mahatma Gandhi that India may be large-spirited enough to accept whatever there is in Miss Mayo's book of stimulus to fresh efforts for reform. Truth is still stronger than falsehood. Goodwill is more powerful than prejudice. No single book, however disgusting and untrue, can long stand in the way of the movement of the peoples of the earth toward better mutual understanding and greater mutual respect.

In confidence that you share this faith."

AHMADNAGAR,   Yours etc.,
5th December, 1927.   A. H. CLARK.

*

Lord Sinha, who has held the highest offices under the Crown—being the only Indian ever appointed the Governor of a province, and who at the time of his death, which occurred recently, was a Member of the Judicial Committee of the Privy Council, on landing in Bombay (December 30, 1927) was interviewed by a representative of the *Indian Daily Mail.* We copy below that part of the interview which is relevant here:

I entirely agree with Mr. Gandhi that Miss Mayo has had a good sniff at all the filthy drains of India, that her picture is totally out of focus and I am sorry to say that the book is a deliberate, calculated lie.

" The whole of it?" asked our representative —" Yes, the whole of it," declared Lord Sinha with emphasis, " the whole of it as is pictured. It is a lie, and a false picture."

" But I think undue prominence has been given in India to her exploit. It has helped her to sell her book and to further her propaganda. When I say all this I should like to add that it is foolish to suggest that either Government of India or the India Office in London has had any hand in the publication of this book. I am sure that the book has caused great embarrassment to the British Government. You are giving that book the prominence which it does not deserve. She has libelled and maligned almost every great man in India.

" There have been several Americans on board and they all said that the picture made by the book cannot be true. I also know every single Anglo-Indian official who has lived in India considers that the book is not only false but even mischievous."

Asked to point out instances from the book which he held to be absolutely false, Lord Sinha replied that he just remembered one statement made by Miss Mayo which was a lie, namely, that Indian mothers taught their children unnatural vice. " I can conceive of nothing more atrociously false. I asked half a dozen English members of the Indian Medical Service, who have spent, each of them, more than 25 years in India as to whether they have ever heard of such a thing and they all said that they have no more heard of them than I, and they are convinced that it is absolutely false."

*

Dr. James H. Cousins, Irish poet and author, who is a keen student of Indian culture, and knows this country intimately by long residence and educational experience, writes in a prefatory note to an essay on *The Path to Peace:**

"The whole edifice of falsehood erroneously labelled *Mother India* rises naturally from a foundation of race prejudice and mental dishonesty which is none the less dangerous and reprehensible because it may be subconscious. The post-script expression of friendliness to India in the book is a thin apologia for the manipulation of pathological elements in a nation's life in order to make a case for her continued retention in a state of political dependence. This thesis emerges as the actual, if it was not originally the deliberate, intention of the book; and it is supported by the ancient and dishonourable expedients of *suggestio falsi* and *suppressio veri*. The authoress attributes to all India certain customs that belong only to a section of the people. She calls India a 'world-menace' because of certain elements in her sanitary habits, but gives no hint that the 'world-menace' of the influenza epidemic of 1918 that cost India six million lives arose outside India.

* Madras: Ganesh & Co.

She criticizes the water supply of Madras, but is silent on the disclosure last year that milk watered with dirty stable hose had been responsible for typhoid fever in New York. She pillories the sacrifice of goats in a Kali temple, but approves of the practice of flesh eating which condemns an infinitely larger number of animals to torture and death in Europe and America for the satisfaction of appetite...

"It would be quite easy, quite futile, and quite criminal, for me to take from my file of cuttings from American papers (with their records of bribery and corruption, vulgarity, impurity, robbery, smuggling, adulteration and murder) a case in proof of the recent declaration of an American judge that America is the most criminal country in the world, and to shape this case towards an expressed or subtly implied conclusion that the United States should be reverted to the state of affairs before the Declaration of Independence. I agree in advance with the reply that these things do not represent the United States; and I claim the same logic in regard to India...

"The fact that there are glaring evils in India needed no ' ordinary American citizen ' for its demonstration. Indians have been working for their removal for generations with as much zeal as reformers in America have been working to eliminate the scheduled six thousand murders per annum, and reformers in England have been trying to remove the canker of venereal disease. I know well all that can be catalogued in laboratory manner regarding human depravity in India, for

I have worked for twelve years in humanitarian causes in the country and am as familiar with its statistics as with its reality. But I cannot prostitute my intelligence to the inept conclusion that because there are sins in India, the people should therefore be kept in political subjection. I am not a politician in the political sense. I am a student of human evolution and a searcher for the perfect way towards human perfectness, and I assert that the needs of the case in India are just the reverse of the implications of *Mother India*. Human experience has always shown, and modern psychology confirms it, that responsibility is the parent of efficiency, not its offspring..."

*

A statement with regard to Miss Mayo's book, *Mother India*, signed by Rev. Dr. N. Macnicol and Mr. P. O. Philip, Secretaries, and Miss A. B. Van Doren, Hon. Officer, has been issued to the Press in the name of the Executive Committee of the National Christian Council of India, Burma and Ceylon, the only dissentient member being Bishop J. W. Robinson, ' who does not find that he can assent to its terms.' The Lord Bishop of Calcutta and Metropolitan of India is the Chairman and Dr. S. K. Dutta is the Vice-Chairman of the Council, and the Executive Committee includes Rev. Chitamber, Bishop of Dornakal, Rev. J. F. Edwards, Dr. C. R. Greenfield, Bishop of Madras, Rev. J. Mackenzie, Rai Bahadur A. C. Mukerji, Messrs. K. T. Paul, B. L. Rallia Ram and Rev. H. C. C. Velt. We take the following from that statement:

"It has never been denied either by Indians or by foreign missionaries that great social evils exist in India, and it is a matter of common knowledge that strenuous and organized efforts are being made by groups of Indian reformers to get rid of them. Yet we, representing a body of men and women who are in close touch with the people and are conversant with their every-day life, unhesitatingly assert that the picture of India which emerges from Miss Mayo's book is untrue to the facts and unjust to the people of India. The sweeping generalizations that are deduced from incidents that come to the notice of the author, or that are suggested by the manner in which these incidents are presented are entirely untrue as a description of India as a whole. At the end of the book Miss Mayo admits that she has left untouched other sides of Indian life, and for that very reason we can affirm that Indian life does not present the dark and the evil aspect which this book suggests, and that the ugly and repulsive and disgusting aspects of it that are emphasized in the book are not the predominant things in Indian society.

"Beauty and culture, kindliness and charm, religion and piety are to be found alike among the highest and the humblest. Miss Mayo leaves no room for these in her picture."

*

In a communication to the Press, Mrs. Margaret E. Cousins, Secretary to the Women's Association in India, referring to Miss Katherine Mayo's *Mother India*, says :

"Although the authoress has made the wrongs done to women in India as the subject of the major portion of her indictment, yet Miss Mayo did not have an interview with any representative Indian woman, like Mrs. Naidu or others. If she had, she should have been wiser. Indian women feel they are being exploited for the delay of self-government to their country."

Mrs. Cousins repudiates the charge that Indian women look for motherhood within nine months after reaching puberty, and says the majority of millions of people do not allow motherhood until after 16. If it were otherwise India would have perished centuries ago. She concludes: "While we repudiate her book, we must turn every ounce of our zeal towards the rooting out of those social evils which are undoubtedly in our midst."

*

Rev. Stanley Jones, a missionary with considerable Indian experience, in the course of a letter to the *Leader* of Allahabad, says:

"My views of *Mother India* may be summed up briefly as follows:

"(1) Taking the individual statements up one by one, it is not easy to disprove them. Here and there inaccuracies and exaggerations may be found, but they would probably stand as a whole. This refers only to the statements of facts themselves, and does not refer to the authoress's generalizations about those facts, which I consider to be often erroneous.

"(2) While conceding this, I feel the book to be very unfair, to say the least. The picture that one gets from reading the book is not a fair or true picture. What happens in the mind of the Western reader who has no facts to set over against the statements of the book may be seen from the words of one Western reviewer: ' India is putrid, worse than Sodom or Gomorrah,' etc. This is a libel on a whole people. No one from the West would feel other than indignant if facts were drawn from the underworld of the West along with police court statistics and set before the world as a true picture of life in the West. This is the unfairness of the book. There is another India not in the book; if that other India had been put in we could not have complained. But the India that I know is not there. And that India I love and respect and honour.

E. STANLEY JONES."

October 5,
Ipoh (Federated Malay States).

*

Mr. Edward Thompson, British novelist and playwright, who served for a fairly long time as an educationist in India, and is at present Professor of Bengali Literature at Oxford, writes in the course of his review published in the London *Nation and Athenæum* for July 30, 1927:

" The indictment takes so wide a sweep, and is so consistently ungenerous, that the book becomes one long ' nagging.' If you can convince them that you do sometimes see their point of view, and have a genuine sympathy with them, and an unpatronizing love for their country and the best things in their civilization, you can utter the hardest and frankest criticisms, and Indians will listen. Officials, professors in Indian colleges, and missionaries all know this. But you get no hearing if you 'nag.' Once Miss Mayo gets away from the treatment of woman the signs of first-hand research grow few. The prince who predicted that within three months of the British leaving India there will not be ' a virgin or a rupee ' in Bengal probably spoke truth; but the English reader is prejudiced to find the stale yarn brought forward, and with so (characteristically, I am afraid) pontifical an air. ' Here is a story from the lips of one whose veracity has never, I believe, been questioned.' Well, it ought to be questioned now, even though her ' informant, an American of long Indian experience,' heard it when visiting a Mahratta prince, a man of great charm, cultivation and force. The story has been told on every steamer that has carried passengers between England and India during the last twenty years; eighteen months ago I heard an M. P. tell it of a Rajput, Sir Pertab Singh. Miss Mayo has no perception of Mr. Gandhi's courage of force, she quotes freely his scathing condemnations of child-marriage, untouchability and other abominations, but sneers at him because he thinks railways and machinery evil and yet uses them. Then, is India the only country where students consider the possible commercial value of a university career? Are there not students at Harvard, Yale, Oxford who are worried as to whether their education is going to result in a decent job? And Miss Mayo is so without imagination or sympathy with another race's point of view that she cannot see that perhaps self-respect prevented *some* Indians from being enthusiastic over the visit of the Prince of Wales—who, after all, belongs to the blood of their conquerors. She writes of that visit in a manner almost maudlin, which will only amuse any English public other than that whose Bible is the illustrated society papers. She has taken over all the 'die-hard,' virulent contempt for the Bengali race and assumes that this contempt is universally felt by the native princes. Bengalis are important ministers in Indian States—even in Udaipur. She shows no sign of suspicion that possibly Bengal, or even English education in India has ever produced anything but ' babus ' and ' failed B.A.'s ' and graduates. ' In the Philippines and in India alike little or no current literature exists available or of interest to the masses, while in both the countries many dialects have no literature at all.' *No* important Indian language is without at least a considerable literature; and Tamil—in the poems of Manikkavasahar and other Saivite devotees; Hindi—in the *Ramayana* of Tulsidas, a singularly noble poem which every autumn is acted in the village of the United Provinces during an ecstatic fortnight; Bengali—in its versions of the *Ramayana* and *Mahabharata*, of which hundreds of thousands of copies are sold every year, and in the exquisite songs of Ramprasad, which you can hear on any Indian road—all have literature in which the masses take keen delight.

"On page 258 Miss Mayo gives an epitome of the history of India under British rule which was obviously picked up at a dinner-table. She quotes, with ponderous solemnity, the promise of 1784 that 'no native...shall, by reason only of his religion, place of birth, descent, colour, or any of them, be disabled from holding any place, office, or employment under the Company.' She adds, 'A bomb indeed, to drop into caste-fettered, feud-filled, tyrant-crushed India!' Yes, and it would have been a bomb to drop into any collection of India's rulers if it had been seriously meant for another century or more. This promise had to be repeated in 1833, and again in 1858; in 1822, and 1824 Sir Thomas Munro, Governor of Madras, wrote with acute feeling of the entire closing of every office above the lowest to Indians, and on May 2nd, 1857 (eight days before the Mutiny broke out), Henry Lawrence wrote angrily of the same state of things. Miss Mayo ascribes 'the Sikh Rebellion in 1845' to 'this shock of free Western ideas.' Against whom did the Sikhs rebel? They were an independent people.

"To sum up. Hindu child-marriage and callousness to misery inflicted on animals—but we have our field sports—deserve the fiercest condemnation. But it was a mistake when Miss Mayo let her magnificent case be lost in a welter of general condemnation. She had no right to forget that despite all the unfairness of Indian politicians, *some* have exhibited unselfish and courageous patriotism and a high standard of fairness towards opponents. She lost her case when she wove into it a bitter conviction that the white man's rule is so overwhelmingly good for inferior breeds that it is only wickedness that makes them dissatisfied."

*

Mr. D. F. McCelland, the American Secretary of the Madras Y.M.C.A., speaking at a public meeting in Madras referred to *Mother India* in these terms :*

" After the reference by our lecturer, Sir T. Sadasiva Aiyer, to the recent book by Miss Katherine Mayo, it is incumbent upon me as an American to make a few remarks. *That a countrywoman of mine should, after a brief stay in India, write so unfairly and offensively of this country is a source of deep humiliation.* I have been able to read the book only in part, as I have loaned the copy, which I had borrowed, to Mr. Andrews, who has taken it off with him. But it is clearly apparent that Miss Mayo saw only a part of India and could not see that part in proper perspective. In many things her accuracy as an observer will not bear scrutiny and her many highly exaggerated conclusions give an utterly false picture of India as a whole. I have been in India since 1915 and have moved during these years among all classes. I have no hesitation in protesting vigorously against the unfairness of her book. Generalizations that may be taken for fact by readers abroad are too often statements of personal opinion based upon prejudice or partial examination. A very offensive book could be written as

* The report is taken from the Madras daily, *The Hindu*.

well of Americans or of any other Western nation and then we, of the West, would rightly protest against such unfair representation. Human sin and social evil are universal, and writers who generalize would do well to keep that in mind... I wish to express to this audience my own sense of great regret that an American citizen should deal so unfairly and with such prejudice in presenting India to the Western world."

*

Speaking at Geneva to a group of students from all parts of the Empire, the Hon'ble Sir C. P. Ramaswami Aiyar, Indian Government's delegate at the League of Nations meeting, said:

" In order to furnish to outsiders a true picture of Miss Mayo's *Mother India* it is perhaps most useful to employ a figure of speech. Assume that a guest is invited to my house and is shown the drawing-room and the living quarters and has the additional opportunity of seeing the garden and its embellishments and assume that when taking leave of the host he catches sight of the open drain in a corner. Assume, moreover, that this person to whom my hospitality has been extended proceeds to write a book about what he has seen and concentrates on the drain and ignores the other features of the house and garden—that would be to act as Miss Mayo has done. In saying this I do not for a moment ignore or minimize the many social evils and handicaps from which India is suffering. Some of these evils are as old as humanity and some aspects of these evils are as prominent in Europe and America as in India;

but every right-minded Indian patriot is willing and anxious to right these abuses and is working for their eradication. In such an endeavour Indians have been helped by men and women of other races, but amongst such helpers cannot be counted persons like Miss Mayo with filthy minds who in all probability are suffering from inhibited instincts and who have no eyes but for evil, dirt and degradation."

*

Mrs. J. C. Wedgwood, writing in *The People*, Lahore, for January 5, 1928, observes :

"Many Englishwomen are feeling strong indignation at the way in which Indians have been misrepresented by Katherine Mayo, an American, in her book *Mother India*. We wish you to know how deeply we resent her untruthful vilification of Indian life and the false picture she has drawn of Indian ways and Indian thought. Even if everything evil which she has related were true, yet, by the omission of the good she gives to her readers utterly wrong ideas, and causes them to despise Indians, both Hindu and Muhammadan, as 'weak, ignorant and fanatical.' Women as well as men are made to appear superstitious, sensual and slavish,—without desire to be otherwise...

" For example, a reader of her book would come to the conclusion that there were *no* happy marriages in India, but always a tyrannical and cruel old husband ill-treating a terrified child-wife. Miss Mayo ignores the beautiful relationship which most often exists between an Indian husband and wife, the tender protectiveness of the one, and the responsive devotion and loyalty of the other. Indeed, the undying, unquenchable love of an Indian wedded pair is traditional, and is recognized among all nations. It is the theme of many a beautiful legend and song. Miss Mayo is, perhaps, the more anxious to have this conveniently forgotten, because it throws into glaring contrast the unfaithfulness and easy divorce of so many American marriages. To these ' modern ' women, the idea of serving their husbands would seem ridiculous, rather they seek to enslave the man, and get all they can from him, then leave him for fresh game...

"Another evil exaggerated by Miss Mayo is the caste system, and again there is just as much cause to attack America for the same thing. White Americans despise, and will have no contact with, negro Americans—they are the ' untouchables ' in that country. But Miss Mayo is so busy picking holes in Indians, she has no time to look at home. She quotes Indian after Indian who defends ' untouchability ' and one only— Mr. Gandhi—who denounces it...

" It would be quite easy for any one of you who had the time and the opportunity to write a *Mother America* which should show only the dark side of that country—its worldliness and unparalleled crime, its lynchings and divorces, its prostitution and its slums, etc., and make such a travesty of the truth about the U.S.A. as Miss Mayo has done about India, but it would not be good to lower yourself to her level. Rather, as I

suggest, you should make her ashamed by publicly
expressing your regret for her lack of wide vision,
and try to open her eyes to the truth... People will
then feel amazed as well as disgusted that Miss
Mayo should prefer to search with a muck-rake
and shut her eyes to all the beautiful flowers and
fruits with which India abounds."

*

Major D. Graham Pole, a Labour candidate
for Parliament, writes in *The New Leader*, London,
for August 19, 1927 :

"After a perusal of *Mother India*,...one might
be led to the conclusion that the ideal of self-
government for India could have no existence
outside the minds of visionaries or fanatics. It
is reassuring to remember, however, that some
years ago the writer, Miss Katherine Mayo, visited
the Philippines and wrote a book about that visit
also. It was called, *The Isles of Fear*, and was,
in effect. a defence of American imperialism.
Miss Mayo has now, after her Indian visit, done a
like service for British imperialism in *Mother
India*.

" No wonder the book is regarded as a god-
send by those reactionaries who wish to maintain
our hold over India, who have given up their
former excuses, and now tell us plainly that ' the
basic fact is that India is not socially fit for self-
government,' and that political concession must be
postponed by this country until Indian conditions
improve. ' We must not betray India under the
pretext of giving her a political boon,' one of the

APPENDIX I

Conservative journals tells us in reviewing this book.

"Sir John Maynard, K.C.S.I., a retired Indian Civil Servant, who has spent the greater part of his life in India and has filled every office until he retired a member of the Governor's Executive Council in the Punjab, says that he finds it hard to write with restraint about this book. I concur. I have travelled through India from north to south and east to west on no fewer than six different tours during the last sixteen years, and have lived in Indian households both in British India and in the Indian States. I could write a book on India with conclusions as different from Miss Mayo's as could possibly be imagined—and, if I wished, as partial. I might confine my observations to Indian life as I saw it through these houses in which I stayed, and even so, it would give a truer picture of India than Miss Mayo could draw from what she has seen.

"She is interested in Indian society only where it is unhealthy. She creates her 'atmosphere' in the first chapter with a sketch of what is to us, as well as to many Hindus, a revolting religious rite, although it is not in the least characteristic of India, and is practised only by the lowest and most ignorant of Indians. As with religion, so with social customs. To give an idea of marriage in India she has recourse to the hospitals and to the reports of medical authorities, although in the nature of things it is only exceptional cases which come under their notice.

"One would think from Miss Mayo's book that there is hardly a person in India who is not suffering from venereal disease—a suggestion which, Sir John Maynard writes, would be contradicted by any medical practitioner who had worked in Inida. Sir Reginald Craddock, a recently retired Indian Governor, writing to the *Morning Post*, also insists that the picture given by Miss Mayo is too drab and that she has 'concentrated on the darkest side,' whilst the reviewer in the *Times* admits that the impartial judge will detect 'signs of overstatement.' To write, as she does, that Indian women of child-bearing age cannot safely venture, without special protection, within reach of Indian men is, to my knowledge, a gross and unfounded slander. If Miss Mayo came to Britain and visited the hospitals she could paint as dark a picture of British life: if she spent some days in a Police Court there would be very little light and shade in her revelations of British family life. Or, to take her own country, what idea of American civilization could we not derive from that most American product, the film? It is extremely ironical that, at a moment when Miss Mayo's book is giving us this appalling picture of Indian civilization, the Government of India have found it necessary to introduce legislation to deal with the importation of American cinema films owing to their demoralizing influence on Indians!

"On political matters Miss Mayo shows as little balance. She has visited the Indian legislatures, central or provincial, and tells us that sitting through their sessions, an outsider comes to feel like one observing a roomful of small and rather mischievous children who by accident have got hold of a magnificent watch. ' They fight and scramble to thrust their fingers into it, to pull off a wheel or two, to play with the main-spring; to pick out the jewels.' I have seen the Indian legislatures at work, and am bound to say that they compare very favourably either with our local councils or with the Imperial Parliament itself. The Hon'ble Mr. V. J. Patel, President of the Indian Legislative Assembly, has just concluded a visit to this country. Much of his time was spent in the House of Commons and his amazement was intense at the lack of order he found there compared with that of the Assembly over which he so ably presides. When we are told by Miss Mayo that hour after hour and day after day the Swarajist Benches in the Indian Legislative Assembly spend their energies in sterile obstructive tactics, while for the most part the rest of the House sit apathetic, we wonder if Miss Mayo is aware that in the matter of obstructive tactics those who at present sit on the Treasury Bench in the British House of Commons are the past masters. And, if she would like to feel the dead weight of apathy, she has only to attend an Indian debate in the House of Commons where, if she is lucky, she may find as many as 20 out of 415 Conservative members present—mostly yawning or half-asleep.

"Miss Mayo believes that Britain has tried to hustle India into politics, and she tells us that the East resents being hustled, even in reforms. She attributes the failure of Dyarchy not to its inherent defects—defects which are admitted by everyone, from the late Lord Curzon to the Governor of the United Provinces, who described it as a cumbrous, complex, confused system—but to Mr. Gandhi's 'ill-starred adventure into politics.' One looks in vain for any mention of General Dyer and Amritsar. But had Miss Mayo made inquiry of almost any Indian she would have been told that the terrible Amritsar Massacre of 1919 has had more to do with opposition to the reforms than has anything else.

" The authoress discounts the complaints of Indians as to the 'drains' on their economic resources. Army officers, in addition, are spending their private incomes there, over and above their pay. On the next page she contradicts herself when she draws attention to the fact that the children of officers in the British Army or in the Civil Service have to be sent home to England to be educated—where a considerable part of their pay is necessarily spent. But as recently as March '21 last Lord Winterton, in the House of Commons, gave figures showing that there are between 4,000 and 5,000 retired military officers in this country who are drawing annually from Indian revenues and spending it in this country, a sum amounting to almost £2,000,000; whilst there are over 3,000 retired members of the Indian gazetted services, retired and living in this country drawing annually £1,500,000. Surely these are serious drains on the finances of India, to say nothing of the large number of Joint Stock Banks,

APPENDIX I

Mercantile Houses, Factories, etc., whose profits flow to this country.

"The late Lord Lytton, when Viceroy of India, wrote to the Government here a Despatch, in which, speaking of the expectation and claims of Indians to a fair course of promotion to the higher posts in the services of the Government of India, he said :

'We all know that these expectations never can, or will, be fulfilled. We have to choose between prohibiting them or cheating them; we have chosen the least straightforward course.'

" And he added :

'Both the Governments of England and of India had to take every means in their power of breaking to the heart the promises they had uttered to the ear.'

"This book, it seems to me, will be yet another excuse for breaking to Indians our oft-repeated pledges of equality between Indians and Europeans in India.

"The Conservative Government will endeavour to hold on to all that we have got, not for the sake of India, but for the sake of the financial interests that are involved. It is for the Labour Party to see that our pledges are honoured—to allow the Indian people to take up their own burdens and responsibilities, to become custodians of their own welfare.

*

Mr. H. S. L. Polak, a British solicitor, who has visited India several times and has had opportunity to come into contact with Indians in three continents, in the course of a letter to the *Manchester Guardian* writes:

" Miss Lilian Winstanley takes exception to Dr. Tagore's accusation that Miss Katherine Mayo was impelled by ' race hatred ' and other malignant motives in writing *Mother India*. She quotes in defence of Miss Mayo the fierce criticism of their American fellow-citizens by certain well-known American writers.

" The instances cited are not parallel. The victims of those writers can hit back. Miss Mayo's victims, on the contrary, whether in the Philippines or in India, cannot; and Indians who have read the book, or excerpts from it, are united in believing that that was one of the motives that impelled Miss Mayo to write it. They assert that, under the guise of preparing, for no convincing reason, an objective sanitary report, she has written, in fact, and intended to write, a political pamphlet in line with the corresponding political pamphlet that she wrote earlier on the Philippines. Whatever may have been Miss Mayo's motive, she has, in Mahatma Gandhi's words, written ' an untruthful book,' and she appears to have distorted facts and statements to suit her purposes...

" But, while the replies to *Mother India* will probably receive little notice, Indians are only too well aware of the subtle propaganda-use here, in America, and on the Continent, that is being made of *Mother India*. Again and again my Indian friends, high in the service of the State and the esteem of their countrymen, have come to me bitterly indignant at being asked to explain, if they can, the various statements in the book by questioners who assume their correctness as though it was irrefutable and its writer clothed with plenary inspiration. How far this poison has gone it is difficult to judge; but of one thing I am sure—that, whatever may have been Miss Mayo's motive, the wide circulation and the propaganda-use of the book have promoted and intensified race hatred in India is beyond dispute, and the consequences of this are incalculable..."

APPENDIX II

DEPRESSED CLASSES

Miss Mayo has insinuated in many places that the Hindus generally, and the ministers of the Reformed Government particularly, stand in the way of the progress of the untouchables or the depressed classes. The following quotations taken from the speech of the Hon'ble the Education Secretary to the Government of India in a debate which took place in the Legislative Assembly on the 23rd February, 1928, shows how unfounded Miss Mayo's insinuations are. The debate was raised by a resolution moved by a Hindu member to the effect—

"That this Assembly recommends to the Governor-General in Council to issue directions to all Local Governments to provide special facilities for the education of the untouchables and other depressed classes and also for opening public services to them."

In practically opposing this resolution the Education Secretary said : " For the Government of India the problem is not a problem to provide special facilities for the education of the depressed classes. It really is a problem of providing educational facilities for all classes."

Further on in giving figures of progress of education among the depressed classes the Education Secretary said :

APPENDIX II

"I take 1917, as it were, the datum line, and 1926 as the year for which the latest report is available. Let me state generally that within this period (between 1917 and 1926) the number of schools belonging to the depressed classes reading in recognized schools has risen from 2,95,000 in 1917 to 6,67,000 in 1926—in other words a more than 100 per cent. increase—and I think it will be only fair at this stage to state that a considerable part of the progress which has been made in the provision of facilities for the education of the depressed classes and the increase that has taken place in the number of students belonging to the depressed classes have taken place SINCE THE INCEPTION OF THE REFORMS IN 1921."

In another part of the speech the same Hon'ble Member said :

" The barriers of SOCIAL PREJUDICE ARE BREAKING DOWN and to-day we find the position THAT MEMBERS OF THE DEPRESSED CLASSES ARE READING IN THE ORDINARY SCHOOLS...AND THE REVERSE PROCESS IS ALSO GOING ON, NAMELY, THAT MEMBERS OF THE SUPERIOR CLASSES ARE READING IN SCHOOLS WHICH ARE SPECIALLY MEANT FOR THE DEPRESSED CLASSES. Let me give the figures. In the United Provinces there were roughly 56,000 pupils belonging to the depressed classes in 1925 and of these 56,000, 33,000 were reading in ordinary schools and 23,000, or less than half, were reading in special schools. In the case of the Punjab the figures are still more striking. Out of roughly 19,000 odd students 16,000 were reading in ordinary schools and 3,000 odd were reading in special schools...

Practically every province, Sir, has opened special schools. Personally I am not much in love with these special schools, the reason being that I look forward to the day when the social prejudice would have softened sufficiently for members of all classes and communities to read in the same school. However, as I say, the first step which the Local Governments [which mean the Indian Ministers of Education] have taken is to establish and start special schools. The second step which they have taken is to give special scholarships and to remit fees in the case of students belonging to the depressed classes. The third step which they have taken is to liberalize the rules for grants-in-aid to schools and also other special subsidies to schools which teach pupils belonging to the depressed classes. The fourth step which they have taken is to give special capitation grant."

Speaking of the United Province, which is one of the most orthodox provinces in India, the Education Secretary said :

" There the creidt is due primarily to the ministers under whose instructions this work is being done......36 out of 38 district boards have appointed special supervisors in order to foster education among the depressed classes."

Pandit Madan Mohan Malaviya is by common consent the head of the orthodox community in India and it would be interesting to our readers to know what his views on this question are. In the course of a long speech on the resolution he observed :

"Sir, I have very great pleasure in offering my support to the resolution which is before the House. It is a matter for regret and reproach to the Government and to the country that such a resolution should have to be brought forward at this advanced period of the history of the world. It is a matter for reproach to both of us, and I wish that we should each, in criticizing the other, frankly recognize our share of the responsibility. It is undoubtedly true that for a long time past the depressed classes, as they are called, have been living under conditions which are very depressing indeed. The social customs and rules, as they have been understood, or wrongly understood among a section of us Hindus, have largely been responsible for it in the past. But, Sir, as more than one speaker has pointed out, Hindu public opinion has undergone a very great change on these questions, and to-day it is a matter for sincere satisfaction to Hindus that a large number of their public men of all classes, and among them a large number of Brahmans, are working for the amelioration of the depressed classes. There are many societies and missions working in which the higher classes of Hindus, as they are called, have been taking an active and prominent part to ameliorate the condition of the depressed classes. My friend, Lala Lajpat Rai, has referred to these efforts, and mentioned the name of the one large-hearted donor, Babu Jugal Kishore Birla, eldest brother of our colleague. Babu Ghanshyam Das Birla. He alone has been spending between Rs. 20,000 and Rs. 25,000 *every month* for ameliorating the condition of the depressed classes."

Mr. H. G. Cocke: Is it Government?

Pandit Madan Mohan Malaviya : "I am speaking of what Babu Jugal Kishore Birla, brother of our friend, Babu Ghanshyam Das Birla, has been spending for the last five years for the amelioration of the condition of the depressed classes. There are numerous other individuals and societies which have been working in the same direction, and I am happy to be able to say that Hindu public opinion has undergone a very great change. The House has heard from Pandit Thakurdas Bhargava what that change means. There are thousands of men in the higher classes of Hindus who make no distinction between a brother belonging to one of the depressed classes and another brother of the higher classes.

" Many of us have long recognized that this question of the amelioration of the condition of the depressed classes is largely a question of education. I can say that this has been recognized by every sensible man who has looked at this question. The other day I quoted from a speech which I delivered in 1916 in the Imperial Legislative Council in which I said that

> 'the question of the elevation of the depressed classes depends largely, almost wholly, nay I say, depends wholly upon education. That is the one solvent which will solve this problem, and most certainly do I wish and pray that the Government will do as much more as it can towards the spread of education among these classes. I also urged that the

schools of the Government and of the community should be open to the children of the depressed classes as much as to any other children.'

"That was in 1916—i.e., before the Reforms. But let me say,—and it pains me to say it—in connection with this question of the elevation of the depressed classes, that while I gladly recognize that a few officers of the Government have individually expressed a great deal of sympathy with them, and while the Local Governments have taken some steps to improve their condition, what they have actually done for them is very very small compared to what they should have done...

"I draw attention to these facts to show that, while the Government of India as a whole and many officials of the Government of India individually, repeatedly expressed deep sympathy with the cause of the education of the people, and while the Government of India's records are full of resolutions recognizing that it was their duty to extend it and expressing their desire that it should be extended, as a matter of fact the Government of India did very little to promote general mass education. And what is worse, when, as I have said, a resolution was brought forward in 1910, by Mr. Gokhale in the Governor-General's Council, the Home Member at the time, Sir Harvey Adamson, opposed the resolution. A year later Mr. Gokhale brought forward his Bill for permitting compulsory and free primary education to be introduced in certain areas. It is sad to recall that the Government opposed that Bill also. Mr. Gokhale's resolution of 1910 was withdrawn, but when the motion that his Bill of 1911 be referred to a Select Committee was brought forward the Government members voted against it. It is painful to recall how that modest Bill which sought only to give permission to certain Local Boards under certain conditions to make elementary education free and compulsory was defeated by the votes of the Government. Only 13 of us—humble representatives of the people—voted for the motion to refer the Bill to a Select Committee, and 38 persons—at the head of whom stood His Honour the Lieutenant Governor of Bengal—and which included all the officials, and I am sorry to say, certain Indian members, voted against the motion, and killed the Bill. Now that was in 1912. In 1918, my friend, Rai Bahadur B. N. Sarma, brought forward a resolution in this Council that one of the post-War reforms should be the introduction throughout British India of free and compulsory primary education immediately after the War. That resolution again was opposed by the Government..."

The reference to Pandit Thakurdas Bhargava by Pandit Malaviya was with reference to that part of Pandit Bhargava's speech in which he said that he was not only prepared to shake hands with untouchables but also to eat with them. Pandit Bhargava said:

" So far as the Hindus are concerned to-day it is not correct to say that the Hindus are not in favour of equal treatment being meted out to the depressed classes. Now, Sir, I speak for every section of the Hindus. I do not belong to the advanced section. I BELONG TO THE ORTHODOX PART OF IT BUT I MAY SAY THAT YOU WILL NOT FIND ANY HINDU WORTH HIS NAME IN THE WHOLE COUNTRY WHO IS NOT READY TO CONCEDE EQUALITY OF RIGHTS TO ALL MEMBERS OF THE DEPRESSED CLASSES. (An Honourable Member: " Will you shake hands with them?) What is shaking hands. I am ready to dine with them. To-day...the question is out of date and you will be glad to know that thousands like myself are doing their mite in their own unostentatious way. I would rather inform the Hon'ble Member that there are societies in various districts of the Punjab which have taken up this question and which have done perhaps more than what the Local Governments have done in this matter."

In moving an amendment I made the following speech :

" Sir, my friend the Mover made it clear what the object of this resolution is. We do not admit that sufficient has been done either by the Government of India or the Governments of the provinces in this direction. Moreover, we also complain that there is great diversity of practice between different provinces as to what local governments are doing in this matter, and there seems to be great confusion of ideas between local administrations about what they should do and therefore it is necessary to clarify this by a clear pronouncement of the Government of India. I must say that to my mind that pronouncement is very disappointing. It shows that although a very great and loud claim has been made for the solicitude of the Government of India for the depressed classes—the trustees of 60 millions of depressed classes—yet sufficient is not being done to bring them educationally at least to the level of the other communities of India, or to give them equal privileges by virtue of their being citizens of India.

"I will first take the Education Secretary's figures. First of all I might clear this point by saying what I mean by special facilities. It is a recognized principle of the Government of India, which has been stated in many despatches on education, that classes which are backward in education must be taken in hand by Government and brought up to the level of other classes. It is the considered policy of the Government of India and has been put into practice in different provinces for the last twenty or twenty-five years, nay, even more, by different measures taken by different provinces for the purpose. It is now too late to say that there are general institutions that are open to all classes of His Majesty's subjects, that they are quite sufficient for the purpose of giving education to the depressed classes, and that special facilities are not required. It is shown that special facilities are being given and are required. In certain places those special facilities are being provided, and Government is alive to the necessity and importance of providing special facilities in these places. But what are those special facilities that have been so much dilated upon as having brought about remarkable results? I would remind the House that there are only three provinces out of nine in which special steps are alleged to have been taken to provide facilities for the depressed classes, and one of them is the United Provinces, where great credit is due to the minister. I want to pay my tribute to him openly. In the case of the other provinces, Bombay has only one Division in which anything special is being done, and in Madras the Commissioner of Labour has been asked to look after the depressed classes.

"I ask the House to consider whether the fact, that in three provinces out of nine any special care is taken for the education of the depressed classes, is satisfactory. This is a very meagre record, and I don't think that any Government should be proud of it. In only one province something adequate has been done, and that is the United Provinces. That also has been done by the exertion of the minister and also by private agencies."

Mr. G. S. Bajpai: "I would like to correct one mis-apprehension which my friend seems to be labouring under. It was not the purport of my remarks to say that special measures had been taken only in three provinces. What I said was that a special staff had been appointed in three provinces. In addition to that I stated that certain measures of a general character, such as the offer of special scholarships, remissions of fees, opening of schools, liberal grant-in-aid had been resorted to; these I said were common to more than three provinces."

Lala Lajpat Rai: "If my Honourable friend had waited, he would have found that I was coming to that point. What he has explained to us does not at all explain the matter fully. He has stated that in three provinces only, special staff had been appointed to look after the education of the depressed classes. If he goes into the Education Report he will find that almost in every province a special staff has been appointed by the Government to look after the other classes considered to be backward, but only in three provinces has any special staff been appointed to look after the depressed classes. That is a point which is worthy of note.

"Now we will come to what has been done in the matter of special facilities. I will dispose of the special concessions first; with regard to that I submit that the practice in different local governments is not quite uniform, and in all places there are not special scholarships granted for the benefit of the depressed classes. I will read to you another question which was put in the same session of the Punjab Legislative Council, in which the question read to you by the Honourable the Mover was put, about the enrolment of the depressed classes in the Police :

' *Lala Mohan Lal:*—(a) Will the Honourable Minister for Education be pleased to state if it is a fact that the Government has fixed some scholarships for the boys of the criminal tribes?

(b) If the reply to the above be in the affirmative, will the Honourable Minister be pleased to state if they intend to extend this privilege to the boys of the members of the depressed classes?'

' The answer by the Honourable Mr. Manohar Lal was :

(a) Stipends are awarded.

(b) Members of the depressed classes are eligible for fee concessions under article 12, chapter IV of the Punjab Education Code.'

" The House will see how cleverly the Minister evades the question that was put to him. The question was, if special scholarships similar to those provided for the children of the criminal tribes were also provided for the children of the depressed classes. He did not reply to that question but he referred to the general concessions that were provided in the provincial Educational Code.

"Sir, great importance has been attached to the rise in the number of the scholars of the depressed classes. It has been said that within the last decade, since when the Government of India discovered the existence of the depressed classes on account of the announcement of August 1917, and on account of the Reforms being on the anvil, since that time the number of scholars of these depressed classes has increased from about 3 lakhs to about 6 lakhs, that is 100 per cent., as my friend said. Yet, Sir, it is being dinned into our ears every day and disseminated broadcast all over the world that there are 60 millions of these depressed classes who are protected by this Government against the tyranny of the superior Hindu castes; and in these ten years, since this enumeration has taken place, the Government is very proud of having put one per cent. of this community as scholars in schools. Is that an achievement which the Government is proud of, considering the boast they always make and the interest they profess to take in these classes, saying that it is their concern? Then, Sir, I want this House particularly to remember that this increase in the number of scholars of these depressed classes is not due to the efforts of the Government alone. I do not deny that something is being done by the Government, but I think that that something is extremely insufficient. The increase in the number of the scholars of these depressed classes is due very largely to private effort. I may tell my Honourable friend, if he does not know it, that various Hindu organizations have been trying not only to encourage the introduction of these scholars of the depressed classes into the ordinary schools and to remove any bans and prejudices that may be existing against them, but also to open up special schools and to provide special scholarships for them. I know of one individual (Hindu) who has been spending within the last five or six years from Rs. 15,000 to Rs. 25,000 a month on the education of these depressed classes and that is the eldest brother of my friend,

Mr. Ghanshyam Das Birla. So the Government cannot take exclusive credit for having increased the number of scholars of these depressed classes. The cause of this increase is due, in part at least, to the Hindu organizations that have been working in this direction very zealousy and devoting funds —they are also entitled to the credit. I wanted to know exactly what part the Government has played in the advancement of the depressed classes and what they are at present prepared to do. The reply to that question is practically nil; because as far as the expenditure is concerned, we have been told grandiloquently that 30 lakhs had been sanctioned for education by the Government of India; but we were not told this more relevant point of how much of that money had been spent for the advancement and education of the depressed classes. Not even my friend, Mr. Joshi's question has been answered as to how much of that has been spent on primary education. The bulk of that money is being spent on education, no doubt; but surely the Education Department could have given us the figures of how much is being spent on primary education and on the education of the depressed classes; that information is not forthcoming. I know that something like 6 lakhs out of this 30 lakhs have been given to two universities; I do not quarrel with that and I am glad they have got that money; but after providing for them, you must also provide more for the depressed classes and for primarry education. I want to know from the Government of India what example they are going to set to the different local governments in this matter and that is why I propose a definite sum of one crore of rupees to be sanctioned for the education of these depressed classes from Central funds; surely that is not too much—one crore of rupees for six crores of people whom you announce under big headlines in the newspapers to be under the special protection of the Government and whom you use for your political propaganda. I could surely ask the Government to sanction one crore of rupees for the immediate uplift of these people by providing them with education in order to uplift their social and economic conditions. It is not a very big demand considering the proportion of the population—6 crores out of 24 crores which are under British rule. They amount to one-fourth of the population on your figures and if we ask you to sanction one crore of rupees in order to give them a start so that they may afterwards be taken into the schools under the ordinary rules, surely that is not a very big demand. And it is a test of your sincerity and of your alleged concern for the interests of the depressed classes. I want the Government to play up and show us that they are really anxious; that their claims are sincere and *bona fide;* that they are not playing a political game, but that they are really interested in the education and uplift of the depressed classes. That is my point in bringing forward this proposal to spend one crore of rupees on their education. Do Government really want that these depressed classes should be educated, should be uplifted and be brought to the level of other communities? If so, let them accept my amendment. But the Government of India is not

accustomed to do things of that kind; they are
not in the habit of doing things of that kind; they
simply want to use catch phrases for their own
political ends; but when it comes to doing anything tangible, there is nothing doing. There are
a large number of other things; there is the army,
there is the navy, and there are so many other
things on which money can be spent and must be
spent; but when it comes to the education of these
classes for whom Government of India here and
the Secretary of State at Whitehall profess so
much solicitude, then there is an evasion of the
question or there is a plain refusal and an
absolute "No." I hope the people of this country
and the people of the world will take note of the
state of things and will value the professions of
the Government of India at their proper worth.

" Now coming to the figures that have been
given by the different provinces, I do not want to
go into them now, because I have not got the time;
otherwise I could have shown that the different
provinces have practically neglected the depressed
classes. The only two provinces which have
made some progress are Bengal and the United
Provinces. The Honourable Member pointed out
rather scoffingly that the Punjab had not done
much. I may tell him that in the Punjab we have
done much more than the Government has done
for the education of the depressed classes. We
have provided special schools; we have given
scholarships; we have opened special wells for
them which the Government never provided for
them considering that these were the classes who

were so much oppressed by the tyrannical Hindus. The Honourable the Home Member said the other day that the complaint of the depressed classes was not so much against the Government as against the Brahmanical caste system and against the Brahmans. Well, here I want to test your good will and your sympathy for these depressed classes. Here is something tangible to be done; do it please. We are as much interested, perhaps even much more interested than you are, in the elevation of the depressed classes; we believe that untouchability is a great slur, and a great blot on the fair name of Hinduism, and the sooner we remove it the better. We are also interested in bringing them up to our level because we want our ranks to be solidified and to come up to one level, so that we may be able to take India with us as a whole at an early date. We are much more interested in the elevation of the depressed classes than any Government can possibly be; but we want to know what you are doing when you are making empty boasts that you are interested in the uplift of these sixty millions of the depressed classes, as against us who are striving to raise them and to bring them up to our own level.

"Now, Sir, I do not want to say much more, as my time is very limited. I want to say only a word or two about the other points which I have raised...

"I was just going to say a word about roads and wells. This point has been raised in my amendment for this reason that the Hindu members once brought up a resolution in the Punjab Legislative Council that all public wells in all municipalities and district boards should be thrown open to all communities including the depressed classes, and the resolution was resisted by the Government and lost. As regards roads several times attempts have been made in the Madras Presidency to have all roads opened to the depresssed classes, in fact some people in their zeal for bringing about this reform, have gone to jail; but the main obstruction has come from the Government; and that is why I want the Government of India to enunciate a policy which will apply to the whole of India and to which all local governments and administrations will conform. Of course the word " Local " is a wide term and will include all those administrations which are directly or indirectly under the Government of India and therefore they can spend their money on those areas which are in their charge directly.

"One word more, Sir, and I have finished. I want a special list of untouchables and other so-called depressed classes to be made. because I am perfectly certain that many of the classes who are classified as untouchables at present are really not untouchables. The figure has been swollen for political objects as I said the day before. In 1917 the figure was estimated to be somewhere near 30 millions; in the census of 1921 the exact figure came to about 52 millions; then it was simply stated in the Report somewhere that the figure may be estimated to be somewhere between

52 and 60 millions; and Mr. Coatman in his annual report on India has just put it definitely at 60 millions. In the next census it may rise to 100 millions because there is an object behind it. So I want that a special inquiry should be made to find out who are untouchables and who are not.

"With these remarks, Sir, I commend my amendment to the acceptance of the House.

APPENDIX III

THE GOVERNMENT OF INDIA AND CASTE

Some time ago, in the course of an article in *The People*, Lahore, dealing with the attitude of the Government of India towards social reform among Hindus, I said that both by their military and civil policy the Government was bolstering up the caste system. A Labour M. P., asked the Under-Secretary of State for India in the House of Commons if that was a fact. The Under-Secretary of State for India gave an answer which was not true. Probably it was no fault of his. The information supplied to him by the India Office was incorrect. Upon this I addressed a letter to the Military Secretary to the Government of India in the Legislative Assembly to which he has sent the following reply which I give below *in extenso*:—

New Delhi, the 7th March, 1928.

MY DEAR LALA LAJPAT RAI,

Will you please refer to your demi-official letter, dated, the 24th February, 1928. As I explained in answer to Mr. Ram Narayan Singh's question No. 880 on September 6th, 1927, the Government of India do not themselves draw any distinction between 'martial' and 'non-martial' classes. Recruitment is at present restricted to certain classes because the Indian Army is of limited size and the military authorities must necessarily procure from their expert point of view, the best material they can get. It is not denied that other classes would also make good soldiers (though not as good as those at present recruited). The Government of India have no particular literature about the classes enlisted in the Indian army. Instructions to Recruiting Officers are embodied in the 'Recruiting Regulations, Indian Army,' a copy of which will be found in the Assembly Library, and the class composition of each regiment is shown at the top of the pages in the Indian Army List on which the 1st battalion of the regiment appears.

I also forward, for your information, a statement showing the main classes which are now enlisted in the Indian Army and the arms of the service in which they are enlisted. Each of the main classes is of course subdivided into various sub-classes or clans, *e.g.*, Pathans include Khattacks, Yusufzais, Bangash, etc.; Punjabi Mussalmans comprise Rajputs, Awans, Tiwanas, Jats, etc. Similarly with the Sikh and Hindu classes. The various denominations of the sub-classes and clans probably run into hundreds.

Yours sincerely,
G. M. Young.

Regulation No. 14 runs as follows :

"14. Units should recruit from all sub-divisions of classes and from the whole of the area allotted to them, but must not recruit outside those classes or areas without permission.

"The classes and tribes authorized to be recruited by units are shown in Appendix XIV— (will be issued separately).

"The statement of classes recruited for the fighting arms of the Indian Army gives the following list of Hindus and others who are considered eligible for being recruited to the different arms of the Indian Army :—

Statement of classes recruited for fighting arms of the Indian Army.

Main class recruited.	Whether recruited for					
	Cavalry.	Artillery.	Sappers and Miners.	Signals.	M. G. Platoons British Battalions.	Infantry and Pioneers.
Mussalmans.						
Punjabi Mussalmans	yes	yes	yes	yes	yes	yes
Pathans	yes	...	yes	...	...	yes
Punjabi Mussalmans	yes	yes	yes	yes	yes	yes
Hindustani do.	yes	yes	yes	...	...	...
Rajputana do.	yes	...	...	...	...	yes
Dakhani do.	yes	...	...	...	...	yes
Madrasi do.	...	...	yes	yes	...	yes
Hazaras	...	...	...	...	...	yes

	Whether recruited for					
Main class recruited.	Cavalry.	Artillery.	Sappers and Miners.	Signals.	M. G. Platoons British Battalions.	Infantry and Pioneers.
Hindus and other Classes.						
Sikhs	yes	yes	yes	yes	...	yes
Dogras	yes	...	...	yes	...	yes
Garhwalis	...	...	yes	...	...	yes
Kumaonis	...	...	...	...	yes	yes
Rajputs	yes	yes	yes	...	yes	yes
Brahmans	...	yes	...	...	...	...
Jats	yes	yes	yes	...	yes	yes
Mahrattas	...	yes	yes	...	...	yes
Ahirs	...	yes	...	...	yes	yes
Gujars	...	yes	...	...	...	yes
Madrasi Hindus	...	...	yes	yes	...	yes
Madrasi Christians	...	...	yes	yes	...	yes
Burma classes	...	...	yes	...	...	yes
Gurkhas	...	...	...	...	...	yes

Leaving aside the Sikhs, the Madrasi Hindus (what the term means and comprises is not intelligible) and Burma classes (which again is rather vague) it comes to this that no Hindu who is not a Rajput, Brahman, Jat, Ahir or Gujar can be recruited in the Punjab, the United Provinces, Bengal, Bihar and Orissa, Gujrat, Bombay, Sindh, and N.-W. F. Province. Amongst Brahmans only certain sub-castes are eligible, and those too only for the Artillery.

APPENDIX III 541

As far as the Cavalry is concerned only Sikhs, Dogras, Rajputs and Jats are eligible. These distinctions are made even more prominent in the nomenclature of the different regiments and companies.

It will be thus seen that the statement made by the Under-Secretary of State for India in the House of Commons was entirely misleading.

The Indian Army not only maintains "class" distinctions but it also maintains the distinctions of castes and sub-castes. It thereby militates against attempts to reform the caste system. The other day the Sainis of the Punjab, passed a resolution asking for admission into the Army.

Similar distinction is made in the Police and other Civil Departments of the Government. The following question and answer taken from the proceedings of the Punjab Legislative council are significant of the Government's sympathy for the depressed classes :—

Page 687 of the Council Debates, 23rd February, 1928 :

"*Q*.—Will the Hon'ble Member for Finance be pleased to state if members of the depressed classes are taken in the police? If not, does the Government intend to direct that, in the matter of recruitment of police constables, the members of the depressed classes should also be taken?"

"*A*.—Members of the depressed classes are not enrolled in the police. When there is evidence that the depressed classes are treated on an equal footing by all sections of the community, or when the Government is satisfied that enrolment of members of these classes will satisfy the requirements of efficiency and be in the best interests of the composition of the service, Government will be quite prepared to throw open recruitment to them, provided they come up to the physical and other standards required of all recruits.'

Yet another proof. In answer to a question put by a non-official member of the Legislative Assembly about the eligibility of the Bhandaras of Ratnagiri district (an admittedly sea-faring Hindu class) to the lower ranks of the Indian Marine, the Military Secretary said :—

No. 324, 25th August, 1927. (*a*) The answer is in the negative as Government do not propose to recruit Hindu castes into the lower ranks of the Indian Navy at present.

Caste distinction is most strictly maintained in the administration of the Punjab Land Alienation Act. Except certain specified "castes" notified by Government as "agricultural tribes" no one can buy land from a member of an agricultural tribe under the Act.

APPENDIX IV

One of the charges levelled against us by Miss Mayo relates to the lack of interest on the part of educated Indians in the movement for the education of masses. That the charge is entirely groundless can be more than abundantly proved by facts and figures. The non-Government Schools Conference held toward the end of February, 1928, at Lahore under the Presidentship of Mahatma Hans Raj is a complete refutation of the charge. The Chairman of the Reception Committee, Mr. K. L. Rallia Ram, an Indian Christian, who has for a very long period been connected with education in the Punjab, has conclusively shown the hollowness of that charge. He says " out of 1,11,166 pupils attending schools in the Punjab 85,710 are attending private schools," and he then adds that 'it is hardly too much to say that the greater part of the success of the province is to be attributed to the existence of private schools which have made a real contribution to the cause of education.' Further on he observes that 'the educational sphere of work of non-Government schools as well as district board schools—which more or less are of the same category—covers a far wider range than that of the Government schools; so wide in fact that out of every 11 students in the province 9 are receiving education in private schools. In this connexion it would be interesting to note that the Government is spending about

Rs. 14 lakhs on 71 Government schools, while 214 private schools get only Rs. 10 lakhs as Government grant-in-aid'. I have not included the income from fees in Government schools which amounts to about 7 lakhs.

INDEX

A

Adams, Brooks, 323
Africa, treatment of coloured people in, 141, 145, 147-59
Age of Consent, raised in England in 1885 from 13 to 16, 181; attempts to raise in India, 182; opposed by British officials, lviii, 182, 184, 190, 191
— In America, history of legislation, 182; attempts to lower it from 16 to 14, 182; in Kansas, from 18 to 12, 183; compared to that in the West, 215
Al. Carthill, on India's poverty, 352; on Indianization, 462
Al. Smith, 133
America, education in, 52, 56; Dr. Ellis on, 53; expenditure on, 67, *note*; of Negroes in, 105; of Red Indians, 137
America, feeling against Catholics in, 132
America, Gandhi's message to, lxviii, lxix
American ideal, compared with that of ancient Hindus, 49, 50
American journalism, 269-71
America, mechanization of life and love of sensationalism in, 124
American sex morality, 215-219; girl mothers, 218; popularity of divorces on the increase, 221; films provide exaggerated sex stimulus, 237; ban on films in India, 237, 374
American trade interests in India, 373
America, treatment of Negroes in, 106-39; of Red Indians, 136
America, untouchables in, 105-106, 136
American women, Prof. Munsterberg on, 6; take part in lynching, 126, 127
Ampthill, Lord (Governor of Madras, 1905), on sanitary code of Hindus, 285
Amritsar Congress, resolution on Reforms in, 453, 458
Amritsar Massacre, 452-53
Andrews, Mr. C. F., on British rule in India, 439
Anglo-Indians, number of, in India, 95; sexual morality of, 250-52; " in India every [Anglo-Indian] woman under fifty has a 'boy,'" 251; 'women unsafe near British soldiers' quarters, 252; Dr. Cornelius on, 252
Anglo-Russian rivalry in India, 471, 483
Ansari, Dr. M. A., on British rule in India, 423-425
Army, the, *see* Defence of India
Arya Samaj, Miss Mayo omits mention of, in social reform

movement, 98; uplift work of, lvii, 100

Asquith, Mr., on inefficiency of British officials in India, 435

Assembly, Indian Legislative, social reform bill in, opposed by Government, 182

B

Bajpai, G. S., on depressed classes, 527

Balfour, Miss M. I. (a woman doctor of Bombay) challenges Miss Mayo, 188-89

Banerjea, Sir Surendra Nath, 406

Basu, Major, B. D., 401 *note*

Behar, education of depressed classes in, 100

Belgian, treatment of natives in—Congo, 144

Bengal, elementary education in, 25, 32; education of depressed classes in, 99, 100, 533; prosperous under native rule, 311; Macaulay on mismanagement and corruption in Company's rule 313-14

Besant, Mrs. Annie, 185

Bhargava—Pandit Thakur Das, on depressed classes, 524-525

Birkenhead, Lord, on Reforms, 469

Birla, Babu Jugal Kishore, munificence of, for depressed class education, 521, 522

Blackstone, on conditions of woman in England, 179

Blaschko, Dr. Alfred, on increasing prostitution in Europe, 228

Bloch, Dr. Iwan, on irregular sex relationship in the West, 221, 224, 228, 238, 240; on sexual offences in Europe, 266; on pornographic literature and advertisements, 232-33; on venereal diseases in Europe, 240-45

Blunt, Mr. Wilfred Scawen, on India's poverty, 357; on British rule in India, 437-39

Bolts, William, on hardships by the Company's servants on the people, 326-29

Bombay, elementary education in (in 1823-28), 25, 32; education of depressed classes in, 99, 100

Bose, Dr. Sir J. C., F.R.S, on *Mother India*, xxxvi

Bose Institute, Calcutta, 57

Bose, Miss (Principal, Lahore Victoria School), contradicts Miss Mayo's statement about her, li, lii, 208

Boston, Municipality declared bath tubs illegal, 182

Brago, Sergeant, on the Company's 'cruel' trade operations, 324-25

Brahmans, and education, Miss Mayo on, 16-17; and education, 18, 19; not responsible for present day illiteracy, 24; as teachers accepted no fees, 20; as village priests, 29, 94; their attitude t o w a r d s the 'Pariah' not more cruel than that of the Klansmen towards Negroes, 136

Brahmanic system of education, 18-23; survives even after Buddhism, 24

INDEX

Britain, Great, *see* England

British Empire, the, treatment of coloured people in—much worse than that of 'untouchables' in India, 139-42; Indians treated as helots throughout, 141; in Asia, Gibbons on, 474-77; foreign policy governed by considerations of safety of—in India, 471, etc.; India in—a world-menace, 470, 483, etc.

British rule in India, *see* India

Bruce, J., 320, 323

Buddhism, position of women in, 184

Buddhist system of education, 22; not merely theological, 23; attracted scholars from China and abroad, 23

Bureau, M. Paul, on sexual immorality in France, 221-23; on pornographic literature and photographs, 229-32; on abortion in France, 248; on infanticide in France, 248-49

Burke, Edmund, on E. I. Company's trade policy, 329-30

Burma, literacy before British rule in, 23

Butler, Sir Harcourt, on 'red tapism' in India, 451

C

Calcutta University Commission, misquoted by Miss Mayo, 74, 75

'Carnaticus,' justifies 'divide and rule' policy in India, 403

Catholics, Roman, caste among, 94; number of in India, 96; missionaries, 100; feeling against in America, 132; hated by Protestant 'Klan,' 134, 135

Caste, 81; evolution of, 82; M. Senart on, 83-85; originally in India as a form of social and industrial organization, 87; not so rigid in Epic period, 156; marriage relations without restrictions of—in *Smritis*, 164; among Muhammadans and Christians, 92; in Ancient Rome and Athens, 83-84; in modern European countries, called 'class,' 87; Booker T. Washington on caste in America, 107; in Japan, 88; now disappeared because of political and economic independence, 90, 91; Government in India, encourages caste for its owr ends, 91, 92; in the Army, 537-41; in the Navy, 542; in Police, 528, 541-42

Cattle, Mr. Desai on—quoted by Miss Mayo, 290-91, consume considerable portion of grain required for human consumption, 296; Lupton on, 295-97; not increased proportionately to population, 297; not sufficient for tillage, 297; not prospered under British rule, 299; exporters purchase best stock, 299; ignorance responsible for bad treatment of, 298; Mr. Chatterjee on, 298-99; large number raised in U. S. A. for meat industry, 293

Central Provinces, education of depressed classes in, 99, 101

Chamberlain, Sir Austen, on India, 8, 319

Chatterjee, N., on cattle in India, 298-99

Chesney, Sir George, on motives of British rule in India,. 452-55

Christianity, and women's status, 178

Churchill, Winston, 255, 257

Clarke, A. M., on *Mother India*, 493-95

Coatman, J., 97

Coke, Lt.-Col. John, justifies 'divide and rule' policy, 404

Colgate, Mr. (famous toothpaste manufacturer) on clean teeth in India, 280 *note*

Colvin, Sir Auckland, on Indian poverty, 354

Committee on Sexual Offences against Young Persons, 257, 260-67

Congo, Belgian, treatment of Negroes in, 144

Congo, French, treatment of Negroes in, 144

Congress, Indian National, 187; on Reforms, 453, 456-57; adopts Non-co-operation, 457; on Indianization, 396

Congress, Martial Law Enquiry Committee, 252

Conti, Nicolo de, on India's prosperity before British rule, 308

Connell, A. K., on railway finance and 'cheap capital,' 389

Coote, W. A., (of National Vigilance Association), on London brothels, 225; men attracted by press announcements in London brothels, 225

Cornelius, Dr. 252

Cotton, J. S., on India's condition under British rule, 353

Cousins, J. H., on *Mother India*, 497-500

Cousins, Mrs. Margaret, E., on *Mother India*, 501-02

Cow, Miss Mayo on starvation of cow in India, 290; Miss Mayo on care of cow in America, 291; condition of— in Akbar's time 299-300; ignorance and poverty responsible for bad condition of, 298-99: slaughter of—on a large scale, a new factor in India, 298; question ignored by Indian Government, while in U. S. A. a primary concern of the State, 293; quality and milk producing capacity of—fast deteriorating in India, 299; best milkers slaughtered, 290

Cow urine, 'Holy men drink,' —a lie, 291

Coward, Noel, 236

Cromer, Lord (Finance Minister for India, 1882), on India's annual income per head, 365-66

Curtis, Lionel, xx, xxi; conspiracy suspected between him and Miss Mayo, xxiii-xxv, lxi, lxii

Curzon, Lord, on India's annual income per head, 366, 367; quoted by MacDonald, 430; on Reforms, 469

D

Dahlen, George, on "Press-Fridoline," 225

Davids, Rhys, on India in Buddhist period, 303

Dean Miller, on Negroes in America, 130

Debt, India's Public, R. C. Dutt on, 343; amount always increasing 343; how increased after Mutiny, 344-46; Wingate on, 346

Defence of India, Miss Mayo on Army in India, 374; K. T. Shah on expenditure on, 375-77; more than half of total revenues spent on, 64; expenditure compared to that in other countries, 374, 375; large expenditure a 'drain' on India, 379; Army employed in other parts of the British Empire, 377; Esher Committee on, 377; and foreign aggression, 482-83; all control in the hands of the British, 463; caste in Indian Army, 537-41

Depressed Classes, *see* Untouchables

Devadasis, institution though rotten, exaggerated by Miss Mayo, 199; Frazer on, 200-03; his version materially differs from that of Miss Mayo, 203; unknown outside Southern Presidency, 203; even in South, unknown in Malabar, 203; no better and no worse than prostitutes in Europe and America, 204; similar evils spread among wider portions of society in the West, 223; Madras Council trying to abolish, 204

Dickinson, Prof. G. Lowes, on religion in India, 278; on incompetency of the English people to rule India, 428

Digby, William, on 'economic drain,' 333, 334; estimates the amount of 'drain,' 348; on India's annual income per head, 366, 368; on railway finance, 388

Dill, Sir S., on Roman caste system, 86

Ditcher (Mr. Pat Lovett) in the *Capital*, on Miss Mayo, 272-74, 492-93

Divorce, on the increase in Europe and America, 221

Doleris, Dr., 246

Drain, economic, from India, 323, 331-49; is a subject of bitter controversy, 331; Mr. Hyndman pleads for substitution of native rule, as a remedy, 332-33; amount ever increasing, 340; Englishmen on, 331-42, 365; amount estimated, 340-49; does not represent the interest on capital invested and services rendered, 347; military expenditure as such, 375; in shape of raw produce, 379, 380; in shape of 'cheap capital' for railways, 382-86; in shape of 'store purcahse in England,' 387; in shape of public services, 393-94; increasing with the increasing cost of administration, 393; further increased by Lee Commission's proposals, 398

Dubois, the Abbé, 179, 194, 210; his opinions on Hindu religion unreliable, xxxvii, xlii; even he does not support Miss Mayo, xliii-xlvi, 252; on Hindu education, 16, 36

Du Bois, Dr. W. E. B. (a famous Negro writer), 123, 127

Duff, Alexander, on educational policy to be pursued in India—Roman example recalled, 44

Dufferin, Lord, made enquiry into economic condition of India, 358

Dutt, R. C., on Public Debt of India, 343

Dyarchy, unworkable, 465-69; *see* Reforms

Dyer, General, 452

E

Education, ideals of, 12, 59, 60; is a function of State, 11, 58, 66-8; by private agency an impossibility, 66-67, 190

Education, in England, down to 1870, 12; in 1917, 61, 62

Education in India, Raja of Panagal on, quoted, but misquoted by Miss Mayo, xlvi, xlvii, 17; Abbé Dubois on, 16

Education in India, Rev. Keay on Brahmanic system of, 18-22, 23, 24; Buddhist system of, 24; excellent indigenous system of, 26-33; as it was financed, 30; at the time of British arrival, 28, 30, 34-35; its decay under British rule, 33, 36; in the Punjab under Maharaja Ranjit Singh, 35; literacy in Burma before British rule, 23; under British rule, indigenous system destroyed by the policy of the British Government, 33, 36, 42-46; Duff on, 44, Trevelyan, Grant, and Macaulay on, 42, 45; Dr. Ellis on, 52, 53; neglected by Government, history of primary education in India, 69; introduction of compulsory primary education opposed by Government on the plea 'that time has not yet arrived,' 69, 190; efforts of Mexican Government compared with those of Indian government, 56; expenditure in India on,—represents, 4 as. per head for Indians, 55; and Rs. 25 per head for Europeans in India, 56; expenditure in England on, 60-63; and by U. S. A. Government, 67, *note;* scale of pay in Indian schools compared with that in American and British schools, 78-79; pay of the village teacher, 79; private agencies' efforts for, 57; Mass education, 543-44

Education, progress of the German Nation due to—, Ellis quoted, 52

Education of women in India, Miss Mayo on 36-37; education of Hindu women prior to British rule, 37-38; education never denied to Hindu women, 185; indigenous system of, 38; its decay and causes of its decay under British rule, 39, 40

INDEX 551

Education of women in England, a recent thing, 12-13, 181

Education of untouchables, 71, 72, 98-99, 518-36; of 'American untouchables,' i.e. Negroes and Red Indians, 112, 137

Electorate, Communal, responsible for Hindu-Muslim dissensions, 400; helped by Government, 400; introduced first time in India, 406; instigated by Lord Minto, 406; is a dissension-creating device, 407

Ellenborough, Lord (Governor-General of India, 1842), on attitude of Hindus and Muslims towards the British, 400; suggests 'divide and rule' policy, 400

Elliott, Sir Charles, on Indian poverty, 354

Ellis, Dr. A. Caswell, on progress of the German nation due to education, 52: on worthlessness of natural resources without education, 53

Ellis, Havelock, on premarital relationship in the West, 212-13, 215. 220; on prevalence of polygyny in the West, 220, 221: on prevalence of venereal diseases in the West, 243-45

Elphinstone, Lord (Governor of Bombay, 1859), justifies 'divide and rule' policy, cites Roman example, 404

Elphinstone, Mountstuart, on India's past prosperity, 308; on Indian roads, 308-9

England, education in, 12, 58-63; condition of women, *see*
women; supported slavery, 107; economic condition of— in the 16th century, 320; a backward country, Robertson, 321-22; Brooks Adams on scarcity of money in, 322; prosperity of—built on Indian treasures, 324, 332; economic 'drain' from India to, *see* 'drain'; prostitution in, 225-28; venereal diseases in, 245

Eta, the depressed classes in Japan, 89

Epic period, position of women in the, 155-57

Europe, marriageable age risen in, owing to spread of education, 190; prostitution in, 225-28; monasteries and churches used as brothels, 203-4; over-sexed life in, 238-40; venereal diseases in, 240-45; was in a state of barbarity till recently, xvii-xviii

F

Fazl-i-Hussain, Hon. Sir (late Minister of Education, Punjab and now Executive Councillor), 71, 72-73

Fakhruddin, Sir Muhammad, on the Reforms, 466

Fisher, Rt. Hon. H. A. L., on education being the business of the State, 58; on ideals of education. 59, 60; on education in England, 61, 62; on learning and earning, 63

Franchise, *see* Suffrage

Francis, Mr. Philip, compares native rule in India with that of E. I. Company, 334;

on India's condition under Company's rule, 334

Frazer, Sir James, on Devadasis, 200-03

France, (and French), treatment of natives in—Congo, 144; atrocities in Africa, 147-48; sexual morality in 223-25; vice, an organized industry in, 223-25, M. Bureau and Bloch, quoted on pornographic literature and pictures, 229-33; obscenity in the drama and on the stage, 235-36; abortion and infanticide cases, 246-49; expenditure on defence, 376

Frontier Province, North-West, 'desires no advance,' says Miss Mayo, 412; Muslim League demands Reforms in, 412

Flexner, on irregular sex relationships in London, 225-26

Fullarton, Col., on India during Hyder Ali's reign, 311

Fuller, Sir Bampfylde, on 'favourite wife' of British Government in India, 409; on Englishmen's incompetency, 429

G

Gait, Sir Edward, on child marriage in India, 187-88

Gandhi, M. K., xxi, xxix, 103; on *Mother India*, xxx, xlix-li, 267; Miss Mayo's reply in *Liberty*, to his criticism, lxvi-lxvii; rejoinder to Miss Mayo, lxviii-lxx; passive resistance movement, 452

Ganga Ram, Sir, on agricultural education in India, 48

George, Lloyd, on 'steel frame,' 393, 461

Germany, progress due to education, 52; condition of women in medieval times, 178; sexual morality in, 213-14, 220; popularity of pornographic literature and pictures in, 232-33

Gibbons, H. A. on India, as a factor in shaping Britain's foreign policy, 471-77

Gide, M. Andre, on the atrocities of French administrator in Africa, 147-49

Gokhale, G. K., and primary education, 69, 523-24; on Railway finance and 'Cheap capital,' 388

Goldman, Emma, on prostitution in churches, 204

Gorki, Maxim, denounced by the American Press, 271

Gour, Sir Hari Singh, his Bill to raise marriageable age opposed by officials, 191

Grant, Charles, on educational policy of British Government, 42, 45; on economic drain, 336

Greece, child marriage in, 187

Gruening, Miss, 123, 127, 129

H

Hall, Dr. Cuthbert, on British rule in India, 480-82

Hamilton, Lord George, on India's annual income per head, 366

INDEX

Hamilton, General Sir Ian, on India's defence, 482

Harrington, A. H., on India's miserable condition, 358

Hastings, Warren, on Company's misgovernment, 314, 317, 318

Haworth, Paul Leland, on American Negroes, 110-12

Hearn, Lafcadio, on caste system in Japan, 88-89; on Japanese unfitness for democratic government, 90

Heber, Bishop, on the prosperity of Bharatpur under native rule, 317-18

Hecker, Miss Eugene, on miserable condition of women in ancient Rome, 178, 179, 180, 181; on lower age of consent in Christian world, 182; on bill in U.S.A to lower age of consent, 182-83

Hellpach, Willy, on oversexed life in Europe, 238

Hindus, singled out for attacks by Miss Mayo, 1, 2, 15; Dubois's opinion unreliable about, xxxviii; ideals compared with those of the West, 49, 50; Assemblymen's efforts for education of Untouchables, 70, 73; their efforts to raise the age of consent, 182, 183; and depressed classes *see* Untouchables; and caste system, *see* caste; and Christianity, 93; and child marriage, *see* Marriage; their attitude towards the British, 399, 400; high standard of cleanliness, Lord Ampthill and other authorities quoted, 278-87

Hindu Medicine and Science, discoveries in, 285-88

Hindu-Muslim Dissensions, Hindus placed on equality with Muslims by Alivardy Khan, 313; sheet-anchor of British policy in India, 411; Miss Mayo chuckles over, 398; unity in Martial Law days, 399; Government's steps to destroy unity, 399, 411; some eminent British statesmen on 'divide and rule' policy, 399-408; a creation of British rule, says, John Maynard, 408-09

Hindu women, treated with great consideration, xlii; education of, 37; in Vedic times, 155; property rights recognized, 154; freedom of movement enjoyed by, in Vedic and epic times, 155-56; attained positions of highest distinction, 155; *see also* Woman in India

Hiuen Tsang, on freedom of choice of husbands by Hindu women, 159

Hobhouse, L. T., 10

Howell, on prosperous Bengal, 312

Howell, A. P., on education in pre-British India, 30, 31

Hume, A. O., on Indian poverty, 354, 55

Hunter, Sir William, on cleanliness of Hindus. 284; on Indian poverty, 353, 356, 390

Hurd, Carlos F., on lynching, 124, 126

Huxley, Aldous, on Englishmen's incompetency, 430

Hyndman, H. M., on 'economic drain,' 332-33, 348; on India's poverty, 350-55; on Englishmen's incompetency to rule India, 427-28

I

Ibbetson, Denzil, on evolution of caste, 81; on safeguards to child marriage in India, 190

Ibn Batuta, on India's prosperity, 309

Illiteracy, Miss Mayo on, 36, 74; the Brahman not responsible for, 24, 25; Government responsible for, 53

Imam, Sir Ali, on Simon Commission, 431; on Reforms, 467

Inchcape Committee for Retrenchment, on railways, 387; on purchase of stores, made in England's dear market, 387; on increase of salaries of public servants, 396

Imperialism, the greatest 'world-menace' known to history, 140; forces rising against, 484

India, education in, see Education; widespread propaganda being carried on against—in Europe and America, lx, India and the British Empire, see British Empire; the market of England's raw-produce, 379; a 'World-menace,' xxxiii, chap. XXXIII; Public Debt of see Debt; poverty of, see Poverty

India in historical times, State dealt with social life and public health, etc., 8, 9; education in, see Education; achievements in medicine and science in, 285-87; Rhys Davids on India in Buddhist period, 303; ancient State not despotic, 307

India under Muhammadans, compared with England under Normans, 304; cruelties of Muslims much less than their Christian contemporaries, 305; should not be compared with 19th century England, 306

India in pre-British days, had enormous wealth and prosperity, British authorities quoted, 307-36; education in, see Education; village system in, 28

India under British rule, conquered by *Indian* money and blood, 343; mismanagement, cruelties and atrocities of East India Company in India, 310-36; manufacturers treated as slaves, 329; silk-weaver's thumbs cut off, 327; Bolts on, 326-27; trade ruined, 330; past prosperity of India vanishes, 310-49; India not benefited by British rule, says Malcolm, 388; conditions of the lowest classes becoming worse, says Cotton, 353; India played a great part in success of England's Industrial Revolution, 319; John Shore on exploitation of, 335; Muslims take the same view on Simon Commission as Hindus, 412-16; Englishmen on incompetency of the English to rule India, 427-37; Sullivan pleads for India's restoration to Indians, 336; Indians excluded from services, while Englishmen preferred, 335, 393-97, 460; claim of Trusteeship examined 413-15; Chesney and Joynson Hicks on the motives of British rule in India, 453-57

Indian Finance, under Reforms, controlled by Government, 462; of railways, *see* Railways; Transferred departments inadequately financed, 64, 466

Indian Marine, caste consideration by Government, 542

Irwin, Mr., on India's poverty, 361

J

Japan, depressed classes in, 89, 90; Hearn on her unfitness for democracy, 90; caste and its disappearance in, 90; expenditure on defence, 375

Jinnah, M. A., 411

Joynson Hicks, Sir William, on motives of British rule in India, 456-57

K

Kalidas, the great Indian poet and dramatist, 158

Keay, Rev. F. E., on Brahmanic system of education in India, 18-26; on popular system of elementary education in pre-British India, 24-26, 27; on literacy in Burma before British rule, 23

'Ku Klux Klan,' a secret society in America, 132; organized against the alien, the Catholic, the Jew, and the Negro, 132; pledged to eternal maintenance of white supremacy, 134; lynching methods, 114, 132; membership estimated, 134 *note;* has considerable influence on politics, 134; attitude towards the Negro 'Pariah,' 136

L

Lansbury, George, on Englishmen's incompetency to rule India, 432

Lawrence, A. J., on Indian's poverty, 359

Lecky, on Indian mutiny and its cost borne by India, 344-45

Leitner, Dr. G. W., on literacy in the Punjab before the British, 33, 34; on indigenous system of education, 26 *note*, 28, 32; on female education in India before the British, 38 —and on its decay under British rule, 39; on native genius and learning, 33, 34, 35, 36; on widow remarriage in India, 193 *note*, 194, 197; on lofty conception of marriage among Hindus, 196

Leys, Dr. Norman, on treatment of natives in Africa, 149

Lily, W. S., on test of prosperity and India's poverty, 350

Lindsey, Ben, Judge, on sex relationship among schoolboys and girls in America, 217-21; being a radical reformer abused by American Press, 271

Literacy, among Indian masses before British rule, 23-25, 34, 42

Lovett, Pat, *see* Ditcher

Ludlow, on village system in pre-British India, 28

Lupton, Arnold, on food supply of India, 295-97; on poverty, 351, 353; on national income of India, 366; on India's industrial backwardness, 379

Lynching, 114-28; number of cases in America, 115; of women, 126; American women take part in, 124, 127

M

Macaulay, Lord, on educational policy to be pursued in India, 45; on E. I. Company's misgovernment, 313, 338; on Company's gains, 320, 321, 324; on gains of Lord Clive, 327-28

McClelland, D. F., on *Mother India*, 506

MacDonald, Ramsay, on officials' responsibility for dissensions in India, 408; on foreign rule in India, 427; on incompetency of Englishmen to rule India, 429

McPherson, Sir Hugh, on Reforms, 465, 466

Madras, elementary education in (1822-26), 24, 31; Devadasis in, 200, 203, etc.

Malaviya, Pandit Madan Mohan, on depressed classes, 520-24

Malcolm, Sir John (Governor of Bombay, 1827), on British policy of education in India, 46, 47, 48; on peace and prosperity of Maratha territory before British rule, 315, 16; on ruin of Malwa after occupancy, 316; says British rule has not benefited India, 338

Mallet, Sir Louis, on Indian government, 433

Manu (the great Hindu lawgiver), on women, 160; on mother's first claim to honour, 165; on property-rights of wife, 166; on remarriage, 171; on personal cleanliness, 281; on evils of sexual indulgence, 283

Mann, Dr. Harold, (Director of Agriculture, Bombay), on miserable condition of people, 370-71; on 'empty stomachs,' 371-72

Manohar Lall, (Minister for Education, Punjab), on India's 'grinding' poverty, 364

Marriage, Hindu ideal of, a sacrament, and indissoluble, 169; complete merging of two personalities, 172-74; Manu on, 171; marriage laws of Romans, 176-78; among Germanic people—women not free, 178-79; 'not real love marriages' in the West, says Nardau, 220

Marriage, early child, having pernicious effects on the physique of Indians, 188, 213; but not so general as represented, 166; not an ancient institution, Macdonell,

Keith and Risley quoted, 186; among Romans, 176, 179; early marriage among Greeks and Romans, 186-87; in England, lviii, 188; in India means generally a kind of betrothal, 187; yet denounced in India, lviii; marriageable age and motherhood age, 188-89; rise of marriageable age in Europe due to education, 190; attempts to raise in India and their opposition by Government, lviii, 190-91; Hindu States introducing reforms, 191

Marriage of Widows, remarriage common in earlier times in India, 169; Narad on 170; Miss Mayo's statement, absurd, lxv-footnote, 193-95; restricted now only to high castes, lviii, 192, 196; Dr. Leitner on, 196 *note;* restrictions being removed, lviii

Marris, Sir William, on Reforms, 466

Martial Law, 453

Martin, Montgomery, on economic drain, 341

Mayhew, Arthur, 75

Maynard, Sir John, on *Mother India,* xxxvi; on Hindu-Muslim Dissensions—'a creation of British rule,' 408-09

Mayo, Miss, a tool of the 'Jingoes of America' in British hands, xix-xx; came on a mission of political propaganda, xx, xxii, xxx, lxi, 80, 102, 426; her defence of British administration, 3, 426; on British achievements in India, and criticized, 293-96; explanation of great popularity of her book, xviii-xix; her way of argument criticized, 5, 6; her wrong dealing with figures exposed, 55-56; her trick of dealing with quotations exposed, xliv-lvii, 76, 205, 209; even Dubois—her favoured authority—cleverly handled, xliv-xlvi; adopts tactics of 'Scandal Bureau,' 271; betrays ignorance of Hindu law, 198; and of agricultural conditions in India, 292; and of Indian history, 301, 302; and of India's economic situation, 373; criticized by and replies to M. Gandhi in *Liberty,* Gandhi's rejoinder, xxx-xxxv, lxvi-lxx

Mercantile Marine Committee, 462

Mexican Government's efforts for education, 56

Meyer, Prof. Bruno, on sexual irregularities in the West, 221

Military, Indian, *see* Defence; caste in recruitment, 539-41

Mill, James, on wretched condition of people under British rule, 311; on England's backwardness in 17th century, 322

Minto, Lord, 406

Montagu, Rt. Hon. Edwin, xx; on defective character of Indian government, 431; Mesopotamia debate—speech of 443-44; on announcement of 1917, 446-47

Montagu-Chelmsford Report, on Indian Reforms—recommends Indianization, 396, 446, etc.

Moore, on India's prosperity under Tipu's administration, 311

Morel, E. D., on treatment of natives in British Africa, 142-48

Morison, Sir Theodore, on 'economic drain,' 348

Mother India, 2, 74, 195; how it was written, xxvi; opinions of some eminent persons on, xxviii-xxxvii, xlix, li, and Appendix I; criticism on it of some most reliable Indians refused publication by British Press, xxvii, lxii

Muddiman Commitee on Reforms, 465

Muhammad Ali, Maulana, 406

Muhammadans, Muslims; rule in India, *see* India; women's education among them before British rule, 38; position of women, 38; 'must be suppressed' said Lord Ellenborough and Thomas, 399-400; 'primary movers in Mutiny,' 401; are to be patted, 404; Mr. MacDonald on special favours to, 408; Sir Bampfylde on the *'favourite* wife of British Government,' 409; take the same view about British government as Hindus, chap. XXIX; and British rule, 484

Munsterberg, Prof., on American women, 6

Muslim League, prepares joint scheme of Political Reforms, 443; demands Reforms in N.-W. F. Province, 413; boycotts Simon Comssion, 418

Mutiny, Indian, of 1857 caused by Englishmen's fault, 344; cost to suppress it borne by India, 45; John Bright on the cost—calls it a 'grievous burden' on India, 346; Muhammdans primary movers in—401

N

Naidu, Mrs. Sarojini, 185

Naoroji, Dadabhoy, his writings ignored by Miss Mayo, 373; on India's national income, 367; on 'cheap capital,' for Railways, 388 89

Napier, opposed introduction of steam power in Navy, 182

Narad, on medical examination of man before marriage, 163; on remarriage of widows, 170

National Christian Council of India, on *Mother India,* xxxvi, 500-01

National Medical College, at Calcutta, 57

Nataranjan, K., on unreliability of Abbé Dubois's authority, xl, xlii, xlv; criticism of Miss Mayo, liv

Nearing, Prof. Scott, 9

Negroes, in America, their education neglected, 105, 106; cruelties against them unparalleled in India's history, 108, 124-29; denied

INDEX

citizenship rights, 107-11; oppressive laws against, 111; separate accommodation for them on railways, etc., 114; excluded from public schools, hotels, and churches, segregation of, 112-13; lynching of, 115-31; women lynched, 127; some think it impossible to treat them as equals, 129; called 'a sacrificial race' by Dean Miller, 130

Nesfield, Mr., on caste, 82

Nivedita, Sister, on Indian Widows, 194

Nobili, Robert de, forged 5th Veda, xli

Non-co-operation, 458, 460

Nordau, Max, on marriage in Europe, 220

O

Obscene publications, advertisements in French Press, 230, 232-36; drama, M. Bureau on, 235-37;—and their circulation, 230; photographs most popular in Central Europe, 232; newspapers, 234-35; see also Pornography

Oliver, Lord, on government's favouritism of Muslims, 409

Orme, on manufacture of cotton goods in India, 321

P

Panagal, Raja of, quoted by Miss Mayo on Brahmans' opposition to education, 15-17; repudiates Miss Mayo's statement, xlvii, 17

Pankhurst, Miss Christabel, on venereal disease in England, 244

Patel, V. J., 69

Patro, S. P., on India's poverty and indebtedness of the people, 364

Pearson, Charles, on State and social duties, 13

Pietro del Valle (17th century Italian traveller), on India's peace and prosperity, 310

Pioneer (Allahabad Anglo-Indian daily), on poverty 'under the yoke of British mismanagement,' 356, 57; Mr. Harrington in—, on India's poverty, 358, 59; Mr. Grierson in—, on India's poverty, 362

Polak, H. S. L., on *Mother India*, 515-16

Pole, Major D. Graham, on *Mother India*, 510-15

Pornography, well organized in Europe as a successful trade, 232-33. See also Obscene literature

Pouresy, Mr. Emile, quoted by Bureau on publication of obscene literature in France, 232

Poverty of India, 350-72; annual income of the people per head not more than Rs. 30—different estimates, 354-68; and over taxation, 355-57, 362-63, 414, 415

Pratt, J. B., on widows in India, 195; on mothers in India—'nowhere in the world more revered,' 197

Premarital sexual indulgence, opportunities rare for—in India, 212, 216; almost universal in some countries in West, 213, 216; commended in the West by Radical sex thinkers, 213

Prostitutes—Prostitution, Devadasis, 200, 203-05; widespread in the West, 223; Dr. Blaschko on, 228; developed to a gigantic social institution in the West, 228; Dr. Bloch on secret prostitution, 228; Press in the service of, 224-25; in temples and churches, 203-05; brothels in guise of baths, schools, and treatment establishments, 225, 227

Punjab, education before and after British rule, 27-37; of women, and its decay, 36-40; number of depressed class boys in schools, 99

R

Ragozin, on position of women in the Vedas, 153

Rahimtoollah, Sir Ibrahim, examines British claims of trusteeship, 413-18; criticizes economic policy of Britain, 414; on India's capacity to bear taxation, 416

Railways in India, history of, 382-86; Mr. Wacha on the history of, 386; 'cheap capital' exposed, 383-85; Mr. Connell on, 389-90; no solution of famines, 391-92; administration entirely in hands of Europeans, 463; passengers shabbily treated, 382-386

Railway, Board, all European, 463

Rallia Ram, K. L., 72; on mass education—non-official efforts, 543

Ratcliffe, S. K., on *Mother India*, xix

Reddi, Dr. Muthulakshmi, 185

Reddi, Sir K. V., on Reforms, 466-67

Red Indians, mercilessly treated in America, 136; supplied with bad lands and insanitary surroundings, 137; their education neglected, 137; Mr. Russell on inhuman treatment of their boys in schools, 137; their property under control of Government, 138

Reforms, 440-69

Reforms Enquiry Committee, 465

Reforms Pamphlet (of India Reform Society), 303; about India's past prosperity, 304-06, 308; 309

Reinsch, Dr. Paul S., on British rule, 481-82

Richey, Mr. (Education Commissioner to Government of India), on want of finances for educational development, 65; on progress of education in Bombay, 70; on the scale of pay in village schools, 78

Risley, Sir Herbert, on Roman and Grecian caste, 83, 85; on Indian caste system, 85; on widow remarriage, 176; on child marriage, 187-89

INDEX

Robertson, 321-22

Rome—Roman caste system, 83, 84; condition of women, 176; early marriage in, 176; educational policy of Rome as the British ideal in India, 43-4; 'Divide et Impera' policy, 403, 405

Ronaldshay, Lord, on dyarchy, 469

Rose, on indebtedness in India, 360

Ross, Prof. E. A., xiii

Rowlatt Bill, 452

Roy, K. C. (of the Associated Press), contradicts Miss Mayo, xlviii

Ruding, 322

Russell, H. L., on treatment of Red Indian boys in American schools, 137-38

Russia, venereal diseases in 245 *note;* abortion cases in, 247; and Britain, 477, 478, 489, etc.

Rutherford, Dr. V. H., on British inefficiency, 435-37

S

Salisbury, Lord, on 'economic drain,' 342

Sanger, Dr., 203

Sanitation, present day bad sanitation due to poverty, 287-88; public health neglected by government, 288; expenditure on it by government, 288-89; Miss Mayo and Hygiene of Hindus, 278-89

Sarda, R. B. Har Bilas, proposes a Bill in the Legislative Assembly to raise the marriageable age and opposed by official bloc, 182, 191

Sarma, Rt. Hon. Sir B. N., on India's National income, 368; on compulsory education, 524

Seeley, Prof. J., on English rule in India, 427

Senart, on caste system, 83-5

Sexual morality, in India, Miss Mayo takes delight in dilating upon sexual depravity of Indians, 210;—a vital part of her argument, 210; her sweeping generalizations, 211; Hindu scriptures preach continence, *Manu* and *Sushruta* on continence, 283-84; conditions much better as compared with the West, 212, 213, etc.; of Anglo-Indians in India, 249-52

Sexual morality in the West, Pre-marital sex relationship, 212-15;—in American schools, Judge Lindsey on, 215-19; girl mothers in America, 217; contraceptive methods commonly known to American girls, 218; 'no girl a virgin after sixteen in Germany,' 220; divorce becoming popular in the West, 221; 'half of sexual intercourse outside legal marriage' says Ellis, 221; prostitution in the West, *see* Prostitution; obscene publications in the West, *see* Pornography; abortion and infanticide, 247-49; venereal diseases in the West, *see* Venereal diseases

Sexual offences against children, Miss Mayo on,—in

India, 254; in England, 255-67; offences becoming serious in England, 263; difficulty in punishing the offenders in England, 259-62; intercourse with children as a cure for venereal disease in England, 264-65; in America, 268

Shafi, Sir Muhammad, on Simon Commission, 419

Shah, Prof. K. T., on economic drain, 348-49; on annual income per head, 367-68; ignored by Miss Mayo, 373; on military expenditure, 375-78; on respective expenditure, on Englishmen and Indians in Public Services, 393-95

Shaw, George Bernard, 237

Shirras, Findlay, on India's national income, 368

Shore, F. J., on exploitation of India by England, 335-36

Siegfried, Andre, 111, 134-35

Sikhs, position of women among them, 38; female education, 38

Sinclair, Upton, on American journalism, 269; on American 'Scandal Bureau,' 270-71

Simon Commission, 464; attitude of Muslims towards, 418; boycotted by Muslim League, 418, 20; Sir Ali Imam on, 420-23; Sir Shafi on, 419

Sinha, Lord S. P., on *Mother India*, xxxvi, 495-97; injustice done to him by Miss Mayo, lvi

Sinha, Sachchidanand, on Reforms, 467

Sircar, N. N., on Lord Sinha's reference in *Mother India*, lv

Sitalvad, Sir Chimanlal, quoted by Miss Mayo, 2

Skeen, Sir Andrew (Chairman of the Skeen Committee), on very slow progress of Indianization in India, 378

Skeen Committee, 379, 464

Sl very in America, 104, 130; abolished in theory only, 108; slaves when emancipated were compelled to leave the State, 108; British Judges upheld its continuance in Sierra Leone, 149

Smith, V. A., on India's ancient prosperity, 302

Social Reform societies in India, lvii, 102-03

Stanley, Jones, on *Mother India*, 501-02

Strachey, Sir John, on Indian famine, 391; on 'divide and rule' policy, 404

Stridhan, 156

Suffrage of women, a recent thing in England, 181; in India, 185

Sullivan, John, on economic prosperity of pre-British India, 336; pleads for restoration of British territory to native rule, 336; on economic drain, 337

Sunderland, Dr. J. T., on economic drain—'the greatest cause of impoverishment,' 342; on poverty of Indian people, 366-67; proves incompetency of British rule in India, 434, 437

INDEX

Sutra, meaning of, 157; first attempt of Aryans at scientific codification, 157; position of women in *Sutra* period, 157

Suttee, unknown to Vedas, 155; not so general as represented, 166; originally entirely voluntary, 166

Swaraj, 104

T

Tagore, Rabindra Nath, and Miss Mayo, xxxv, xxxvi, xlix, lii-lv, 487-92

Tata, J. N., spent a good deal to provide scientific education, 57

Technological Institute, Calcutta, 57

Thakore of Gondal, on cleanliness of Hindus, 279-84

Thapar, Dewan Bahadur Kunj Behari, O.B.E., contradicts Miss Mayo, lii, 208-09

Thomas, Henry Harrington, on attitude of Hindus and Muslims towards the British, 401-03

Thompson, Edward, calls *Mother India* one long nagging, xxxvi, 502-06; on British rule in India, 436-39

Thorburn, on poverty and famines, 362; on high taxation, 363, 364

Thornton, on 'cheap capital' for Railways, 384-85

Torrens, W. M., M.P., on India in the past, 307

Toynbee, C.S.I., on insufficiently fed people of India, 362

Transferred department in provincial Governments, revenues inadequately provided, 64, 466; ministers not free to act, 467-69

Trevelyan, C. M., on State efforts for country's progress in England, 12-13

Trevelyan, Sir Charles, on educational policy to be pursued in India so as to render India amenable to British rule, 43, 44; Roman parallel cited, 43-44

Tucker, St. John (Chairman of East India Company), on increasing quantity of economic drain, 340-41

U

United Provinces, education of depressed classes in, 99-100

Untouchables, numbers in India, 96-98; Miss Mayo on, lxvi, 37, 70, 71, 93, 95; Hindus not opposed to education of, 70-73; in schools, 99-100; in Police Service, 528, 541-42; used as a weapon against Indian aspirations, xvi, 96, 100-02; a blot on Hinduism, 102, 140; Hindus trying to remove it, lix, 102; Negroes and Red Indians in America treated as such, 105, 107, 136; in Japan, 88-90; official figures for, 536

Usher, on the position of Negroes in U. S. A., 108

V

Varna, see Caste

Vedas, position of women in, 151-55, 176, 18; on object of married life, 153-54; Suttee unknown in Rigveda, 155

Venereal Disease, Miss Mayo on, 240; not as widespread in India as in the West, 240-42; Dr. Bloch on the origin of syphilis, 240-43; ten times more frequent among British troops than in Indian troops, 244; Dr. Bloch, Havelock, Ellis, and Dr. White on—in Europe and America, 242-45; 75 per cent. population infected in England, 245; in Russia, 245 *note;* sexual intercourse with children considered a cure for venereal diseases in the West, 266-67

Village school, its working in pre-British India, 30-32; neglected by the government, 32

Village system, in pre-British India, 28; elementary education an important function of, 30-32

Villiers, E., on Reforms, 468-69

W

Wacha, D. E., on Indian railways, 385-86, 388; on indifference of railway management, 386

War, India's contribution in the, 443, 447

Ward, on 'habitually underfed' people of India, 360-61

Ward. William, on literacy in Bengal, 26 —

Washington, Booker T., on Negroes, 107-08

Wedgwood, Rt. Hon. Col. J. C., xxviii; on *Mother India*, xxxvi, 254, 508-10; on Lord Irwin, 434

Wheeler, Sir Henry, on Reforms, 465-66

White, Dr. Douglas, on venereal diseases in the United Kingdom, 244

White, on India's poverty, 360

White Slave Traffic in Europe, 221-23; in England, government's circular to warn young girls, 226-28

Widows, remarriage of, *see* Marriage; Miss Mayo's diabolic exaggeration about, 197-98; their lot not so hard as depicted, 194; their life of sacrifice, 192; attacks on their morality—product of evil mind, 192; their high morality, 192; their condition different in different castes, 193; their property rights recognized, 198; Mr. Pratt on, 194, 195; Sister Nivedita on, 194; Dr. Leitner, on, 196-97

Williams, Mr. Rushbrook (formerly Publicity Agent of the Indian Government), on *Mother India*, lxv *note*

Wilson, A. J., on economic drain, 341-42, 348; on railway finance, 388

Wilson, H. H., his protest against suppression of Indian languages and exclusive encouragement of English, 45-6; on economic drain, 341

Wingate, Sir George, on economic drain, 339-40; on Indian Mutiny and Public Debt, 346

Wingfield-Stratford, Miss Barbara, on low standard of Anglo-Indian morality in India, 250-52

Woman in India, worshipped by Hindus in different forms, lvii; was free in her choice of mate in early times, 151, 158-59; Hiuen Tsang's testimony, 159; her position in epic period, 155-57; *Manu* on, 160-62, 166; 'as Mother placed on a higher pedestal,' 165, 197; her first claim to honour, 165; Mr. Pratt on, 194-95; her property rights recognized, 167-68, 184; her rights of adoption, 168; marriage and remarriage of, *see* Marriage; as wife enjoys an equal status, 172-74; in the past also enjoyed better position than her European sister before Mid-Victorian era, 176, 183; even better in some respects in Vedic times than European women in Europe to-day, 176; as legislator, 185; performing important public duties, 185; *see* also Hindu Women

Woman in the West, 'vote' for, a very recent thing, 176, 181; among Romans, could be put to death by father or husband, 177; usually married young among Romans, 177; was not free to choose her mate, 178; according to Christian thought woman is the cause of fall of mankind, 178; was not allowed to give evidence or security or to act in Court, 178; her rights of property were not recognized among Germanic people, and among English people, 180-81; wife-beating still a common offence in England, 180; her present position entirely the growth of the last 75 years, 184; Negro women in America, *see* Negroes; Prof. Munsterberg on American women, 6

Womenteachers in India, reason for the paucity of, lxiii, 74, 76, 77-78

Y

Yaqub, Maulvi Muhammad, on Hindu-Muslim Unity, 420

CALCUTTA :
Published by Messrs. Banna Publishing Co., 5-2, Garstin Place, and printed by Shadi Ram Monga at Messrs. Lal Chand & Sons, 76, Lower Circular Road.